DAY BY DAY WITH

WILLIAM BARCLAY

DAY BY DAY WITH

WILLIAM BARCLAY

Selected Readings for Daily Reflection

Edited and introduced by
Denis Duncan

HENDRICKSON PUBLISHERS

Day by Day with William Barclay
Hendrickson Publishers, Inc.
P.O. Box 3473
Peabody, Massachusetts 01961-3473

Copyright © 2003 John Hunt Publishing Ltd.

Texts taken from *Every Day with William Barclay*
and *Through the Year with William Barclay*
Compilation copyright © Denis Duncan 2003

The English (UK) version is published under the title
Morning and Evening by
John Hunt Publishing Ltd., Alresford, Hants, UK.

Typography: Andrew Milne Design, Worthing, W. Sussex

ISBN 1-56563-978-2

First printing – October 2003

Printed by WS Bookwell Ltd., Finland

CONTENTS

The Magic of William Barclay

You cannot analyze magic. Break it up into what seems to be its component parts as you will, you still will not find out what makes magic, magic. There is an indefinable something somewhere that makes the parts into a magical whole.

This was true of the late William Barclay. He was, in a real sense, magic. Brilliant mind, humble heart, massive brain, childlike faith, capable musician, football fan, theologian, thinker, hard worker - all these are elements that contribute to the man. But the whole man was far more than the sum of those aspects of him just listed. There was an elusive element that made the difference. It was his personal magic.

What was it that contributed to the magic of William Barclay? First, surely that he spoke the most profound thoughts in the language of the people.

William Barclay was a great human being. Nearly all his life (except for his first five years in Wick in Caithness) was spent in the vital earthiness of the West of Scotland, a place where humanity is real. To those at a distance from Glasgow, the thought of life in that great city seems daunting. But to those who "belong to Glasgow" there is no more human, warm, friendly place on earth. Life has often been hard there, but it has made real character and real people.

William Barclay lived as a boy in Motherwell in industrial Lanarkshire and near to the Glasgow in which he taught with such distinction. To hear William Barclay speak was to feel the earthiness and reality of life. So he speaks to humanity with understanding. Distinct from man because of the brilliance of his mind, he was, at heart, just one of "Jock Tamson's bairns". He was a man who knew people, their feelings and their needs.

The magic of Barclay was expressed, secondly, in his common inheritance with suffering humanity. He was deaf (but never pity him, please, for that which he called a blessing!). It was that which made him part of human pain.

He and his wife (now also dead) lost a daughter in a drowning accident off Northern Ireland. That was a terrible blow, perhaps the hardest he had to bear. But it gave him an understanding of human sorrow that helped him to bring comfort to people in pain. So when William Barclay appeared on television, there came through the earthy voice and sympathetic heart, the accents of authenticity. This man spoke with authority. He knew, as an academic but also as a human being, what he was talking about, and so he was heard.

The magic of William Barclay lay, thirdly, in his humility. He stood level with the greatest men in his professional sphere, yet he was everybody's friend and available to whoever wanted him or needed him. This is not always true of those whom men call "great". It was part of the greatness of William Barclay.

So I offer you in this volume, the Barclay magic. Some items will speak to one, some to another. All will not like everything. Most will like something. From the inexhaustible treasures of the photographic mind of this "modern miracle" there will, I hope, be given to you still greater benefit.

William Barclay died early in 1978 after an illness that had been restricting him to some extent in his last years. But he continued his work, particularly on the Old Testament part of his *Daily Study Bible*, and in fact he worked to the end - up to some three days before he died.

William Barclay lives on however through the written word. He will continue to be — as he had become in his life — an apostle to millions. Thanks be to God for him.

This book brings together two earlier works, *Through the Year with William Barclay* and, *Every Day with William Barclay*.

It has been an extended privilege to work with these thoughts once again. I hope it will be an added blessing for you to use them as you will.

Denis Duncan

Happy New Year

MORNING

I was cleaning my car in the street at my front door, using one of those amazing brushes which lift off the dust like magic. A very small girl came up and watched me.

"My daddy's got one of these brushes to clean his car too," she said.

"That's very nice," I replied. And, with a view to making conversation, added, "And what kind of car has your daddy got?"

"Oh," said the little girl, "he hasn't got the car yet, but he's got the brush to clean it."

If you can't get all you want, start with what you can get! If you can't achieve the big thing of which you dream, "get cracking" on what you are able to do. TODAY!

EVENING

For a happy life, three things are necessary: Something to hope for. Something to do. Someone to love.

Something to hope for
Alexander the Great, in a mood of generosity, was once handing out gifts. To one he gave a fortune, to another a province, to another a position of high honor. A friend said to him, "By doing this you will have nothing to yourself." "Oh yes I have," said Alexander. "I have kept what is greatest of all. I have kept my hopes."

The beginning of the end of life is when we live in memory rather than in hope: when our memories are an escape from prison rather than a stimulus to further living.

Something to do
A terminally ill office-cleaner wrote when she knew death was near:

> Don't pity me now.
> Don't pity me never.
> I'm going to do nothing
> For ever and ever.

Anyone who can look back to days of enforced inactivity knows that work is not a curse but a blessing.

Someone to love
Browning writes: "He looked at her: she looked at him: suddenly life awoke." When love enters life, there comes a new thrill; a new humility; a new awareness of possibilities undreamed of. How great is the blessing of someone to love.

Motivation

MORNING

One of the most alarming parables Jesus ever spoke was the Parable of the Talents (Matthew 25:14-30). In that parable the striking thing is the condemnation of the man who hid his talent in the earth and did nothing with it.

No doubt that man said to himself: "It's all very well for these lads with five and two talents; but I've only got one talent. What's the use of me trying to do anything? It's hopeless to do anything with one talent; it's not worth trying."

That is the kind of thing that a Christian never dare say.

Once Jesus said: "Go ye therefore, and teach all nations" (Matthew 28:19). To whom did he say it? He said it to eleven ordinary men. What if *they* had said, as they had every right, humanly, to say: "It's hopeless"?

Once the risen Lord said: "Ye shall be witnesses unto me both in Jerusalem, and in all Judaea, and in Samaria, and unto the uttermost part of the earth." To whom did he say that? To one hundred and twenty men (Acts 1:8, 15). What if they had said: "It's useless for us to set out on a campaign to win the world"?

The characteristic of the Christian is that he always "gets cracking" on what he can do. The result? Miracles!

EVENING

Rodin, the famous sculptor, talking about the strange barrenness that in his day affected the productions of literature and of art, in one sentence, gave his explanation of it. "My compatriots have lost the art of admiration," he said.

One of the most tragic features of life is the loss of wonder. When we are young, we live in a thrilling and wonderful world. As we grow older, we begin to live in a world that has grown gray and commonplace. But the change is not in the world. It is in ourselves.

The classic expression of this loss of wonder is in Wordsworth's "Ode, Intimations of Immortality". We come into this world "trailing clouds of glory from God who is our home". And then the shadows begin to close:

> Shades of the prison-house begin to
> close
> Upon the growing boy . . .
> The youth who daily from the east
> Must travel, still is Nature's priest,
> And by the vision splendid
> Is on his way attended;
> At length the man perceives it die
> away,
> And fade into the light of common
> day.

The vision is lost, and the wonder is gone. How tragic!

When the fire goes out

MORNING

A poet who expressed deep pessimism was A. E. Houseman. He writes:

> When first my way to fair I took
> Few pence in purse had I,
> And long I used to stand and look
> At things I could not buy.
> Now times are altered; if I care
> To buy a thing, I can
> The pence are here, and here's the fair,
> But where's the lost young man?

Life had brought him many things, but on the way something had been lost. That something was himself and the wonder of youth. When *that* wonder is gone, all is gone.

W. B. Yeats tells how John Davidson, the poet, said to him: "The fires are out; and I must hammer the cold iron."

His days of greatness were at an end.

EVENING

Fielden Hughes has written a most interesting book called *Down the Corridors*, in which he sets out his experience as a schoolmaster. He writes:

I should aim not to kill life with pedantry, but, as my business was to produce whole men, nothing that happened to awake wonder and pleasure in me was likely to be wasted. Besides, the worst thing that can happen to a schoolmaster is that he should lose his own sense of wonder, and should cease to be excited about living.

If that should happen to him, all he has is his dreary stock-in-trade, which boys only want if he can set it on fire. They won't have it damp or dead, or when it has nothing to appeal to the excitement and fire which live in their hearts and minds. . .

We go on with our jobs till we are sixty at least; and it may be till we are sixty-five. But there is in every teacher's life a day when he ought to retire, and he probably knows it. That may be his sixty-fifth birthday, or it might occur when he is in his thirties. It is the day when the fire goes out.

It is sad. But it is a reality that has to be faced, for everybody's sake.

The sense of wonder

MORNING

Somehow we must keep the sense of wonder alive. It is, in fact, not so very difficult to do this.

The more we know about this astonishing world the more we are bound to wonder.

An ordinary passenger train going day and night without stops would take about nine years to reach the moon, 300 years to reach the sun, 8,300 years to reach the planet Neptune, 75,000,000 years to reach Alpha Centauri, which is the nearest of the fixed stars, and 700,000,000 years to reach the Pole Star.

Who will not be astonished in a universe like that? There is a text in one of the Psalms: "Thou hast made us to drink of the wine of astonishment" (Psalm 60:3), It is a draught of that wine that all men need the more as the years begin to close about them. But, if we look at God's world, and even more, if we look at God's love, we too will be lost in wonder, love and praise.

For the more we know of the love of God, so amazing, so divine, the more we must stand astonished.

EVENING

We are living today in a world which is in a hurry, a world which worships speed. The tempo of life has never been faster, and the pressure of life has never been more intense.

There is something fundamentally wrong about all this.

Newman once described culture as a "wise receptivity". There is far too little time in life when we wait passively to receive.

Yeats writes in his autobiography: "Can one reach God by toil? He gives himself to the pure in heart. He asks nothing but our attention."

But so many of us are living a life in which there is no time to glance at God, much less to contemplate him.

Everyone knows the lines which W. H. Davies the tramp-poet wrote with such a simple loveliness:

What is this life if, full of care,
We have no time to stand and stare?

That is what very few people in this modem world have time to do.

Which is sad.

Making time

MORNING

There are certain things in life for which we must make time.

We must make time to think

So many people are so busy living that they have no time to think *how* they are living.

Plato said that the unexamined life is the life not worth living.

No business could ever survive if sometimes it did not take stock, and if sometimes it did not check up on the whole policy and purpose behind it.

Time to think is essential to life, if life is to be what it was meant to be.

We must make time to pray

John Buchan once described an atheist as "a man with no invisible means of support".

The tragedy of life is that so many people who would resent being called atheists are trying to live life without contact with the invisible world and with God.

We live in a worried and frightened age, and many of these things are due to no other cause than that men have lost contact with the eternal strength.

We must make time to talk

Samuel Johnson, who knew John Wesley quite well, used to say that Wesley had only one fault — he had no time to sit back, cross his legs, and talk.

One of the strange phenomena of modem life is that good talk is very nearly a thing of the past. It would stimulate our thoughts and bring us nearer each other, if we took a little more time to talk.

EVENING

But we must make time for one thing more.

We must make time to do nothing

Pascal once said that more than half this world's ills come from the fact that people cannot sit in a room alone.

There is a place in life for complete relaxation, for a deliberate letting go of the tensions, for a wise idleness, for a restful passivity.

Many a man's mental and physical troubles would be eased, and possibly ended, if only he could persuade himself for a little time to relax and to do nothing.

The Bible is full of advice to us to do this very thing. "Be still," said the Psalmist, "and know that I am God" (Psalm 46:10). "Stand still," said Moses to the people scurrying about in their terror, "and see the salvation of the Lord" (Exodus 14:13). "Come ye yourselves apart into a desert place," said Jesus, "and rest awhile" (Mark 6:31).

God grant us more stillness in this hurried life of ours. Only so, will life become what it is meant to be.

Verdicts on life

MORNING

I have come-across a whole series of sayings which might serve as verdicts upon life.

Yeats tells how a certain critic described Ibsen's play, *The Doll's House*, as "a series of conversations terminated by an accident".

To some people, that would accurately enough describe life. They meet. They talk. The chances and the changes of life meaninglessly intervene. They pass on.

There can be no progress in a life in which there is no goal, for there is nowhere to reach.

Let us look at some verdicts on life.

Macbeth, as the shadows close about him in Shakespeare's play, says:

Life's but a walking shadow, a poor player,
That struts and frets his hour upon the stage,
And then is heard no more; it is a tale
Told by an idiot, full of sound and fury,
Signifying nothing.

Life to Macbeth was a drama of unrelated moments with no sense and no plot.

What a poor verdict on life!

EVENING

But the verdict quoted this morning is not the Christian verdict on life.

In one flashing sentence Paul gave the Christian verdict on life when he was writing to his friends at Philippi: "For me to live is Christ" (Philippians 1:21).

For the Christian, life begins with Christ
It is the Christian conviction that life only becomes life more abundant when Christ enters into it; that Jesus Christ gives to life an adventure and a meaning and a significance and a relevance and an aim and object which it never had before he entered into it.

For the Christian, life continues in Christ
Life is lived in his presence and in his company. No task is faced alone. No sorrow is borne in isolation. No journey is made as a lonely pilgrim.

For the Christian, life ends in Christ
In the end he goes, not to the dark, but to Jesus Christ, the light of the world.
To live in the light *is* life abundant.

Destiny and rules for life

MORNING

Sir Philip Gibbs tells how, between the wars, he attended a debate. The debaters were a distinguished company — Rose Macaulay, Margaret Irwin, C. Day Lewis, Margaret Kennedy, T. S. Eliot. The subject of the debate was: "I find this is a good life, or, I do not."

Sir Philip says: "Not one of them could find a good word to say about this life. True, they jested; but they jested like jesters knocking at the door of death."

There is nothing other than the Christian faith which can give life real value.

Christianity supplies man with a task, the task of serving God and serving his fellow men.

Christianity supplies man with a standard, the standard of the perfection of Jesus Christ.

Christianity supplies man with a strength, the strength of the continual presence of the Risen Lord.

Christianity supplies man with a destiny and when this life is done, life in the presence of God.

EVENING

I give you three rules for life.

We must never be self-centered in our happiness

Even while we are happy, there are others whose hearts ache. The time when we want to laugh is for others a time for tears.

In our happiness, we must never be so self-centered that we forget others' pain.

We must never be selfish in our prosperity

The Romans had a proverb which said that riches are like salt water — the more you drink, the more you thirst. How true! Those blessed with much do not always find it easy to give away.

John Wesley's rule was to save all he could and give all he could. When he was at Oxford, he had £30 a year. He lived on £28 and gave £2 away. Then his income increased to £60. But he still lived on £28 and gave away the rest.

It is always wrong for prosperity and selfishness to go hand in hand.

We must never be self-righteous in goodness

How harmful is the so-called Christian who harps on about his goodness. How little does he realize that the man who is furthest from God is the man who thanks God he is not like others.

Goodness implies humility. It is the one who can say, as the publican in the parable did, "God be merciful to me, a sinner," who is truly justified before God.

Mistakes and restoration

MORNING

If I have time, I like to go to football matches. One match I saw in London involved a recently signed young center-forward. He was trying with all his heart and soul and strength. He did get one magnificent goal, then a short time afterwards he missed a chance which a child could have accepted. He blazed the ball past an open goal from about three yards out from the goal.

He stood there the picture of dejection, his head bowed and his shoulders drooped.

In the same forward line there was a forward who was a famous international, and who had played for that team very much longer. When this famous international saw the dejection of his young colleague, he ran up to him and flung a comforting arm round his shoulder, gave him a pat on the back, and said a few words of encouragement to him. The young center-forward squared his shoulders, shook himself and charged into the game to play twice as hard as before.

What an example to Christian people!

"Brethren," said Paul, "if a man be overtaken in a fault, ye which are spiritual, restore such an one in the spirit of meekness; considering thyself, lest thou also be tempted" (Galatians 6:1).

That is indeed the Christian way.

EVENING

Once, in the House of Commons, Gladstone made a most important speech. In the course of it he had to quote certain figures, and the figures he quoted were quite wrong and quite inaccurate. His opponents were not slow to seize on his mistake and to make things very difficult for him.

Now the figures had been supplied to Gladstone by his private secretary, whose duty it was to brief his chief, so Gladstone might well have turned and rent that young man for involving him in this public humiliation.

But, instead, that night Gladstone wrote him a very gracious and kindly letter telling him not to worry, that all men made mistakes, that as far as he was concerned, the matter would never be mentioned again.

If a man be overtaken in a fault — what happens usually? So often he is criticized, torn to pieces, cold-shouldered, even ostracized!

A teacher can do an infinite amount of damage by coming down savagely, sarcastically, or over-severely on a pupil's mistake, when a word of encouragement might have sent the child out to do better in the days to come.

A parent can do infinite damage by an over-critical attitude to his or her children.

"Restore such an one . . ." That is the Christian way.

Believing and receiving

MORNING

Goodness is too often a spasmodic thing. The chart of our goodness is like the temperature chart of a patient with a high fever. We are capable of reaching the heights of goodness, and we are just as capable of taking a sudden nose dive into the depths.

There are young people who bank on the love and the kindness of their parents. They know that, whatever they do, they will get away with it; and, often unconsciously, they trade on that knowledge. Most of us are a little like that with God.

Everyone knows the well-worn saying of Heine. He had not been a good man, and yet he seemed not in the least worried. When he was asked why he was so unworried, he answered: "God will forgive. *C'est son metier.*" It is his trade.

Consciously and unconsciously we trade on the mercy of God.

But the New Testament is clear. "Bring forth therefore fruits meet for repentance" (Matthew 3:8). "By their fruits ye shall know them" (Matthew 7:20).

J. D. Drysdale complained about what he called the danger of "only believism".

The Christian belief is belief that issues in action, that is proved by action.

If it isn't, it is not belief at all.

EVENING

It is more blessed to give than to receive, but there is no virtue in refusing to receive at all.

There is a certain amount of pride in refusing to receive

One of the things that the church at Laodicea said was: "I don't want your gifts. I need nothing" (Revelation 3:17), and that was not seen as righteousness, but as a serious error. It wasn't a compliment; it was a condemnation.

It is a fine thing to give; but it can be the mark of pride to refuse to receive.

One of the characteristics of truly great people is that they can receive graciously

I know a very famous man in the academic world who by no means always dresses like an academic. In a London railway station he saw an old lady in difficulties and offered to carry her bag. When he had put it in her carriage for her, she gave him sixpence — which he gravely and courteously received rather than embarrass the old lady who offered it.

Jesus could receive.

He could take a boy's picnic lunch because it was all that the boy could offer and with it he would work a miracle (John 6:1-14).

There is a courtesy in receiving as well as in giving.

It is sometimes more blessed to receive than to give.

Fire! Fire!

MORNING

We had a fire in our house, a fire which brought along the fire-brigade. The paraffin stove in my study went up in flames — the fault was mine not the stove's!

My wife and I succeeded in dealing with the flames, so that the worst of the danger was averted, but the stove itself and the rugs in which we had smothered it were still smoldering, and, for safety's sake, we decided to telephone for the fire-brigade.

I rang 999, told the voice at the other end of my trouble, and received the answer: "We'll deal with it."

In six minutes, the fire brigade arrived.

The firemen dealt with the situation with extreme efficiency and with courtesy.

I discovered parables and symbols that night!

I discovered that, in certain situations in life, if you are wise, you *shout for help.* You may feel very silly, and more than a bit of a fool doing it, but, if you want to avoid worse trouble, you ask for help.

That is the way it should be with God. Many of our troubles in life come from the fact that we try to do things by ourselves, when we ought to call in the help of God.

EVENING

Over that fire I discovered too that, when I asked for help, it comes *with speed.*

When we ask for God's help, time and time again God answers, and answers at once, as many can testify.

One of the loveliest things in life, and in human nature, is the way that a mother hears a child's cry in the night. The mother may be asleep, but let the child cry, and immediately the mother is awake, and on the way to see what the matter is.

"Before they call," says God, "I will answer; and while they are yet speaking, I will hear" (Isaiah 65:24).

I discovered another thing.

Once all the bother was over, and there was time to speak to the firemen, I was very apologetic about it. I was especially apologetic about sending for the fire-brigade when the worst was past, and when there was nothing left but the smoldering remains to deal with.

But the firemen were insistent that we had done the right thing.

"If you are in the slightest doubt," they said, "never hesitate to send for us. That is what we are here for."

When in doubt, it is always safer to call for help. The God whose glory it is to help, knows nothing but joy when we call.

Faith of firemen

MORNING

A short time after the firemen had left, we had the routine visit which follows from the officer of the salvage corps. He came into my study, made a note of the trifling damage, and looked at my desk.

The open Bible was lying there.

"I see you've got the Book," he said. "You'll not come to much harm so long as you have that there."

I don't know that man's name, but, out of our fire, there came again a great truth.

There are things which can wreck a life even more disastrously than a fire can wreck a house.

But no one will find it easy to wreck our lives, so long as we have "the Book".

And so long as we have beside us and within us, the One of whom the Book tells.

EVENING

Once a man came to Spurgeon and told him that he was saved, and that now that he was saved, he wanted to help to bring people to Jesus Christ.

Spurgeon looked at him.

"What are you?" said Spurgeon.

"I'm an engine driver," said the man.

"Is your fireman a Christian?" asked Spurgeon.

"I don't know," said the man.

"Well," said Spurgeon, "find out; and if he's not, start on him."

A man who lived in a tenement in a respectable artisan district in a certain great city was touched for Christ. He immediately began to go to a church which was near at hand.

In that church about the first person he met was the man who lived in the house across the landing. That man was an elder in that church, and never in years had he mentioned the church to his next door neighbor, and never had he made any attempt to guide him or lead him or persuade him into it.

What a failure in Christian responsibility!

Christians ought to be missionaries. If they aren't, they are failures.

So start . . .

Just where you are!

Start there!

Compensation: human and divine

MORNING

There is a Glasgow church in which I have sometimes preached. In it the organist was blind.

I have always been amazed by the fact that you only needed to tell him once the hymns you wished sung. And he knows the whole order of service.

You can't hand him a list. He couldn't read it. But simply repeat the hymn-list once, and it is firm in his memory.

I was preaching there one morning, and with me was the minister of the church. After I had fixed up the morning list of hymns, the minister was arranging the evening praise list with this amazing blind man.

The minister said: "I would like this evening to have 'For those we love within the veil.' That's hymn number 216."

"No," said the blind organist in his soft Highland voice, not 216, 218."

This blind man carried in his memory the number of every hymn in the hymn book.

But when I spoke to him about his amazing memory, he refused to think of it as amazing at all.

He simply felt it was a compensation for his blindness.

It was therefore his blessing.

EVENING

I was once with a Youth Fellowship in one of the Church Extension churches on the south side of Glasgow. There must have been at least 200 young people there, many of them from a housing scheme which is alleged to be a rather tough spot.

I never got a better hearing from any audience in all my life.

One of my questioners was a young lad who was spastic. It was an amazing thing, a thing commanding unbounded admiration, that this lad, with his terrible handicap and his awkward uncoordinated movements, could possibly take part in an open discussion like that, and could openly witness as to how he prayed to God to help him to conquer his handicap — and God had helped him most amazingly.

I talked to the boy afterwards, and he told me that he had only one ambition, to be a minister. Then he said to me: "I'll bet you I can do what you can't do." I said: "I wouldn't be surprised at that. What is it you can do?"

He said: "I can read a page of any newspaper once, and then repeat it by heart."

If, by the grace of God, that lad ever becomes a minister, he has got a gift that is going to stand him in good stead.

God always gives compensations.

Human weakness and spreading the gospel

MORNING

I happen, as you may know, to be deaf, so deaf that, without a very wonderful hearing aid, I am quite helpless and cannot hear anyone. But there is one tremendous advantage in being deaf. If you are deaf, your power of concentration is far more than doubled, for the very simple reason that you never hear all the sounds which are so distracting for other people!

There is a big compensation for a writer in being deaf!

I think that if we worked this out a bit, we might get a surprise.

If God has taken something from us, he gives us something else back.

That was one of the great discoveries that Paul made. Paul was a sick man, a man with a trouble which was like a stake (it is a "stake" rather than a "thorn") turning and twisting in his body. He prayed to God to take that terrible pain away. Again and again he prayed that it should be taken away. It wasn't taken away. But out of that terrible experience of pain and agony, which was to haunt him all his life, Paul discovered something — he discovered the grace which is sufficient for all things and the strength which is made perfect in weakness (2 Corinthians 12:1-10).

We will often find compensations if we think more of what life has given us and less about what life has taken away.

EVENING

As a church member, you are one of a community pledged to the spread of the gospel

Do you realize that serious fact, that a church member *is* one of a community pledged to the spread of the gospel?

We are members of the church because we are pledged to the spread of the gospel.

Where are we going to spread it?

I know of many cases where people were, as they claimed, "converted". They were asked what they were going to do tomorrow, now that they were converted. The answer invariably was: "I'm going to say my prayers and read my Bible."

That is a very inadequate description of the Christian life. You could do that and never move outside of your own house or room. That could be sheer escapism.

Of course we must say our prayers and read our Bibles — but the object of doing so is to go out into the world and to live for Christ in the shop, the office, the factory, the school.

It is there that our Christianity is seen — or not seen.

We are in the church, not only for what we can get out of it, but also for what we can bring out of it to others.

Vulnerable to people and to God

MORNING

One of the strange features of human life is its vulnerability.

A man is vulnerable to goodness

O. Henry, that master of the short story, has a tale about a lad who used to stay in a country town, and who had once been a good boy.

He came to the great city, fell in with bad company, and learned to walk the wrong way — and to walk it very successfully. He was an excellent pickpocket and a thief. He had done well and he had never been caught. He was pleased with himself. For he was at the top of his thieving profession!

One day he was going down one of the city streets. He had done well. He had just stolen a wallet and snatched a bag, and he was pleased with himself.

All of a sudden he saw a girl of his own age. He looked again, and he recognized her. She had sat beside him in the same class in the village school, in the old days when he had been young and good and innocent. He had only to look at her to see that she was still the same sweet, simple girl that she had always been.

She didn't see him; but the very sight of her suddenly made him catch a glimpse of himself. He suddenly saw himself for the petty thief that he was. He leaned his burning forehead against the cool iron of a lamp standard. "God!" he said, "how I hate myself."

In spite of what he was and of what he had done, he was still vulnerable to goodness.

To find we still have that vulnerability is something for which we ought to thank God.

EVENING

Life would be much simpler if we could sin in peace.

A man is vulnerable to God

You can never tell when suddenly God will break in. No man is ever safe from God.

That is what the Psalmist meant when he said: "Whither shall I go from Thy Spirit? or whither shall I flee from Thy presence? If I ascend up into heaven, Thou art there: if I make my bed in hell, behold, Thou art there. If I take the wings of the morning and dwell in the uttermost parts of the sea, even there shall Thy hand lead me, and Thy right hand shall hold me. If I say, Surely the darkness shall cover me, even the night shall be light about me Yea the darkness hideth not from Thee: but the night shineth as the day; the darkness and the light are both alike to Thee" (Psalm 139: 7-12). There is no escaping the divine pursuit.

We belong to God

MORNING

During the Second World War I had something to do with a canteen which was run for the troops in the town in which I was then working. Early in the war, we had billeted with us in our town a number of Polish troops who had escaped from Poland.

Among them there was a Polish airman. When he could be persuaded to talk, he would tell the story of a series of hair's-breadth escapes. He would tell of how somehow he had escaped from Poland, how somehow he had tramped his way across Europe, how somehow he had crossed the English Channel, how he had been shot down in his airplane once and crashed on another occasion.

He always concluded the story of his encounters with death with the same awe-stricken sentence: "I am God's man."

Here was a man who felt that God had dealt so wondrously with him that he belonged henceforth to God.

Every one of us is God's man.

EVENING

We are God's because God has created us
The Jews had a lovely thought. They believed that no child could ever come into being without the action of the Holy Spirit of God.

"There are three partners in every birth," they said, "the father, the mother and the Holy One, blessed be He."

God alone is the creator of life, and this life which we enjoy was given to us by God.

We are God's because God has preserved us
Whoever we are and wherever we are. God has brought us through all the chances and the changes of life to this present hour.

Sometimes when we look back and see what we have come through, we are compelled to say: "If I had known what was coming, I would have said that I could never face it."

But God brought us through it all, still on our feet and still able to bear up.

H. G. Wells tells of an experience of his. He was on a liner which was entering the port of New York in a dense fog. The ship was creeping forward, feeling her way through the fog. Suddenly out of the fog there loomed another vessel, and the two vessels glided past each other with hardly a yard to spare.

"It made me think," said Wells, "of the general large dangerousness of life."

Life is indeed a dangerous thing, but God has preserved us in danger, has upheld us in sorrow, has healed us in sickness, has brought some of us back even from the gates of death.

God has preserved us. We belong to God.

Redeemed and made whole

MORNING

We are God's because God has redeemed us

The essential fact of Christianity is that God thought all men worth the sacrifice of his Son. God thought it worth the life and the death of Jesus Christ to bring men home to himself.

When we are using something which we have borrowed and which belongs to someone else, we are specially careful of it We do not much care if we crack or scrape or tear or damage something which belongs to ourselves. That does not matter. But if the thing belongs to someone else we exercise a double care.

We ought to be like that with life.

This life of ours does not belong to us. We did not create it, and very certainly we did not redeem it. When we look back, we see very clearly that by ourselves we could never have sustained it.

This life belongs to God. That is why we should use it with reverence and with care, because it does not belong to us.

We should also remember that we dare not waste or soil that which does not belong to us, that which cost so much.

EVENING

A churchman told me of something that he himself had seen at Kelvin Hall during Billy Graham's crusade there.

As my preacher friend sat there, he could not help noticing that this man and his wife were not on good terms. It was not that they were quarrelling or anything like that; but they were treating each other with the frigid courtesy of almost complete strangers. There was obviously a barrier between them; it was clear that this was a marriage which had failed.

The service went on, and the time for decisions was reached. For a minute or two nothing happened. Then this well dressed, hard-headed businessman turned to his wife and said, still with the courtesy which one uses to strangers: "Excuse me please, I must go." And he rose from his seat and started down the long aisle to the front of the hall.

Perhaps twenty seconds passed, and suddenly the woman rose and awkwardly crushed her way past my preacher friend out into the aisle. With a kind of pathetic, stumbling, half run, almost like one blind, she ran after her husband. As she came up with him she caught his hand with a little pleading motion like a child; and these two went hand in hand to declare their faith in Jesus Christ.

What lies behind that little incident I do not know; but one thing is quite clear — here were two people who in discovering Jesus Christ discovered each other. When the barriers between them and God went down the barriers between each other crashed down also.

Unexpected loveliness and hidden strength

MORNING

Mark Rutherford has a novel in which he describes a second marriage. The woman had already been married and she had a teenage daughter. The second husband could make absolutely nothing of the girl. She seemed a sullen, boorish, unlovely character without one single redeeming feature.

Then one day her mother fell ill. Overnight that girl underwent a complete transformation. She became the perfect nurse. There was a new radiance in her. Nothing was a trouble. No service was too menial. She served and she shone in her service.

To have judged her by first appearances would have been completely to misjudge her.

They say that there is a certain kind of stone. When you take it first in your hand it looks like a dull and lusterless piece of stone. It has no life, no sparkle, no brilliance. But if you keep turning it over, you will finally get it into a certain position when the rays of light strike it in a certain way, and it will begin to shine and sparkle like a diamond. The sparkle is there if you will only look for it long enough.

People are like this. Everyone has some gift. Everyone does something well. Everyone has some redeeming feature.

EVENING

Jesus had the ability to see the real person.

Not many people would have seen pillars of the church in an impetuous soul like Peter, or a pair of blusterers like James and John with a nickname like "sons of thunder".

But Jesus did.

Not many people would have picked a dour pessimist like Thomas to be a right-hand man.

But Jesus did.

Not many people would have wished to pay a visit to a quisling tax-gatherer like Zacchaeus or to have had a traitor like Matthew among his closest friends.

But Jesus did.

Jesus had the power to see the hidden strength and beauty in every life, and to waken the sleeping hero in the soul of every man.

Pride

MORNING

Let us think, one by one, of the Seven Deadly Sins.

At the head of the list is pride.

Pride is, in a sense, the *only* sin. Pride is the ground in which all the other sins grow, and the parent from which all the other sins come.

Basically, *pride is the exaltation of self.* It is the setting of too high a value on oneself.

One of the useful things that I have learned from being in the doctor's hand is that no one is indispensable!

A man is always in a dangerous condition when he begins to think that the universe is revolving around him.

Self-importance is pride. The trouble is that, if we allow ourselves to begin to think that we are indispensable in all sorts of things, we can, in the end, render ourselves unable to do the things in which we really are indispensable!

It is not a bad thing to learn that the world gets on quite well without us.

EVENING

The natural result of pride is contempt for other people. There is no sin quite so unchristian as contempt.

There is a pride in birth, which can become snobbery.

There is a pride in knowledge, which can become intellectual arrogance.

There is a pride in achievement, which can become self conceit.

There is a pride in money, which can become the belief that we can buy anything.

All these different kinds of pride have only to be looked at honestly to be seen to be ridiculous. No one has any more ancestors than anyone else! The most learned man is learned only within a very narrow sphere.

The greater a man's achievement, the more he must see that there is still much to do.

The real essence of pride is *rebellion against God.*

The root of *all* sin is the idea that we know better than God. We could even put it in a less "religious" way than that. The mistake of pride is that it defines and neglects the whole mass and weight of human experience.

The lesson of human experience is that, if a man breaks the laws of God, he suffers for it.

If he breaks the laws of health, he suffers.

The way to happiness and to peace of body, mind and spirit is to accept, humbly, the laws of God.

Pride is the sin of the man who is a moral and an intellectual fool.

Wrath

MORNING

Wrath is repeatedly condemned in the New Testament. Twice in Paul's letters two kindred sins are mentioned and forbidden side by side, and it is interesting and illuminating to see the difference between them. Both in Ephesians 4:31 and Colossians 3:8 wrath and anger are mentioned side by side.

In these two passages "wrath" is *thumos* and "anger" is *orge*. In Greek there is a clear distinction between these two words.

Thumos is from a Greek root which means "to boil", and it describes the anger which blazes up quickly and just as quickly subsides.

The Greeks themselves likened it to a fire kindled with straw, a fire which crackles and blazes for a moment and then dies. *Thumos*, is then a burst of temper, a blaze of anger, a momentary outbreak of uncontrollable passion.

Orge, on the other hand, is described as the anger which has become inveterate. It describes the anger which lasts for a long time, the frame of mind which nurses its wrath to keep it warm, the attitude of mind which cannot forget or forgive a wrong or an injury, and which maintains its anger sometimes even for a lifetime.

The teaching of the New Testament is that the quick blaze of an inflammable temper and the long-lasting anger of a bitter heart are *both* to be condemned.

EVENING

In his correspondence with the Corinthians, Paul numbers *thumos* as one of the things which wrecks a church (2 Corinthians 12:20).

In his letter to the Galatians, he numbers it among the sins of the flesh which are opposed to the Spirit (Galatians 5:20).

In First Timothy it is insisted that when a man prays there must be no orge in his heart (1 Timothy 2:8), and James insists that the Christian must be slow to anger *(orge)*, for the anger of man can never work the will of God (James 1:19,20).

The Greeks were not far wrong when they denned anger as "a brief madness". When a man is angry, he is not in full control of himself. When that happens he does things and says things, to others and about others, which, in his calmer moments, he knows to be wrong.

Even if he does not actually do them or say them, he thinks them, or he wishes to do and say them. Jesus taught that the sin of thought is every bit as serious as the sin of action.

There are many people who justify bursts of temper and blazes of anger by saying that it is "their nature", and "they cannot help it". If the New Testament is right, they cannot be, at one and the same time Christian and bad — or quick-tempered.

Let such people learn to think before they speak. Let them think of the hurt and the harm their words cause, and of their own sorrow after the anger is over. Above all, let them ask for the help of Jesus Christ.

Envy

MORNING

Envy is repeatedly forbidden in the New Testament

In the New Testament there are two words for "envy", and there is an interesting distinction between them.

The first and the commoner is the word *phthonos*, together with its kindred verb *phthonein*. This word is altogether bad. It is a word which could not conceivably be used in a good sense. It describes an ugly thing.

It was this *phthonos* on the part of the Jewish orthodox religious authorities which brought about the crucifixion of Jesus (Matthew 27:18; Mark 15:10). This *phthonos* is the sin of the false teacher (1 Timothy 6:4); it is the sin of the unregenerate and the Christless world (Romans 1:29; Titus 3:3); the Christian must strip it off and lay it aside forever (1 Peter 2:1).

The second word is the word *zeios*. It is the word which is used when it is said that "love knows no envy" (1 Corinthians 13:4). It is the sin which Paul fears may wreck the fellowship of the Corinthian church (1 Corinthians 3:3; 2 Corinthians 12:20). It is the sin which must have no part in the Christian character (James 3:14,16).

But *zeios* is not by any means always a bad word. It can in fact be a noble word. It is the word "zeal" in its Greek dress. It can describe the noble aspiration after the highest, the splendid emulation of a great example, the longing to rise to the heights which have been set before us.

The tragedy is that noble aspiration can so easily become ignoble envy, that fine emulation can so easily become evil jealousy.

EVENING

There are three things about *envy* that we ought to note.

How much of our criticism of others is due to unconscious envy?

Sometimes we criticize or belittle or even jeer at someone who is successful. We may criticize the methods of such a man, the theology of such a man, even the character of such a man. Let a man examine himself, and let him be very sure that his criticism is not born of envy.

Envy comes from failing to count our own blessings, and failing to realize that there is something which we can do and do supremely well

Foch said that the whole secret of war is "to do the best one can with the resources one has".

The root cause of envy is the exaltation of the self

So long as we think of our own prestige, our own importance, our own reputation, our own rights, we will necessarily be envious.

Lust

MORNING

It is important that we should be clear about the meaning of the word "lust".

In the minds of most people "lust" tends to be almost exclusively identified with bodily and physical sin, with sexual indulgence and immorality. But the word "lust" has a far wider meaning than that.

Lust is the desire for anything that a man has no right to desire. It is the desire for a legitimate thing in an illegitimate way.

Lust is a right desire wrongly used.

There is a physical lust

The basic fault in physical lust and in sexual immorality is that it deliberately uses other persons as a means towards gratifying an entirely selfish desire.

Any relationship between two people, if it is to be a Christian relationship, must be a partnership. Any relationship in which one person does all the taking and another all the giving is essentially wrong.

EVENING

When does love become *lust?* Love becomes lust when one person wishes to use another person simply for the gratification of desire. If two people love each other, that love must beget a partnership of body, mind and spirit. It must be a total partnership, in which each partner finds a new completeness in life.

When a person uses another person for no other reason than to gratify one purely physical instinct, then love becomes lust.

There is spiritual lust

Spiritual lust can be seen in what we commonly call ambition, the desire "to get to the top", the desire for power over other people, the desire to use other people for our own personal private ends and purposes.

Here again the fault is exactly the same. In all things our relationship with other people must be partnership. Whenever we wish to make use of them; whenever we try to use them as means towards an end; whenever our aim is to get things out of them rather than to share things with them, then spiritual lust, the desire for the forbidden thing, has entered it.

A man must want to make the best of his gifts. He must want to make the biggest contribution to life that he possibly can. But the basis of that desire must be not selfish, but selfless; not acquisitive but generous; not isolation from men but identity with men.

Gluttony

MORNING

It was Aristotle who described every virtue as the mean between two extremes. On the one hand there is the extreme of "excess", on the other there is the extreme of "defect", and in between there is "the golden mean", or as we would rather call it, "the happy medium".

We can consider gluttony best in relation to Aristotle's golden mean.

In regard to things that satisfy the body, there are three possible attitudes.

There is asceticism

Asceticism is the attitude of mind that believes that the body should be deliberately starved and ill-treated, that to eat at all is a bad thing, and that the perfect ideal would be to eliminate food altogether!

This was the attitude of the monks and the hermits of the early church, when they left the company of men and went out to live in the desert.

The New Testament gives no justification for this.

Jesus was happy to be at a wedding feast, and, when the multitude were hungry, his first thought was to give them food, and food in plenty.

EVENING

There is gluttony itself

Gluttony is greedy over-indulgence in material food.

In New Testament times a wave of refined gluttony swept over the Roman Empire. That was the time when men sat down to feasts of peacocks' brains and nightingales' tongues.

Gluttony is eating for eating's sake. It is "living to eat" instead of "eating to live".

The extreme of excess is just that.

There is enjoyment

One of the great sayings in the Bible speaks of God "who giveth us richly all things to enjoy" (1 Timothy 6:17).

The Jews were not given to asceticism and to deliberate starvation. One Rabbi said to a would-be ascetic very wisely: "God will one day call us to account for all good things that we might have enjoyed, and did not enjoy."

Given this *principle of enjoyment* everything falls into place.

It will teach us how to use all *foods and drinks*.

Enjoyment involves a wise, temperate, disciplined use of all good gifts.

The Christian ethic avoids asceticism and gluttony alike, and remembers that God gave us all things richly to *enjoy*.

Greed

MORNING

There are some sins that have a certain attraction and fascination. A man to the end of the day might have lingering longings that he might indulge in them. But avarice is the least attractive of all sins.

No one would wish to be branded as a man of greed. No man could possibly envy the life and the character and the mind of the miser.

Avarice, which is the sixth of the seven deadly sins, need not end in a man being a miser, however. Avarice is undue and illegitimate greed for money.

Avarice grows from certain wrong ideas about money and about what money can do.

It grows from a wrong idea of the meaning of the word enough

Enough has been wisely, if cynically, defined as always being a little more than a man has!

The curious thing about money is that however much a man has, he would be perfectly happy and quite all right — so he thinks — if he only had a little more. Often he rises to the "little more", and still he wants a little more!

Epicurus, the Greek philosopher, said something, which shows an infinite knowledge of human nature; "If you wish to make a man happy, add not to his possessions, but take away from his desires." "To whom little is not enough," he said, "nothing is enough."

Let no one underrate the value of money. Poverty is no blessing. Even sorrow, as the proverb has it, is easier to bear when there is a loaf of bread.

But let a man remember that it is the truth of experience that, for him who thinks in terms of money, enough is never achievable.

EVENING

Avarice grows from a wrong idea of the source of happiness. However much material things help happiness when it already exists, they do not create happiness.

The Greeks had their famous story of Midas of Phrygia. He loved money, and he asked the gods to give him the gift of turning everything he touched to gold. They gave it to him. It was wonderful. He touched the flowers and they became gold; he touched the ordinary crockery and it became gold.

But then he tried to eat and drink, and no sooner did he touch the food and the drink than it became solid gold. His little daughter ran into the room; before he could stop her she ran and kissed him; and there she stood a little statue of solid gold.

In the end he besought the gods to take the gift away.

Avarice grows from the idea that money is the source of security.

People feel that to have plenty of money is to be able to enjoy life and to feel safe.

Even the best and the wisest of us needs to remember that it is folly to lay up treasure on earth and not to seek to be rich towards God.

Sloth

MORNING

In modern lists of the seven deadly sins the seventh sin is listed as sloth; but, if we look at the older lists, we will find it described by another name, the name "accidie". "Accidie" was once a commonly used English word.

The sin which "accidie" describes may nowadays lack a definite name, but it is still easily recognized, and there are many who will have experienced it.

One of the classic expositions of it is by John Cassian, and he describes "accidie" as it affects the monk and the hermit and the man of God.

"Accidie", he says, describes the frame of mind in which a man comes to dislike the place where he is and to despise the people with whom he associates.

He feels that the place where he now is is a dull and arid place.

He feels that the society in which he now has to mix is without grace and spiritual perception.

He feels everything would be so much better, if he could get into a better place and move against more spiritual people.

He comes to feel that he is not getting anywhere; and he slips into a way of saying that he is no use to anyone and that he would never be missed.

In the end he becomes idle, unable to concentrate on anything. He wanders about looking for someone to talk to, unable to work himself and unwilling to let anyone else work.

EVENING

"Accidie", or sloth, is much, much worse than just plain laziness.

There is a streak of laziness in the most energetic of people. But "accidie" is the attitude of the man who has lost the joy of living and of working and of meeting people, who has even lost the joy of worship and of prayer, and who is bored with life in general so that he feels that there is nothing worth doing and nothing left to live for.

It is a very common and a very modem attitude. A doctor has said that boredom is the modern illness, and that he believes that medicine will find a cure for cancer long before it will find a cure for boredom. A Christian may fall into many sins, but it is incredible that a Christian should be bored. The man who has fallen into this sin of "accidie", this weary hopelessness about life, has forgotten two things.

He has forgotten why he ever came into this world

Every man who ever came into this world was sent into this world by God to do some special task. Every man is, as it has been put, a "dream of God".

He has forgotten where he is going to

He is going on. When life ends here, it will begin somewhere else; and all he has got to take with him to that other place is himself.

Is our church dead?

MORNING

A certain minister was called to a certain church in America. He was warned that the congregation was dead, but nevertheless he regarded the call as a challenge and he decided to accept it.

He soon discovered that the church was dead. No planning, no toil, no exhortation, no urging could kindle a spark of life or waken any response.

He told the congregation that they were dead, and that he proposed to carry out the funeral of the church.

A day was fixed. Into the church there was brought a coffin; the church was decked with mourning wreaths.

The time of the "burial service" came. The church was crowded as it had not been for years.

The minister carried out the "burial service". Then, at the end, as a last token of respect, he invited the congregation to file past the open coffin. As they did so, they received a shock. The coffin was open, and empty. But the bottom of the coffin was not wood, it was glass. It was a mirror. As each man looked into the coffin of the dead church he saw — his own face.

We often speak of the church as if the church was a kind of separate and independent entity, as if there was something called "The church" which was quite different from ourselves. But the fact is that we are the church. The church is people. It is its members.

If a congregation is dead, it is because its members are dead.

EVENING

Are we giving the church tolerance or intolerance?
The church is full of people who think that there is no way of doing things but their way. To change a customary or traditional way of doing things is worse than heresy. But the way of doing things that annoys us may be the way of doing things which brings salvation to someone else's soul!

No one has a total monopoly of the truth or of doing things in the right way.

Are we giving the church our prayers or our forgetfulness?
It is no small gift to uphold your minister's hands in prayer.

It is no small gift to come to the church service after praying for the Spirit of God to dwell among his worshipping people.

A ministry that is wrapped around in prayer has every chance of being an effective ministry.

If we think our church is dead, perhaps it is waiting for the life that we can bring to it.

Harmony and serenity

MORNING

One of the most famous badges and coats of arms in the world is the badge of Achimoto College in West Africa. It was designed and conceived by that great man, Aggrey.

The badge of Achimoto is the picture of part of the keyboard of a piano with its black and its white notes. And the symbolism of it is this: You can extract some kind of tune by playing only on the black notes; and you can extract some kind of tune by playing only on the white notes; but if you are ever to produce a real tune and real harmony, you must use both black and white notes.

Therein lies the truth. But the truth is not easy; and even when the broad principle is accepted, there still remain many problems — such as inter-marriage — which are very far from any real solution.

It is not easy for people who were the leaders of the world and who were conscious of their superiority to learn a new gospel of equality.

There is, in human nature, as there always has been, a suspicion of the stranger. The Greeks considered it part of the very structure of nature that they should hate the "barbarians", that is the non-Greeks.

Homer tells of the wars of the Greeks and the barbarians and Socrates insisted that all Greek boys should read Homer so that enmity might be for ever perpetuated.

In the search for unity, ancient claims and prejudices die hard. Only in Christ are all things and all men gathered into one; and, if the church does not lead the way in the new crusade for one world in Christ, no one else can.

EVENING

There is an old legend which tells that, when the people of Nazareth were hot and bothered and irritated and annoyed, they used to say, when Jesus was a baby: "Let us go and look at Mary's child." Somehow serenity came back.

When little things annoy us, the time has come to look at Jesus, to remember he looks at us. In his presence is the secret of the quiet mind. As an old evangelical chorus has it:

Turn your eyes upon Jesus
Look full on His wonderful face
And the cares of earth will go
    strangely dim
In the light of His glory and grace.

Being loved and loving

MORNING

Most people don't really want to love; what they want is to be loved; and the two things are quite different

It is true in human relationships

We are always looking for someone to whom we can go and to whom we can tell our troubles, someone who will understand us, someone who will be a cloak to us against the cold winds of the world, someone to whom we can talk, someone who will protect us, and help us, and comfort us, and care for us.

We want to be loved. But we are far less conscious of the duty of making ourselves into the kind of person we want others to be.

We like to go to other people; but when other people come to us do we find them something of a nuisance?

If we are honest, most of us will have to admit that we like the privilege of being loved, but are very unwilling to accept the disturbing duty of loving others. Yet this we must do.

EVENING

It is much the same with us and God

Loving and being loved?

We are very anxious that God should love us, but we are very unwilling really to love God ourselves. One of the most shameful things about most people's religion is that their one idea is to make use of God. They are very eager to get into touch with God when they are in trouble; but when things are going easily and smoothly. God can take a back seat in their lives.

John Wesley has an entry in his Journal which reads like this: "I had much satisfaction in conversing with a woman at Cowes, who was very ill, and very serious in mind. But in a few days she recovered from her sickness — and from her seriousness together."

Why bother about God and the serious things, when you don't need them?

Real love is a dangerous and a disturbing thing. It awakens a sense of unworthiness. It lays on us the obligation of selfless and unwearied service.

All true love involves giving as well as receiving. We must examine ourselves in our relationships with our fellow-men and in our relationships with God, lest we have drifted, all unconsciously, into a position in which we desire all the privileges of being loved and in which we refuse all the responsibilities of loving.

Doubt self, trust God's Son

MORNING

It is good to be an adventurer. The world could not do without its adventurers. But there are some roads that must be marked "No Entry".

It is tempting to play with fire. It is tempting to experiment with experience. It is tempting to try the forbidden things, just to see what they are like.

But there are some adventures — conscience will tell us what they are — which must not be made. They may not ruin, but they will leave a mark.

Susannah Wesley was one of the great mothers in history. One day one of her daughters wished to do something which was not altogether bad, but which was not right. When she was told not to do it, she obviously was not convinced. It was late and she and her mother were sitting beside a dead fire. Her mother said to her: "Pick up that bit of coal." "I don't want to," said the girl. "Go on," said her mother. "The fire's out; it won't burn you." "I know that," said the girl. "I know it won't burn me, but it will blacken my hands." "Exactly," said Susannah Wesley. "That pleasure you want won't burn, but it will blacken. Leave it alone."

By all means let us be adventurous, but let us remember the roads that are marked "No Entry".

Let us listen when the voice of conscience unmistakably says: "Thus far and no farther."

EVENING

There are two ways in which a man can say, "My son".

Erchie and his wife had had a son, but the lad had run away from home to sea and they did not know where he was.

On a Saturday evening, Erchie and his wife would go out for a walk, and somehow their steps always took them down to the docks. And Erchie knew, although nothing was said, that his wife was always looking for the lad who had run away. And Erchie used to say to himself: "I wonder, if the laddie kent what a heartbreak he was to his mother, if he would bide away so long."

Sadly and with a broken heart, Erchie would say, "My son!"

There was a Son of whom God could speak with all joy.

At the moment of his baptism the voice of God came to Jesus: "Thou art my beloved son; with thee I am well pleased" (Mark 1:11).

There was a son of whom God could say with pride and joy, "My Son!"

Divisions in fellowships

MORNING

There are fences between the different churches, so that to this day we cannot come together in common to sit at the table of our Lord.

There are fences between the different theologies and the hatred of theologians for each other has become a byword.

There are fences which divide those who have different views of scripture, so that the so-called "fundamentalist" banishes the so-called "liberal" or "modernist" from the circle of salvation, and the so-called "liberal" or "modernist" regards the "fundamentalist" as a willfully ignorant obscurantist.

There are fences that divide those who put their faith in different kinds of evangelism, so that the suggestion of any kind of evangelistic campaign is just as likely to split a community as it is to unite it.

We can never properly face the powers of evil when we are split and disintegrated among ourselves.

How shall we overcome these fences?

EVENING

No matter what a man believes we should try to estimate that man at his true worth.

Surely if a man holds a different kind of theology from that which I myself hold, I can still appreciate that man's intellectual worth, his moral greatness, and his spiritual devotion.

Lockhart in his *Life of Sir Walter Scott* tells how Thomas Campbell the poet and John Leyden had a quarrel and would not speak to each other.

Lockhart himself went to Leyden and read to him Campbell's famous poem "Hohenlinden".

When Leyden had heard it, he said: "Dash it, man, tell the fellow that I hate him; but, dash him, he has written the finest verses that have been published these fifty years."

Lockhart duly delivered the message to Campbell, and Campbell said: "Tell Leyden that I detest him, but I know the value of his critical approbation."

There is at least hope that the fences will come down, if, even when we differ from a man, we still appreciate his true worth.

Remove labels and break down fences

MORNING

No matter what a man says he believes, we should try to judge the man not by his professed beliefs, but by what he is himself.

A man in Glasgow had stomach trouble. His life was a misery.

He went to doctor after doctor, and their treatment was quite perfunctory and he was no better.

At last he was recommended to a certain doctor, with the warning that this doctor was a freethinker. He went to him and this is how he recorded this experience:

"He treated me with the utmost courtesy . . . His patients were mostly very poor people, whom, I feel sure, he never charged for his advice; he worked in the slums out of pure goodness; he was never discourteous; he treated me as a fashionable practitioner in the West End might treat a rich patient, and in the end charged me some ridiculously small fee, refusing peremptorily to accept more . . . He was an excellent doctor and a delightful man, and, in spite of his free-thinking, more like a Christian saint than any other being I have ever known."

If only we would stop sticking labels on people and take men as they are, the fences would come down.

EVENING

No matter how wise we are and how convinced we are, we do not possess the whole truth.

No man has the right to assume that he is right in everything and everybody else is wrong in everything.

On August 3, 1650, Cromwell wrote a letter to the General Assembly of the church of Scotland, and in it he said: "I beseech you, in the bowels of Christ, think it possible you may be mistaken."

This is not to plead that we should cease to be sure of things ourselves, but it is to plead that we should cease to believe that everyone else is wrong.

One of the greatest things that Paul ever said about Jesus Christ was written when he was thinking of the new unity of Gentile and of Jew in the Christian church: "He hath broken down the middle wall of partition between us" (Ephesians 2:14).

It is in destroying fences, not in erecting them, that true Christianity lies.

Adventure and effort

MORNING

One of the great and epic feats of the war was in the breaching of the Mohne Dam in 1943 by the squadron of eighteen aircraft under the command of Wing-Commander Gibson, who won the Victoria Cross for his exploit. This action put the Rhur valley out of commission and did much to hasten the end of the war.

The aircraft had to dive 2,000 feet, and to fly at exactly 240 miles an hour exactly sixty feet above the water. Mines had to be dropped so that they just touched the wall of the dam. It was done; but it was done after two months of night and day practice and preparation. No fewer than 2,000 hours were spent in practice. No fewer than 2,500 practice bombs were dropped.

Eric Linklater who tells this story in his book *The Art of Adventure*, goes on to ask: "Is it, then, true to say that the art of adventure is a careful and sufficient preparation for adventure?"

That which looked like a dramatic improvisation of a moment was in fact the product of weeks of toil.

EVENING

The great masters knew all about real effort. Horace advised all authors to keep what they had written beside them for nine years before they published it — advice which a journalist with a weekly column can hardly take!

Plato's *Republic* begins with a simple sentence: "I went down to the Piraeus yesterday with Glaucon, the son of Ariston, that I might offer up prayer to the goddess." Yet on Plato's own manuscript, in his own handwriting, there are thirteen different versions of that single sentence. He toiled at the sentence until every cadence fell on the ear aright.

Thomas Gray's "Elegy" is one of the immortal poems. It was begun in the summer of 1742; it was finally privately circulated on June 12, 1750.

It took no fewer than eight years to achieve these few immortal stanzas.

In any kind of life there is always the danger of a flabby kind of drifting.

It was A. J. Gossip who taught me practical training for the ministry when I was a student at Trinity College in the very early 1930s. I have to my great loss forgotten much of what he told us, but one thing has stuck vividly to me. His advice to every minister was: "Put on your outdoor boots or shoes immediately after breakfast."

It was psychologically sound advice.

It is so fatally easy to adopt a slippered attitude to life, and to forget that, as the old Greek Hesiod put it, "In front of virtue the gods immortal have placed sweat."

Time

MORNING

Nearly all the great men have been haunted by the sense of the shortness of time — and the uncertainty of time.

It was Andrew Marvell who said:

But at my back I always hear
Time's winged chariot hurrying
near.
And yonder all before us lie
Deserts of vast eternity.

As we grow older, and as time grows ever shorter, there are certain things which we should remember.

We should never leave things half-finished — in case they are never finished.

We should carefully choose what we are going to do — for there is no longer time to do everything, and we should do the things which really matter.

EVENING

When we work out how we spend time, the results can be startling. Take three very simple things.

Take the time we spend in eating

Let's say we spend 10 minutes at breakfast, 20 minutes at our midday meal, 20 minutes at tea, and 10 minutes at supper; that is 60 minutes or 1 hour per day, 7 hours a week. It means that in a life of 70 years we will have spent 3 years eating!

Take the time we spend sleeping

Let's say that we sleep for 8 hours every night; 8 hours is one third of the day; one third of our time is spent asleep. That is to say, in a life of 70 years we shall have spent almost 24 years asleep!

Take the case of learning

We only go to school for the equivalent of 43 days in the year;

It is startling when we work things out! No wonder we say, *tempus fugit* — time flies. There are three things we should always remember about time: We only get so much time, and when that is finished we cannot get any more. None of us knows how much we are going to get. If there is something to be learned, we must learn it now; for the longer we put it off the harder it will be to learn it. "Now is the time!"

Preaching and speaking

MORNING

It is almost a first law of speaking that the shorter a speech or sermon or address has to be, the more careful preparation it demands. In such a case, a man has to know exactly what he wants to say and exactly how he wants to say it.

There are very few sermons that would not be improved by being shortened. Jesus could say more in a two-minute — yes, a thirty-second — parable, than the wordy speaker can in an hour.

Samuel Johnson wrote in *The Vanity of Human Wishes*:

"Superfluous lags the veteran on the stage." No one would wish to eject someone who is doing good work; no one would wish to be hard; everyone will be gratefully aware that there are men who have worked for twenty, thirty, forty, fifty years in one place — and it has not been one single day too long. But there comes "Time up!"

It is one of the tragedies of the ministry that the church has never made it possible, or been able to make it possible, for a man to retire when he wished. As things are, he has to keep on because it is impossible financially for him to do anything else.

I hope I shall know when it is time to get off the stage.

EVENING

It is a duty to speak.

We must speak in time

There comes a time when it is too late to speak, and the damage is done. Prevention is always better than cure.

I think it was Fosdick who said that it was always a better plan to build a fence at a dangerous bend with a steep drop than to keep an ambulance waiting at the bottom of the drop to pick up the bodies after the smash.

We must speak at the right time

A word spoken at the wrong time can do very much more harm than good. We must have the wisdom to choose our time; and any word of warning must always be spoken in private, and never flung out in public, when it can produce nothing but resentment.

We must speak in the right way

Certainly we must speak the truth, but equally certain we must speak the truth in love (Ephesians 4:15). Whenever the truth is spoken in such a way as to hurt and wound, whenever the main accent of the voice is criticism, whenever we seem to speak down to the other person, then warning and rebuke and advice are bound to fail.

The kinder the warning the more effective it will be.

The comforter and comfort

MORNING

The Holy Spirit is the person who enables us to cope with life.

Of course, that is exactly what "Comforter" meant in the seventeenth century; for the word "comforter" has in it the Latin adjective *fortis* which means brave; and a comforter was one who put courage into a man.

I am not forgetting how precious the word "Comforter" is, and I am not forgetting how great a function of the Holy Spirit comfort is, in the modern sense of the word. But to limit the function of the Holy Spirit to that, takes much of the strength and iron and virility and gallantry out of the doctrine of the Holy Spirit.

It is very difficult to set an English translation for *parakletos*; it may well be that Moffatt was right when he translated it simply but cogently and beautifully as "The Helper".

We would add power and relevance to the doctrine of the Spirit, if we once and for all banished the word "Ghost", and if we ceased to limit the work of the Spirit by too much use of the word "Comforter" in relation to him.

EVENING

We may never acquire a grasp of foreign languages but, if we are going to help people, there are certain languages which we need to be able to speak.

We must be able to speak the language of doubt

It is very difficult for a man who has never experienced a twinge of doubt to talk to a man whose mind and heart are tortured by questions.

A faith is not the highest kind of faith until it has been tested. We should never be ashamed of having doubts. They are the way to real certainty.

Tennyson said rightly that there is often more faith in honest doubt than in the unthinking acceptance of a conventional creed.

We must be able to speak the language of temptation

Wesley said of a certain man that he was a good man but a stranger to much temptation. For that very reason he was unable really to help others.

The way to real goodness lies through the victorious battle with temptation.

We must be able to speak the language of sorrow

Barrie told how his mother lost the son she loved. "That is where my mother got her soft eyes," he said, "and that is why other mothers ran to her when they lost their child."

The ability to comfort others is a costly thing. It comes through having had sorrow oneself.

Ezekiel said, "I sat where they sat." That is the way of help.

Parergon and taking pride

MORNING

Acquire a *parergon*. You don't follow me, do you? Well, it is like this. When I was in Wales once, I met a professor of Applied Mathematics who was the author of a commentary on the Letters to the Corinthians, and a professor of Biochemistry who, Sunday by Sunday, was a most acceptable lay preacher.

In my own university I know two professors who are expert church organists, one a professor of Naval Architecture, the other a professor of Obstetrics.

The whole point is that they are so distinguished in their own chosen line just because they do two things at once. The extra, thing they do is the very thing which keeps them at concert pitch for the main work. And it is that extra thing which is called in Greek a *parergon*.

There is a legend about John the apostle, that one day someone found him playing with a tame partridge and criticized him for not being at work. His answer was, "The bow that is always at full stretch will soon cease to shoot straight." Everyone needs some sort of relaxation, and the more he is dedicated to his own job, the more he needs it.

Acquire a secondary interest in life, a *parergon*. You will work all the better for it, and leisure will become, not a problem, but an integral part of the fullness of life.

EVENING

One of the happiest men I ever knew, a man who took the greatest pride in his job, was a man in a garage in a town where I used to live. He was not a mechanic; nothing so high up as that. His job, six days a week, was to wash dirty motor cars.

What a pride he took in that job! He washed them with such thoroughness and such pride that you could run your hand along the inside of the mudguard on the wing and withdraw it spotless!

His gift was the gift of washing cars!

But how he used it and gloried in it!

Someone has said that what the world needs, and what God needs, is not so much people who can do extraordinary things, as people who can do ordinary things extraordinarily well.

One of the commonest things in life is the fact that many a person who is much in the public eye could not do his work for a single day without someone who, all unseen, does the greatest task that God ever gave anyone to do — the task of making a home which is really a home.

Take pride in whatever you have to do!

Positive attitudes

MORNING

One of the greatest gifts in life is to have strength and gentleness combined.

It is good to have strength of purpose without being stubborn

One of the great dangers in life — and it is a danger to which people in churches are particularly prone — is the danger of condemning everything that we do not understand, the danger of thinking that there is only one way of belief and only one way of doing things.

It is good to have strength of faith without being self-righteous

It is one of the great tragedies of the Christian life that very often those whose faith is strongest and most "evangelical" are quickest to accuse others of heresy, of modernism, of liberalism, and to insist that anyone who has not had the same experience as they have had has had no Christian experience at all.

There are—blessed be God!—many ways to God. No man has any monopoly of belief or of experience.

A man requires both strength and gentleness before he can be a pillar in the house of God.

EVENING

There is a magnifying glass in the mind, not just in old age but at all ages.

There are people who magnify the amount of work they have to do

To meet them you would think that they had the whole world on their shoulders; that no one ever had so much to do or had to work such long hours.

It is not really a wise occupation, for the more work we have to do, the more necessary it is to stop talking about it and to get on with the job.

Paul has something to say to these people. Whatever happens to you, he said, remember it has happened to plenty of other people before, and it will happen to plenty of other people again. It is only part of the human situation. God will always send you a way out (1 Corinthians 10:13), he adds.

There are people who magnify slights and insults

In many ways they are the most difficult people in life to deal with. If, in any group of people, there is someone of whose feelings we have always got to be careful, if anything we do say has every chance of being twisted into something we never meant, then there is a tension which is quite intolerable.

Resting

MORNING

G. F. Garbett, who was Archbishop of York, met many important people in his long life. He was in Rome when President Roosevelt of the United States died. He called on the United States ambassador, Alexander Kirk, to express his sympathy.

Garbett tells us what Kirk said. "He spoke very feelingly of Roosevelt. He told me he had great interior powers of recuperation." In 1940 Kirk saw him carried to his cabin on his yacht in a condition of extreme exhaustion, very old and tired. In an hour's time he came out a new man, looking twenty years younger. His daughter remarked: "Father is like that; since his illness [Roosevelt had polio] he has trained himself to rest intensively; that is how he goes on."

To rest intensively — that is a strange and wonderful and a most significant expression. Why is it that, for so many of us, rest is so comparatively ineffective, and that even after rest we are still tired?

What does it mean to rest intensively?

There is no point in resting the body if the mind is not at rest. There is no point in going to sit down, or to lie down, if the mind is still incessantly active and if thoughts are restlessly chasing each other through it. It is just as necessary to stop the mind thinking as it is to stop the body acting.

We can only rest the mind by making it think of the things which make for peace.

EVENING

Rest does not necessarily mean doing nothing, although there are times when it does. Often the best rest is change of activity.

Few men achieved more work than James Moffatt, the translator of the New Testament. One who knew him well said that, in Moffatt's study, there were three tables. On one was the manuscript of his translation then in progress. On another was the manuscript of a work on Tertullian on which he was then engaged. On a third there was a manuscript of a detective novel which he was writing.

Moffatt's way of resting was to move from one table to another!

Tiredness is often as much staleness as anything else — and the way to defeat it is not to do nothing, but to do something else.

It is almost a law of life that a man is all the better for having more than one thing to do — even if the other thing be no more than a hobby which is dear to his heart.

Real rest must always be contact with power. Real rest must therefore be contact with God so that our strength may be renewed by contact with a power beyond ourselves.

Repeatedly Jesus had to go into a lonely place to meet God — and what was necessary for him must be far more necessary for us.

Real rest is rest in God.

The Word

MORNING

Dr. F. C. Grant has written a book entitled *How to Read the Bible.* In this book he includes the advice given by Philip Melancthon: "Every good theologian and faithful interpreter of heavenly doctrine must of necessity be first a grammarian, then a dialectician [that is, weighing different interpretations], finally a witness."

Let us look at that program.

The student of the Bible must be a grammarian

That is to say, his primary object must be to find out the meaning of the words, to discover what the Bible means.

Canon B. H. Streeter was once asked, "What do you recommend as a method for the devotional study of the Bible?" His answer was, "The accurate, painstaking critical study of the Bible is its devotional study, for the first thing to enquire of Scripture is its meaning. What could be more important for its devotional interpretation and application than this?"

One of the most serious sins against the light and against the Spirit is the failure to use the helps for Bible study which the great scholars have given us. If we fail to study the meaning of the words of Scripture, then we will be in very serious danger of making Scripture mean what we want it to mean, and not what God wants it to mean.

EVENING

The student of the Bible must be a dialectician

That is to say, he must be willing to weigh one interpretation against another. There are many so-called students of Scripture who would strenuously deny the doctrine of Papal Infallibility, but who claim a like infallibility for their own interpretations.

No man ever became a scholar by assuming that he was always right. There is nothing in this world more beneficial spiritually and intellectually than listening to someone with whom you disagree!

In the study of the Bible it is a duty to listen to every side of the question, and not to be deliberately blind to that which it does not suit us to see.

The student of Scripture must be a witness

The Nestle editions of the Greek New Testament, to which New Testament students have for so long owed so much, begin their prefaces by printing at the top of the page that saying of Bengel, the prince of commentators: *"Te totum applica ad textum; rem totam applica ad te,"* which translated means: "Apply yourself wholly to the text, then apply the whole to yourself."

We study the Bible to find in it the picture of Jesus Christ, his offer of salvation for our souls, and his guidance and his commands and demands for our life.

Everything in perspective

MORNING

"It is an excellent thing to have an optimist at the front provided there is a pessimist in the rear."

There is wisdom in this observation by Lord Asquith, the famous British Prime Minister. If you were to embark on some great operation, it would do no harm to have both sorts of men in your company.

There is value in the kind of man who sees possibilities in everything.

He is the kind of man who, when faced with a problem, is creating all kinds of ingenious solutions. They may not all be practical, but they are always worth a look.

There is the kind of man who is willing to plunge into anything with the sketchiest of preparations.

There is, however, also the man who sees difficulties in everything.

He refuses to make a move until the last detail is prepared and under control.

He must see his way clearly, not only to the next step but also to the one after that.

He is cautious, slow to commit himself, prone to see the possibility that all will end in failure.

The Greeks liked to divide men into two kinds — those who need the spur and those who need the rein. Both kinds were found in the apostolic company.

There was Peter and there was Thomas. Both played a part in Jesus' band. The good leader can use both kinds complementarily.

EVENING

How tragic it is that, in life, we get so much out of proportion. It happens over the things on which we expend time and trouble.

If one had but one prayer to pray, he might best pray that God would make him sensitive enough to see the difference between the things that matter and the things that don't: or to put it the other way, to cultivate a sense of proportion.

It happens over the things that interest people.

Lloyd George, the famous British Prime Minister, once invited Ramsay Macdonald, also a Prime Minister during his political career, to discuss some important issues — especially unemployment. "Did you make any progress?" Lloyd George was asked. The fiery Welshman blazed with indignation. "Progress?" he said; "he insisted on discussing the old Dutch masters!"

Well, the Dutch masters are worth discussing — but at the right time. Lloyd George, overwhelmed by the mass unemployment he faced, felt this was fiddling while Rome burned.

How necessary it is to put first things first in life!

How essential it is to cultivate and operate a sense of proportion !

Changing for the better

MORNING

It is quite a handicap not to be able to turn round!

The Bible is clear that to turn round is just about the most essential action in this life.

The promise of the Law is happiness and prosperity "if thou turn unto the Lord thy God with all thine heart and with all thy soul" (Deuteronomy 30:10).

The Bible is full of the word "turn". And how could it be otherwise? The word "conversion" is derived from the Latin verb *convertere* which simply means "to turn".

In life there are certain turnings which are essential.

We must turn from ourselves to others
The Christian life cannot be the selfish and the self-centered life; it must be the life of care and concern.

We must turn from the past to the future
The Christian characteristically looks forward. He is well aware of the sins and failures of the past; his penitence is real and heartfelt; and yet he knows that, in the grace of God, for the Christian the best is always yet to be.

We must turn from the world and look to God
The Stoics used to say that the only way to live was *sub specie aeternitatis*, that is, under the shadow of eternity. It is easy to slip into a life where God is hardly ever remembered, and yet, because man is mortal, one day he must meet God, and, therefore, he cannot dare to forget God.

EVENING

Swoppets are little toy figures. Mostly they are cowboys and Indians on foot and on horseback. But the thrilling thing about them is that they all come to pieces; and you can take one figure's head off and put it on to another figure's body. Or you can take one rider off one horse and put him on another.

Whenever I see Swoppets I begin to wish that you could do the same with human beings. I begin to wish that it was possible to take one part from one person and another part from another person, and so to make up a combination that was far better and far more complete than either was alone.

I wish we could join together A's determination and B's gentleness.

Our trouble so often is that we are half good. If only we could put the best of two people together we would get real and total goodness.

People aren't Swoppets and we can't take bits from each of them and add them together. But Jesus Christ can make new men.

Barriers

MORNING

I have come across, in an old notebook, a copy of a certain prayer from W. H. Elliott's autobiography *Undiscovered Ends*. It ran like this:

O God, who hast made of one blood all nations of men, mercifully receive the prayers that we offer for our anxious and troubled world. Send Thy light into our darkness, and guide the nations as one family into the ways of peace. Take away all prejudice and hatred and fear. Strengthen in us day by day the will to understand. And to those who by their counsels lead the peoples of the Earth grant a right judgment, that so through them and us Thy will be done. Through Jesus Christ our Lord, Amen.

We have our international barriers.

If ever we needed to pray that prayer, we need to pray it today. It is a prayer that God may guide men at last to live in a world where the barriers are down.

EVENING

We have our ecclesiastical barriers

It is not very logical to fulminate against political *apartheid* and to practise ecclesiastical *apartheid*. So long as the church is disunited within herself, she can have little influence as an advocate of unity amongst men.

We are rapidly coming to a situation in which man-made defenses are nothing better than man-made destructions, and in which men seek to ensure the safety of the future by methods which may well blast the future out of existence. We are coming to a situation in which man-made compromises can do no more than momentarily stem a rising tide which ultimately cannot be stayed.

Nothing is more certain than that the world must either become one world or perish.

As far as the Christian is concerned, the supreme tragedy of the whole situation is that the church, as it stands just now, is quite unfitted to take the lead in the great crusade for unity under God, for very certainly it will not heal the divisions of the world until it heals its own.

If the leaders of the churches can find no way to unity, then we must pray that there will come such an upsurge towards unity from the ordinary people that the instinct of the heart may achieve what the arguments of the mind have failed to achieve.

Down with these barriers!

Reading

MORNING

One Methodist historian credits John Wesley with the publication of no fewer than 371 works, thirty of them jointly with Charles Wesley; and it is to be remembered that this was the work of the man who traveled more miles and preached more sermons every year than any man has ever done.

John Wesley insisted that his helpers and preachers should read, and read constantly. "Steadily spend all morning in this employ," he writes, "or at least five hours in the twenty-four."

Wesley knew well that the man has not yet been born who can continue to give out as a preacher without taking in as a student and scholar. But Wesley insisted that not only his helpers and preachers should be readers, but that all his people should read. "The work of grace would die out in one generation," he wrote, "if the Methodists were not a reading people." "Reading Christians," he said, "will be knowing Christians."

There are great values in constant and wide reading.

EVENING

The man who reads will never be lonely
Between the covers of books he will find people who will become very real to him; and thoughts which will ever keep his mind employed.

The man who reads will never be bored
The man who finds pleasure in a book has a pleasure that is open to him at any time. No man can use his leisure with profit and without boredom who never reads a book.

The man who reads will never be ignorant
He will be in constant touch with minds far greater than his own. A preacher without a library is like a workman with no tools. The preacher who ceases to read will also soon cease to preach in any real sense of the term. He is a bold man who thinks that he can afford to neglect what the great minds of the past and of the present have left to him.

Perhaps the decline in preaching is due to the fact that so many of us spend too much time at committees and too little time in our studies.

To the Christian there is always the Book of all books, the Bible, to be read.

He may study it for a lifetime but he will never exhaust it. The more strenuously and determinedly he studies it, the more it will give him.

The letter writing ministry

MORNING

A letter can convey our congratulations

When we have some success, or when something good happens to us, one of the happiest things is to know that there are others who are sharing our joy and who are wishing us well.

It has been said, rightly I think, that it is much easier to weep with those that weep than it is to rejoice with those that rejoice. In a world where envy and jealousy are far too common, a stamp can do a lot of good if it tells our friends that we are glad some success or some happiness has come to them.

A letter can convey appreciation

There are few things which uplift a man's heart like a word of appreciation and of praise. Such a word does not make a man proud or conceited; it is much more likely to keep him humble because he is well aware how little he deserves it.

A letter can convey sympathy

In the day of sorrow, there is comfort in the awareness that others are thinking of us and remembering us and sharing sorrow with us in so far as it is humanly possible to do so. A stamp should certainly be used to send our sympathy to someone who is surrounded by sorrows.

EVENING

Write at once, answer at once

I talked earlier about the word of sympathy, of thanks, of congratulation. It should be written at once, so do it at once! If you don't do it at once, you probably won't do it at all!

Write legibly — especially your name and address

Illegible writing is discourtesy. You can't answer a letter if you don't know who and where it came from!

Say whether you are Mrs. or Miss! The number of ladies who simply sign their name and put no status is amazing! It has landed me in a lot of trouble!

There is a text in the New Testament about letters that no Christian should ever forget. Paul wrote to his Corinthian friends, "You are a letter from Christ" (2 Corinthians 3:3). It is through us that Jesus Christ communicates with men. Jesus is God's word, and we are Jesus' letters. This is the privilege and the responsibility of the Christian.

To live is . . .

MORNING

Some years ago there was, in Glasgow at Hampden Park, one of the greatest matches of the century, the final of the European Cup between the German team Eintracht and Real Madrid, the greatest club team in the world.

Of all Real Madrid's famous players none was greater and none more famous than Puskas, the Hungarian. It was he who was usually the architect of victory and the scorer of goals.

On the morning after the great European Cup Final, Puskas was interviewed by one of the great newspapers. And Puskas was very willing to talk, for, he told the reporter, "When I don't play football, I talk football. When I don't talk football, I think football."

For Puskas football was the ruling passion; football was his life. That is why Puskas was the master footballer.

In this life there are many ruling passions which may grip and drive and govern a man. It was said of Southey, the author, that he was never happy except when he was writing or reading a book.

It is true that a man will never become outstandingly good at anything unless that thing is his ruling passion. There must be something of which he can say, "For me to live is this."

EVENING

What does it mean to say, "For me to live is Christ"?

It means that we never forget his Cross and all that he did and suffered for us
There is more than a little to be said for the Roman Catholic custom of carrying a crucifix, in order that we may never forget the Man upon the Cross, and how on the Cross he suffered for us men and for our salvation.

It means that we never forget his presence
It means that at morning, at midday and at evening, night and day, we are conscious that we are in his sight, and that he is with us. Everyone feels the presence of Jesus Christ at some special moment in life. Everyone feels him near in the church, at some sacred spot, at prayer. But for true Christians it must be true, as it was true for Brother Lawrence, that he feels Jesus Christ as near when he washes the dishes and does the most menial task as at the Blessed Sacrament.

It means that we take no step without submitting our action for his approval
Men act from many motives in this life — the desire for gain, the eagerness for honor and prestige, the love of comfort, the desire for safety, from motives of prudence, of ambition, of self-protection. The Christian motive can be no other than the approval of Jesus Christ.

Life and its goals

MORNING

For me, this past week has been a kind of summary of life, for circumstances have brought me into close contact with great universal realities in life—Birth and Death.

There was the baptism which reminds us of birth

There is nothing in the world so moving as to hold a little child in one's arms. There in one's arms there rests an amazing bundle of possibilities for good or for ill. And the challenging thing is that the realization of these possibilities rests almost entirely in the hands of the parents.

There was the funeral to remind us of death

As Epicurus said long ago, "In regard to death everyone of us lives in an unfortified city." Here is the assault against which we have no defense; here is the end which we cannot escape.

There is nothing here for complaint or regret or fear; for this is part of the essential human situation into which every human being enters. But again there is challenge, the challenge to be ready whenever the call comes for us, at morning, at midday, or at evening.

EVENING

There are many possible ends in life. A man's goal may be money, or knowledge, or prestige, or position, or discovery.

Leslie Weatherhead in his book *A Private House of Prayer* tells of a conversation which took place in a university common room. Someone posed the question, "What do you want to be?" Many answers were given, many of them not unworthy — academic distinction, an athletic prize, a professor's chair. Then one quiet, shy, sensitive man spoke. "You fellows will laugh at me," he said, "but I want to be a saint."

Here are three definitions of a saint:

A saint is someone in whom Christ lives again.

A saint is someone who makes it easier to believe in God.

A saint is someone who lets the light shine through.

To be a saint is simply to walk the way of life with Christ — and that indeed is the true end of life.

We must always remember that life is not finished until it comes to its end.

The danger of life is that, to the very last moment of it, disaster can come. A famous man absolutely refused to allow his biography to be written during his lifetime, although his achievements would well have justified the telling of its story. He always said, "I have seen too many men fall out on the last lap." "Eternal vigilance is the price of liberty." Eternal watchfulness is the price of honor. That watchfulness must last to the end.

Learning and questions

MORNING

Real teaching is not teaching a pupil what to think; it is teaching him *how* to think. Any teacher who is out to make the pupil think and believe the same as himself is a bad teacher. The good teacher is out to help the pupil to think for himself.

True education is not so much putting things into the pupil as it is drawing things out of the pupil.

One of the greatest mistakes is to confuse teaching and indoctrination. Teaching builds up character and independence; indoctrination destroys both. What then do we have to do to help our education?

We have to be ready to learn from advice
There are many people who go to others for advice. But for all that, they do not really want advice. They want to be told that they are doing well; that they ought to go right ahead and do as they are doing.

We have to be ready to learn from example
This is particularly true of what we might call bad example. We see or hear of someone who has made a mess of things, and whose downfall was due to something which has some part in our own lives. Instead of taking warning, we so often in effect say, "It can't happen to me," and go on doing as we are doing. That is the way to trouble.

We have to be ready to learn from our mistakes
The wise man is the man who never makes the same mistake twice.

EVENING

The great characteristic of the teaching of Jesus is the parable.

The parable is a story that invites a question. At the end of a parable there always comes the question, spoken or implied: "Well, what do you think?"

What set me off on this line of thought was a section in Dr. H. Cecil Pawson's excellent little book *Personal Evangelism*. Here are some of his half-finished sentences:

(1) church-going is to me . . .
(2) So far as Sunday is concerned, I . . .
(3) Total abstinence is to me . . .
(4) Can you conceive of a condition in your life in which it would be true to say "I've lost everything"?
(5) When I am depressed I . . .
(6) My greatest ambition is . . .

There are Professor Pawson's questions. If we try to answer them, and are honest in doing so, it could be a revealing and a salutary experience. *You try it!*

Needed: Christian ethics

MORNING

One of the worst possible features of modern life is the flood of thoroughly bad literature that issues from the printing presses. There are few towns in which you cannot discover without difficulty a bookshop which deals in books which are barely on this side of pornography and sometimes not on the right side at all. There is a deliberate stimulation of that which is worst.

Life is full of infection. In modern life it is quite impossible that the young person should escape contact with this infection.

There is the responsibility of real education not only in letters, but in life
One of the saddest and most tragic of all situations is that which arises when a young person comes back to a parent or a teacher with life in ruins, and says, "I would never have been in this mess, if you had only told me what you ought to have told me."

There is above all the responsibility of making Jesus Christ a living presence in life
If we can introduce our young people to Jesus Christ, and if we can teach and train and enable them to walk every way of life in his company and aware of his presence, then they will have a prophylactic which will preserve them from any infection which may attack them.

The more civilized and the more sophisticated the world becomes, the more the world needs Jesus Christ.

EVENING

In life there must be a correct balance between adventurous experiment and respect for experience
Young people are natural experimenters; it would be wrong if they were not. But they cannot neglect the wisdom and the voice of experience unless at their peril.

The Highway Code is not about that which is advisable. It is something which has to be observed if chaos on the roads is not to occur. Similarly the code of the Christian ethic must be observed, if life is not to become a jungle.

The Highway Code is not, however, law. It is the statement of the principles which must govern the use of the roads, if life on the roads is to be safe.

The Christian ethic is not rules and regulations concocted to limit and to circumscribe Christian freedom. It is a presentation of principles, which, in each circumstance, the individual must work out and apply for himself, on the principle that the Christian must live and love as Jesus Christ lived and loved.

There is a Highway Code; no sane driver neglects it. There is a Christian code of living
Permissiveness is no virtue, if it permits that which experience has proved to be fatal.

The church should never hesitate to say that society neglects this code for life at its peril.

Concentration and leadership

MORNING

In concentration there are two essentials.

The first essential is *interest*. No one can really concentrate on anything unless he is interested in it. Given interest, concentration automatically follows.

Interest often comes from *taking the long view of things*. There are many things which are not in themselves interesting, but which become interesting when they are seen as means towards something beyond themselves. Piano practice is not interesting in itself, but it gives no difficulty to the person whose heart is set on being a great pianist. Athletic training is not in itself interesting, hut it will present no difficulty to the person who is determined to excel in athletics.

But we can concentrate only if our work is done when it should be done

The only possible way to concentrate is to do each task when it ought to be done and complete it then, for the subconscious memory that there is something which should have been done and has not been done, is itself enough to wreck concentration.

Concentration in all things is necessary. The greatest concentration of all is the concentrating of the eyes of the soul on Jesus Christ.

Look unto Jesus.

EVENING

Leadership is a gift. Some men have it. Others don't. But most of us could have more of the capacity to lead if we understood the secrets of leadership.

The leader whom men will respect is the one who is himself involved in the job

George VI was a king who had an impediment in his speech. It was not a stutter. It was really a stop.

One day he was seeing over a certain film studio. By an unfortunate coincidence, the engineer who was showing him round had exactly the same impediment. In his nervousness the engineer found he was becoming worse and worse.

King George put his hand on the man's shoulder. "It's all right, friend," he said. "I know what it's like."

The leader for whom men will work is the one with the personal touch

One of the things that made Field Marshal Montgomery a great leader was simply that his men practically knew him by sight. He did not sit in headquarters issuing directions. He came and met them.

Letters are no substitute for personal contacts. The man who leads is the man who is near and known.

The leader

MORNING

A leader must have insight to see what ought to be done

Half the battle is won when we discover what is wrong and what needs to be done. Some of us drive motor cars without any idea of what is going on under the bonnet. When something goes wrong and the car stops, we are helpless. We have to send for the motor mechanic; he opens the bonnet; he immediately diagnoses the trouble; and often it is so simple that, if we had been able to see what was wrong, we could have fixed it for ourselves!

In life we can only see what needs to be done by looking at things with the eyes of Jesus Christ, and in the light which he supplies. It may well be said that the first step towards mending any situation is nothing other than praying about it.

A leader must have resourcefulness to devise a way of doing what needs to be done

It is far too common a reaction to a bad situation that nothing can be done. Cavour said that the first essential of a statement is "the sense of the impossible". As P. G. Wodehouse's famous Jeeves used to say, "There is always a way."

We may well remain defeatist when we tackle things in our own strength, but the grace of God in Jesus Christ is sufficient for all things.

EVENING

A leader must have the courage to risk it

Few people like the truth, and few people like reformations. "Truth," said the Cynics, "is like the light to sore eyes." Therefore, the man who speaks the truth always takes a risk. Most people prefer to remain comfortably undisturbed. Therefore, the reformer always incurs dislike.

George Bernard Shaw said, "If you do not say a thing in an irritating way, you may just as well not say it at all, since nobody will trouble themselves about anything that does not trouble them."

A leader must have magnetism to fire his followers

That magnetism comes from only one source. It comes from a burning conviction of the rightness of the cause and a transparent sincerity of purpose. No one can kindle men to enthusiasm unless he is on fire himself. No one can light a flame in the hearts of other men unless he has a fire in his own bones. And no one will follow a leader whose sincerity he does not trust. The time-server, the man who is dominated by personal ambition, is always seen through but men will admire the burning enthusiast even if they feel that he is wrong.

It can be seen at once that leadership is a costly thing. It begins with self-dedication to Christ, for real leadership is based not on the exaltation of self, but on the obliteration of self.

Tradition and foundations

MORNING

Tradition is important. Let us see why.

Tradition preserves what is fine

To enter into the tradition of a great school, or a great ministry, or a great congregation, is one of the most inspiring things of life. Here is something to live up to. Here is something one must not let down.

But tradition can fossilize something that has lost all point

Even today a bride is on a bridegroom's left arm in order to leave his right arm — the sword arm — free to meet a crisis! The dress of the Moderator of the General Assembly of the Church of Scotland is still, for some extraordinary reason, a fossilized version of eighteenth-century court dress!

There is many a tradition that is meaningless now because its origin has been forgotten. Yet it goes on!

This can be bad!

Tradition can therefore be an inspiration or a handicap

A man can be lifted up by it — there are times when even to put on a certain uniform does something to a man: or it can become a barrier to progress — "we never did that here!"

Encourage traditions that are fine.

Discourage those that are fossilizing.

EVENING

When we are up against it, it is the simplest things we want, like water from the village well

This is true of religion.

It was my job to teach in a university. I know well how essential scholarship is. But I sometimes wonder if religion is really as difficult and as complicated as all that, and I sometimes wonder how much of our "technical" scholarship is really relevant to the human situation.

When we are up against it, our minds and memories go back to childhood's days

Thomas Carlyle traveled far from the little village of Ecclefechan, in the south of Scotland, but he used to say that what kept him right was his mother's voice across the years: "Trust in God, and do the right."

Happy is the man who has a childhood's faith on which to look back — for no life is stronger than its foundations.

The simple things, the foundations — these are the things that matter when the hard times come.

Unshockable families

MORNING

If there is a virtue that a teacher and a parent and any kind of friend should have, it is that of never being shocked.

This does not for a moment mean that you have to agree with everything that everyone, perhaps especially young people, says

It does not mean that, when they make some outrageous suggestion, and when they want society to be completely permissive, you say, "That's quite all right. Go ahead!" It will in fact mean that you often find yourself in strenuous and violent disagreement with them, and that you often find yourself arguing for a precisely opposite point of view.

Argument is the great activity of friendship.

It does mean that you willingly and freely grant to the other person the right to think for himself. The last thing you want to do is to stop anyone thinking for himself

People don't think too much; they think too little. If they thought a little more strenuously and a little more clearly, they would probably think themselves out of the things which are wrong.

Wrong ways and decisions are the result of too little, not too much, thinking. So when people start thinking for themselves, the last reaction we ought to have is to be shocked.

EVENING

How wonderful it would be if parents could always be called the friends of our children. There is so often an almost unbridgeable gap between parent and children. They become strangers to each other. There are reasons for that gap.

There is the inevitable gap between the generations

There is the gap between the "then" and the "now". Parents do not bridge that gap by being determinedly "with it". There is, in fact, nothing more embarrassing than, in the old phrase, "mutton trying to look like lamb."

A gap there is, but each generation must be itself. Age trying to behave like youth is worse than youth aping age. We must be ourselves.

If a parent is to be a friend to his child, there must be communication

The tragedy of modern family life is that so very often parents and children drift so far apart from each other that, in the end, they cannot even make conversation; they have nothing to say to each other. This is a situation that must not arise.

Happy is the child whose parents are not only his parents, but his friends too.

The past and the future

MORNING

I remember the time when an airplane was an incredible sight. I remember when motor cars were rarities.

I remember the first wireless sets.

I remember the first ballpoint pens — how rare they were and how expensive!

I remember when you could buy cigarettes for eight pence for twenty and petrol at one shilling and two pence for a gallon.

Do I feel nostalgic about all this? Would I put the clock back if I could? Certainly not!

For there are other things I remember.

I remember when there was no health service.

I remember when people could not have proper medical attention because they could not pay for it. I remember when my work, week after week, included visits to sanatoria, for tuberculosis *was* a scourge then! I remember children with rickets and diphtheria. I don't want to go back to that!

That great teacher and preacher, A. J. Gossip, jumped on someone who once said that things could never be the same again. "Thank God," said Gossip, "that things can never be the same again."

EVENING

The day seems to be coming when work will be able to be done with no more effort than sitting and watching. If that day comes, there will be trouble.

Juvenal, the famous Roman satirist, prayed the famous prayer for *mens sana in corpore sano*, a sound mind in a sound body. Now we cannot have a sound body without exercise. The health problems of *homo sedentarius* are already well enough known. And we cannot have a sound mind if there is absolutely no interest at all in work, and if it can produce nothing but boredom.

At the moment there is a balance. It may be difficult to get at one and the same time a sound mind and a sound body. But there are those whose work is so mentally interesting that they can forget the lack of physical effort, and there are those whose work is so physically demanding that they can forget its repetitive nature. But when work becomes physically immobile and mentally boring then trouble will come.

It seems that the more complex and sophisticated living becomes, the harder it will be to find real life.

Generous service

MORNING

St. John's-Renfield church in Glasgow celebrated its one hundred and fiftieth anniversary in 1969. A very interesting brochure, with a brief but vivid history of the congregation, was issued to mark the event.

Among the many interesting things in that account is the story of the opening of Free St. John's church in George Street on June 8, 1845. The collection that day was made up as follows:

Banknotes: 2 at £100, 22 at £20, 7 at £10, 95 at £5, 444 at £1.

Gold: 1 old guinea, 10 sovereigns, 23 half-sovereigns.

Silver: 52 crowns, 1 American dollar, 420 half-crowns, 627 shillings, 393 sixpences, 53 fourpences, 2 threepences, 1 two pence.

Copper: 48 pennies, 42 halfpennies, and 1 farthing.

To this had to be added £ 12.3.4d in the evening collection and £8.2.0d of donations from people who were absent — a grand total of £ 1779.17. 10d. — *and one farthing*.

This farthing fascinates me. Who gave it and why did he give it?

There are three possibilities.

Perhaps someone was so incredibly mean that, into the collection, he put the smallest coin of the realm.

It could stand for a modern version of the widow's mite (Luke 21: 1-4).

Perhaps on that memorable Sunday someone literally turned out his pockets, giving the notes, the silver, the copper that was in them — to the uttermost farthing. If so, this stands for the person who gives everything he has got to his Lord and keeps nothing back.

Happy is the man who gives himself and his all — to the uttermost farthing. One farthing. In which group are you?

EVENING

Sir Giles Gilbert Scott, the great English architect, had an extraordinary distinction. He designed Liverpool Cathedral and the street telephone kiosk!

Vast grandeur and unadorned utility came from the same man.

No truly great man ever despises small things

Giles Gilbert Scott gave his genius to a great modern cathedral, but was equally dedicated in producing a telephone kiosk.

In a cathedral men talk to God: in a telephone kiosk, they talk to each other

The man who is at variance with his brother can't be in fellowship with God. The man who is in fellowship with God will be in fellowship with his brother man.

The kiosk and the cathedral stand for communication between man with man and man with God. We cannot have the one without the other.

A helping hand

MORNING

Confession, so they say, is good for the soul. I am one of those people who are no good about the house.

A painting job had to be done in a room in our house and another member of the family decided on a do-it-yourself policy. Well, the job was done and, in my view, it was not well done.

I was, therefore, as I said, forced into action, and promptly — after some well-chosen words of criticism — did the job myself over again. And, though I say it myself, did it very well indeed!

That, I can now see, is exactly and precisely the wrong way to do things.

It is always wrong to delay action until something goes wrong. It is always wrong to be lazy and selfish enough to do nothing until in the end something has to be done. It is far better to act in time, before things go wrong.

Prevention is better than cure every time.

EVENING

I remember reading a tale about D. L. Moody. A man came to him with a very sorry story. "What would you do, Mr. Moody," he asked, "if you had got into a mess like that?" "Man," said Moody, "I would never have got into it." (All the same he helped the man to the utmost.)

There are so many things which need never have happened, if action had been taken in time.

Many a labor and industrial dispute would never arise, if some grievance were personally dealt with in time. Many an international crisis and even a war would be averted, if someone had the sense to act in time. Many a situation in a church has been allowed to grow to serious proportions, when, if it had been dealt with in Christian love and charity and prayer at the beginning, it could have been cured straightaway. Many a young person has made shipwreck simply because a parent or older friend did not want the trouble and the unpleasantness of speaking a word of warning and rebuke in time.

It is always wrong to be propelled into action from motives of criticism
Action which is really the result of criticism, whether the criticism is expressed or whether it is unexpressed, is always the action of superiority and conscious superiority at that. And we get nowhere that way. Action must always be in love and in sympathy. So long as we stand above people, we cannot really help them. We can do something for them, but that is a very different story from helping them.

The action which is fundamentally the action of criticism may be efficient enough, but it can never speak to the heart.

I hope that I have learned my lesson.

Seeing it through

MORNING

I told you of my experiment in house painting. Now the paint which I was using was a rather special kind of paint which is guaranteed not to drip. That, of course, is a very useful quality in a paint. But it is thick, not liquid, almost like a jelly, and there are right ways and wrong ways of using it. From that paint I learned certain lessons, and they are lessons not only for painting but for life.

I learned that you must know how to do a thing or your work will be quite ineffective

I had to learn how to use this paint.

Normally, in painting, you can sweep the brush backwards and forwards like a pendulum. But you couldn't do that with this paint. If you drew the brush in one direction, you laid it on; but if you swept the brush backwards in the reverse direction, you promptly brushed it off again, and so you "got nowhere fast". But if you kept laying it on, always in the same direction, you got a wonderful job.

It is very essential to get knowledge, but it is at least as essential to learn how to use knowledge in the right way.

I learned that you cannot paint in a hurry

If you hurried it might look all right when the paint was still wet, but when it dried, it was streaky instead of even, and the underpaint showed through. It was a thoroughly unsatisfactory job.

Haste was hopeless!

EVENING

I learned from my painting that you cannot leave a job half done

If you left it half done and then began again, the join was quite easy to see. If you began a job, you had to finish it.

One of the sorriest things in life is the number of things that we begin and never finish. Life is littered with things half done. Most of us are much better starters than finishers. When we were young, we used to begin a collection of this or that or the next thing, and we would be enthusiastic for a week or two, and then the thing would be thrown into a cupboard or pushed away into a drawer and forgotten. That may be all right for a child, for a child has not yet learned to have any concentration, but it certainly will not do for a person who is supposed to be a mature man or woman.

"Blessed is he who endures to the end" (Matthew 24:13). It is the man who sees things through who comes to happiness and to success in the end.

First things first

MORNING

One of the most dangerous jobs in the war was sailing in convoys; and the worst danger of all was sailing in the convoys bound for Russia, for then, if a ship was torpedoed, a man perished quickly in the icy waters, unless help came at once.

One day a chaplain came to a man who was sailing in those convoys and asked him for any special impressions. "I don't think," said that man, "that there is anything I can tell." "But," said the chaplain, "I know that you have been bombed and torpedoed and machine-gunned. There must be something." "That was all in the day's work," the man said. "But there must be something," said the chaplain, "that made some lasting impression on you, something that you will remember all your life." "Yes," said the man, "there is something, or rather, there are two things that I shall always remember. The first is the sound of men's voices in the sea at night, when you can't stop to pick them up . . . and the other is the sound of people's voices complaining in the shops at home."

Into the man's mind there had burned itself the contrast between men dying in icy waters and men and women complaining about trifling and petty inconveniences. People grumbled at quite unimportant things while men were dying at sea, and sacrificing their lives.

There is hardly anything so necessary as the ability to distinguish between that which is important and that which is not.

EVENING

There can be that tragic lack of proportion in the things to which people give their effort and their strength.

Many a social worker will spend hours on other people's families and no time on his own.

Many a man will spend his whole strength and thought and energy on this world and forget completely that there is a God and that there is a world to come.

Perhaps there never was an age in which there is such a lack of sense of proportion as there is today. It is easy to say, "We never had it so good", if you are thinking only in material terms. If you are thinking in spiritual terms, it is a very different story.

If a man had one prayer to pray, he might well pray that God would keep him vividly awake and alive in mind and spirit so that he can see the difference between the things that matter and the things that, in the long run, do not matter at all.

What do I work for?

MORNING

I heard recently about a certain lady. She was a quiet, gentle, unobtrusive person. One day she said, "You know, when I see the people who are somebody, I'm very grateful that I'm a nobody." What did she mean? I offer my guesses!

She was perhaps thinking of the people whom success has spoiled

Abraham Lincoln once said cynically, "You can see what God thinks of money, when you see the people he gives it to."

You are perfectly right to magnify your office — but not to magnify yourself! When you get a step up in life, ask yourself a question: "Do I regard this advancement as a means of exercising more power or as a means of rendering more service? Do I regard this as a means of getting more or of giving more?"

If you remember that a Christian is among his fellow men as one who *serves*, then success will not spoil you!

If we accept the Christian view of man, then there is no such person in life as a nobody

As a workman of any kind, there is no doubt that we could be more or less readily replaced. But if there is anyone in this world who loves us, there is someone in whose heart we cannot be replaced. We matter to someone. And even if on earth we know that loneliness which has none to love and none to care, we matter to God.

You can lose everything and still have God. If you have God, you cannot be a nobody.

EVENING

Some people really work for themselves

It is a hard thing to say, but almost every church and every voluntary and charitable organization contains a certain number of people who seek for office and for place because they have no chance of any prominence in the world and the church, or the voluntary organization, is the one place where they can be somebody.

In the end there is only one way to work, and that is to work for Jesus

Always our question must be, "Lord, what do you want me to do?" Always our work must be taken and shown to him. The only thing which should matter to us is his "Well done!"

The Bible

MORNING

What you get out of the Bible depends on what you bring to the Bible. The Bible has an extraordinary way of providing a personal message to each of its readers.

The Bible speaks to our interests and our abilities.

One of the curious things about the Bible is that so many craftsmen will find things about *their* skill and *their* crafts in it.

The doctor finds his skills discussed in Leviticus. The lawyer and the judge will feel at home in Deuteronomy.

The preacher can study the message of the teaching of the prophets.

The soldier and the military leader will find battles and campaigns to analyze.

The traveler . . .

The archaeologist . . .

The geographer . . .

The builder . . . Why, the description of the detail of the Temple is a fascinating mine of information for any craftsman to wonder at!

The housewife will find herself in the parables of our Lord.

What a wonderful book to touch life at so many points! No one need ever feel the Bible irrelevant. For it deals with what we know and do.

EVENING

What you get out of the Bible depends on what you bring to it (we said). The Bible touches life at so many points that there is hardly anyone who will not find something relevant to his own life and work in it (we said).

The Bible speaks to our needs whatever they may be.

The Bible gives comfort in a time of sorrow, guidance in a time of difficulty, challenge when we have lost the place, the means to praise when we want to rejoice.

You cannot find an area of life that does not find, in the Bible, a relevant comment on our needs.

This is the wonder of this wonderful book.

The more we take to the Bible the more it will give us

The Bible can give to the simplest soul and the most uninstructed a word for the way, but delve deeply into it and there is matter and meaning that will stretch the greatest intellectual. A means to simple worship, it is also a mine of information — archaeological, historical, geographical, biological and so on.

The story of the Bible is that there is no one who goes to it in need and in faith whom it does not find.

Prayer (1)

MORNING

The wonderful thing about God is that he can listen to all men's prayers at the same time.

It is never too late and never too early to pray to God

Sometimes we fear to visit a person too early in the morning or too late at night or during their busy time, lest we be nothing better than a nuisance to them, lest we interrupt their work, and lest they be too busy to see us.

No one is too young and no one is too old to pray to God

Sometimes we say of children that they should be seen and not heard, to quote that old Victorian tag again. But Jesus said, "Let the little children come to me."

Sometimes people grow old and all their loved ones and their friends pass on and they have no one to talk to. Loneliness is one of the supreme problems of age.

No child is too small to talk to God; no aged one is too forgotten to talk to God. The fears of childhood, the problems of youth, the weariness of the middle years, the loneliness of age — they can every one of them be brought to God, and God will hear.

That is precisely why prayer should be not only a thing of the crisis and the emergency, but be part of the daily life of every man.

The wonder of God is that he listens to each one of us as if there was only one of us to listen to. He is the hearer of prayer — the world's prayer, and my prayer.

EVENING

A great many people stop praying because they think that prayer does not work. But this happens because they have a wrong idea of prayer.

Prayer has its laws. Here are two of them.

Prayer is not God doing things for us: prayer is God helping us to do things for ourselves

It is a first law of prayer that God will never do anything for us that we can do very well for ourselves. God is not the easy way out.

Prayer is not simply unloading our tasks on to God. Prayer is the means by which God enables us to do them for ourselves.

Prayer does not change circumstances. It changes us

The circumstances are the same, but we approach them with new courage, new strength and a new ability to cope with them.

Prayer helps us meet difficulties in a new way.

Prayer (2)

MORNING

Here are two more "rules of prayer."

Prayer is not escape. It is conquest

Prayer is not a mechanism for helping us to avoid a demanding situation. It helps us to face and overcome that situation.

Suppose we are in a difficulty. Suppose we go to some trusted friend for help and guidance. When we leave that friend, we have not escaped from the situation, for it is still there to be faced, but somehow that time with our friend has made the situation less daunting and more tolerable.

Similarly prayer never offered any man escape from a difficult set of circumstances. It offered him strength to face those circumstances and to conquer or to endure them.

Prayer is not so much talking to God as listening to God. It is not so much telling God what we want him to do, as listening to see what he wants us to do

In prayer, we have, of course, to begin by talking, but we always have to end by listening. Prayer is literally saying, "God, what wilt thou have me to do?"

EVENING

Here is the prayer which a small boy actually wrote: "O God, help us to be good and to help other people." In many ways it is the perfect prayer.

It does not say "Make us"; it says "Help us"

The boy has grasped the fact that prayer is not getting things done for us; prayer is getting the strength to do them for ourselves.

The prayer does not say, "Help me"; it says, "Help us"

Our prayers would be very much more effective if they had in them less of the "me" and more of the "us".

The prayer asks simply for help to be good

If things are right at the center, they will be right at the circumference. There may be many things we need, but we need to be made good most of all; and, if we are good, all other things will take their proper place.

It does not say "Help others", it says, "Help me to help others"

When we pray for others, we must always at once try to answer our own prayers.

The best prayer of all is, "Help me to help."

Attitudes to people and work

MORNING

The most God-like thing in the world is the passion to help others.
You remember the four lines of doggerel that C. T. Studd, that prince of missionaries, loved:

Some want to work within the sound
Of church or chapel bell;
I want to run a rescue shop
Within a yard of hell.

There is a phrase in the creed. I know that it is a difficult phrase, and that even the exact meaning of it is far from certain — "He descended into hell." Whatever may be the exact and precise meaning of it, here is a picture of Jesus Christ scouring even the depths of hell with the message of salvation, going to the literal utmost to help and to save men.

Life is for ever full of the contrast between divine selflessness and human selfishness. When Paul wishes to describe Jesus in all his Godhead, it is not in terms of glory that he describes him; it is in terms of the abandonment of glory, the acceptance of the humiliation of humanity, the toil of servitude, the agony of the Cross (Philippians 2:5-11). It is precisely there that the God-likeness of Jesus essentially lies.

EVENING

The important thing is not that something should be done perfectly, but that it should be done as well as we can do it

Very often we don't try to do something, on the excuse that we cannot do it very well. But our first duty is not to do the thing very well, but to do it as well as we can do it.

When Henry VIII asked Miles Coverdale to produce an English translation of the Bible, Coverdale knew very well his own limitations and his lack of the necessary scholarship in Hebrew and Greek. "Considering how excellent knowledge and learning an interpreter of scripture ought to have in the tongues, and pondering also mine own insufficiency therein, and how weak I am to perform the office of translator, I was the more loath to meddle with this work."

But then he goes on: "But to say the truth before God, it was neither my labor nor desire to have this work put in my hand; nevertheless it grieved me that other nations should be more plenteously provided for with the scripture in their mother tongue than we; therefore when I was instantly required, though I could not do as well as I would, I thought it my duty to do my best, and that with a good will."

Coverdale knew that he was but ill-equipped; but he did his best, and his best became a masterpiece.

Victory

MORNING

The young man I had to examine had graduated Master of Arts with Honors in Mental Philosophy. It was as he entered his course of study for the ministry that I marked his Greek and English Bible papers.

He scored 94 per cent in the first and 86 per cent in the second. What I have not yet told you is that he is totally blind.

Handicaps are meant to be overcome

How often seriously handicapped people have done great work and so won great victories.

Julius Caesar was an epileptic.

Douglas Bader, that wartime flying ace supreme; won his greatest triumphs after he lost his legs and had to use artificial ones.

All handicaps bring compensations

I am almost completely deaf. But this means I can sleep without trouble in a noisy hotel by a railway station! And I can concentrate far better on work and study for I have no distractions. And at boring committee meetings, I can switch off my hearing-aid!

EVENING

If a man has a handicap and is determined to conquer it, nature becomes his ally.

I know a person who had to have a very delicate and serious eye operation. For a long time this involved lying in a hospital bed with her eyes bandaged so that not a ray of light might come near them.

This friend told me that, in less than a week, she could tell exactly what nurse was walking along the corridor simply by the sound of her feet, and could even identify a person by the person's touch on the bedclothes. It was as if the other faculties sharpened and strengthened themselves to make up for the faculty which had ceased to function.

Nature loves the person who refuses to give in. No man is beaten by a handicap until he admits defeat, and he need never do that.

The apostle Paul beat his "thorn" because he brought two things to it. He brought his own determination and he brought that amazing grace of God in which he was able to do all things, because his weakness was made strong in the strength of God (2 Corinthians 12:9; Philippians 4:14).

If we have some handicap, we and God can do something about it together.

Reality

MORNING

Tillotson, the great Archbishop of Canterbury, was one day talking to Betterton, the great actor, in the eighteenth century. Tillotson asked Betterton, "Why is it that I, when I am preaching about the greatest things, leave people quite unmoved, while you, when you are acting in what is nothing more than a play, can move them to the depths of their hearts?" "Sir," said Betterton, "you are telling them stories, while I am showing them facts."

What a condemnation of human nature, what a commentary on the human heart, that the action of a play should be more real to people than the working out of the eternal drama of the love of God!

What is the reason for this?

There are two reasons, I think.

There is the deadening influence of familiarity

Most of us have heard the story so often that the cutting edge of it is gone.

There is the strange fact that for so many people the Bible stories happen in a kind of land of make-believe

They happen in the same twilight land as the fairy tales do; they lack the reality of events which are sharply historical.

EVENING

Owing to a certain traffic problem in the avenue where we live in Glasgow, I wrote to the local police; and almost by return post there came back a very charming and courteous letter, actually thanking me for complaining and saying that something would be done — and it was done, and at once.

Over a rather unsatisfactory matter in Post Office practice here in our Cathcart area I wrote to the local postmaster. In a very few days I had a letter back, again actually thanking me for complaining, and saying that the matter had been attended to.

The last instance is almost beyond belief! I had certain correspondence with the Inspector of Taxes! Now I want to admit that I had been very dilatory in dealing with this correspondence and I deserved a sharp rebuke. But when I did answer, and when I did state my claims, the Inspector of Taxes actually wrote back expressing the opinion that in my claims I had been "rather harsh on myself, and suggesting that I should claim far more than I did."

We should never allow the bad incidents in life to blind us to the vast amount of good that there is in life. We should never allow the conduct of one bad or discourteous person to make us condemn the whole institution to which he belongs.

There is so much that is good about. I hope you find it too.

Caution and chance

MORNING

We must be very cautious, very careful, how we touch and handle and treat things which are very precious

How carefully a teacher or a parent should touch and handle the mind and the innocence of a child! How carefully we ought to touch and handle friendship and love lest the loveliest of human relationships should be hurt or damaged or impaired!

The lovely things of life must be handled with all care.

We must be very cautious how we meet the dangerous things in life

It is to warn of approaching danger that most signs on the road are erected. It is very easy to play with fire, to flirt with danger.

I read in the correspondence columns of a newspaper a very wise story. An old lady in the old days advertised for a new coachman. There were three applicants. She asked each of them the same question. "How near," she asked the first, "could you drive to the edge of a precipice?" He answered that he could drive within an inch of the edge. She asked the second the same question. He also claimed that he could drive to within an inch of the edge. She asked the third the same question. "Madam," he said, "I cannot tell you, because I always keep as far away from danger as I possibly can."

The third man got the job.

EVENING

No man can take a chance when it comes to him unless he has made himself ready to take it when it does come

One of the grim things in life is that there are any number of people today who wish that they had worked a bit harder and studied a bit harder when they were young, because now they are passed over for promotion because — to use a colloquial phrase — they have not got what it takes.

No man can take a chance when it comes unless he is there to take it

A man will wait for long enough, if he waits for inspiration to come to him. Inspiration comes to the man who is prepared to work until it comes to him. The preacher, the writer, the student will find that the likeliest place to find inspiration is at his desk. He must avoid the habit of not going to his desk until inspiration has come; he must go, and inspiration will come — out of mental perspiration!

The man who refuses to blame himself will seldom get anywhere

There is a kind of person who blames everyone but himself. He lives in a world in which everything seems to be permanently against him.

Self-examination would often be the best way to a change of what is called luck.

Getting through work

MORNING

There is a law of life. There are some things you can do and see any time; there are other things which you only get the chance to do and see once; and if you are ever going to see and do them, you must take that chance, or it does not come back.

If a word of praise or thanks has to be spoken, it had better be spoken now — for life is an uncertain business, and you may never get the chance to speak it again

While we have them, we ought to tell them of our love and gratitude.

Very often a word of warning should be spoken now

One of the tragedies of life is when someone slips into some ruinous mistake because those who might have warned him did not speak in time. It is quite true that we may be rebuffed, and it is quite true that we must be careful how we speak, for there is a hard way of speaking that will do more harm than good, but it is better to speak and be rebuffed than not to speak at all. We have said this before, but it is worth emphasizing again.

Very often there are gifts which should be given now

There is an old Latin proverb which says *qui cito dat bis dat*, which means, "He who gives quickly gives twice." A gift which is given in the moment of need is of double value. If we put off giving it, it may be too late to give it at all.

EVENING

If you keep steadily on at a thing with repeated efforts, even if each effort is not much in itself, it can do big things in the end

In Glasgow University, the famous Lord Kelvin used to illustrate the effect of small forces on large masses. In his classroom he would have a huge heavy lump of metal weighing as much as a hundredweight and more suspended from the ceiling. He would have a basket full of paper pellets; and, to the great joy of the class, he would begin to bombard the heavy iron mass with the little pellets of paper.

At first nothing happened; then after a time the iron mass would begin to tremble; then it would begin to move; and finally it would begin to swing in a wide arc, and all through the effect of repeated blows with the little paper pellets.

The little things can achieve the big things, if we keep on — but you have to keep on, for, if you stopped bombarding the iron mass with the paper pellets, it would stop moving.

It is the little, constantly repeated efforts which count.

If you keep steadily at a thing, it is amazing what changes you can, in the end, achieve.

Divine friendship and sacraments

MORNING

The most precious thing in the world is a friend to whom we can go at any time, and never feel a nuisance; someone to whom we can turn just whenever we need him; someone to whom we can talk about anything; someone who will never laugh at our dreams or mock at our failures; to say it again, someone to whom we are never a nuisance.

We all know the person who is really half-watching the clock all the time we are there; the kind of person who implies, if he does not actually say it, that he can give us ten minutes and no more; the kind of person who, all the time, is quite obviously thinking of his next appointment and his next engagement; the kind of person to whom we are really more of a nuisance and a bother than anything else.

There is a wonderful incident in the life of Jesus (Mark 6:31-34). The crowds were so pressing and so insistent that Jesus and his friends could not even get peace to eat a meal. So Jesus took his friends into the boat and they went across the lake to a lonely place to rest awhile, to get a little peace and quiet. But the people saw him go and they raced round the lake and they were there when he arrived.

So many people would have found the crowd an unmitigated nuisance and would have left them in no doubt that it was so. But when Jesus saw them, he was moved with compassion for they were "as sheep without a shepherd". He was tired and harassed and hungry; he wanted peace; but even then the people who needed him were not a nuisance. *It is so with God.*

EVENING

I remember being in Newcastle-upon-Tyne once and looking at a monument to the famous Earl Grey of the Reform Bill. It was on a tall pillar which soared hundreds of feet into the air. When you looked up to the top of that pillar, you saw two bright lights outstretched on metal arms, shining at the top of it; and if you looked a little more closely, you saw that there were two other arms with two other unlit lights upon them. I wondered what this meant.

Whenever there was a fatal road accident in Newcastle, then the two white lights were switched off and two red lights switched on. So in Newcastle they knew when someone died on the road. The red lights meant that a life had been lost.

This is what Jesus did when he took bread and wine and used them as symbols of his body broken and his blood shed for men.

When people saw it shining red, it was a reminder that another had died on the roads, and it was meant to warn every motorist who saw it to drive more carefully and every pedestrian to walk more watchfully. So the broken bread and the poured out wine are the symbols of the broken body and the shed blood of Christ, and are therefore the supreme warning of what sin can do.

Variety and playing second fiddle

MORNING

T. R. Glover used to say that one of the first laws of life was to remember that "whatever you think, someone thinks differently".

This is true in all kinds of ways in the church.

It is true of worship, with the great prayers of the church, and with language sonorous, dignified and ecclesiastical

Other people like a simple form of worship where there is more room for spontaneity and for extempore prayer. In this there is no right or wrong.

The liturgists must not despise the simple folk, and the simple folk must not go about saying that anyone who likes liturgy and ritual is half way to Rome! Let us each worship God as he finds God and let him not criticize or despise the other.

It is true of the life of the church

Some people think that the church should have a highly organized social life. They like to find their parties and their socials, and their dances and their entertainment in the church, as they love to find their worship on the Sunday. Others have a much more austere view of the church and think that these things are out of place in the church and think that the church's activities should be confined to "religious" meetings.

There is room for both. Those who like everything in the church must not inveigh against the "narrowness" of the others. Those who do not like these things must not in a superior way criticize the "worldliness" of their brethren.

EVENING

Almost always behind some brilliant, scintillating, publicized character there is someone standing in support.

During the war one of the most colorful generals was the American General Patton. He swept through Europe like a gale of wind with his pearl-handled revolver and his flair for publicity. Someone once asked him, "How do you do it? Where on earth does the petrol come from to feed your motorized columns?" "I don't know," said Patton, "I've got a chap who looks after that."

Behind the vivid Patton there was a quiet man, whose name no one knows, who kept the whole army moving. It is like that in the most varied walks of life.

It is not the job that matters. What matters is how we do it.

Most of us will never see the first place. Most of us will have to be content with the second place. Most of us will never have the spotlight on us; most of us will have to work behind the scenes. But at the end of the day there is not a doubt that the unseen work will be seen, and the unrewarded work will be rewarded.

Whatever our task is, God needs it and God needs us; the point of life is not the task, *but how the task is done.*

Values and truth

MORNING

We live in a world in which values have gone mad. But from all this one basic fact emerges — the world sets its highest value on that which entertains.

What the world is willing to pay for is entertainment. Men will pay anything to be amused.

There is the strangest parallel with the Roman society of the time when Christianity came into this world.

It would be difficult to find any age in world history when so much was spent on food as it was then. Tacitus tells us of single banquets which cost as much as £500. Seneca tells us of dinner at which the dishes included peacocks' brains and nightingales' tongues. Suetonius tells us that the Emperor Vitellius set on the table at one banquet 2,000 fish and 7,00 birds and that in a reign of less than a year he managed to spend more than £3,000,000 on food. The elder Pliny tells of seeing a Roman bride, Lollia Paulina, dressed in a bridal dress which was so richly jeweled that it cost £423,000.

An age which pours out money on its pleasures is a decadent age.

It is hard to avoid the conclusion that *we* are living in an age of decadence and of escapism. And as Christians, there lies our challenge and our chance.

EVENING

Once Buddha was in a town where there was a conflict of warring theological views between the monks. So Buddha told them the parable of the Rajah, the blind men and the elephant.

One day the Rajah called the servant, and bade him assemble, at his palace, all the men in the town who had been born blind. Then he commanded that an elephant should be brought in. Then the Rajah made one blind man touch the head of the elephant, another the ear, another the trunk, a tusk, a foot, the back, the tail, and the tuft of the tail; and to each one the Rajah said that he was touching the elephant.

When they had all felt the elephant, the Rajah said to them, "Have you all studied the elephant? Now tell me your conclusion." The man who had touched the head said, "It is like a pot." The one who had touched the ear said, "It is like a fan." And each blind man thought that what he had touched was an elephant.

That, said Buddha, is what men are like about the truth.

Just as each blind man insisted that the part of the elephant he had touched was the whole elephant, so men insist that the little bit of truth that they have seen and grasped is the whole truth.

It is extraordinary that any man should think that he has grasped the whole truth.

Recipe for reform

MORNING

It was as long ago as 1890 that William Booth published *In Darkest England and The Way Out* and it is as relevant today as on the day when it first saw the light.

William Booth saw that the social gospel is not an addendum to the Christian message, an optional extra; he saw that it is an essential part of the Christian message.

"What is the use," he said, "of preaching the gospel to men whose whole attention is concentrated upon a mad, desperate struggle to keep themselves alive? You might as well give a tract to a shipwrecked sailor who is battling with the surf which has drowned his comrades and threatens to drown him. He will not listen to you. Nay, he cannot hear you any more than a man whose head is under water can listen to a sermon. The first thing to do is to get him at least a footing on firm ground, and to give him room to live."

Booth was one of the first men to see that salvation is total salvation, salvation of body and soul.

He went on to lay down some essentials in any plan for reformation.

First, it is essential that any scheme put forward must change the man when it is his character and conduct which constitutes the reasons for his failure in the battle of life

EVENING

Here are the four other principles laid down by William Booth.

Any remedy must be commensurate with the evil with which it proposes to deal
So often attempts to do something do no more than scratch the surface.

Any such scheme must be capable of being permanent
Little is to be gained by momentary emergency measures. Something has to be done which can become part of life permanently.

Any such scheme must be immediately practicable
It must not be a dream; it must be something that is capable of being put into operation now.

Any assistance given to one section of the community, must not interfere with the needs and interests of another
Concentration on the need and interests of any one age, or section, or class of society must never be at the cost of the neglect of any other parts of the community.

These were Booth's items in the "recipe for reformation". They are as relevant today as they were in 1890. If somehow all the churches and all the resources of the state were to get together on these lines, things might happen. Things *would* happen. Is it impossible?

Recipe for the individual

MORNING

I have been drawing again on the magnificent advice of William Booth as we find it in the selection of his writings called *The Founder Speaks Again.* Now we come to the center of the circle, the individual person.

When Booth was twenty years of age, on December 6, 1849, he drew up the following series of resolutions.

"I do promise," he wrote, "my God helping:

"Firstly, that I will rise every morning sufficiently early (say twenty minutes before seven o'clock) to wash, dress, and have a few minutes, not less than five, in private prayer.

"Secondly, that I will, as much as possible, avoid all that babbling and idle talk in which I have lately so sinfully indulged.

"Thirdly, that I will endeavor in my conduct and deportment before the world and my fellow servants especially to conduct myself as a humble, meek and zealous follower of the bleeding Lamb, and, by serious conversation and warning, endeavor to lead them to think of their immortal souls.

"Fourthly, that I will not read less than four chapters in God's word every day.

"Fifthly, that I will strive to live closer to God, and to seek after holiness of heart, and leave providential events with God."

EVENING

I now put some of Booth's resolutions into my own version. Here they are:

Begin the day with God
Only then will we see everything in its true importance and in its true proportion.

Avoid gossip
One of me grim facts or life is that most people prefer to pass on something bad about other people than something good.

Be a witness and a missionary for Christ
It has been said, "The greatest handicap that the church has is the unsatisfactory lives of professing Christians."

Study the Word of God
The Bible is the Christian guidebook for life, and the Christian must study it to find God's word for him.

Standards and truth

MORNING

There are three qualities without which any civilization is bound to disintegrate. They are the cement that holds any society together.

There is honesty, without which all business, all trade, all commerce, all human relationships must simply disintegrate

Now there are any number of people who are prepared to take a dishonest chance or to put through a dishonest deal themselves, and who yet depend on the core of decent honorable people to hold society together and to make life possible.

There is the spirit of service

Unless there are those who are prepared to do something for their fellow-men without pay, without gain, and without hope of reward, that is to say, unless there are at least some people who are prepared to live unselfishly, the whole structure of social welfare and social responsibility breaks down.

There is chastity

Unless there is chastity and purity and fidelity, there must follow the destruction of the home, and the destruction of the home would mean the end of society as we know it.

The church is the custodian of those standards. Not even those who break them would wish to see them destroyed.

EVENING

It is only in the Bible that truth is clearly revealed and clearly seen. Wherein is that 'specially true?

The Bible gives us the true view of man

There is no book so realistic as the Bible. The Bible is clear that there can be no higher purpose than that for which man was created, but it is also clear that something has gone badly wrong.

The Bible gives us the true view of the world

As the Bible sees it, the world is neither to be despised nor is it to be worshipped. Earth is neither a desert dreary, nor is it the paradise of God. Parable after parable of Jesus shows us the world as the training and the testing ground of eternity.

The Bible gives us the true view of God

Or rather it is truer to say that the Bible tells how in Jesus Christ the true view of God came to men. Jesus Christ said, "He who has seen me has seen the Father" (John 14:9).

Stewardship and tests of conversion

MORNING

Is it not true that we can all afford what we want to afford?

It is very easy to find that we cannot afford to do what we do not want to do and to give what we do not want to give. It is very easy to find reasons why it is really an economy to buy what we want to buy.

Is it not true that we can afford for ourselves what we find it quite impossible to afford for others?

Expenditure on self is always possible even when expenditure on others is impossible.

How much do we give of our time to our church?

Apart from our attendance at church on Sunday, do we give to the work of Christ and his church as much time as we give to television, to the cinema, to golf, to tennis, to gardening, to a motor run to the coast? Are there some of us who from Sunday to Sunday give literally no time to the work of the church and to the service of Christ and his people?

How much do we give of our talents?

Do we give at all of such talents of hand and mind and voice as we possess to Christ and his church? If we sing, do we sing for Christ? If we teach, do we teach for Christ? Do we give as much of talents to the church and to Christ and his people as we give to our favorite hobby?

EVENING

There are three obvious tests of conversion.

The first test is. Does a man pay his debts?

This is really what Zacchaeus did. He restored at once that which he had fraudulently taken.

The second test is. Does a man mend all his quarrels?

Nothing could be blunter than the First Letter of John."If anyone says, "I love God," and hates his brother, he is a liar" (1 John 4:20).

No man is a converted man so long as he has in his life an unhealed quarrel with a fellow man. Conversion does not relate a man only to God; it also must relate him to his fellow men.

The third test is. Does it make a man a better workman?

Human nature left to itself is both selfish and lazy. It is Paul's advice to Timothy: "Do your best to present yourself to God as one approved, a workman who has no need to be ashamed" (2 Timothy 2:15).

Greatness and beauty

MORNING

I remember once doing some work for the Royal Army Chaplains' Department in Germany and going to a place called Ostenwalde where there was a church house in which excellent work was being done. And when I was there I remember being thrilled because the bed in which I slept had once been — as he then was — General Montgomery's bed!

Every time we enter a church and worship there, we are putting ourselves in touch with the saints and the heroes and the prophets and the martyrs. We can say to ourselves, "I belong to that fellowship to which those who loved and died for their faith in every age and generation belonged". When we sit at the sacrament, we can say to ourselves, "I am doing exactly what Jesus did with his disciples in the upper room long ago."

For the Christian this contact with greatness is even more universal. We live in the world which is the work of God. The men and women amongst whom we live and move are the children of God.

The world in which we live is the handiwork of God. Everywhere we go, we can say, "Here is God."

EVENING

As the years go on, we make ourselves a certain kind of face. An expression assumed often enough leaves permanent marks on the face.

Worry will leave its mark upon a face in the vertical lines etched upon the forehead

You can always tell a worried man by his face. Yet we forget that a worried Christian is a contradiction in terms. For the Christian, there is a way to the peace that passes understanding.

Discontent will leave its mark upon a face

Many a pretty face has been spoiled by a permanent look of discontent. Yet the Christian will count his blessings — and he will always have some blessings to count.

Resentment will leave its mark upon a face

There are some people who are resentful against life, against their fellow-men, against God. They live life in the permanent conviction that they have never had a square deal from anything or anyone.

But joy, too, leaves its mark upon a face

There are those who always look as if they are going to smile. "A happy man," said Robert Louis Stevenson, "is a better thing to find than a five pound note."

More than communism

MORNING

A new charter of the Russian Communist Party was prepared, laying down what a Communist should believe and how he should behave. It was reported that the charter had seven points, and the seven points are more than worth setting down.

The first demand is loyalty to the cause of Communism both in Russia and in other countries.

The second is conscientious labor for the benefit of society.

The third is collectivism and comradely mutual assistance. "One for all and all for one."

The fourth principle is honesty and truthfulness, moral purity, unpretentiousness, and modesty in public and personal life.

The fifth demand is for mutual respect within family circles, and concern for the upbringing of children.

The sixth principle is intolerance of injustice, parasitism, dishonesty and careerism.

The last demand is for fraternal solidarity with the working people of all countries.

Here is nothing, except the demand for loyalty to Communism, which a Christian could not accept and which, in fact, a Christian is bound to do.

Does the Christian take his Christianity to the office and the factory with him as the Communist takes his Communism? I very much doubt it.

EVENING

Behind the Communist creed there are two basic principles
There is the principle that a way must be found in which people can live together. And above all, there is the principle or responsibility. Apart from anything else this creed clearly lays down the duty of every man to be the best possible workman that he can be, and to do the best possible day's work that he can do.

There are very, very few people who accept that duty and obligation in our so-called Christian Western society. With us it has become almost a principle that a man does as little as he can and gets as much as he can.

If this Communist creed is carried out in practice, it actually provides a more Christian philosophy of work and responsibility than exists in alleged Christian countries.

The conclusion is clear and challenging. It is simply this: to put it colloquially, the Christian has "got to go some" to beat this creed
Christianity can only prove its superiority to Communism by proving that Christianity produces better and happier men and women.

Fire and dynamite

MORNING

One day recently my minister friend was telling me that his niece was giving him advice on how to preach! And her advice was: "If you can't put fire into your sermon, put your sermon in the fire!"

A better epigram and better advice it would be hard to find!

Fire can warm a person

On the great day in Aldersgate which changed John Wesley's life, Wesley said: "I felt my heart strangely warmed."

A great German critic said of the First Letter of Peter that its outstanding characteristic is warmth.

There can be no great preaching without warmth, nor can there be any real teaching without warmth. Warmth does not mean that a man will rant and shout and gesticulate and generally throw himself about. There can be a quietness and a stillness which have in them a white-hot intensity which no one can mistake.

Heat fuses things together

Usually an alloy will be made out of two metals by heat. There is a lesson there. If ever there is to be union amongst us, that union must come not so much from cold logic as from the warmth of the loving heart. When our hearts reach out to each other in love, we will get further than ever the arguments did.

It is only the warmth of love that can fuse two personalities or two churches or two congregations together.

EVENING

What is the difference between fireworks and dynamite?

Both of them make a noise

But in the one case the noise is what you might call an ineffective noise; it has no discernible result. In the other case the noise is an extremely effective noise, for with the noise things happen. There can be a kind of preaching which, as Shakespeare once said of life, is "full of sound and fury, signifying nothing".

The greatest danger of fireworks is to those who play with them, not realizing their potentialities for harm

The greater danger of the firework type of preaching is to the man who becomes a slave to it. He loses the conception of what preaching is.

To preach is in Greek kcrussein, which is the word which is used for a herald's proclamation on behalf of the king. Let a preacher remember that he is the herald of God and he cannot then go far wrong.

The church is . . .

MORNING

"The church is made up of those who, because they love Jesus, love God and love each other."

I do not think that I have ever heard a better definition of the church.

The church is made up of those who love God

Do we really love God?

If we love anyone, that person is the center of our thoughts and the center of our lives.

Is God in the very center of our lives?

Voltaire, as everyone knows, had little use for religion. He was one day walking with a friend when they passed a church. Voltaire raised his hat as they passed.

"I thought," said the friend, "that you did not believe in God."

"Oh," said Voltaire, "we nod, but we do not speak."

Would it be true to say that very many of us have a nodding acquaintance with God, that God is on the circumference but not in the center of our lives? Can we honestly say that we love God?

EVENING

The church is made up of those who love each other

How do we really feel towards our fellow-men? Sometimes we despise them. Sometimes we even hate them. Sometimes we tolerate them. Sometimes we respect them and even admire them. But do we really love them?

The church is made up of those who love God and who love their fellow-men, because they love Jesus

The tremendous thing about Jesus is that he does two things.

He shows us what God is like

Before Jesus came, we might have thought that God was distant and remote and unknowable — but not now. We have only to look at Jesus and to say: "God is like that."

He shows us what a man should be like

In Jesus we see true manhood as it ought to be. It is Jesus who shows us what man is like and what God is like. Maybe the trouble is that we do not love God enough and we do not love men enough simply because we do not love Jesus enough.

Persevere and don't doubt

MORNING

I was looking for a certain street in London. I asked a policeman for directions. I told him where I wished to go and asked him where the street was. "Why, sir," he said, "I saw you pass; you were on the right way to it just now; but you turned back too soon."

You were on the right way, but you turned back too soon

That is a good description of the reason for a great deal of failure in life. The trouble about life is that we so often turn back too soon, that we so often put in one effort too few.

It is that way with knowledge

There is a story about a famous man who was studying when he was a young man, and who was finding it pretty heavy going. He had almost made up his mind that it was all too much for him, and that he would quit. He was idly turning over the pages of his textbook and he was much dejected.

He came to the last leaf, and suddenly on the inside cover of the book he saw pasted a narrow strip of gummed paper. He was curious as to what might be below it, and he stripped it off. When the paper was removed he found himself looking at one short sentence: "Go on, young man, go on!"

He went on and the day came when he became famous. He was on the very edge of turning back too soon — but he went on.

EVENING

It is that way with thought

A certain lady who became a very famous scientist tells how she was started on the path that led to real knowledge.

She was out for a country walk with her father, himself a famous scientist, when she was very young. Quite suddenly he looked down at her, and apropos of nothing at all, said to her: "My dear, never believe anything anyone tells you." He meant: "Don't accept things at second-hand; don't make your knowledge a carried story; think things out for yourself; and don't be satisfied until you have done so."

The reason why the faith of so many people collapses in the hour of trial is simply that it is not theirs.

The cure for doubt is not to push a thing into the back of the mind and to refuse to think about it. The cure for doubt is to think a way through the doubts. We would have a faith that would be more secure if we did not turn back from thinking too soon.

Rejecting and accepting

MORNING

It is that way with goodness

The great example of this is the Rich Young Ruler. He wanted goodness. He came to Jesus and asked his guidance. Jesus quoted the commandments which are the basis of respectability.

The young man said that he had kept them all. "Well, then," said Jesus, "go and sell all your possessions and give them away." And the young man went away sorrowful, for he had great possessions. If he had honestly put his thoughts into words, he would have said: "I want goodness; but I don't want it as much as all that."

He turned back too soon.

Jesus Christ wants men and women who will go all the way with him.

The tragedy is that the world is full of men and women who turn back too soon.

EVENING

John Pollock, in his biography of Billy Graham, tells of an incident from his Harringay (London) Crusade.

At the time of the appeal two men who had been sitting side by side both rose to go forward. As it happened, one was a professional pickpocket. The pickpocket turned to the other man as they began to walk forward and said: "I must give you back your wallet which I took a few minutes ago!"

Here was conversion with immediate results!

When Zacchaeus really encountered Jesus, the first thing he did was to say: "The half of my goods I give to the poor; and, if I have defrauded anyone of anything, I restore it fourfold" (Luke 19:8).

Here again was conversion with immediate results.

When the Philippian jailor was confronted with the action of God and when he believed, he and all his family were baptized. And then he took and washed the wounds of Paul and Silas, the weals on their back that the lash had left, and took them into his house, and set a meal before them (Acts 16:33,34).

Here again was conversion with immediate results.

The significance of these stories is the practical character of the results of conversion. The people in question reacted not in a pious way but in a most practical way.

The real tests of conversion are not that a man should start attending prayer meetings and Bible study groups, although he may, of course, well do these things.

The real tests are in life itself.

Educated ministers

MORNING

A young minister I know well is a very good scholar. He told me about his university days when he was in the Arts Faculty. He had done well and he had come to a stage when he had to decide whether or not to take an honors degree in a particular group of subjects. Rightly or wrongly, he decided not to do so. He felt that the wider study of an ordinary degree might serve him better for the work of the ministry than the highly specialized work of an honors degree.

The student went to interview the professor in whose department he might have taken an honors degree and told him of his decision. The professor was clearly disappointed. He looked at the young man and said: "We do still need an educated ministry you know." Here was a teacher who clearly felt that no qualification was too high for the ministry.

It is impossible to equip a man too highly for the work of the ministry.

EVENING

The preacher is of necessity a teacher; and the teacher must be equipped to teach

If anyone asks him: "What do you mean by that?" he must be able to tell them. The Bible is his textbook, and the Bible was written in foreign languages and in a foreign land centuries ago.

He who would expound it truly must know something of the situation in which it was first written.

The Holy Spirit helps him who helps himself; and it is when a man brings to the Bible all the intensity of study of which he is capable that the Spirit co-operates with him and opens scripture to him.

The preacher is a teacher who must teach the same people twice a Sunday over many years

Unless he is going to be dully repetitive he must have a wide knowledge of many things.

It is likely nowadays that the minister will have to teach in a school sometimes not as a member of staff but as the parish minister

A dangerous and even disastrous situation arises when he has to confront a group of young people who are far better educated than he is, for no one can teach people unless the people respect him.

The task of the minister was never more difficult than it is today. A complete equipment for it was never more necessary.

Knowledge will not do everything, but when that knowledge becomes what a great evangelist called "Knowledge on Fire", then things really begin to happen.

God's Spirit is looking for minds to use.

The finer the instrument, the more the Spirit can use it.

Grumblers and martyrs

MORNING

A Scottish lady who emigrated with her family to America, and who has been very happy in the land of her adoption, has told me of a phrase which has become almost a catch-phrase in her family.

In the early days, when she had first come to America, and before she had settled down, she used to do a bit of grumbling and regretting. And when she got into one of these moods her husband used always to say to her: "Well, there's a boat home!"

That phrase became a kind of catchword in that household. The lady herself and her husband in due time had a family; and the children, though never allowed to forget their Scots ancestry, grew up as Americans.

When the daughter of the family was still only a little girl a British visitor came to the house. This particular visitor was very discourteously criticizing American politics in general and President Eisenhower in particular. The small girl could in the end stand it no longer, and she turned to the critical visitor and spoke the family watchword: "Well, if you don't like it, there's a boat home!"

If we are for ever grumbling about our job, we would be well advised to get out and get another.

EVENING

There is one area in which I believe what I said yesterday to be especially true.

If we are unhappy in any congregation, then the sooner we leave it the better for everyone concerned.

There are people who criticize the minister and his preaching; who find fault with the worship of the church; who criticize the choir and the organist; who tell everyone that the minister never visits, that the office-bearers are a poor lot, and that the congregation is standoffish and unfriendly.

If they feel like that, the remedy is in their own hands. They can leave!

An unhappy and dissatisfied church member is a bad church member. He can be a focus of discontent, infecting others with his own dissatisfaction.

There are some people who get a good deal of pleasure out of being martyrs.

There are some people who would not be happy without a grumble.

That will not do in the church.

The church offers us a wide choice. Somewhere within it, we can find the place where we are happy.

The tough ministry (1)

MORNING

Some time ago a friend of mine quoted to me a saying which I had not heard before.

We were talking about a mutual friend who not infrequently gets into controversy, but who is himself not very able to stand criticism.

In talking of him my friend said:

"Well, if you can't stand the heat, you should keep out of the kitchen."

If we can't stand the conditions of anything, we should not undertake to do it.

If we are not prepared to accept the conditions of any kind of work, we should not start that kind of work.

This set me thinking about the conditions we must accept if we are to work with people at all, and especially if we are to enter the ministry of the church.

If a man can't keep his temper, he should stay out of the ministry

A bad-tempered minister of Jesus Christ is clearly a contradiction in terms. The person presiding over any community or committee will set the tone of it.

If the man at the top is liable to fly into a temper then the whole atmosphere is vitiated. This certainly cannot be Christian.

EVENING

If a man can't stand criticism, he should keep out of the ministry

All leadership is open to criticism; and any man who proposes to make any kind of performance in public will certainly be criticized.

Of all professions the ministry is most liable to criticism, for the simple reason that people expect a standard from the ministry that they do not expect from any other profession.

It is a compliment to the ministry that such a standard is expected. A big man can accept criticism; he does not want to be surrounded by yes-men. He will realize that very often sensible criticism will save him from many a fault and mistake.

As for the other kind of criticism, the criticism that is malicious, niggling, trouble-making, prejudiced and unjustified, let a man learn to bear it in the confidence that, in the last analysis, the only criticism he need really fear is the criticism which finds an echo in his own conscience.

The tough ministry (2)

MORNING

There are some more areas in which we should "keep out of the kitchen".

If a man cannot do routine work, he should keep out of the ministry

This may be put in another way. If a man has no self-discipline, the ministry is no job for him.

Most people have to work for a master, an employer, a superior. The minister is his own master. There is no one to make him work but himself.

There is no job in the world in which it is so easy to put things off and to leave things undone and to waste time as it is in the ministry. To be an efficient minister a man has to have the gift of doing the routine work as it comes with complete self-discipline.

If he does not do his work under his own orders, there is no one else to make him do it.

EVENING

If a man is looking for quick and visible results, he should keep out of the ministry

There are sure to be times when the visible result will come. But for the most part the minister must sow in patience beside the waters of hope and leave the harvest to God. And often it will only be after long years that he has the blessedness of seeing the effect of what he has done.

If a man is looking for personal prominence, he should keep out of the ministry

Too often the attraction of the ministry is the pulpit. The young man's vision is the vision of himself holding some congregation spellbound.

In any event by far the most important part of the work of the ministry is done out of the pulpit, and often no one ever hears of it or knows it except the person who is helped.

As for the pulpit, the more a man draws attention to himself, the less he draws attention to Jesus Christ.

To make these demands seems almost to demand the impossible, but it has to be remembered that, if God gives a man a task to do, he also gives him the strength to do it.

The true church

MORNING

You can find in John Bunyan's thought about the church four things.

The church "is (i) separated from the world (ii) as a fellowship of believers which was (iii) gathered together in freedom (iv) to live a life of holiness".

The church is separated from the world

Bunyan writes in his commentary on Genesis: "The work of the church of God is not to fall in with any sinful fellowship, or to receive into their communion the ungodly world, but to show forth the praises and virtues of him who hath called them out from among such communicants into his marvelous light."

But let it be noted, this separation is not the separation of detachment; it is the separation of involvement. It does not mean that the church is disengaged from the world, and leaves the world.

Jesus did not pray that God would take his people out of the world, but that God would keep them from the evil of the world (John 17:15).

The church is a fellowship of believers

In the Bedford church where Bunyan was minister the members, when they became members, "determined to walk together in the fellowship of the Gospel". They jointly first gave themselves to God and then to one another.

In the church we meet God and we meet men. In the church it ought to be always possible to find both human and divine friendship, to find the friendship of God and the friendship of men.

EVENING

The fellowship of the church is gathered in freedom

It is a voluntary association of men in faith and in holiness. So far did Bunyan go in this direction that he would not even say that baptism was necessary for entry to the church.

Nothing that belongs to outward circumstances, nothing "circumstantial", makes any difference.

Those within the church are to live a life of holiness

Here we are back to the separation idea. The Greek word for "separate" and the Greek word for "holy" are the same. Separation, "difference" is holiness.

Richard Baxter said that the necessary qualification for church membership is that Christians must be visible saints. And to be a visible saint is to live by "the right and Gospel pattern".

As Bunyan put it the church is a fellowship "gathered or constituted by, and walking after the Rule of the Word of God".

There is the ideal of the church.

Questions and shallow theology

MORNING

Teaching does not consist so much in telling people the right things as it does in asking people the right questions.

"A teacher," J. F. McFadyen once said, "should be an animated question-mark."

Socrates was one of the world's great teachers, and he was one of the world's most famous questioners. He used questions for two purposes. He used them to demonstrate to a man how much the man actually knew without knowing that he knew it.

In the famous dialogue, by question and answer he drew from the slave, who knew no geometry at all, the solution and the proof of the theorem of Pythagoras, that the square on the hypotenuse of a right-angled triangle equals the sum of the squares on the other two sides.

By question after question, the proof was extracted from a person who had no idea that he knew it.

Socrates also used questions to confront a man with himself, to drive the man into a position in which he would be compelled to see his own inconsistency and his own folly.

It was through questions that Socrates taught.

So did Jesus. The great characteristic of the teaching of Jesus, that by which as a teacher he will always be known, is the parable.

The parable is a story which invites a question. At the end of a parable, there always comes the question, spoken or implied: "Well, what do you think?"

EVENING

We get at man much more deeply and much more really through their hearts and their emotions than through their minds and their intellects.

This is just one of the notes that are missing in so much modern preaching and so much modem theology.

Rhadakrishnan, the great Indian thinker, once said: "Your theologians seem to me like men who are talking in their sleep."

J. S. Whale talks about running around the burning bush taking photographs from suitable angles instead of taking off our shoes from our feet because the place whereon we stand is holy ground.

He talks of theologians who put their pipes in their mouths and stick their feet up on the mantelpiece and talk about theories of the atonement instead of bowing down before the wounds of Christ.

The need for heaven

MORNING

C. S. Lewis, in *The Great Divorce*, has an odd scene. A busload of people from the Grey City of Hell are taken to the entrance of heaven. They are offered admission to heaven, but with one exception, they all refuse it. The people in heaven are the Solid Persons, so radiant and so solid that they make the visitors from hell look like insubstantial shadows. One of the pale ghosts from hell is met by one of the Solid People from heaven. The pale ghost from hell had at one time been the employer of the Solid Person on earth, and the Solid Person had in his time on earth actually committed a murder.

The pale ghost was astonished that he was in hell while the man who had once been his employee and a murderer was in heaven.

"Look at me now," he says. "I gone straight all my life. I don't say I was a religious man and I don't say I had not faults, far from it. But I done my best all my life, see? I done my best by everyone, that's the sort of chap I was. I never asked for anything that wasn't mine by rights. If I wanted a drink I paid for it and if I took my wages I done my job, see? . . . I'm asking for nothing but my rights . . . I'm not asking for anyone's bleeding charity." The Solid Person answered: "Then do. At once. Ask for the Bleeding Charity."

Hell is full of people who believe that they never needed anyone or anything, that they were able to live life by themselves.

Heaven is the place for the man who knows his need and who is willing to ask.

EVENING

The lack of a sense of need is a strange thing, for life is designed to awaken in us the sense of need.

We cannot cope with things alone
The responsibilities of life threaten to crush us; the sorrows of life threaten to submerge us; the anxieties of life bring the failure of nerve; the tasks of life leave us weary and exhausted.

We cannot find the way alone
We are meant to ask: "Lord, what do you want me to do?"

We cannot stand the scrutiny of God alone
No man can stand in the presence of the living God unashamed and unafraid.

We have to say: "God be merciful to me, a sinner."

We have to know our need.

Quo vadis?

MORNING

Where are you going? That could be the most important question in life.

Where are you going, if you are young? Where are you going in your studies? Are you studying in such a way that you will make yourself the kind of person for whom life will be a series of open doors: or are you studying in such a way that life cannot be anything other than a series of dead-end jobs?

Where are you going in your interests and your hobbies? Are you giving your interest to things which are such that they will last for a lifetime, or are you giving it entirely to things that you are bound to grow out of, and in which there is necessarily a diminishing satisfaction?

Where are you going in your friendships? Are they such as to enrich life, or are they such as to surround life with risk?

It is essential to start out in the right direction. When you are young, the question, "Where are you going?" is very important indeed.

EVENING

Where are you going, if you are in the middle years?

It is in the middle years that life becomes most strenuous. Before we know what life is like, we are under the delusion that the higher up we get, the easier it is. The opposite is true. The higher up we get, the harder we have to work. It is one of the paradoxical dangers of modern life that a man reaches a maximum position of responsibility when he is slightly past his physical peak and is therefore not quite so able to support it.

In the middle years the question is whether we are going to go on to kill ourselves, or whether we are going to be wise enough to know when to slacken the tension and lay down the task, at least in part.

Where are you going if you are near the end? The Christian faith has never any doubt of that. "Good night," wrote F. B. Meyer in one of his last letters, when he knew the end was near, "I'll see you in the morning."

Quo vadis?

Attitudes of love and need-love

MORNING

C. S. Lewis in his book *The Four Loves* identified three attitudes in love.

There is need-love.
There is gift-love.
There is appreciative love.

In terms of human love, the love of a man for a maid, need-love would say: "I cannot live without you."

Gift-love would say: "The most important thing in the world for me is to make her happy."

Appreciative love would rejoice in the existence of the person, and give thanks for the beauty and the loveliness and the goodness of the person, even if it was well aware that the person was not for it, and could never be for it.

In terms of God, need-love is driven to God by a sense that it cannot deal with life without God.

Gift-love finds its joy and its happiness in serving God.

Appreciative loves gives thanks and glory to God for his very existence and for his handiwork in his creation.

EVENING

Let us look at these three kinds of love.

It is with need-love that most people start

The cry of the human heart is indeed "I need thee every hour".

"Whom have I in heaven but thee?" says the Psalmist, "there is nothing on earth that I desire besides thee" (Psalm 73:25).

Lincoln frankly confessed: "I have often been driven to my knees in prayer, because I had nowhere else to go."

It is characteristic of human beings that they have to be dependent on someone. The man who is self-sufficient is a very rare creature, and hardly a normal creature. Dependence on God is of the very essence of religion. Dependence on some person is of the very essence of humanity.

Gift-love and appreciative love

MORNING

Gift-love is an essential part of love.

The love that thinks only in terms of taking is not true love; love instinctively thinks in terms of giving. It seems to express itself in the gift.

In human love, there is a certain danger in this. There is a kind of human love which is so anxious to give and to protect, that it may in the end create in the person loved an almost complete dependence. It can smother instead of develop the personality of the other.

Love gives in order to strengthen and not to weaken.

Gift-love is love which is well aware that, in God's service, we find our perfect freedom, and, in doing his will, our peace.

For the only gift that any man can bring to God is the gift of himself.

EVENING

There is appreciative love.

In a sense, this is the love that has to be cultivated. Need-love is instinctive; gift-love arises naturally in the heart of any man who has any idea of love at all. But appreciative love is different.

The difference lies in one direction. There is, in human nature, an almost universal tendency to take things for granted.

In human relationships we take the love and the care and the continual service we receive for granted. In divine relationships likewise we take the world and all the gifts of nature for granted.

We take as rights, in our relationships with both men and God, those things which are in fact gifts of grace.

We would do well to think again until we reawaken the sense of debt within our hearts.

The need-love which takes because it must; the gift-love which gives because it can do no other; the appreciative love which consciously remembers and gives thanks — yes, we need them all.

Loveliness in action

MORNING

Ibsen makes Julian utter a criticism of the Christians.

Julian was the Roman Emperor who wished to put the clock back and to bring back the pagan gods. "Have you looked at those Christians closely? Hollow-eyed, palecheeked, flat-breasted all; they brood their lives away, unspurred by ambition; the sun shines for them but they do not see it; the earth offers them its fullness but they desire it not; all their desire is to renounce and suffer, that they may come to die."

There are Christians who are morally without a fault, but they are curiously unlovely. You could never put your head on their shoulders and sob out a sorry story. If you did, you would freeze to death.

In the Greek of the New Testament, there are two words for "good". There is *agathos*, and *agathos* simply describes the moral quality of a thing as good.

There is *kalos*, and *kalos* means not only "good" but also "winsome" and "attractive".

In *kalos* there is always loveliness, and it is *kalos* which the New Testament uses again and again to describe the Christian goodness.

In real Christianity there is always a winsome attractiveness.

This is a lovely thing.

EVENING

It is told that once a woman came to Henry Drummond to ask him to visit her husband who was dying. Drummond said that of course he would come.

But he asked the woman why she had asked him when he had never even seen the husband and did not know the dying man at all.

"O, sir," she said, "I would like him to have a breath of you about him before he died."

Drummond was not much of a scientist and maybe he was still less of a theologian, but Drummond had a sheen and radiance on him that made men want him with them.

Jesus loved the world.

He played with children when he was on the way to Jerusalem to die.

He was happy at a wedding feast.

The outcast men and women who were sinners did not cross the street to avoid him; he was their friend.

Someone has defined a saint as "someone in whom Christ lives again".

And we never show men Christ until we make goodness a winsome and a lovely thing.

Joy for today and tomorrow

MORNING

If we are to win men there are certain notes that we must regain.

We must regain the note of reality

The preaching and the teaching that matter are the preaching and teaching which come from a man to whom his subject obviously matters.

A great philosopher once said that no man need try to teach unless he has a philosophy of his own or of someone else's which with all the intensity of his being he wishes to propagate.

We must regain the note of urgency

Richard Baxter wrote:

> I preach'd as never sure to preach again,
> And as a dying man to dying men!

It was Bunyan who heard the voice: "Wilt thou leave thy sins and go to heaven or wilt thou have thy sins and go to hell?" After all, it is not only something desirable which we are presenting to men; it is something essential, something which is a choice between life and death.

We must regain the note of joy

Bunyan's conversion was begun when he heard the old women sitting in the sun talking about what God had done for their souls, and "Methinks that it was joy that made them speak".

EVENING

I once saw by the roadside an advertisement for a well known and well-tried patent medicine. It ran like this:

"How you feel tomorrow depends a lot on today."

That is one of the great practical rules of life with a threat and a challenge in it at one and the same time.

Our tomorrows must of necessity depend a great deal on our todays.

Our future depends on how we use our memories today

The psychologists tell us that the golden age of memory is from the years seven to eleven.

Ignatius Loyola well knew that when he uttered his famous dictum that if you gave him a child for seven years he did not care who got him afterwards.

We should be storing our memories as early and as soon as we can. And we should be storing them with the right things.

Profound reconciliation

MORNING

Our future depends on how we use our minds today

In this world there is nothing easier to acquire than a shut mind.

I was standing in the entrance hall of our college one day talking to two theologians. The one was a young man with a questing and a seeking mind; the other was an old man of the most rigid conservatism, some might say, obscurantism.

The older man asked the younger man what he was lecturing on at the time; and the younger man replied that he was in the midst of a course on the modern theologians, Barth and Brunner, Buber and all the rest of them.

The older man looked down from his great height and said with a certain contempt for all things new: "The old is better."

Many a young minister's heart has been near to broken by the battle cry of so many churches: "We never did that here before."

A man must keep his mind open. That is not to say that he should change his principles like a theological weathercock; but it is to say that we should be learning to the end of the day.

Sclerosis of the arteries can kill a man's body and sclerosis of the mind can kill his intellect and atrophy his soul.

EVENING

Bryan Green had conducted a campaign in America over a period; and at the end of the campaign there was a meeting where people were asked to say in one or two sentences what that campaign had done for them. One by one they bore their witness and their testimony.

Then a Negro girl rose; she was not much of a speaker; she could hardly put the words together to make a sentence of public speech; and she said: "Through this campaign I found Jesus Christ and Jesus Christ made me able to forgive the man who murdered my father."

Jesus Christ made me able to forgive.

John Donne said in his "Devotions": "No man is an island, entire of itself."

But life can so easily become a sea in which we live as islands separated by the gulfs of our misunderstandings.

It is only Jesus Christ who can reconcile us to God — and in the end to one another.

Self-giving and sacrifice

MORNING

It is often said that it is impossible to bear something for someone else. Is that true?

In Jocelyn Gibb's *Light on C. S. Lewis*, Nevill Coghill tells a story C. S. Lewis once told him.

Lewis married late in life. In his marriage he found the very perfection of love, but too soon the wife he loved so much died of cancer.

Once when Lewis was with Coghill he looked across the quadrangle at his wife. "I never expected," he said, "to have in my sixties the happiness that passed me by in my twenties."

"It was then," writes Nevill Coghill, "that he told me of having been allowed to accept her pain."

"You mean," said Coghill, "that the pain left her, and that you felt it for her in your body?"

"Yes," said C. S. Lewis, "in my legs. It was crippling. But it relieved hers."

The Beatitude says: "Blessed are the merciful." The Hebrew word for mercy is *chesedh*.

In his commentary on Matthew, T. H. Robinson writes of this word: "*Chesedh* is the perfection of that mystical relation of one personality to another which is the highest of all possible grades of friendship. It means a systematic appreciation of other persons, the power, not merely to concentrate blindly on them, but to feel deliberately with them, to see life from their point of view."

EVENING

The discipline of the working life will be nothing without the discipline of the spiritual life.

W. B. Yeats spoke of "the exhausting contemplation. No man can face the tasks of life without a background of the discipline of the life of the spirit".

This sounds difficult and demanding — and so it is. But we do well to remember David.

David wished for ground on which to erect an altar. He went to Araunah the Jebusite to buy the ground, and Araunah offered him it for nothing.

David answered: "I will surely buy it of thee at a price; neither will I offer burnt-offerings unto the Lord my God of that which cost me nothing" (2 Samuel 24:18-25).

Not a little of our failure comes from the fact that we seek to offer to men and to God that which cost us, either nothing, or far too little.

God's wind

MORNING

In Jane Austen's novel *Emma*, there is a sentence that may well serve as a text.

Mr. Churchill has just suggested that a window should be opened and the polite Mr. Woodhouse objects. "Open the windows!" he expostulates. "But, surely Mr. Churchill, nobody would think of opening the window at Randalls. Nobody could be so imprudent."

There are quite a lot of places in which people don't want the windows opened. One of them is the church!

There are many things in the church that could do with a breath of fresh air.

We should let the wind blow on our church services

We retain the ancient pattern that may be all right for the person who is brought up in the church but is largely irrelevant for anyone who comes in for the first time.

The lack of adventure in the presentation of the gospel is one of the causes of the falling numbers who go to church.

We should let the wind blow on the Scriptures

It is time that the Authorized Version was laid honorably aside for the unparalleled work of literature that it is, and the new versions brought in for all teaching purposes and for all the public services of the church.

Unless Scripture is contemporary, it is nothing.

EVENING

We should let the wind blow on our liturgy

There are few things that do more to remove reality from the services of the church than the archaic irrelevance of so much of the liturgy. If a form of worship had been used for centuries, that is one very likely reason why it is irrelevant for today.

We should let the wind blow on our sacraments

One of the most distressing facts in my own church, the church of Scotland, is that the sacrament of the Lord's Supper is attended by more members of the church than any other service is, and that, at the same time, hardly anyone knows what is going on. The devaluation of this sacrament has been very sad.

God preserve us from a church where it is imprudent to open the windows.

The church ought to be a body of people living eagerly and vividly in the present and not a holy and antiquarian huddle of people whose spiritual home is centuries ago.

Lewis Cameron

MORNING

There are two interesting and significant incidents in Lewis Cameron's autobiography, *Opportunity My Ally*.

While Lewis Cameron was still a lecturer in Agriculture in Leeds, he was on holiday in Aberdeen. Friends invited him and the lady who was to be his wife to come to the evening service in Holborn United Free church at which Dr. A. W. Scuddamore Forbes of the West Parish church of St. Nicholas was to preach.

In a church that could seat a thousand people there were about forty people present. Dr. Forbes preached on the text: "Jonah rose up to flee unto Tarshish from the presence of the Lord" (Jonah 1:3). Suddenly Dr. Forbes laid aside his manuscript and said: "Why are all these pews empty? The people like Jonah have fled from the presence of the Lord refusing to face his challenge. Why are our Divinity Halls empty? Young men are more concerned about their own material advantages and selfish pleasures than with the advancement of the Kingdom of God!"

In that moment something happened to Lewis Cameron, and he decided to enter the ministry.

A congregation of forty in a church seating a thousand — but at that service one man's life was changed.

EVENING

One Sunday evening in January 1946 Lewis Cameron set off from Edinburgh for St. Luke's church, Milngavie. It was snowing hard. It was doubtful if he would get through and he only did get through by following a snowplough.

When he did get to the church it was to discover that the heating system had broken down and that there was only a handful of people in a building that was only a few degrees above freezing point. He was to speak on the Social Service of his church, and it seemed hardly worthwhile.

The next morning he received a phone call from a Glasgow lawyer who was one of the trustees in charge of a certain trust: and the upshot was that as a consequence of a sermon to a handful of people in a freezing church on a snowy January night the church of Scotland received £104,226 for its social work.

A handful of people — but a tremendous result.

Numbers are not everything. It can be in the smallest congregation that the biggest things happen.

The action of the Spirit of God is not dictated by numbers.

Few or many, God is there and God can act.

Does it work?

MORNING

I have just been hearing about a small boy whose father is a minister, and who is also exceedingly interested — as indeed all sensible people are — in railway engines (I am!).

It so happened that where he lived a new church was being built. He and his father were train-spotting one day, and a magnificent new engine appeared.

The father pointed out to the boy — I am not quite sure that the figures are accurate but that does not affect the point — that the engine had cost about £60,000 to build. And said his father: "That's as much as the new church cost."

The boy thought for a minute and said: "Well, I would rather have the engine. I think that it's worth the money far more than the church."

"How do you make that out?" his father asked him.

"Well," said the boy, "the engine works!"

The acid test of anything is "Does it work?" Or, as Jesus put it: "You will know them by their fruits" (Matthew 7:20).

EVENING

The test of a theology is "Does it work?"

Does a theology teach men what to believe or, as it has been put, does it teach them what to disbelieve?

Does it send men out to the market-place to live and to serve, or does it lock them up in a study or a class-room, interested more in theories than in people?

Is it involved in life, or is it divorced from life? Is it communicable to the ordinary man, or is it the esoteric mystery of the intellectual élite?

The test of a church is "Does it work?"

Does a church send its members out into the community to live for God and to live for men, or does it gather them in an isolated community of unworldly so-called holiness? Does it raise barriers, or does it destroy barriers? Does it send out people whose lives are like lights in a dark place (Philippians 2:15)?

The test of a profession is "Does it work?"

One of the best and the most notable things in modern evangelism — it has, in fact, always been a characteristic of evangelism rather than of the church — is the opportunity for decision. But the test of a man's profession is not his willingness to stand up and declare for Jesus Christ in a meeting.

If we really want to know whether a man has made a true decision and a true profession, then the people to ask (as I am never tired of saying) are his wife, his children, his employer, or the community in which he lives.

Generosity

MORNING

In the Old Testament the duty of generosity is laid upon men.

In the fifteenth chapter of Deuteronomy, it is laid down that every seventh year in Israel should be a year of release, when debts are cancelled and wiped out.

It is quite obvious that, as the seventh year drew near, many a prudent and cautious man would be very unwilling to lend anything to anyone, in case the borrower took advantage of the year of release and deliberately never paid the debt. But even then the law is that, if at such a time a poor man in need comes and asks for help, the heart must not be hardened and the hand must not be shut, but the hand must be opened and he must be given sufficient for his need (Deuteronomy 15:1-11).

The Christian ideal is a generosity which does not count the cost. Jesus said: "Give to him that asketh thee, and from him that would borrow of thee turn not thou away" (Matthew 5:42).

The cautious man of the world would only give, and only stand surety, if he was quite certain that he would lose nothing and would get his money back in full, and, if possible, with interest.

The Christian duty is to give generously, even when there is every chance that there will be no return.

EVENING

Christian teaching is that it is better to be generous than cautious, that it is better to take the chance of being swindled than to risk turning away empty one who is genuinely and honestly in need.

Why should that be so?

It is the reverse of what the world reckons as wisdom and sense.

It is so because that is precisely what Jesus does for us.

On one occasion the very word "surety" is used of Jesus (Hebrews 7:22). When Jesus came to this world, and when he died for me, he took the risk of whether or not the hearts of men would respond to this colossal act of love.

When God so loved the world that he gave his Son for men, he risked everything on the response of men.

The love of God did not forbear to give lest it should be the loser.

God gave and God did not count the cost; Jesus loved and kept nothing back.

Let the world stick to its prudential maxims. The Christian must accept the risk of the generous heart and the open hand, even as God in Christ accepted it.

Three laws and conversion

MORNING

To the Athenians, Solon was the supreme lawgiver. He was to the Athenians what Moses was to the Jews. He came to power when the state of Athens was steadily degenerating, and by drastic measures he reconstituted the city. The rich had become richer and more powerful, because by lending money they had succeeded in concentrating all wealth in the hands of the few and had reduced the ordinary people to a state not far from serfdom.

Solon took the bold step of canceling all debts. He made it illegal for any man to give his own body as surety for his debt.

Many poor Athenians had given themselves as security for their debts; when the time for payment came, and they were not able to pay, this meant that they themselves passed into the hands of the money-lender, and so were sold as slaves. This practice Solon forbade.

Solon laid down three unique laws.

He enacted that, *in any time of dispute within the nation, the man who took neither side should be disfranchised and should lose his rights as a citizen.*

Solon declared that *men must speak no evil of the dead.*

He laid it down that, *if a father did not teach his son a trade, then the father had no right to claim support from his son in his old age.*

There is no doubt that Solon was one of the great creative lawgivers of the world. Solon's experience of life, and Solon's wisdom were crystallized in the wisest of all sayings: "Know thyself." To Solon the most important thing of all was self knowledge. Solon was profoundly right. Nothing is more necessary than that a man should know himself.

EVENING

Clyde S. Kilby in *The Christian World of C. S. Lewis* tells of the first stage in the conversion of C. S. Lewis.

"It seemed to Lewis that God was as surely after him as a cat searching for a mouse." He then quotes Lewis's own words: "You must picture me alone in that room in Magdalen, night after night, feeling, whenever my mind lifted for even a second from my work, the steady, unrelenting approach of Him whom I so earnestly desired not to meet. That which I greatly feared had at last come upon me." As he knelt down in prayer and admitted that God was God he felt himself in his own words "the most dejected and reluctant convert in all England."

There is no "standard" way of being converted.

We must not force the grace of God into one mould.

God works in many ways.

Weakness, strength and growth

MORNING

We must know our own weakness

If we know our own weakness, we will go far to being saved from two things.

We will be saved from temptation

If a man knows his own weakness, he will know the situations which he must avoid.

If a man knows that certain things make him lose his temper, he will do well to avoid them.

If we know our own weakness, and wisely remember it, half the battle with temptation will be won.

We will be saved from frustration

To know our own weakness will protect us from desiring or undertaking that which is not for us.

Many a man would have been much happier in life, if he had been satisfied with a job he could do, and had not attempted a job that was beyond his powers, and which could bring nothing but worry and defeat.

We must also know our own strength

Too much self-distrust is quite as bad as too much self-confidence. What the world loses because people will not accept responsibilities of which they are quite capable is incalculable. Often the refusal to accept office springs from a genuine feeling of unworthiness, but far too often it springs from laziness and from unwillingness to make the effort.

EVENING

We must find a way to know ourselves

The only way to know ourselves is to have a standard with which to compare ourselves, and thus to see our own weakness.

We have that standard in Jesus Christ.

To see ourselves and to see life in the light of Christ is to see ourselves as we are, however painful that experience may be.

It is a duty to know ourselves but it is equally necessary to realize that no man need stay as he is

The Christian can know himself through Christ, and through Christ he can also know how that self of his can be made new.

He can grow in grace and in the likeness of Christ.

Good parents

MORNING

I received a letter from America. It was from a man who had read something which I had written, and who had noticed my name. He wrote to ask if I was the son of W. D. Barclay of Motherwell in Lanarkshire, Scotland, who had been a bank manager in Motherwell, and who had preached the gospel in many churches there.

It so happens that I am. For seventeen years we lived in Motherwell when I was a boy. My father was a banker by profession, but at heart he was a preacher, and his name was known as a preacher all over Lanarkshire.

It is a quarter of a century since he died, but there are many places, especially in Lanarkshire, and indeed all over Scotland, where I am still my father's son.

I thank God for this, for to few lads can there ever have been granted to have had a father and mother such as I had.

"Let us now praise famous men," sang the Son of Sirach, "and the fathers that begat us" (Ecclesiasticus 44:1).

EVENING

There are few greater gifts in this world than the gift of godly parents.

Heine, the German philosopher, once said that a man could not be too careful in the choice of his parents!

It is not given to us to choose them, but, when God has blessed us with them, he has given us a gift for which no gratitude can be too much.

J. M. Barrie said that when you looked into his mother's eyes you knew why God had sent her into the world — to open the eyes of others to all lovely things.

G. K. Chesterton used to tell how, when he was a boy, he had a toy theatre with cardboard characters. One of the characters was the figure of a man with a golden key. He had long since forgotten what character the cardboard figure actually stood for, but always he connected the man with the golden key with his father, because his father unlocked all kinds of wonderful things to him.

We should be grateful for our parents.

A good father

MORNING

There is a double duty laid upon us in relation to our parents.

There is the duty of honoring our parents while we still have them

Barrie wrote after his mother's death: "Everything I could do for her in this life I have done since I was a boy; I look back through the years and I cannot see the smallest thing left undone."

There are few — very few — who would venture to make a claim like that. But to be able to make it is something that all should aim at.

There is also the duty of seeking to be parents on whom our children will look back with gratitude and with joy

In our generation that is both easier and harder than it was for a previous generation.

The relationship between parent and child is very different from that which existed even thirty years ago. It is much easier, much less distant, much freer, much less restrained and much less constrained.

The advantage of this is that it makes friendship with our children much easier.

The disadvantage is that it makes discipline, when it is necessary, much more difficult.

But somehow the parent must solve the problem of being at one and the same time the partner and the guide of his child.

EVENING

There is laid on the parent, too, a heavy responsibility. It is by the name "Father" that we address God; and the only way in which a child can put meaning and content into the word "father" is from what he learns of its meaning from his own father.

It is one of the grimmest commentaries on fatherhood that Luther could hardly bring himself to pray the Lord's Prayer and to say, "Our Father", because of the sternness, the strictness and even the cruelty of his own father.

Joseph of Nazareth, of whom we know so little, and who is so much in the background of the gospel story, must have been a wonderful father, when Jesus so naturally and so simply gave the name "Father" to God.

Negative and postive criticism

MORNING

An American professor called Ilion T. Jones quotes a saying of that great American-preacher, Clovis G. Chappell: "No man has a right so to preach as to send his hearers away on flat tyres. Every discouraging sermon is a wicked sermon . . . A discouraged man is not an asset but a liability."

There could hardly be a more un-Christian way of living than to go about in such a way as to depress and to discourage other people.

In the Royal Navy there is a regulation that no officer shall speak discouragingly to any other officer in the discharge of his duties.

In the Senior Service discouragement is forbidden. Yet the world is full of discouragers.

There are those who discourage every great plan and every great dream
There are the experts in the pouring of cold water on other people's visions. There are so many people, in the church especially, whose favorite adjective is "hopeless" and whose watchword is "impossible".

It is far better to fail in some great attempt than not to try anything at all.

If we do try to do something it is amazing what can happen.

No man knows what might happen in the church and in the world, if people would only stop pouring so much cold water.

EVENING

There are those whose one ability in life is to find fault
They have eyes that are focused to find fault, and tongues which are tuned to criticize.

The strange thing is that they consistently concentrate on what a man has not done, and forget everything that he has done. If on any occasion he has made a mistake, they never forget it, and they never allow him to forget it either.

No one in his senses should resent criticism. Professor Jones, reminds us that "during his first few years in London, Spurgeon received a weekly letter from an anonymous critic, listing the young preacher's faults. In later years Spurgeon thanked God for his self-appointed critic, and regretted that he could not express appreciation to him in person. His criticisms were invaluable, and made a distinct contribution to Spurgeon's speaking effectiveness."

The aim of criticism should always be to encourage a man to do better. The last thing that criticism should ever do is so to discourage a man that he has not the heart to try again at all.

Criticize by all means — but criticize in love.

Good communication

MORNING

There are those who hit a man when he is down

When I was a boy I had a personal experience. In those days I played cricket. There was one season when nothing would go right. J. M. Barrie once said in one of his cricket speeches: "The first time I saw Bradman bat he made one; the next time I saw him he was not so successful."

I had had three successive weeks when I was not so successful, and I was discouraged. There was a wise and old cricketer in charge of the team. The next week I was surprised to see my name on the team list at all, because I had expected to be dropped.

The afternoon of the game came; the list of the batting order was put up. I went to look at it, fully expecting to see myself lowered in the batting order to the tail of the team, as a series of noughts deserved. Lo and behold I discovered from the list that that wise old captain had moved me up to number one to open the innings.

He was wise! I squared my shoulders and went out and made up for at least some of the noughts — and it was encouragement that did it.

When a man has been a failure, then is the time, not to discourage, but to encourage him.

"Be of good cheer," said Jesus (John 16:33). Keep your heart up, said Jesus. That is what we should always say to our fellow-men.

EVENING

If Jesus had lived and taught in the twentieth century he would have constructed and told very different parables.

They would have been about shop-assistants and typists and secretaries and garage mechanics and engineers.

No translation can do anything about this. It is not the words that are strange, it is the whole world in which Jesus lived.

It is usually the case that, to understand a gospel parable properly, we need instruction in Palestinian manners and customs. I wonder if there should not be an attempt, not to rewrite the Bible, but to re-express the Bible in terms of today, especially with children.

I am quite sure Jesus would have remade his own stories. Should we not have such a vivid doctrine of the Holy Spirit that we should seek the guidance and the help of the Holy Spirit to enable us to re-express the eternal and the unchanging truth for the child of today?

And for the adult too.

Opportunity knocks

MORNING

I had the privilege once of listening to an address on the evangelism which was being planned and carried out in a certain English diocese. The address was given by a man who clearly had a fire in his bones.

In his address he told us, with sorrow, a story which is tragic from the point of view of the Christian church.

In a certain town, which is the main town of the diocese, the civic authorities decided to begin youth club work.

When this was known, the Christian Council of the town sent the diocesan missioner to interview the civic authorities to ask if the churches might be allowed into these youth clubs to give a certain amount of Christian instruction or at least to hold epilogues in them at the end of the evenings.

The answer of the civic authorities was "No", but they were prepared to hand the whole business of the youth clubs over to the church, lock, stock and barrel, to run. If the churches would run the clubs, the civic authorities would give finance and accommodation and every possible backing.

The missioner returned to the Christian Council thrilled. As he said himself, the whole youth work of the area had been handed to the church on a plate!

All that was wanted now were volunteers and leaders to come forward and to seize this magnificent opportunity. But when an appeal was made, not one person came forward to help. The offer of the civic authorities had to be regretfully declined. The church had lost an opportunity which was never likely to recur.

EVENING

In his book *Then and Now*, John Foster tells of an amazing historical instance of this Christian failure.

In 1271 Pope Gregory the Tenth received a request from Kublai Khan, the ruler of the Mongols, the widest Empire in the East the world has ever seen. Kublai Khan sent Nicolo and Maffeo Polo as his ambassadors to the Pope.

His message ran: "You shall go to your High Priest and shall pray him on our behalf to send me a hundred men skilled in your religion . . . and so I shall be baptized, and, when I shall be baptized, all my barons and great men will be baptized, and then their subjects will receive baptism, and so there will be more Christians here than in your parts."

The whole East was being offered to Christ. Yet the Pope did nothing. In 1289 Pope Nicholas the Fourth did send missionaries, but they were far too late and far too few and the chance was lost.

What a difference it would have made if all China and the East had been gathered in to Christ. How different history and world politics would be today.

God's presence and hope

MORNING

There are so many who never get past the childhood stage of when God is in the sky. But if God remains "in the sky" forever, then we lose him, because he would not be much use there anyway.

The God "up there" is a pretty irrelevant God.

If we would keep the presence of God real and vital and living. God must come out of the sky into the world — which is just what he did in Jesus.

"The Word became flesh and lived amongst us" (John 1:14).

As Tennyson put it:

Speak to Him thou for He hears, and Spirit with Spirit can meet —

Closer is He than breathing, and nearer than hands and feet.

Yes, he is.

EVENING

The church must surely be the one institution which cannot know despair.

In the Christian faith there is hope for the world

It is possible to look at the world and to feel that men are possessed by a kind of suicidal insanity which cannot end in anything other than a disintegrated chaos.

But Christ has the remedy for the human situation. The application of that remedy is the business of the church.

In the Christian faith there is hope for men

Time and again I have quoted that sermon title in one of Fosdick's volumes: No man need stay the way he is. Often a person will defend himself or herself by saying: "I can't help it. I'm made that way. That's my nature. I can't change myself." That is the final heresy.

True, a man can't change himself. But if Christ cannot change him, then the whole claim of Christianity is a lie.

But if the church is to change the world and to change men and women, it must be changed itself

The more one sees of the church, the more one senses a deep-down attitude of defeat. There are so many people in the church who have simply accepted the situation.

Of course, the situation will not change without blood and sweat and tears on our part.

God give us, not the defeatism which accepts things as they are, but the divine discontent which in the life and the strength of Jesus Christ will battle to change them.

Educational trends

MORNING

There can be a certain pessimism about education.

One of George Bernard Shaw's characters says cynically: "He who can, does; he who cannot, teaches." He implies that the teaching profession is staffed by those who failed in every other.

But there are certain wrong trends in education.

Education must never be indoctrination

With characteristic violence of expression, Shaw makes one of his characters say: "The vilest abortionist is he who attempts to mould a child's character."

It is true that the teacher's task is to teach the child to think, not to teach him what to think.

To stimulate the young person to do his own thinking is the task of the teacher — which, of course, is not to say that certain foundations have not still to be laid.

EVENING

Education can be over-factual

Mr. Brown tells us of Dickens's Mr. McChoakumchild in Hard Times whose one aim was to implant facts, facts, facts, and who put imagination high among the deadly sins.

Of course, there are basic facts which are needed for the business of life, but a fact does not become important until it is appropriated in a situation.

The vision must be trained as well as the memory.

There is, too, a kind of education which is almost entirely memorization

Shaw speaks with violence about this kind of education which, he says, can be acquired "by any blockhead who has a good memory, and who has been broken in to school drudgery". "These memory tests," he goes on to say, "only enable teachers and scholars to be certified as proficient when they should have been certified as mentally defective."

There is a kind of examination whose sole purpose is to provide an opportunity for the person taught to write down exactly what he has heard. But as Epictetus said: "Sheep do not vomit up the grass to show the shepherd how much they have eaten. They turn it into wool."

Real knowledge does not consist so much in remembering everything as in knowing where to find the right answer.

Habits and learning from the past

MORNING

A friend of mine told me recently about an experience one of his friends had in Canada. It happened in the far north, and it happened at that time of year when the whole country was covered in snow.

Some men had gone out for a walk. Their way took them through a wood which was carpeted in snow and where every tree was like a Christmas tree.

One of the company was smoking a cigarette. He finished it and then he threw it on to the ground, but with the greatest possible care he crushed it with his foot until every last and smallest spark was finally extinguished.

The visitor to Canada looked on in astonishment. "Look," he said, "why on earth did you go to such trouble to extinguish your cigarette? The whole place is covered in snow. It could not possibly set anything alight. Why all this care?"

The Canadian said: "It's like this. If I came out here in the summer-time and I dropped a lighted cigarette the chances are I would cause a disastrous forest fire. And therefore I have deliberately habituated myself never to drop a cigarette end anywhere without making quite certain that it is totally extinguished. And now," he said, "I do it completely automatically."

This man had taught himself a saving habit.

EVENING

A book entitled *Richard Wilton*, a forgotten Victorian, was written by Mary Blamire Young, his great-granddaughter, on the basis of family letters and memories. Clergymen of the olden days can teach us something! True, they had no insistent telephone calls, no constant committee meetings, no evening organizations. But in the day of these clergymen of a century ago three things stand out.

They did not forget to study

Richard Wilton's day begins with his spell at his commentary — and by the time that letter was written he was an old man. Study was always an integral part of his day.

There runs through both letters a great pastoral concern. These men shared the simple lives and the simple needs of their people. The schoolchildren are taught, the gardener's allotment is admired, the woman who coughed in church must be helped. The minister is the pastor.

Whatever progress there had been, that pattern of the ministry, now more than a century old, still stands for good.

Beauty

MORNING

I have always loved the story of Dean Ramsey. The good Dean loved his roses and it was a high mark of favor when he would say to a guest, "Come into the garden; I would like you to see my roses".

But one day a very lovely lady was visiting him. "Come into the garden," he said, "I would like my roses to see you!" — which is one of the loveliest compliments ever paid.

Still it does make one wonder why people will flock in crowds for aids to beauty which is skin deep, and remain quite indifferent to the beauty of the soul which makes life lovely.

Beauty which is skin deep is not difficult to acquire, if you have the money

You can buy it in a box or in a bottle, at the shop of a hairdresser or a beautician. On the other hand, the loveliness of the soul, the great inward graces of life, which make all life beautiful, are not easy to come by. They need to be paid for in self-discipline, in self-denial, in effort, in struggle, in prayer. It is so much easier to get the thing in the box.

EVENING

There are things which are not so satisfactory about the beauty that is skin deep.

For one thing, it only masks the reality beneath it. You can paint and powder on a lovely complexion, but that does not change the dull, lack-luster skin beneath the coating.

For another thing it is very impermanent. It has to come off at night, if only to put a mud-pack on! Soap and water will soon remove it. But the great graces of the heart and mind are an indelible part of life which nothing can remove.

Skin-deep beauty is sought to impress others

Maybe it does — for a moment; maybe it does make others turn in the street and look — and even whistle! But when the years go by, the people we really remember are the people who are gentle and gracious and wise and kind. Real loveliness outlasts synthetic beauty.

Even if it is outward beauty we are looking for (and why shouldn't we?), it is impossible to get it without the inward beauty

Inner discontent will etch upon the face lines that the beautician cannot remove. Crossness and irritability and bad temper will mark a face with wrinkles that a plastic surgeon cannot remove.

If we really want beauty, it must begin from inside. There can never be a permanently lovely face without a lovely soul.

Perseverance

MORNING

The Syro-Phoenician woman wanted Jesus to heal her sick daughter (Mark 7:24-30); but she was not a Jew and Jesus' mission was in the first place to the Jews, and he told her that his help was not at the moment for her.

"You can't take the children's bread," he said, "and throw it to the dogs."

"True," she replied, "but, sir, even the dogs under the table eat the children's scraps!"

"For saying that," said Jesus, "you may go home content." And she went home to find her daughter healed.

The Syro-Phoenician woman would not take "No" for an answer

Columbus would not take "No" for an answer. For eighteen years he tramped round the courts and the great houses seeking for financial help to fit out a squadron to discover the new worlds on the other side of the seas.

Booker Washington would not take "No" for an answer. He wanted a university education. He heard of a college which would accept Negroes. He walked there, hundreds of miles. When he arrived there, the college was full up; but he pleaded so hard that they gave him a job sweeping the floors and making the beds and cleaning the windows, and in the end he got in as a student, because he would not take "No" for an answer. Once, seeking to find a way to do something, he carried out more than seven hundred experiments, all of which ended in failure. "Now," he said cheerfully, "we know seven hundred ways not to do it," and carried on until he got the right way.

EVENING

If we want really to get somewhere, we must be of those people who won't take "No" for an answer.

The Syro-Phoenician woman found the value of a cheerful answer

We very often fail to get something because we meet a first refusal with a burst of bad temper or with black looks or with obvious resentment, and because we turn away with every line of our body showing how angry we are. If instead of that, we answered with a laugh and a jest, we might very well get what we want.

Perseverance plus cheerfulness will get a man almost anywhere. Even if they don't get him all the way, they will still make him laugh wherever he arrives.

The world needs people like that.

Imitation

MORNING

What kind of example are we setting our children?

What are we making our children think of marriage and of the relationship of husband and wife within the home?

Do we make them think of marriage as a relationship in which two people are for ever bickering and quarrelling about this, that and the next thing, a relationship in which two people spend their lives snapping at each other? Or do we make them think of marriage as a relationship in which two people are in perfect harmony and perfect accord with one another?

Is the child being brought up all unconsciously to think of marriage as an uneasy and unhappy and uncomfortable relationship and to think of the home as the arena of a series of squabbles and fights? Or is he being brought up to think of marriage as the most perfect of relationships and the home as a place of comradeship and togetherness and peace?

That is the question; each of us must answer it for ourselves.

EVENING

What are we making our children think of work?

Are we making them think of work as something in which it is the right thing to do as little as possible and to expect as much reward as possible? Are we teaching them to think of work as something in which it is a clever thing to "pull a fast one" on our employer or our boss? Are we teaching them that profitable little dishonesties are clever and praiseworthy so long as you get away with them?

Or are we teaching them that there is in fact no satisfaction like the satisfaction of a task well done, that there are people who are more concerned to do a job well, than to watch the clock and to count the wage, that petty dishonesty is something with which a Christian must have nothing to do?

This is the question; each of us must answer it for ourselves.

What are we making our children think of the church?

Are we making them think of the church as something to which we have to be grudgingly compelled every now and then to make some gift? Or are we making them think of the church as a place to which, like the Psalmist, we are glad to "go up", a place where we find our friends, and that to help it is a pleasure and a privilege?

Imitation is a God-given faculty for it is by imitating that we learn. We who are parents must remember the responsibility of being imitated by the children whom God has entrusted to our care.

Moderation but . . .

MORNING

There is a great deal of value and a great deal of truth in the advice which tells us to avoid extremes, to study moderation in all things, and always to seek the golden mean.

The person who oscillates between glowing enthusiasm and complete despair is an unsatisfactory person. The person who plunges from radiant joy to unrelieved gloom is a difficult person. We say of such people that they have no halfway house. Such people are often at the mercy of trifles, and they rocket their way through life swinging from one extreme to the other.

It is quite true that the man who pursues a steady, even course, the man whom nothing uplifts too much, and nothing casts down too much, the solid and imperturbable, and — to use a modern vivid coinage — the "unflappable" man, is indeed a valuable person to have beside you in any undertaking.

EVENING

But although there is truth in the advice which bids us to seek the golden mean and to avoid extremes, it is by m means the whole truth. The Greek suspected enthusiasm; the one man whom the Greek could not understand was the fanatic.

There is a sense in which for the Christian enthusiasm is the one essential quality, and the fanatic is the man who matters most of all

The great point at issue is this — the attitude of mind behind the advice to avoid extremes is the attitude of mind which regards playing safe as the most important thing in life. If, for instance, we always pursue a cautious prudence in speech, we will certainly never offend anyone else, and we will certainly never get into trouble ourselves. But, at the same time, we will never be able to say the things which rebuke men's sins and challenge their minds, and stir their hearts.

If we insist on following the middle and the cautious course of action, we will quite possibly make no glaring mistakes, but we will never at any time produce the heroic and the sacrificial actions which really matter in their effect of men. The one thing that the Christian cannot ever do is to play safe.

"All things in moderation" is prudent advice, and it has it value; but all things for Christ with an even reckless extravagance is the law of the Christian way.

Charm and more than charm

MORNING

Charm is one of the greatest of all gifts

Everyone knows the people who have charm. To meet people with charm is a happy experience. They can bring the sunshine on a rainy day. They can make other people their willing servants. They can persuade people to do what anyone would have thought they could never dream o doing.

There is a strength in charm like the strength of the sun which melts the ice.

But charm is one of the most dangerous gifts that any person can have

There are two dangers in charm.

The first is that a person should use it to get away with something they have done. Often a person with charm can talk and smile and "blarney" his way out of any situation, so that there comes a time when he comes to depend on that. He thinks that he can talk his way out of any trouble he has got into or any mistake that he has made.

The second danger is that a person with charm should try to make his charm a substitute for deeds, that he should try to make pleasant words and attractive mannerisms and fascinating smiles take the place of the things he ought to do.

Goodness *and* cleverness, charm and efficiency — a Christian ought to have all these qualities.

EVENING

Paul was quite certainly not a handsome man. In the third-century work called the "Acts of Paul and Thecia", there is a description of Paul which is so unflattering that it must be genuine: "A man of little stature, thin-haired upon the head, crooked in the legs, of good state of body, with eyebrows joining and nose somewhat hooked." Certainly, from the point of handsome looks, no one would have looked twice at this man Paul.

Still further, strangely enough, it seems that Paul was not even a very good speaker, and that he was certainly no orator. The Corinthians said of him that "his bodily presence is weak, and his speech of no account" (2 Corinthians 10:10).

Paul's effectiveness came from one thing. It came from an unanswerable experience of Jesus Christ.

Polish and elegance can often leave a congregation quite cold; experience and sincerity can never fail to move men.

Saying "no", saying "yes"

MORNING

A good test of a person is whether or not he instinctively says "No" when he is asked to do something.

Men and women can be classified into two groups — those who instinctively say "Yes" when they are asked for help, and those who instinctively say "No". I sometimes think that if I were choosing a colleague to work with, the first thing I would ask about would not be his university degrees and certificates, and his academic distinctions, but, "Is he obliging or disobliging?"

By far the best kind of person to have around is the kind of person who is always ready to say "Yes" when you ask him to do something.

But the tragedy of life is that it is not only to our fellowmen that we so often say "No"; we so often say "No" to God. We know that conscience is directing us somewhere; we know, in our heart of hearts, that there is a call to do something, but so often we say "No".

You can see this happening even with our prayers

So many people try to use prayer in the wrong way altogether. They continuously try to use prayer as a way of escape, as a way of averting something that they believe is going to happen. Their whole attitude in prayer, conscious or unconscious, is that they are always begging God to change his mind to suit them.

For them, prayer is a way of saying to God, "Your will be changed." It is not a way of saying to God, "Your will be done."

EVENING

When Jesus invited men to follow him, what he offered them was a job to do. "Come," he said, "follow me, and I will make you fishers of men." (Matthew 4:19). He did not keep them with him: he sent them out, and sent them out with the clear warning that there was trouble ahead (Matthew 10:5-42). His last words to them were, "Go! Preach!" (Matthew 28:19). What he left them was a task, the task of being witnesses for him and to him (Acts 1:8).

Repeatedly Jesus spoke to men just as much about what they could do for him as about what he could do for them. He appealed to men to come to him, not only for what they could get, but also for what they could give.

In the present situation there are things for which we might well appeal to men to take their stand with Jesus Christ and with his church.

Men are needed today to preserve the moral standards by which society is held together.

Men are needed today to preserve the standards of liberty and of freedom which cost so much to achieve.

We have a right to say today, "Come and stand with us for the standards without which freedom and liberty cannot survive."

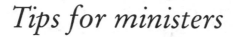

Tips for ministers

MORNING

George Johnstone Jeffrey was a saint and a man of devotion. His advice is most practical. He had a favorite text—he quotes it twice in his lectures — "Hast thou commanded the morning?" (Job 38:12).

He uses this text in the most down to earth way. "I am weighing my words," he says, "when I say that if there is one habit more than another that has been of value in the art of preaching it is that of early rising."

A minister is his own master as far as time is concerned; and there is no profession in which it is so fatally easy to waste time

The office-worker has to be at his desk at a set time; the factory worker has to be at his bench or his machine at a given time. There is no one and nothing to compel the minister to start work at any time — except his conscience.

The minister should be as meticulous in getting to his desk at a fixed time as any office or factory worker is.

The minister is at everyone's beck and call, not eight hours a day, but twenty-four hours a day

His job is comparable with the job of the doctor, in that it is never done. He can never close his door and he can never refuse an appeal for help. Meticulous he must be as to when he begins, but he has no claim at all as to when he is to end.

EVENING

J. H. Jowett said, "I have been greatly impressed in recent years by one refrain which I have found running through many biographies. Dr. Parker repeated again and again, 'Preach to broken hearts.'"

Ian Maclaren said, "The chief end of preaching is comfort."

Dr. Dale said, "People want to be comforted . . . They need consolation — really need it, and do not merely long for it."

People need comfort in sorrow

There would be one way to ensure that sorrow never entered into life and that would be never to love anyone. Wherever there is love, there will also be sorrow. This means that almost everyone in this world will at some time, know tears and a broken heart.

People need comfort in sin

In every congregation, there are those who are suffering from a sense of sin — in some, an acute agony, in some a dull hopelessness. But it is there. There are those in whom realization of, and penitence for, sin has never been awakened. It must be awakened. But, after the awakening, there must come the message of comfort.

A good advert?

MORNING

The Christian is a living epistle known and read of all men, an open letter, an advertisement for Christianity (2 Corinthians 3:2,3).

We are so to live that when people see the good we do they may give praise to our Father in heaven (Matthew 5:16).

Just how do we measure up to this demand that the Christian life should be the only effective advertisement for Christianity?

Advertising consists in making a claim

Christianity claims that it gives rest and joy and peace and power. Is there in our lives a calm serenity, a radiant happiness, a power to cope with life that the non-Christian does not possess? Or are we just as worried and anxious, just as gloomy and grumbling, just as liable to collapse as the next man?

We cannot expect others to want Christianity, if it apparently makes no difference at all.

Advertising makes comparisons

By implication one product is compared with another so that by the comparison its superior quality may be seen.

We say that Christianity alone can save the world; we claim that it is better than any other religion. You can only judge a religion by the people it produces; there is no other standard available.

Are *you* a good advertisement for Jesus Christ?

EVENING

How like a good watch a good man is!

A watch counts the hours. So does the wise man

"So teach us to number our days, that we may apply our hearts unto wisdom." (Psalm 90: 12).

In the longest life, time is short. Like the watch, we should count the hours.

A watch, when it is damaged, has to be returned to its maker

It must be so all through life with us. When life goes wrong, and when we go wrong, then there is nothing to do but to take it back to God so that he may forgive and he may mend us to send us out to work better in the time to come.

Prophets and power

MORNING

The prophet is a man with a seeing eye

In the Old Testament, the prophets were the men who could see what was happening. They could see the way history was shaping. Others would be busy dashing about trying to arrange alliances and treaties with Egypt, with Syria, or with some other power. The prophet was the man who saw deeper than superficial power relationships. He saw the nation's destiny.

The prophet has a courageous voice

He tells the truth whatever the cost. "We cannot but speak the things we have seen and heard," said Peter and John to the Sanhedrin. The prophet never buys security with a cowardly silence.

The prophet has a dedicated life

Said Isaiah to God when he learned there was work to be done, "Here am I, send me." He had to do not what he himself wanted to do, but what God needed him to do.

God needs people of dedication, like the prophets.

The prophet is a man with a dangerous occupation

Jerusalem was the city that stoned the prophets (Matthew 23:37). Stephen told the Jews that they had consistently stoned the prophets (Acts 7:52).

No one can be a prophet who is not prepared to take a risk for God.

EVENING

Tokichi Ishii had a record of savage and beastly cruelty that was almost without equal. With almost fiendish brutality he had murdered men, women and even children, and had pitilessly and cold-bloodedly removed anyone who stood in his way. At last the law caught up with him. He was captured; he was in prison awaiting execution.

While he was in prison, he was visited by two Canadian ladies who tried to talk to him through the prison bars. They were unable to make even the very slightest impression on him. He merely glowered back at them like a wild animal.

In the end they left a Bible with him, in the faint hope that the Bible might be able to make the appeal that no human words had been able to make.

Then it happened. He began to read, and the story so gripped him that he could not stop. He read on until he came at last to the story of the Crucifixion. It was the words, "Father, forgive them, for they know not what they do," that broke down his last resistance. "I stopped," he said. "I was stabbed to the heart, as if pierced by a five-inch nail. Shall I call it the love of Christ? Shall I call it his compassion? I do not know what to call it. I only know that I believed and that the hardness of my heart was changed."

Providence

MORNING

A story is told of John Ruskin, the famous art critic and artist. One day a lady, who was a friend of his, showed him a handkerchief made of very precious material. A blot of indelible ink had fallen upon it, and the lady was lamenting to Ruskin that the very valuable handkerchief was ruined beyond repair.

Ruskin asked if he might have it. The lady said that of course he could have it, but she could not see why he should want the ruined piece of material. Some days later Ruskin brought the handkerchief back, and on it, beginning from the blot, and making the blot the center of the whole matter, Ruskin had drawn the most intricate and beautiful pattern and design.

God has a way of taking the most unlikely things, and of somehow fitting them into his purposes and using them for his plans. In everything God works for good (Romans 8:28).

God can make pain and sickness work for good

Robert Leighton, the Scots divine, after a serious illness, said, "I have learned more of God since I came to this bed than in all my life before."

It was out of the thorn in his flesh that Paul discovered the all-sufficient grace of God (2 Corinthians 12:7-9).

Many a man has discovered God in illness in a way in which he never discovered him in health.

EVENING

Howard Williams has said that often the whole of the Christian faith is contained in the word "nevertheless".

It happens when prayer seems to be unavailing

Studdert Kennedy wrote of Jesus Christ:

> 'E prayed to the Lord, and 'e
>   sweated blood,
> And yet 'e were crucified.

There is a time when all we can say is, "Nevertheless, not my will but thine be done."

It happens when faith seems to be a losing battle

Studdert Kennedy wrote of himself, "Every man, whether Christian or not, must sooner or later stand in the last ditch face to face with the final doubt. I know that last ditch well. I have stood in it many a time; and I know that before I die I shall stand there again — and again." There is a time when there is nothing left to say but,"Nevertheless I do believe."

The personal touch and the personal life

MORNING

There are some things that make all the difference to life.

We all like to be treated as persons

The great danger in any well-organized welfare state is that men and women begin to be treated as numbers on a list, types of a certain group of some kind or other, entries on a schedule. Everyone knows what a difference it makes when an official treats us as a person, when a doctor seems interested in us as someone with a name and a home and a problem and not as a case. Men and women are individual persons and can only be treated as such.

We all like people to be interested in us

We all know what a difference it makes to be served by a shop assistant who is really trying to help and not by one of these take-it-or-leave-it-I-couldn't-care-less characters who are behind some counters. Charm is really the attitude of one who obviously cares.

We all like to be remembered

It is very pleasant to go into a restaurant where the waiter remembers you, or where the waitress smiles at you like a returned friend. It is one of life's grimmest experiences to be introduced to someone, and then to meet him a second time and find that he has not the slightest recollection of ever having seen you before!

EVENING

One of the insoluble problems of a man who becomes a public figure is that he no longer belongs to himself, or to his wife, or to his family. He begins to belong to the public; and there is a very real sense in which that has to be so.

A great surgeon cannot refuse to carry out an emergency operation because he happens to have planned a family party.

A great police officer cannot refuse a sudden investigation of a crime because he would like to spend a night at home.

A great statesman cannot refuse a tour of the country when he would much rather be with his family.

A parson cannot refuse a summons to comfort the sorrowing and soothe the troubled and the ill on an evening when he has planned an outing with his wife and children.

All talent is a responsibility, and the greater the talent a man has, the less he belongs to himself. Jesus himself said that a man who puts even the dearest relationships of life before him is not worthy of him (Matthew 10:37, 38); but where love is great enough and where love lets itself be known, even this problem can be solved.

Diagnosis and remedy

MORNING

In any illness there are certain steps which must be gone through before a cure is possible.

There must be diagnosis by the doctor

The doctor must be able to put his finger on the spot and to say that this and this is wrong. The most alarming illnesses and the most difficult to deal with are the illnesses in which no one can quite discover what is wrong. You cannot even begin to treat an illness until you find out what is wrong.

There must be acceptance by the patient

The patient must accept the verdict and the diagnosis of the doctor. If he completely refuses to believe that there is anything wrong, and if he persists in going on as if nothing was wrong, then he cannot be cured.

There must come next the prescribed treatment by the doctor

The sole purpose of the diagnosis of the trouble is that the treatment which will work a cure must be prescribed.

EVENING

There must follow acceptance on the part of the patient

If the patient does not accept the treatment, if he refuses to have the operation, if he pours the bottle of medicine down the drain and throws the box of pills out of the window, if he totally disregards the diet prescribed, then he cannot hope for a cure.

A man is not only a body; a man is also a soul, a spirit, a mind. And the state of a man's mind and soul and spirit can be such as to hinder the prescribed cure or even to make it totally ineffective. The spirit, the mind, must be right before the body can be cured.

For a complete cure two things are necessary: the best medical treatment, willingly accepted, and the most intense prayer, faithfully offered.

When that happens, then the spirit is in a condition for the body to be cured. For then the grace of God co-ordinates with the skill of man, that skill which God himself has given.

The great man

MORNING

One of the greatest castles in England is Arundel Castle, and one of the greatest of all the English aristocracy is the Duke of Norfolk to whom that castle belongs.

Once a certain Duke of Norfolk happened to be at the railway station, when a little Irish girl arrived off the train with a very heavy bag. She had come to be a maidservant at the castle.

The castle is about a mile from the station and the little Irish girl was trying to persuade a porter to carry her heavy bag to the castle, for which she offered him a shilling, all the money that she had. The porter contemptuously refused. The Duke stepped forward, shabby as usual in appearance. He offered to carry her bag to the castle, took it and walked beside her along the road to the castle, talking to her.

At the end of the journey, he gratefully accepted the shilling she offered him, never allowing her to know who he was; and it was only the next day, when she met her employer, that the little Irish girl knew that the Duke of Norfolk had carried her bag from the station to the castle and that she had tipped him a shilling!

EVENING

A very wonderful story of a true nobleman that tells us a good many things about this kind of man!

It is never safe to judge a man by externals.

A great man is always a thoughtful man.

There is grace in taking as well as giving.

The truly great man does not think of his place or his prestige.

It is only little people who think how great they are.

It is only unimportant people who think how important they are. There is nothing in this world which is a surer sign of a small mind than the complaint that one did not get one's place; and there is no motive in this world that is more wrong than the desire for prestige.

In the last analysis, to the truly great man, no act of service can possibly be humiliating

No task, if it is going to help anyone else, can possibly be beneath his dignity.

It is enough surely for the disciple that he should be as his Lord.

The man who "fixes his eye upon Jesus" sees that loving service is the loveliest thing in the world.

Shut up

MORNING

No man can love God without loving his fellow men. If he says he does, then he does not know what loving God means. That is why the social gospel is never an addendum to Christianity but always the very center of Christianity.

It is blindness to think that we can meet Christ in the Sacrament if we comfortably forget that he said that what we do and do not do to our fellow-men is done and not done to him

Here is something that Studdert Kennedy himself saw with vivid intensity. He had no time for those whose religion consisted in making their communion and in long prayers and so forth and so on. It was in fact therein that he saw the failure of the church. "We have been calling men to services," he said, "when what they wanted was the call to service."

In his book *The Word and the Work*, he said, "Nobody worries about Christ as long as he can be kept shut up in churches. He is quite safe there. But there is always trouble if you try to let him out."

Was there ever a time when Jesus Christ was more thoroughly shut up in the church than he is today?

EVENING

The tragedy of today is that there is a tacit kind of agreement, conscious or unconscious, that Christianity is impossible. And this agreement is not among non-Christians, but very often among Christians.

It is clear that Christianity is regarded as impossible in the international world

A world which has agreed that the only way to keep peace is to possess so-called nuclear deterrents has clearly come to the conclusion that Christianity can be written off as an impossibility in the relationship between nation and nation.

It is clear that Christianity is regarded as impossible in the political sphere

Any politician who announced that he proposed to judge each issue in terms of soul and conscience and so to cast his vote would quite certainly be told in effect that the party whip was very much more important than his conscience, and that the party line was very much more important than the Christian gospel.

Christianity has become rather an optional extra on the circumference of life than a complete essential, dominating the whole of life. What happens if we let Christ out? That is not the question, for the question for the Christian ought always to be, not, "Is it safe?" but, "Is it right?"

Debit and credit

MORNING

I once visited that amazing parish church in Boston in Lincolnshire, one of the largest parish churches in all England. Boston is still busy, but compared with what it once was it is a little place, for there was a time when Boston was second as a seaport only to London. But still that famous tower, Boston Stump, stretches 275 feet into the sky, a landmark for miles around and a guide to the sailor at sea.

They say of Boston church that it is built in a very special way. They say that there are seven doors to stand for the seven days of the week; twelve pillars in the nave to stand for the twelve months; twenty-four steps to the library to stand for the hours of the day; fifty-two windows to stand for the weeks of the year; sixty steps to the chancel roof to stand for the seconds in a minute; 365 steps to the top of the tower, to stand for the days of the year. So if you know the way that Boston church is built, you cannot look at it without remembering the passing of time.

I have not yet reached the age of decrepitude, but it is worthwhile to stand and think what time has done to me.

There are things on the debit side.

Time certainly takes physical strength away.

I find myself forgetting much more readily than I used to.

I find that I cannot work as fast as once I did; things take just a little longer to do.

EVENING

Here are some things on the credit side after half a century of life.

I find that I am much more sympathetic than once I was

You cannot live for over half a century without seeing how easy it is to go wrong, and when someone does make a mistake now, I am much more likely to say with George Whitefield, "There but for the grace of God go I," than I am likely to condemn.

No one can pass the half century without having sorrowed and suffered, and to have sorrowed oneself is to be a little better able to help others who are going through it. The passing years bring sympathy — and that is no small gift.

I find that I am much more tolerant than once I was

It is not that I am any less sure that certain things are right, and it is not that I am no longer willing to argue as boldy as I can, and even, as Goldsmith said of Dr. Johnson, to try to knock a man down with the butt-end of it, if my pistol misses fire! But I am very much more willing to admit that perhaps I may be wrong, and that there are many more ways to God than the way which I have found.

Easter Day

MORNING

It is one of the strange things in the modern church that we think of the Easter faith only at Easter time.

It is at Easter time almost alone that we think of the Resurrection and of the life to come; it is at Easter time almost alone that we sing the hymns of the Easter faith.

This is so wrong. I think that we have forgotten the origin of Sunday, the Lord's Day. The Sabbath, the Jewish holy day, commemorated the rest of God after the labor of the six days of creation; the Sunday, the Lord's Day, commemorates the Resurrection of our Lord, for it was on that day that he rose from the dead.

In the early church the Resurrection was the star in the firmament of the church. The Resurrection was the one glorious fact on which all worship and all life were founded. To that centrality of the Easter faith, the Resurrection faith, we would do well to return continually.

It is the Easter faith, the faith in the risen and living Lord, which makes us able to meet life

For if we believe that Jesus Christ is risen and living, then we must believe that all life is lived in his presence, that we are literally never alone, that we are called upon to make no effort, to endure no sorrow, to face no temptation without him.

EVENING

It is the Easter faith, the faith in the risen and living Lord, which makes us able to meet death

It is the Easter faith that we have a friend and a companion who lived and who died and who is alive for evermore, who is the conqueror of death. The presence which is with us in life is with us in death and beyond.

A writer tells how his father died. His father was old and ill. One morning the writer tells how he went up to his father's bedroom to waken him. The old man said, "Pull up the blinds so that I can see the morning light." The son pulled up the blind and even as the light entered the room, the old man sank back on his pillows dead. Death was the coming of the morning light.

The Easter faith should be in our thoughts not simply at a certain season of the Christian year; it ought to be the faith in which Christians daily live, and in which in the end they die, only to live again.

Hobson's choice

MORNING

I have by chance discovered the origin of a well-known phrase. In Cambridge the name "Hobson" recurs. There is a Hobson Street. There is a Hobson's Conduit, which used to stand in the center of the market-place and which is now in Trumpington Street.

This Hobson kept a livery stable in Cambridge in the seventeenth century. If you came to him to hire a horse, it was his unbreakable rule that you took the one next to the door — or you got none at all.

It is from this Hobson and his insistence that, without choice, you took the horse next to the door that there comes the phrase "Hobson's choice".

When we are confronted with Hobson's choice, it simply means that we are confronted with a situation in which there are no alternatives, and when we have to accept what is there.

Life quite often confronts us with a choice that is Hobson's choice.

It may happen that through force of circumstances we are left with no alternative.

The world is full of people who, because they did not get what they want, have become soured and embittered and querulous and sometimes even obstructive of others who have what they think they should have.

The Stoics had a saying which sounds merciless but which is true. "If you can't get what you want, want what you can get." It is a good rule for life.

EVENING

It sometimes happens that a man has no choice from the point of view of principle. In this case the compulsion does not come from outside him, but from inside him. It is not, so to speak, physically impossible for him to do anything else, but it is morally impossible.

He is in the situation of Martin Luther who was compelled by inner compulsion to say: "Here I stand; I can do no other; so help me God."

The world and society and politics and the church need men who feel that moral compulsion and who will abide by it, because they find it impossible to do anything else. We need men who cannot be bought, and who will prove that it is a lie to say that "every man has his price". We need men who cannot be seduced. We need men who cannot be frightened out of doing the thing which the moral imperative demands.

When circumstances force it upon us, we must accept it, not doubting that there is opportunity and challenge in what is left as much as there was in what is taken away.

When a moral issue confronts us with it, we must choose the way of conscience and of principle and refuse to leave it.

Two parables

MORNING

In T. R. Glover's *The Jesus of History* he has some very interesting things to say about the parables of Jesus, and, in particular, about the twin parables of the treasure hidden in the field and the pearl of great price (Matthew 13:44-6).

In these two parables Glover sees four things which are of the very essence of achievement in the Christian life.

They begin with the recognition of an opportunity.

The men who found the treasure and the pearl saw at once that this was literally the opportunity of a lifetime.

There are few greater gifts than the ability to see the opportunity when it comes. The same situation can come to two men. One will see it as a disaster and the other as an opportunity; one will see it as something about which nothing can be done, the other will see it as an inspiring challenge to action.

There is the famous story about the army which suddenly fell into an ambush set by its enemies. One commander said to the General: "Alas, we have fallen into the hands of the enemy." The General answered: "Why not say that they have fallen into ours?"

The Christian sees every situation as an opportunity and a challenge.

EVENING

The two parables go on to a resolution. Immediately the opportunity presented itself, the men involved took their decision to grasp it. There was no delay and no dither. The opportunity emerged; the opportunity was grasped. Both men were prepared to pay the price of grasping the opportunity. They sold all that they had to buy the field and the pearl. They were prepared to pay the price of turning the opportunity into reality.

Life gives nothing for nothing. There are still many who turn sadly away (Matthew 19:22), because they will not pay the price the opportunity demands.

The price will always be toil; the price may sometimes be sacrifice; but the price has to be paid.

But when the opportunity is recognized, when the decision is taken, when the price is paid, then the end is joy.

The treasure and the pearl were possessed.

In the parables, the end was success. But even if, in the end, there is no success, there is more joy in attempting something great and failing in it than in not attempting it at all.

To try and to fail is better than not to try at all.

Christians in the ancient world

MORNING

In *The Jesus of History*, T. R. Glover discusses the triumph of Christianity in the ancient world.

It was a highly improbable triumph. How did it happen that a small group of simple and unlettered men could go out into the world with the story of a crucified Jewish criminal and persuade men and women to take that Jesus as savior and Lord?

Glover's answer is that the Christians were enabled by the grace of God to do three things — they out-lived, they out-died, and they out-thought the pagan world.

They out-lived the world

Why were they able to do this? Because they could say of Jesus: "He loved me and he gave himself for me" (Galatians 2:20). Every man had acquired a new dignity and a new worth because he could say that for him, as a person, the Son of God had died.

Further, he believed that the Son of God had loved and given himself for all men. He had therefore a motive for service that no one else had.

He was eager to help the man for whom Christ died. He had a motive of forgiveness such as no one else had. However unpleasant that other man might be, Jesus Christ had died for him.

EVENING

The Christians out-died the world

Tertullian, the famous Roman lawyer, saw the Christians die, and it shook him to the depths of his being. "Every man," he said, "who sees it is moved with some misgivings, and is set on fire to learn the reason; he enquires and he is taught; and when he has learned the truth he instantly follows it himself."

When simple men and women could choose to die like that, and to die in agony, there must be something in that for which they died.

The Christians out-thought the world

The ancient world was credulous and superstitious. The Christian was clear-sighted and fearless.

Lucian tells how he saw on heathen shrines the notice: "Christians keep out." The Christian saw too clearly through the mumbo-jumbo.

In the ancient world the way to destroy your enemy was to attach his name to a demon and the demon would kill him. "Go on," said the Christian, "attach my name to a demon. I don't care. I have a name which is above every name to keep me safe."

The Christian thought fearlessly and clearly. The number of heresies shows the freedom and the vigor with which the Christian thought. He had a freedom of thought and speech that no one else had ever had.

Debt to the past

MORNING

The gauge of railway lines in Britain, that is the distance between the lines, is four feet eight and a half inches. Four feet eight and a half inches seems a very odd distance indeed. How did it come about?

There is more than one explanation of it, but I have just come across an explanation that is very interesting.

The first railway lines were laid, not for steam engines to run on, but for carts to be hauled over them by horses. A horse could haul a much heavier load if the cart or wagon ran on rails rather than on a road. The first rails were therefore laid on wooden boards that had themselves been laid on the top of the ruts which wagons and cartwheels had already made on the roads. The rails were laid to fit the ruts which were already there.

But this only pushes the question one step farther back. Why were the cart ruts four feet eight and a half inches in gauge? It is to explain this that a very interesting suggestion has been made. It has been said that the gauge, the distance between the wheels of a Roman chariot was four feet eight and a half inches, and that it was that which started the whole thing.

Centuries ago the Roman chariots left their ruts on the roads; carts and wagons were built to the same gauge. In due time the rails were laid to that gauge too.

If that is so, there is a direct connection between the Roman chariot and the great modern trains thundering to London sometimes at a hundred miles an hour. There is a direct continuity between them.

EVENING

The present necessarily grows out of the past. No age stands isolated and alone. It stands upon the foundation of all that went before.

That is why the Christian church can never jettison the Old Testament. Without the Old Testament to go before, there could not have been a New Testament at all.

The continuity must be remembered.

This puts us in debt to the past. Each generation is a link in a chain, inseparably attached to what has gone before and to what will come after.

"Others have labored, and you have entered into their labor," Jesus said to his disciples (John 4:38).

We have entered into the labors of others.

Some day, others will enter into our labors.

Life can be too easy

MORNING

Where we holiday there are two golf courses. One is a good course, the kind of course that you could play a championship on. The other is a course for the very young and the very old and the very inefficient. The great feature of the second course is that it hasn't got an inch of rough on it all the way round. Everywhere the grass is cut and short and smooth.

I had been playing all my holiday on the course with no rough, the course on which I could belt the ball without worrying where it landed and I was saying to myself when it was time to go home: "I'm not so bad yet. I can still play." But very soon after we came home, I had a job to do in a town where there are some first-class golf courses. I decided to take my clubs and to have a game when I had finished my work.

I hadn't played three holes when I discovered that on a course, a real course, where there was a fairway flanked by two stretches of deep rough, you couldn't belt the ball two hundred yards away in the direction of mid-off or mid-on (to use cricket terms again!) without getting into serious trouble. If you weren't straight, you were in trouble all the time. And I wasn't straight.

So, as a golfer I was found out.

This goes for life too!

If things are too easy, you won't cope with the real test when it comes.

EVENING

It is never wise to make things too easy for anyone. If you make things too easy for a person, you just unfit him to face the real test. It is never wise to make the task of a child or of a student too easy. It only leads to trouble in the long run.

It is never wise to encourage the idea that you can make mistakes and escape punishment. My easy golf course made me forget that on a real course mistakes are punished. I had to learn all over again that you can't make mistakes and get away with it.

It is no kindness to people, especially when they are in training, to encourage them to think that they can get away with anything. Failure to apply the necessary discipline simply unfits a man for the necessary tests of real life.

If we are wise, we will be constantly on our guard against the peril of wanting things too easy or of making things too easy.

After all, Scripture has it: "Blessed is the man whom thou dost chasten, O Lord" (Psalm 94:12), and, "The Lord disciplines him whom he loves" (Hebrews 12:6).

The way of faith

MORNING

I want to look at some of the things that Bunyan said about faith.

Faith, said Bunyan, "cannot sit still; faith is forcible"

Faith, he said, "is a principle of life by which a Christian lives . . . a principle of motion by which the soul walks forward towards heaven in the way of holiness. It is also a principle of strength, by which the soul opposeth its lust, the Devil and this world, and overcomes them."

Faith is far more than mere intellectual assent to something. Faith is that which drives a man to action; it is that which compels a man to believe so intensely in something that he has to do something about it.

Faith is that which makes the gospel message "contemporaneous"

For the man who has faith, the story of Jesus is not something which happened in the past; it is something which is happening now.

"Faith," said Luther, "taketh hold of Christ, and hath him present, and holdeth him enclosed, as the ring doth the precious stone."

Through faith Jesus Christ lives in the here and now.

EVENING

Faith, as defined by Richard Baxter, includes three things.

Faith is the assent of the intellect

There is an intellectual element in faith. If we cannot in honesty and with conviction and with reason believe in the existence of God and in the historical reality of Jesus, there can be no such thing as faith.

Faith is the consent of the will

Faith must go beyond the mere assent to certain facts. The devils, as James says (2:19), believe in God but they still remain devils. Faith must proceed to action in light of the facts. Faith believes, and then turns belief into action.

Faith, as Baxter says, is a "practical affiance", trusting Christ as Savior

By a "practical affiance", Baxter means a trust which is not theoretical, but which has its effect upon life. Faith is taking Jesus at his word, and believing that he meant what he said, and that his promises are true and his commands binding.

The more we study faith, the greater it becomes.

Trust and friendship

MORNING

Here are two areas in which trust may fail — according to the Bible.

The biblical writers saw the futility of force and power. "Not in my bow do I trust," says the Psalmist, "nor can my sword save me" (Psalm 44:6).

The prophet warns the people that the fortified cities in which they trust will be destroyed (Jeremiah 5:17); and one of the main lines of the prophets is the futility of foreign alliances to beget any real security.

The biblical writers insist on the futility of any human trust. "Cursed is the man who trusts in man," say Jeremiah, "and makes flesh his arm" (Jeremiah 17:5). "Put not your trust in princes," says the Psalmist, "in a son of man in whom there is no help" (Psalm 146:3).

Human help in any event can go thus far and no farther.

On the other hand the whole Bible is full of the joyful voices of men who trusted in God and who were not confounded. "To thee they cried, and were saved," says the Psalmist, "in thee they trusted and were not disappointed" (Psalm 22:5). The trust that will never be disappointed is the trust in God.

This is not to say that the man who trusts in God will live a protected, trouble-free, sorrow-free life; but it is to say that the man who trusts in God will find the strength to meet any situation, however tragic.

Trust in God, not simply for protection, but for that unconquerable strength to meet all that life can do to us.

EVENING

I myself was an only child, but my wife is one of five sisters. I therefore have a charming assortment of nephews and nieces and grand-nephews and grand-nieces!

In 1968 my wife was across in Canada with Jane, our daughter, to visit a sister of hers who lives and works there. Naturally many photographs were taken. In 1969 my wife's sister was across in Scotland visiting her own family and us. Naturally, the photographs were on show.

They were being shown to Julie, one of our grand-nieces, then just about three years old, who lives very near us and who knows Jane well. When Julie saw the photograph of Jane and my wife, she said: "Look! That's Jane and her friend!"

Mother and daughter — mother and friend.

How wonderful!

Confidence and worry

MORNING

There is a right and wrong confidence.

There is the confidence of the man who knows that he is prepared and can deal with the situation

Once someone said to one of these amazing air pilots who fly at such fantastic speeds, "You must take the most frightful risks." His answer was, "The one thing to be quite sure of in my job is to see to it that you never take any risks." He had everything perfectly prepared in so far as it was humanly possible; he was quite sure of his own ability to cope with any foreseeable situation.

That is not a wrong confidence, that is the confidence of the man who knows what he can do.

There is the confidence of the man who is justly aware of his own gifts

When Balzac was a lad he told his father that he proposed to give his life to literature and become an author. His father well knew both the risks and the rewards of authorship. "If you become an author," he said, "and if you take literature as your career, you will either be a beggar or a king." "Very well," said the lad, "I will be a king."

There is nothing wrong in a man knowing what he can do, in willingly tackling a big job, in gladly offering himself for some great service, in the confidence that he can do it.

EVENING

A task which looks quite impossible in the distance somehow or other becomes possible when we actually have to face it

It is an extraordinary thing how in life things which we would have said were impossible become possible when we have got to do them.

It was Edison who said that the only difference between the difficult and the impossible is that the impossible takes a little longer.

A sorrow which looks unbearable in the future somehow or other becomes bearable when it actually happens

Sometimes, when we hear of what has happened to others, and when we think that it might happen to ourselves, we think that if such a thing should happen to us, life could not possibly go on. But life does go on.

No man knows what he can bear, until he has had to bear it; and no man knows what the help of God can be like until in desperation he calls upon it.

The advice of Jesus is good: "Don't worry about tomorrow; let tomorrow worry about itself; sufficient unto each day is the problem and the task which that day brings" (Matthew 6:34).

Doubt and sympathy

MORNING

There are certain languages which we need to be able to speak.

For example, the language of doubt.

It is very difficult for a man who has never experienced a twinge of doubt to talk to a man whose mind and heart are tortured by questions.

It was said of someone that he had "skirted the howling deserts of doubt". And a wise man, commenting on that, said that he would have been much better to go through them and come out at the other side.

A faith is not the highest kind of faith until it has been tested.

We should never be ashamed of having doubts. They are the way to real certainty. Only the man who has had them and faced them can help others.

Tennyson said, rightly, that there is often more faith in honest doubt than in the unthinking acceptance of a conventional creed.

EVENING

There is more than one reaction to pain and anguish.

Some people run away from it

There are people who are frightened of sickness, who can hardly bear to enter a sick-room. In the presence of pain and illness and trouble, their one desire is to get away from it and to keep away from it.

They are not violently to be blamed for this. There is something in them that makes them act like this. But it is something they are bound to try to conquer.

Some people have no sense of sympathy

They are themselves so healthy and so unaware of pain that they cannot understand, and make no effort to understand, the pain of others. They are themselves so sane and well balanced that they cannot understand the nerves or the shrinking of others. They regard the whole thing with complete incomprehension.

These people are almost worse than the first kind. They have an inability to put themselves in the other person's place.

Yet in the Incarnation, this is exactly what God did.

He entered into humanity's pain.

There are the people for whom pain and suffering in others brings out the best

They have the instinct and the ability to help.

It is people like that for whom we all have reason to thank God.

The Bible writers

MORNING

A friend sent me some advice that John Wycliffe laid down for Bible study.

Wycliffe said: "It will greatly help ye to understand the Scripture, if thou shalt mark, not only what is written, but by whom, and to whom, with what words, at what time, where, to what intent, with what circumstances, considering what goeth before and what followeth."

Some centuries later F. J. A. Hort in his introduction to his unfinished commentary on First Peter was to write: To understand a book rightly, we want to know who wrote it, for what readers it was written, for what purposes, and under what circumstances."

This is valuable advice.

It simply means that we can never fully understand a book unless we understand something of the circumstances in which it was written, and of the person who wrote it; and we can never fully interpret a passage unless we take it with what comes after, that is, within its context.

To realize this, begins to make the Bible understood.

EVENING

It makes a difference to know who wrote particular words in the Bible.

"My grace is sufficient to you" (2 Corinthians 12:9).

If someone had written that on whom the wind had never been allowed to blow; if it had been written by a man who had never known want or poverty or pain or toil, we might justly question its validity. But when we know that it was written by a man with a pain like a stake twisting in his body, and with a record of adventure that reads like an epic (2 Corinthians 11:23-28), then it really means something.

It gains its value from the man who said it.

It makes a difference to know to whom particular words were written.

In 1 Corinthians 6:9-11 Paul makes a list of all the most blatant sinners and then writes: "And such were some of you," but now they are as cleansed as they were once polluted, he goes on.

The people to whom that was written lived in Corinth, notoriously and admittedly the most immoral city in the ancient world, the city out of bounds to Roman soldiers on leave because it was so dangerous, the city with the Temple of Aphrodite whose thousand priestesses were sacred prostitutes and who every night plied their trade in the streets of Corinth.

If you were to say that the grace of God is operative in some respectable god-fearing area, it would indeed be something. But if this can be said of a sink of iniquity like Corinth, then this is the trumpet call of moral victory.

The more we know about Scripture, the greater the message of Scripture becomes.

Our bodies

MORNING

Jesus must have been physically fit. In his days in Palestine, the carpenter did not buy his wood from the wholesaler.

He went out to the hillside, chose his sapling, swung his axe, cut it down and bore it home on his shoulder.

That is what Jesus did.

He was no pale, anemic figure but a tall, bronzed young man who could have walked any modern hiker off his feet, I suspect!

One of the tragedies of religion is that there are times when men have thought it almost a religious duty to neglect their bodies.

We may fitly talk of such a thing as the gospel of physical fitness.

If we are feeling depressed, let us remember it may be due not to neglect of our souls but to neglect of our bodies.

"Present your bodies a living sacrifice, holy, acceptable unto God, which is your reasonable service" (Romans 12:1).

EVENING

There is a very surprising young man who is a friend of mine. He would have liked to have been a minister, but life did not run that way for him. He actually works in a big chemist's shop which stays open all night. He works a shift that finishes at eleven o'clock at night.

He still studies as hard as he can. He still takes classes when he can; and he is the only person I know who has set himself to learn Coptic!

Last night I went into the shop where he works to get a tube of a certain preparation which promises to relieve aches and pains. We talked for a moment or two as we usually do, and he said to me: "When I was a boy I used to go to a little mission hall. One of the members was an old man who had lived a pretty wild life when he was young and who had been soundly converted. And one of the things he often used to say was: 'God will forgive you, but your body never does.'"

There is a whole world of truth in that.

John B. Gough, the great temperance orator, became a man of God. He glorified in God's forgiveness; he pleaded with others to accept it; and one of the things he used to say to young men was: "Watch what you are doing. God can forgive you, but the scars remain."

One of the faults of Christianity has often been that it has often spoken as if man was nothing but a soul.

The great Christians knew well that man has a body too. The greatest of them knew how important that body was.

Spiritual dryness and human goodness

MORNING

One night Saint Francis was wakened by cries from the dormitory. When he went in he found a young brother who had practised such asceticism that he was literally dying of hunger. Francis ordered the table to be spread with all the food in the place. He bade the monks sit down, said grace and then he spoke to them.

"Dearest," he said, "we must look after Brother Body or he will turn melancholy and become a drag on us. After all, if we want him to serve us in work and in prayer, we must give him no reasonable cause to murmur."

Philip Doddridge has a sermon on "Spiritual Dryness". In it he says:

Here I would first advise you most carefully to enquire, whether your present distress does indeed arise from causes that are truly spiritual? Or whether it may not have its foundation in some disorder of body . . .

When this is the case the help of the physician is to be sought rather than that of the divine, or, at least, by all means together with it; and medicine, diet, exercise and air may in a few weeks effect that which the strongest reasoning, the most pathetic exhortation or consolations, might for many months have attempted in vain.

EVENING

As I walk up to Trinity College in the mornings I pass one of the busiest crossings in Glasgow. There is a newspaper seller who has his stance there. As often as not, when I pass, he is not there. His newspapers are there, and scattered on top of them there is a collection of copper coins. People take a newspaper and drop their coins there.

I don't suppose that newspaper seller ever loses a coin or is swindled out of a newspaper.

Newspapers themselves are full of stories of thefts and swindles and robberies, but the more you think of it the more you see that life goes on the assumption of the fundamental honesty of men.

Here is a tremendous truth.

We have to explain not only the mystery of human sin. We have to explain the still greater mystery of human goodness
The odd fact in life is that, though we are haunted by sin, we are haunted by goodness, too.

Once when Michelangelo was chiseling away at a great ugly shapeless block of marble, he was asked what he was doing.

His answer was: "I am releasing the angel that is imprisoned in this stone."

There is an angel and a hero in every man.

That is what Jesus knew, and that is the basis on which he acted.

While there is time

MORNING

Shakespeare knew men.
In the first act of *The Tempest*, he draws the picture of the storm at sea. When shipwreck is imminent, he has the grim stage direction: "Enter mariners, wet," and their first cry is: "All lost! to prayers, to prayers! All lost!"

It was only when all was lost that they turned to prayers.

In King Henry V Shakespeare has the immortal scene when the hostess of the tavern and Pistol, Nym and Bardolph talk of the death of Falstaff (King Henry V, ii, 3).

A' parted even just between twelve and one, even at the turning o' the tide; for after I saw him fumble with the sheets and play with the flowers and smile upon his fingers' ends, I knew that there was but one way; for his nose was as sharp as a pen, and a' babbled of green fields. 'How now. Sir John!' quoth I: 'what man! be a good cheer.' So a' cried out 'God, God, God!' three or four times: now I, to comfort him, bid him a" should not think of God; I hoped there was no need to trouble himself with any such thoughts yet.

No need to trouble himself yet with thoughts of God! So many people are like that.

EVENING

How do we know that we have plenty of time?

I think it is Dr. Boreham who somewhere tells of meeting a doctor friend, and seeing that the doctor was much depressed.

Boreham asked what the matter was. The doctor said: "I have just come from a man for whom I can do nothing; and if he had come to me months ago, when he felt the first twinges of the thing that will kill him, I could have cured him quite easily. But he has let it go too far."

So many people connect religion with the ambulance corps and not the firing line of life. It is disastrously easy to put off too long the calling of the ambulance.

The Bible is full of the thought that things must be done while yet there is time.

Must we forget about God until we need him?

Is God someone of whom we only make use?

Is God like a lifebelt or a friend?

There was an old saint who spent much time in prayer. Someone asked why he spent so much. He answered: "I talk to God every day so that when the desperate moment comes he will know my voice."

Two idols

MORNING

Bacon, in a famous passage, pictured the errors and the fallacies that attack the human mind under the picture of the four idols — the idol of the tribe, the idol of the cave, the idol of the market-place, and the idol of the theater.

In the Bacon picture these four symbolic idols do not have quite the meaning that they would seem to have at first sight.

The errors that come from the idol of the tribe are the errors that arise just because man is man, just because he is a member of the general tribe of mankind, just because he is in fact a limited person, both in knowledge and in power.

We make our errors often simply because we forget that we are men; we forget that we are not the creator but the created. We forget that we do not know all, and that God knows best.

A man is a victim of the idol of the tribe when he thinks that he knows better than God, when he forgets that he is a man, and so fails to ask for or to accept the guidance of God.

EVENING

The errors and the mistakes that come from the idol of the cave are the errors that come from trying to make our own idiosyncrasies and peculiarities into general laws and rules. The cave is the cave of self.

This mistake emerges specially in one direction. Man forgets that he is made in the image of God and tries to make God in his image.

A man may make his religion a kind of projection of himself. He thinks that all religion must be his religion.

The most serious example of this is the way in which so much missionary work to all intents and purposes identified Christianity and Western civilization. Christianity was preached, but it was preached in terms of Western clothes, Western manners. Western church structures. Western industry and economics.

When the Salvation Army went to India it rapidly saw that there never could be any real progress until they stopped identifying Christianity and Western civilization and thought in terms of India. An Indian said to Tucker: "We will accept Christ when he takes off his hat, trousers and boots", in other words when he was de-Westernized, and so the Army became Indian to make India Christian.

It is a great lesson.

Christianity must never be identified with our private version of it, still less with the social and economic background we know.

Two more idols

MORNING

The idol of the market-place

The errors that come from the idol of the market place are the errors that arise from the fact that we misunderstand each other's language.

Words mean different things to different people.

Words are the great coinage and communication of the market place, and when we talk we misunderstand and are misunderstood.

We use words in different senses and meanings, so that, as we so often tragically find, we suddenly discover that we have been talking and arguing at cross purposes all the time.

It is a simple but essential rule that in any argument or discussion we should be sure that we understand each other, and know what the other says and means.

EVENING

The idol of the theater

The errors that come from the idol of the theater are the errors which come from false systems of thought which, as it were, follow each other on to the stage of history.

The great necessity is that we should remember that no human system of thought is final, that none has the whole truth, that there is more to God than ever any man has discovered.

If we remember this, it will save us from the mistake that has so often brought tragedy to the church — the error of loving systems more than we love God.

The idol of the tribe, the idol of the cave, the idol of the market-place, the idol of the theater, the mistakes which come from forgetting we are men; the mistakes which come from making ourselves the norm for everything; the mistakes which come from the elusiveness of the meaning of words; the mistakes which come from the undue exaltation of any system — avoid them all!

New life

MORNING

John Masefield in "The Everlasting Mercy" tells of the conversion of the drunken reprobate, Saul Kane. The moment came when Saul Kane was a changed man with one life behind him and another in front of him. He has just left the drinking-place in which he had so often been drunk; but something has happened.

> The bolted door had broken in
> I knew that I had done with sin.

Then he goes on to speak of what the world was like in that moment of change:

> The station brook, to my new eyes,
> Was babbling out of Paradise;
> The waters rushing from the rain
> Were singing Christ has risen again
> I thought all earthly creatures knelt
> From rapture of the joy I felt.
> The narrow station-wall's brick
>   ledge
> The wild hop withering in the
>   hedge,
> The lights in huntsman's upper
>   storey
> Were parts of an eternal glory,
> Were God's eternal garden flowers.
> I stood in bliss at this for hours.

It is a description of the sheer joy of the finding of the life that is new. It is the meaning of resurrection. It is everyman's Easter.

EVENING

New life for C. H. Spurgeon
Once on a wild and snowy winter morning, Spurgeon when he was a lad, set out to go to church. The weather was so bad that he could not reach the church to which he intended to go.

In the church he did find, the preacher had not arrived because he was storm-bound. It was in a substitute church and by a substitute preacher that Spurgeon was converted.

What a gift of God's grace to the church Spurgeon's conversion was to be!

Calling on God

MORNING

As a motorist I have been very fortunate indeed. In twenty-nine years of driving I have only had one accident, and I have never yet been stuck on the road. But once I did run into trouble.

Late at night, when I was on my way home, a fault developed in the electrical system of my car. I knew that sooner or later the car would come to a dead stop and nothing except a tow would move it.

I have been a member of the Automobile Association for as long as I have been driving. I have always paid my subscription; I have always used the handbooks and route books and all the helps to traveling; but in all those years, I have never had any occasion to call for help from the breakdown service.

Then I needed it.
I could call on it.
I got it.
There is here a remarkably close parallel to what happens in life.

For long enough, life can go on smoothly, with an easy routine in which nothing happens with which we cannot deal. The road is pleasantly level. There may be no relaxation, but there is no effort that is beyond us.

There may be no great joys, but there are no great sorrows. There may be no great flashes of vision, but there are no agonizing struggles with evil. We can cope.

EVENING

Then quite suddenly life falls in
There comes a demand for an effort that we know quite well is beyond us. There comes a temptation that we know we cannot struggle against. There comes an illness or a breakdown that lays us low. There comes a sorrow in which the sun sets at midday, and in which life becomes unbearable.

In that moment we turn to God, because, as Lincoln said, there is nowhere else to go. But it will make all the difference in that moment, first, if we know where to go, and second, if through all the years we have kept our contact with God and if we are going not to a stranger but to a familiar friend.

In other words, the better we know God, the easier it is to go to him when we need him so desperately; the more close we have kept our contact with him, the easier it is to find him.

Relying on God

MORNING

"Without me," said Jesus, "you can do nothing!" (John 15:5).

There are certain things for which we need and must have God.

We need God to show us what to do

There are times when it is only God who can give us guidance.

We cannot see a step ahead; only God can see the future and what is ultimately to our good.

It is so often so difficult to see things unclouded by our personal wishes and preferences and prejudices; it is so difficult, too, to see things through our own weakness and our own sin.

The only way in which things can be seen in their true light is in the light of God. Only in his light do we see the light (Psalm 36:9). Only God can give us guidance as to what to do.

We need the courage to do what is right

It is seldom that at the moment the right way is the easy way. It is human nature to avoid trouble and to take the easy way.

It is only God who can give us the courage to do what is right, for it is one thing to know the right and quite another to do it.

EVENING

Only God can give us the strength to bring the right thing to its appointed end

We need the flash of light to show us the way; we need the surge of courage to set us out on the right way. But the really difficult thing is not to begin; it is to continue to the end.

It is only God who can give us power to resist the temptations to take the byways which lead to the far countries of the soul

It was after the thrill of his baptism that the temptations came to Jesus.

It is so often after we have made our decision to do something which is right that there come the temptations which seek to stop us.

If we are walking always in the presence of the living God and always in the companionship of the Risen Christ, then it is possible for us to walk through the world and to keep our garments unspotted by the world, because of the company in which we walk.

One in a crowd

MORNING

Beside the still figure on the roadway, there knelt three people. One was a friend of the victim of the accident and she was very upset and quite helpless. The second was someone from the crowd who had come forward to offer what assistance he could. The third was a policeman who had taken his coat and made it a pillow for the injured woman and who was rendering first aid. That moment was a picture in miniature of life, for it was a study in reactions to the trouble and the distress of other people.

There was the person who had been the cause of the accident

I cannot tell whether he was to blame or not, but he was certainly a very worried man.

Saul Kane, in John Masefield's Everlasting Mercy, was appalled at "the harm I've done by being me". If we would only think about the consequences of things before we act, we would often have to worry less about the results of things after we have acted.

There was the hurrying crowd which never even stopped

Some of them would be too intent on their own business to have time to stop. There are people who deliberately avert their eyes, because their first instinct is to refuse to get involved in anyone else's troubles.

EVENING

There was the friend fluttering helplessly

One of the most heart-breakingly frustrating experiences in life is to see someone in trouble or courting trouble and to know that we cannot do anything about it. But to have to stand helplessly by is one of life's unhappiest experiences.

There was the passer-by who went forward to help — one out of so many.

It is a sad commentary on the essential selfishness and self-centeredness of human nature that only one was found to help.

There was the gaping crowd

It is an odd fact of life that there are certain people who get a bigger kick out of hearing bad news about someone else than they do out of hearing good news. There are few lower occupations in the world than gaping curiously at the troubles of someone else.

There was the policeman

Here was someone whose function was to help and who was equipped to render help. Here was the one whose first instinct would be not to run away from trouble and not to stand and look at trouble, but to run towards it and to do something about it — which is the Christian reaction.

Courtesy

MORNING

More than one attitude can be encountered in evangelism,

There is the evangelist who preaches with an unconscious superiority

He utters his condemning tirades against the sinner, he dangles the sinner over the pit of hell; his stock in trade is largely threat and denunciation. He speaks from a height downwards; his whole assumption is that he speaks from a position of safety to those who are in peril.

Evangelism like that is far more likely to produce resentment than response.

There is a kind of pugnacious evangelism

Its attitude is that there is no salvation outside its particular way of thinking, and that any theology that does not think as it thinks is a lie. It is marked by intolerance and by harsh criticism of all those who differ from it. It attempts to bring men to Christ, but it has not itself the spirit of Christ.

The highest and most effective kind of evangelism is marked by the basic quality of sympathy

It does not stand over the sinner; it sits beside the sinner. It does not draw a distinction between itself and the sinner; it identifies itself with the sinner. It speaks as one hell deserving sinner to another.

EVENING

Dryden once said of Jeremy Collier, "I will not say, 'the zeal of God's house has eaten him up', but I am sure it has devoured some part of his good manners and civility."

A man has a right to his own opinions and he has a right to state them

I can never forget the vivid statement of Voltaire in speaking to someone with whose views he entirely disagreed: "I hate every word you say, but I would gladly die for your right to say it." Take away the right of liberty of opinion and freedom of speech and the very basis of democracy is gone.

It will be a bad day when Christianity has to defend itself by forcibly silencing those with whom it does not agree.

A man has a right to speak his own opinions, but equally he has a duty to listen to the opinion of others

Nothing does a man more mental good than to listen to things with which he does not agree.

There are far too many people, and far too many alleged students and scholars, who refuse to look beyond their own version of the truth. To listen to the other side of the question can be a salutary experience.

It's never too late

MORNING

Part of my duties in Glasgow University was to teach Hellenistic Greek. Not very many people take the class because it is something of a specialist subject, although a necessity for those who want to read the New Testament in its original language.

A letter came to me from a lady who had been a schoolteacher in one of Glasgow's most famous schools for girls. After a long and honorable career in the teaching world, she had come to the age when she retired. And now she was well over sixty years of age.

The letter said that all her life this lady had wanted to study the New Testament in Greek. Now that she was retired, she said, she had time to do so. So she made a request — would she be allowed to attend the class of Hellenistic Greek as a student on the benches?

There was only one answer to that; it would be a pleasure and a privilege to have her. And so, since the beginning of October when the University term began, this lady of over sixty was there on the benches of a University classroom, listening and taking notes with students a third of her age.

This is a magnificent example.

It is never too late to learn.

EVENING

It is never too late to make a new beginning

One of the features of a modern divinity college is the number of older men who come into it. There come men who have been headmasters in schools or who have held high executive and administrative offices in the educational world. There come men who have held high posts in industry, in commerce, in the newspaper world.

Time and again these are the most vivid and vital people in the college. They are beginning a new job when other people are stopping working. Life for them is beginning when life for other people is stopping; and it keeps them young, young in body, young in mind and young in heart.

How different life would be for many people if they saw the end of one career as the beginning of another! They might well see the end of the work which hitherto claimed them as the beginning of the work which they always in their heart of hearts wanted to do.

It is never too late to seek a newer world, in the strength of him who makes all things new.

Going to church

MORNING

I worshipped once, to my great pleasure and profit, in Martyrs' church, St. Andrews. St. Andrews is a world famous holiday resort, as every golfer knows. During the summer months especially, many visitors find their way into the pews of the St. Andrews churches.

I was a stranger in Martyrs' that day. No sooner had I sat down than I noticed a little white card in the book board in front of me, and I noticed that similar cards were laid out along all the book boards. I took it up and read it, and my heart was strangely warmed for the little card ran:

> We welcome you to our church and Fellowship and extend Christian greetings to you.

I did not feel a stranger any more.

After the service I told one of the office-bearers what a fine idea I thought this was, and how much I personally had appreciated it, and he at once went on to tell me about another card which Martyrs' church uses.

This card is put into the pews on Communion Sundays and it runs:

> The minister, kirk session and congregation of Martyrs' church, St. Andrews, welcome you to the fellowship of the Lord's Table.

I know how touched I would have been to find that card in my pew had I happened to come to Martyrs' on a Communion Sunday.

EVENING

There are compelling reasons why church attendance is necessary to keep the Christian life alive, and to fulfill the duties of the Christian life. So it is worth looking again at some familiar reasons for going to church.

There are certain things in life which gain a great part of their value and of their impact from being experienced together

Of course, we can worship alone; and, of course, there are times when we must worship alone. But the fact remains that togetherness is an essential part of worship.

There is a real value in being assured that the Christian faith is not only a personal experience, but the possession of a whole community

We need the church and the church needs us.

Witness and attitudes

MORNING

On the basis of what he sees of them, the man outside the church has come to the conclusion that the claims made for and by Christians are just not true.

Just think of some of the claims that so-called Christianity makes.

It claims that Christianity is the religion of joy, and yet it would be difficult to find a more joyless thing than that which many people produce as Christianity.

It claims that Christianity is the religion of peace, but the majority of Christians are just as worried as anyone else, and the church spends a lot of its time trembling for the ark.

It claims to be the religion of power, but Christians are not noticeably more able to cope with life, nor are they notably more efficient, than anyone else. It claims to be the religion of service, and yet Christians are just as selfish and comfort-loving as men of the world.

It claims to be the religion of love and forgiveness, and yet it is the truth that there is more strife and squabbling in the church than in any other institution in this troubled world. The church where there are no feuds and resignations is the exception rather than the rule.

Nietzsche, the German pagan philosopher, said bluntly, "Show me that you are redeemed and then I will believe in your redeemer." It is not an unfair demand.

EVENING

Do you look for something to criticize, or do you look for something to praise?
For instance, if in your church the choir puts on an anthem or a cantata or an oratorio, do you jump on the mistakes and the inadequacies that are bound to be there, or do you comment on the parts which were well sung, stressing that a very creditable attempt has been made to sing a piece of great music, even if it did not reach professional standards?

Do you encourage or discourage?
When some course of action is suggested, do you promptly see all the difficulties which make it impossible, or do you see the possibilities which make it well worth trying?

Do you count your blessings or do you count your misfortunes?
Adler the famous psychologist, tells of two men each of whom lost an arm. At the end of a year one of them was so discouraged that he had decided that life was not worth living with a handicap like that. The other was so triumphant that he went about saying that he really did not know why nature had given us two arms when he could get along perfectly well with one.

Good and bad witness

MORNING

God is a refiner; man is the metal that must be cleansed; and God's aim is to make man such that he can see his own reflection in him.

What then are the qualities that this true manhood must have?

Our lives are meant to reflect the patience of God

One of the most obvious of all contrasts is the contrast between the patience of God and the petulance of man. If God had been a man, very certainly he would have taken his hand and wiped the world out of existence long ago. When we find people difficult to deal with, we impatiently break out upon them, or we simply have nothing more to do with them. What a contrast with the divine patience of God, who bears with all the world's sinning and will not cast it off.

Our lives are meant to reflect the divine reliability

From beginning to end the Bible stresses the truth, the dependability, the steadfastness, the reliability of God. God does not change his mind; God does not make a promise and then go back on it; what God says he means; and what God promises he will do.

Man means to be loyal, but there is a basic weakness in human nature which makes disloyalty a continuous danger. What a contrast between the divine reliability and fidelity of God and the ingrained shiftiness of human nature!

EVENING

It is easy in every sphere of life to linger too long in the vestibule.

We can do it in friendship

It is characteristic of life that we have many acquaintances, but few friends. Friendship too needs effort. It needs the effort to penetrate into the inner sanctuary of the other person's heart; and it needs an effort to reveal our own heart.

The essence of friendship is the giving and the receiving of nothing less than the whole self.

We can do it with Jesus Christ

In their relationship with Jesus Christ so many people linger in the vestibule. They admire Jesus. Christianity, as Browning put it, has their vote to be true. They would like to be Christians. But Christ demands total surrender; and Christianity means total commitment. And short of that they stop. They keep him in the vestibule.

There was a day when Agrippa said to Paul, "Almost thou persuadest me to be a Christian" (Acts 26:28).

There spoke the man who kept Christ in the vestibule.

A Christian is . . .

MORNING

A Christian is a man who ought to be able to do things that other people cannot do.

A Christian is a person who can bear disappointments in a way that other people cannot bear them

It is very interesting to see how people react when they do not get some position for which they applied and for which they were eager. Some people grow soured and embittered. They spend weeks — some of them the rest of their lives — bewailing the fact that they were so unfortunate, and implying, or even insisting, that they are far better men and women than the person who did get the job.

On the other hand, I know a man who applied for a position, and who might well have expected to get it, and who did not get it, and whose first action was to write a letter of congratulation and blessing to the man who did get it.

The Christian is a man who can bear disappointments, because his heart is cleansed of envy, in a way that is not possible for other men so to do.

EVENING

A Christian is a person who can bear burdens that other men cannot bear

That is because he knows that he is not bearing them all by himself. I have always loved the story of Bishop Quayle, the great American bishop. For years he worried himself to death about his church and his clergy and his work and about all the things that had

to be done. He used to sit up half the night worrying about all kinds of things. Then one night as he sat worrying he tells us that he heard God's voice as clearly as if it had been someone sitting in the same room, and God was saying, "Quayle, you go to bed, I'll sit up for the rest of the night!" And thereafter there was in Quayle a wonderful serenity, for he had learned to cast his burden on the Lord.

The Christian can shoulder burdens which would overwhelm any other man because he knows that there is no burden which he has to carry alone.

The Christian can bear sorrows in a way that other men cannot bear them

Life can never be easy; life is full of the things which try men's hearts. It is not so much a question of going on, for a man has to go on whether he likes it or not; it is a question of the spirit in which a man will go on. Some may go on in resentment, bitterness, defeated hopelessness, grim despair; but in face of the disappointments, the burdens and the sorrows of life, the Christian can maintain the strength, the serenity, the joy which only Jesus Christ can give.

"Whosoever shall compel thee to go a mile," said Jesus, "go with him twain" (Matthew 5:41). This was the most practical advice in the world, for it is the extras of life which make all the difference in the world.

Dependence and independence

MORNING

Dependence and independence have to go hand in hand.

There is no lovelier feeling in this life than to be needed

E. V. Lucas wrote a very lovely kind of parable. "A mother lost her soldier son. The news came to her in dispatches from the war. He had fallen fighting nobly at the head of his regiment. She was inconsolable. 'O that I might see him again,' she prayed, 'if only for five minutes—but to see him.' An angel answered her prayer. 'For five minutes,' said the angel, 'you will see him.' 'Quick, quick,' said the mother, her tears turned to momentary joy. 'Yes,' said the angel, 'but think a little. He was a grown man. There are thirty years to choose from. How would you like to see him?' And the mother paused and wondered. 'Would you see him,' said the angel, 'as a soldier, dying heroically at his post? Would you see him as he left you to join the transport? Would you see him again as on that day at school when he stepped to the platform to receive the highest honors a boy could have?' The mother's eyes lit up. 'Would you see him,' said the angel, 'as a babe at your breast?' And slowly the mother said, 'No I would have him for five minutes, as he was one day when he ran in from the garden to ask my forgiveness for being naughty. He was so small and so unhappy, and the tears were making streaks down his face through the garden dust. And he flew to my arms with such force that he hurt me.'"

EVENING

The one thing that the mother wished above all to recapture was the moment when her son had needed her. There is nothing more moving in life than to hear someone say, "I need you; I cannot do without you."

There is a lovely dependence which should be the aim of every parent in connection with his or her child.

There is no more uplifting feeling than to see someone — a child, or a pupil or a student — facing the tasks of life competently, adequately and gallantly, and to know that you had something to do with equipping him for them

It would be a very wrong thing to aim to keep a child forever tethered to the apron strings, and forever dominated by a father's personality. Our aim must never be to do things for children, but rather to enable them to do things for themselves. Our aim must never be to take a child's decisions for him in every case, but to enable him to take them wisely and bravely for himself.

However lovely dependence is, independence is the aim of the whole process of upbringing and of education.

We must also be dependent forever upon God; and yet, at the same time, we must be able to stand on our own two feet and to meet life as it comes to us.

Exhaustion

MORNING

For Jesus to bring help and healing to others was a costly thing.

When the woman in the crowd slipped up unseen, and touched the hem of his garment, Jesus stopped because he knew that virtue had gone out of him (Mark 5:30).

Paul Tournier in his book *A Doctor's Casebook* tells of a certain experience. He tells about a doctor in Florence who sometimes used the laying on of hands to assist in healing; but he had to give it up because of its effect on himself. "Thus," he told us, "for example, my patient suffering from angina would find that his angina had suddenly gone; but I myself at once suffered a similar attack."

Tournier goes on, "When I told my wife about this, we were reminded of the fact that we had frequently observed: that we regularly had a quarrel ourselves on the evening of a day in which we had been able to help in the reconciliation of another married couple."

No one can help anyone else without virtue going out of him, and without in the most real sense entering into the other person's actual experience. It is in fact in many cases our greatest fault that we seek always to get and seldom to give.

EVENING

We do that in friendship
There is a kind of friendship so-called which has a kind of vampire-like quality. Its one desire is always to be drawing help and comfort and strength from its friend without any reciprocal giving. There is the kind of person who will talk for hours about his own troubles to his friend, but is quite disinterested, if the friend even mentions his. There is the kind of person who will presume largely on the rights of friendship, but who obviously finds it very inconvenient if anything is demanded from him.

We do that with the church
The church has a large number of people who are forever talking about what they expect to get from the church, and what, alas, they do not get. But they are very unwilling to see that the church has any demands on them, and that the church is waiting for something from them. They are very willing to use the church, but they are very unwilling to be of use to the church.

We do that with God.
There are many of us who for long stretches of time conveniently forget God — until we need him. We use God as someone from whom to get, and never think of him as someone to whom to give.

Patient God

MORNING

There is no time when we cannot go to God

God does not work office hours or have his half day off. God neither slumbers nor sleeps; and he is always listening for his children's voices.

There is nothing too small to take to God

John Baillie says somewhere, "If a thing is big enough to worry about, it is big enough to pray about." And very often the surest way to see whether or not a thing is big enough to worry about is to take it to God, for in God's presence things have a way of really appearing in their proper proportion.

There is nothing too private to take to God

We can take to God the things we cannot take to anyone else. We may fear that others might laugh at our dreams and mock at our failures and misunderstand the secret of our thoughts. But God sees the inmost thoughts of men. He knows them and with him we can share the things which we cannot share with anyone else. And there is nothing in the world like having someone to whom we can really and fully open our hearts.

EVENING

There is nothing too shameful to take to God

There are things which we seek to hide from men; there are things which we even seek to hide from ourselves; and often that process of hiding is what drives a man to a nervous collapse and breakdown. But we can tell God the worst as we can tell him the best.

There are in the world good people with hearts like a tideless pool and with blood whose temperature never rises to emotional or passionate boiling point. There are people so constituted that there are temptations which they never experience and which they therefore can never understand. But the great fact about God is that he knows the human situation because in Jesus Christ he fully entered into it, and therefore he can understand.

Of all things about God maybe his patience is the greatest thing. He loves each one of us, as Augustine said, as if there was only one of us to love.

And love is the secret of patience, both human and divine.

Happy face . . .

MORNING

God would have us meet life with the merry heart and the happy face.

To be happy is to do good to ourselves
The writer of the Proverbs has a saying that the Authorized Version translates: "A merry heart doeth good like a medicine." (Proverbs 17:22).

But, if we look in the margin, we find another translation: "A merry heart doeth good to a medicine."

Moffatt has it: "A glad heart helps and heals."

The Authorised Revised Standard Version has it: "A cheerful heart is a good medicine."

A medicine will do far more good to a man with a happy heart than it will do to a gloomy and pessimistic soul.

A doctor can hardly write in his prescription: "To be taken three times a day with a merry heart," but he certainly would, if he could.

It is a medical fact that those who laugh most live longest.

A healthy laugh expands the lungs, and is good for any man.

Every time we greet life with a happy human face we are stretching the span of life for ourselves and giving ourselves the best of medicines.

EVENING

To be happy is to do good to others
"A happy man," said Robert Louis Stevenson, "is a better thing to find than a five pound note."

And, when we come to think of it, he is almost as difficult to find.

There are so many people whose faces are liable to crack, if they allow them to smile. And there are still many congregations who are a little shocked, if they are compelled to smile.

Somehow they cannot connect laughter and the worship of God.

The book of Job tells us that at the foundation of the world: "The morning stars sang together and all the sons of God shouted for joy" (Job 38:7).

"Sing unto the Lord, O ye saints of His," says the Psalmist (Psalm 30:4).

There are people in whose company the sun begins to shine even on a rainy day; and there are people who can put out the sun even on a midsummer day.

There is no one more valuable to meet than the person you leave feeling that life is not such a grim business after all.

. . . and merry heart

MORNING

It is worth remembering that we see our own reflection in other people.

There is a common saying that we have to take people as we find them, and no doubt that is true.

But it is also true that we make people what we find them.

If we find people bleak and unfriendly, all the likelihood is that we are seeing our own reflection in them. If we find people depressing, all the likelihood is that we make them that way.

There is a kind of equal justice in life. Jesus said, "With what measure ye mete, it shall be measured unto you" (Matthew 7:2).

It would do us a great deal of good to remember that our criticisms of others are usually nothing other than criticisms of ourselves.

If we only had eyes to see it.

So, we have to bring to the world a merry heart and a happy face. But if we have to bring it to others, we must first get it for ourselves. And we can only get it from Jesus Christ. One of the most difficult miracle stories in the New Testament is the story of the turning of the water into wine at the wedding feast at Cana of Galilee (John 2:1-11).

Whatever else that story means, and however we are to take it, one thing is quite certain. It means that whenever and wherever Jesus comes into life there comes into life with him a new exhilaration that is like turning water into wine.

EVENING

Grenfell of Labrador once came to John Hopkins University in America looking for a nurse to come back to Labrador to help with the work there.

This is how he put it:

"If you want to have the time of your life, come with me and run a hospital next summer for the orphans of the Northland.

There will not be a cent of money in it for you, and you will have to pay your own expenses.

But I'll guarantee you will feel a love for life you have never before experienced. It's having the time of anyone's life to be in the service of Christ."

There stands the prescription for the merry heart and the happy face!

Color and judging

MORNING

There is no color bar in the mind of a child

This is the proof that the color bar is an artificial and an unnatural thing: for the child it does not exist, so why should it for anyone?

In Trinity College, Glasgow, we had a notable experience. Perhaps the most famous series of preaching lectures in the world is the Warrack Lectures. To the Scottish Colleges on the Warrack foundation there are brought the princes of preachers to give our students help and guidance and instruction in that which will be the business of their lives.

A. J. Gossip, Henry Sloane Coffin, James Stewart, Reinhold Niebuhr, Emil Brünner, and many other great ones have given these lectures. That year the lecturer was the late D. T. Niles, that great ecumenical church leader from Ceylon.

It was the first time in history that the Warrack Lectures had been given by one whose skin was not white.

That was epoch-making in church life. A man from Ceylon had come across the ocean to teach the students of Scotland how to preach. In D. T. Niles the younger churches, the people whose skin is colored, had arrived to teach the people who once had taught them. We will not soon forget D. T. Niles in Glasgow.

EVENING

It is just as wrong to judge anything by externals as it is to judge a book by its cover.

It is wrong to judge a man by externals

A man may look an insignificant character, and yet be a great man.

William Wilberforce, who was responsible for the freeing of the slaves throughout the British Empire, was weak in health, insignificantly small in body, and without any external attractions.

Boswell heard him speak, and after that experience Boswell said, "I saw what seemed to be a shrimp mount upon the table; but, as I listened, he grew and grew until the shrimp became a whale."

It is always wrong to judge a man by his personal appearance, by his clothes, by his physical stature. These are but the external accidents beneath which there lies the real man.

In the Sermon on the Mount Jesus most penetratingly puts externals in their proper place. It is not enough, he says, not to murder; we must never even feel anger in the heart. It is not enough not to commit adultery; the unclean desire must never even enter our heart. This is the test by which we are all judged and by which we all fail.

On trial

MORNING

Barrie, in *The Little White Bird*, talks of the moment when a mother tucks up her child for the night, and when she looks down into the child's eyes with an unspoken question in her own: "Have I done well today, my child?" It would do some of us good sometimes to think a little less of what we want from our children, and a little more of what they want from us.

The child needs guidance

In his autobiography, G. K. Chesterton told of his father. In his childhood Chesterton had a cherished possession — a toy theatre with characters made of cardboard cut-outs and a stage and a curtain and all accessories. One of the characters was a man with a golden key.

Chesterton tells us that he had long since forgotten for what the man with the golden key stood but that the man with the golden key was always associated in his mind with his father because his father unlocked the door for him to so many things.

Chesterton must have had a wonderful father; but every father and every parent should be a guide.

EVENING

The child needs friendship

It is strange and tragic that often parents are the last people to whom a child will turn with his troubles. He will talk more easily to a well-loved teacher, or doctor, or scoutmaster, or some other relation.

One of the most important, and one of the hardest tasks of the parent, is to establish a relationship with the child in which the child will be able to speak of hopes and fears, triumphs and failures, successes and mistakes.

There are few things in this world which can do so much psychological harm as a nagging question in the child's mind which cannot be asked. It will be ultimately buried in the subconscious and there it will do as much harm as some poisonous thing lodged in the body and festering there.

The child needs love

The greatest of all human needs is the need to be needed, the need to feel that one matters to someone. The deepest of all human desires is the desire for security, the desire to feel safe in a circle from which fear is shut out.

There is nothing that the child needs more than simply to know that he is loved. And that is why the poorest of homes with love is better than the most efficient of institutions in which individual love is almost impossible.

Tune in

MORNING

If we want to hear the right things, we have got to be attuned to the right wave-lengths.

If we wish to hear ourselves correctly, our wavelength must be honesty

There are in this world comparatively few people who are honest with themselves. For instance, there are very few people who are honest with their own faults and feelings. They can see the faults of others, but to their own they are quite blind. I had a minister friend who used to have a favorite illustration of this. Sometimes you see a snapshot photograph of a group of people, and it makes them look like a gang of criminals or a collection of mourners at a funeral!

There is a widespread tendency when we look at such a photograph, to say, or at least to think, that it is quite a good likeness of everyone else, but that it is not a bit like ourselves! We are quite prepared to believe that the rest do look like that—but not us! We need honesty in our dealings with ourselves.

EVENING

If we wish to hear others correctly, our wave-length must be sympathy

It is a curious feature of conversation — I find myself at it continuously — that we can hardly wait for the other person to finish telling of his experience or his misfortune or his sorrow because we want to break in and tell of our experience, which is so much more interesting, and our misfortune or sorrow which is so much worse. In this world there are perhaps fifty good talkers for every one good listener. The most useful person in the world is a listener to whom you can pour out your heart.

The reason for our failure is simply lack of sympathy. We are really so concerned with ourselves, and our own feelings and our own affairs, that we have neither the time nor the desire to listen to anyone else.

We need sympathy in our dealings with others.

If we wish to hear God correctly, our wavelength must be humility

The basic mistake that so many people make in regard to prayer is that they think of prayer far too much in terms of talking to God, and far too little in terms of listening to God. Prayer ought to be an activity in which we do not so much talk to God, as God talks to us.

When we are on the right wave-length—and not till then — will we hear the right things from ourselves, from our fellow-men, and from God.

Bridge-builders

MORNING

A very distinguished teacher and theologian was recalling his experiences in chaplaincy service in the army in the days of the war. Very often, he said, in the army, the padre was referred to quite simply as the man of God. He went on to say that when you looked back and sorted out your memories and impressions, you could see that in their padre the men looked for three outstanding qualities.

They looked for a man who knew them and was interested in them as persons

Paul Tournier in *A Doctor's Casebook* speaks of what he calls the modern "massification" of society. The tendency nowadays is for the individual to be lost in the mass. It is so easy for the individual to cease in any sense to be an individual and to become a number on a form, an entry on a file, a specimen pigeonholed in some neat classification. Paul Tournier says that the doctor's great danger is that he ceases to think of a man as a person, and begins to think of him as a gall bladder or a lung case.

We live in an age when people tend to be numbers, entries, specimens. Our fundamental human need is to be treated as a person. Treatment as a person is one of the basic things that anyone has a right to look for in a church.

A man may be a mere number in the world. To God he is a person with a name, and, in the church of God, each person must be a person.

EVENING

They looked for a man who knew their position and who knew what they were going through

They would not have any use for a man who had no knowledge and no understanding of their problems, their experiences, their temptations.

Ezekiel brought the message of God to those who were in captivity; he need not himself have shared that captivity, but what he says is worth repeating: "Then I came to them of the captivity at Tel-abib, that dwelt by the river of Chebar, and I sat where they sat." (Ezekiel 3:15). "I sat where they sat" — that is the secret of being able to bring any help to men. That is what God did in Jesus Christ.

They felt that the padre should be a man who could speak a word for them to God and who could speak a word to them from God

He must be a man who could somehow take their prayers and their needs and their requests to God; and he must be a man who could somehow bring to them from God a message to meet their condition.

That, indeed, is the greatest task of all. To fulfill it a man has to live close to men and close to God. He has to be the pontifex, the priest, the bridge-builder between God and men.

Beauty and kindness

MORNING

A. J. Gossip used to love to tell a story about Mungo Park, the great explorer. He had been journeying for days and miles in the wilds of China, in the most desolate surroundings. Then quite suddenly he saw on the ground at his feet a little blue flower. And, as he saw it, he said gently, "God has been here!"

Even when the world is at its worst, and when life is at its worst, there is still beauty left, and we should never forget it. It is not that to look at the beauty and to think about the beauty is an escape from reality — far from it. Any such glimpse of beauty should move us to three things.

It should move us to the memory of God, the awareness that this is God's world, and that not even the sin and the thoughtlessness and the selfishness of man can entirely obliterate the beauty of God.

It should move us to gratitude, and to the realization that there is always something left for which we ought to give thanks.

It should move us to resolution and to action, so that, as far as we can, we may increase the beauty and remove the ugliness that is within this world.

EVENING

Donald Baillie has a sermon on the text: "What is that to thee? Follow thou me." (John 21:22). He talks about the things that we should never mind, but just keep on following Christ. He writes, "Never mind your perplexities, but follow Christ."

Baillie does not belittle the real and haunting doubts that come at some time to every man. He goes on to say,

"Of course, you have to face your doubts and perplexities quite honestly and quite frankly and try to think them out and get light on them But the great and salutary and reassuring lesson is this: that it is not in just thinking it all out that light comes, and you don't have to wait until you have thought it all out (or you would have to wait for ever). You can go on bravely in the path of duty and purity and love. That must be right — you are sure enough of that. So much of Christ is plain to you, and so far you can follow him with your eyes wide open. And that is how further light comes. He that does the truth comes to the light."

There are many things about which we may not be sure, and there are not a few things about which we may never be sure. But we do know that "kindness in another's troubles and courage in one's own" is always part of the Christian way, and we can get on with that.

At the end of the day, I would take my chance with the man who was no theologian, but who was kind.

The listeners

MORNING

There is somebody listening every time we speak. And surely that is a very good reason for being very careful how we speak.

When we speak an ugly, unclean, impure word, someone hears it — and it sticks in someone's mind

Old Thomas Fuller once said sadly, "Almost twenty years ago I heard a profane jest, and still remember it. How many pious passages of a far later date have I forgotten!" The profane jest had stuck. We can see this happen. It can happen that, to our shocked surprise, a child will suddenly utter an ugly word that he had overheard in the street, and which he was not supposed to hear. We speak a word. That word goes out. "Three things come not back, the spoken word, the spent arrow, and the lost opportunity."

Next time we are about to say something that it is not fitting to say, let us remember that we do not know who may be listening.

EVENING

When we speak a fine and a true word, when we speak a word for Jesus Christ, someone hears it

The classic example of that is what happened to John Bunyan. One day in Bedford he heard three or four poor women talking, as they sat at a door in the sun. At that time he himself was "a brisk talker" and had a surface veneer of religion. "They were far above, out of my reach: their talk was about new birth, the work of God on their hearts," and "of their own righteousness, as filthy and insufficient to do them any good. And methought they spake, as if joy did make them speak; they spoke with such pleasantness of Scripture language." And Bunyan's heart began to shake. It was because he heard the talk of three or four poor women, sitting at the door in the sun, that Bunyan found, not half the way, but the whole way of God.

When we say a fine thing, rebuke an evil thing, commend a good thing, someone is listening; and that very word of ours may be the thing which turns the scale of their hearts, which saves them from temptation, which sets them on the way to God, which lodges in their hearts and, maybe many days or years afterwards, is the memory which saves their souls.

We know that one is listening — and that one is Jesus Christ

He is the hearer of every word we speak. Jesus himself said, "I say unto you. That every idle word that men shall speak, they shall give account thereof in the day of judgment. For by thy words thou shalt be justified, and by thy words thou shalt be condemned." (Matthew 12:35-37).

Influence

MORNING

What we put into a child's mind and a child's life when he is young is there for good.

That is what Ignatius Loyola meant when he made his famous dictum, "Give me a child for the first seven years of his life and I care not who has him afterwards."

From his earliest day we should teach the child to have regard for truth

Boswell tells of a breakfast table discussion with Johnson in the Thrale household. Johnson was insisting on a strict attention to the truth, even in the slightest detail, an attention that he himself meticulously practised. "Accustom your children," he said, "constantly to this; if a thing happened at one window, and they, when relating it, say that it happened at another, do not let it pass, but instantly check them. You do not know where deviation from the truth will end."

Boswell agreed that once you allow variations into any narrative you do not know where they will end. Mrs. Thrale objected to what she considered an undue fussiness, "Little variations in narrative," she insisted, "must happen a thousand times a day, if one is not perpetually watching."

Dr. Johnson thundered. "Well, Madam, you ought to be perpetually watching. It is more from carelessness about truth than from intentional lying that there is so much falsehood in the world."

Dr. Johnson was right. From the very beginning, teach the child an unvarying respect for truth.

EVENING

From the earliest days we should teach the child the meaning of Christian love, Christian consideration and Christian courtesy

Too often the child is treated to the sight of his parents arguing and bickering and criticizing and differing with each other. He may well unconsciously absorb the idea that married life consists of a continual jangling argument.

So often we seem to reserve the right to treat our loved ones with a discourtesy which we would never use to strangers. We must see to it that the child is brought up to have the conviction that the atmosphere of the home is Christian courtesy and Christian love.

From the earliest days teach the child the habit of worship on God's day

Day in, day out we are inserting into the child's mind things which will never come out. See to it that the right things, and the fine things, and the noble things, are inserted there.

Hebrews 11:4

MORNING

In the great eleventh chapter, the writer of the Letter to the Hebrews says of Abel, "He being dead yet speaketh" (Hebrews 11:4).

That is true of many another.

For many of us it is true that, though our parents are dead, they still speak

For many of us it is true to this day that, many years after their death, our parents are still the greatest influence in our lives.

Unconsciously it may be, we still apply to life and its decisions the standards and the principles they taught us. Unconsciously it may be, we still seek their approval in the things we do. God grant unto us to pass on to our children the heritage our parents passed on to us.

Many a teacher, being dead, yet speaks

That is obviously true of a University teacher, who may deeply impress his students with his own thought, and who may even found a school of teaching which will last long after he is gone. But is it also true that the humblest teacher in the humblest school lives on in his or her pupils.

A good teacher is always immortal in someone's life.

EVENING

Many a time a friend, being dead; yet speaks

The influence of a great friendship is not terminated by death.

When Charles Kingsley was asked the secret of the winsome purity of his own life, his answer was, thinking of F. D. Maurice, "I had a friend."

The influence of a great friend is something which overpasses death.

Many a preacher, being dead, yet speaks

No preacher ever knows what he is doing, nor does he ever know where his word is going, or how far it is reaching. But many, although they may never have told him so, owe their lives to the consistent preaching of some faithful preacher and man of God of whom the world at large has never heard, and many in the hour of temptation remember the words they heard.

Every man leaves something of himself in the world. Every man being dead yet speaketh. God grant that when we leave this world we shall leave something which is still speaking for Jesus Christ.

No easy way

MORNING

One of the delusions which most people have is that the great men do things easily. People talk about inspiration as if inspiration was something which enabled people to do things without any effort at all. But all the evidence is that the precise opposite is the truth.

A fact which I had forgotten, and which I have rediscovered, turned my thoughts to this again. The fact is this. We think of Byron and Tennyson as two of the great masters of the techniques of verse making; and yet both of them habitually used rhyming dictionaries! Their rhyming words seem to come with a complete inevitability; they seem to fall into place naturally and effortlessly; but time and time again they were the result of laboriously studying a rhyming dictionary to find a word which would rhyme.

Balzac, the master of the short story, speaks of himself as "plying the pick for dear life like an entombed miner". Not much sound of effortless ease there. Flaubert, that master of French style, speaks of himself as sick, irritated, the prey a thousand times a day of cruel pain", but, "continuing my labor like a true working-man, who, with sleeves turned up, in the sweat of his brow, beats away at his anvil, whether it rain or blow, hail or thunder."

Clearly the work which men look on as inspired is the result of the labor of the sweat of the brow and the struggle of the mind.

EVENING

It is characteristic of all of us that we want an easy way to success in life and in living.

A man came to James Agate, who in his lifetime was probably the most distinguished of all dramatic critics, and asked him for the secret of how to become a dramatic critic. James Agate's reply was that he must study the works of about thirty great dramatists to see what great drama is, before he dared to become a critic at all. The man objected that he would be at least forty before he had got through the list Agate's reply was, "You must be at least forty before your opinions have any value."

No man can reach the greatness without the toil. The truth is that toil is the coin which pays for everything.

It is a lesson we need to learn.

We need to learn it in the religious and spiritual sphere

"The Kingdom of Heaven," said James Denney, "is not for the well-meaning but for the desperate." It is maybe time that we began to learn the lesson that there is only one way that a man can go without an effort — and that is downhill. The way to the stars is steep.

Disaster and being beyond help

MORNING

Any situation is what you make it. The very same situation can be a disaster or a blessing.

One of the great missionary stories is the story of Mary Reed. In India she was haunted and oppressed by the fate of the lepers, for in those days nothing was done for them.

She herself took ill with an illness which no one could diagnose. A visit to a hill station made no difference. She was sent home, and still no one could place her trouble. She had a numbness in one of her fingers and a stubbornly unhealable spot on her face.

At last a doctor realized what was the matter with her. She had contracted leprosy herself.

She was told the news. What was her reaction? Her reaction was to go down on her knees and to thank God that he had made her a leper, for now she could spend her life with the lepers for whom her heart was sore.

Mary Reed went back to India and for many years, herself a leper, she worked among the lepers and was the means of bringing health and hope to them. She thanked God for what looked like a disaster, for in it she saw a boundless opportunity.

Things will happen to us — things may have already happened to us — which look like disaster. Let us remember that nothing is a disaster unless we make it so, and everything is an opportunity if we believe in the God who is working all things together for good.

EVENING

"I can't help you, I can't do anything for you, unless you let me."

That is so often what a parent has to say to a child

A parent knows the way of life, because he has walked it before. He knows the dangers and the perils and the pitfalls and the temptations. He would like above all things to help his child, but so often the child takes his own way and follows his own counsel, and the parent is left wistfully saying, "I can't help you, unless you let me."

That is what God must always be saying

It may be that the greatest mystery of all is the mystery of the freedom of the will. God cannot, however, force his will upon us. God cannot force his guidance upon us. God cannot compel us to accept his way, his love, his grace. So again and again God is saying to his self-willed children, "I cannot help you, unless you let me."

The first necessity of Christianity is submission, and unless we make that submission. God is left saying in sorrow, "I cannot help you, unless you let me."

Wrong directions

MORNING

We so often try to get to our destination in life by going in precisely the wrong direction!

Is it not the case that we may well be taking the wrong direction on the road to happiness?

There never was an age which put its trust so much in material things. We think we will be happy if we get more pay, if we get a new television set, if we at last acquire a car or a house of our own, if we manage this year to have an expensive holiday abroad, or something like that. And yet a man has signally failed to learn the lesson of life, if he does not see that it is not in the power of things to bring happiness to anyone.

You will remember the old story of the king who was dying of melancholy. The doctors tried every cure; and then it was suggested that the king's melancholy could be cured, if he managed to procure and to wear the shirt of a perfectly happy man. So a search was made throughout his realm for a perfectly happy man.

At last they found such a man. He was a tramp on the road, bronzed, carefree, utterly happy. They offered him any price he cared to name for his shirt — only to find that the happy tramp did not possess a shirt to his back!

The way to happiness is in a right relationship with oneself and with one's fellow-men — and we will never get that from things, and we will never get it apart from Jesus Christ.

EVENING

Is it not possible that we may be taking the wrong direction on the road to satisfaction?

Surely the lesson of life is that the way to satisfaction is through hard work, and not through dodging work. The discontent, the unrest which is abroad today, may well be due to nothing other than boredom and the loss of self-respect which are bound to enter into life when a man is putting far less than his best and his whole effort into the work that he has to do. The way to satisfaction is not by easier but by harder work.

The word conversion literally means a turning round about. To be converted means to alter the whole direction of life; it means that we were going in one direction, and we made a right-about turn and started off in the other direction. What are the two directions?

The wrong direction is when we are facing ourselves; the right direction is when we are facing God.

Children and expecting the best

MORNING

What is it about a child that appeals?

There is the child's trust

A child is not suspicious: a child instinctively trusts other people. A child still thinks the world is full of friends. And trust begets trust, just as suspicion begets suspicion.

There is the child's appreciation

As we grow older, we begin to take so many things for granted; but the child still so obviously appreciates any attention that is given to him or her. Maybe people in hotels and restaurants grow weary of guests who accept perfect service without ever a word or a look of appreciation, or even with a churlish complaint, and maybe that is why they are fascinated by a child who so obviously appreciates it all.

It is a bad day when we forget to be grateful to men and to God for all that they do for us, and when we forget to express that gratitude.

There is a child's innocence

A child is still good. I know very well how "bad" a child can be in the parental sense of the word! But beyond it all and behind it all there is the still unsoiled innocence of the child. We see in the child that which we have lost, and that which still haunts us, and that which we yearn to be.

And it is in Christ that we grown-up children can by his grace and power regain the lost goodness and the lost loveliness of life.

EVENING

One of the great characteristic facts of life is that by and large we make men what we expect them to be. If we treat a man as if we expected him to be an unpleasant character, he will very likely be an unpleasant character; and if we treat a man as if we expected him to act like a man of honor, we will probably find him a man of honor.

Suspicion begets suspicion; and a low view of a man produces low men.

There is no more uplifting feeling in this world than the certainty that someone believes in us

God believes in us; he believes in us so much that he sent his son to die for us. Jesus Christ believed in men; he gave them commandments and challenges of staggering height — and he believes that man through him could rise to them.

No Christian can shut his eyes to the sin of the world, but, if the Christian is to be like God and like Jesus Christ, he will expect the best from men — and all the chances are that he will get it.

The long view

MORNING

In every action we would do well to look at the future of our own lives

Many a thing may seem very pleasant at the moment, but it will bring much regret in the years to come. We would be saved from many an error, and we would overcome many a temptation, if we stopped to think how the thing would look, not at the moment, but in another month or another year or even at the end of life.

Many a thing only acquires its true proportion and its true significance when we learn to take the long view of it.

We would do well sometimes to think not only of the future as it affects ourselves, but also as it affects other people

Anthony Gollett tells how he was building a country cottage, and how he was planning to lay out the garden of it. In charge of operations in the garden there was an old man. Anthony Collett had given him instructions to plant apple trees and walnut trees in certain places. But the old man came to him and said, "You did tell me to plant apple trees there; but I have put the walnut trees here, and the apple trees there, for I did think that when you and me were gone, those walnuts would shade them apples."

The old man was thinking how the garden would look years after he and Anthony Collett were gone.

EVENING

It is sometimes good for us to remember that the consequences of the things we do will continue to operate long after we are dead and gone.

A certain American sociologist made an examination of the descendants of a certain drunken reprobate, whom he called Martin Kalikak, who married a woman as bad as himself. This investigation was made in 1920; Martin Kalikak lived about 1770. In the 150 years, Martin Kalikak's descendants totaled 480. Of these, 143 were feeble-minded; 36 were illegitimate; 24 were alcoholics; 3 were epileptics; 82 died in infancy; and 3 were executed for capital crimes. It is easy to see what an unstoppable stream of evil Martin Kalikak unloosed upon this world.

It is for a good man to remember that he leaves a legacy to generations still unborn. He can pass down a taint that will endure from generation to generation; and he can pass down something fine which will be a constant inspiration. It is no bad thing for a man to have his eye on generations still to come.

We would do well sometimes to look beyond them into eternity. We are not only creatures of time, but we are creatures of eternity also; and what we are in time will decide what we will be in eternity. There is every reason in life for sometimes looking into the distance.

Identification

MORNING

One of the commonest activities is the attempt to find classifications into which we can divide people. The fundamental difference between one kind of person and another can be seen in a person's attitude to other people. By and large, that attitude may be one of two things — it may be identification and it may be detachment.

James Agate wrote of G. K. Chesterton, "Unlike some other thinkers, Chesterton understood his fellow-men; the woes of a jockey were as familiar to him as the worries of a judge . . . Chesterton, more than any man I have ever known, had the common touch. He would give the whole of his attention to a bootblack." Anybody, jockey, judge, bootblack, was to Chesterton a person in whom he was intensely interested and with whose feelings and experiences he was determined to identify himself.

In one of his letters, Keats, the poet, said that "a poet has no personality, is a chameleon, finds that he is the billiard ball if he watches a game". That is to say, the poet instinctively and because he cannot help it, identifies himself with everyone he sees. He instinctively enters into their experience, even identifies himself with the balls which are knocked about in a game of billiards.

EVENING

John Woolman, the great American Quaker, was a man with an ever passionate desire to enter into the experience of others, that he might be able to understand and, therefore, to help. He made a voyage across the Atlantic in the steerage of an uncomfortable little ship. The atmosphere of the dark, crowded space between the decks was often almost unbearably foul.

Woolman wrote, "several nights of late I have felt my breathing difficult; and a little after the rising of the second watch which is about midnight, I have got up and stood near an hour with my face near the hatches to get fresh air . . .But I was glad to experience what many thousands of my fellow-creatures often suffer in a greater degree."

He was on a mission to the Indians in which he had to stagger under a great pack like a slave. He staggered on tormented by flies and thirst, suffocated in the airless forest, grilled by the sun. But he was full of joy, "because he had felt in his own body with his five senses what it was to live as a slave".

His one aim was to identify himself with his fellow-men that he might be enabled to help them.

The pagan gods were the gods who refused to share the afflictions of men. Our God is the God who is afflicted in all our afflictions.

For us the glory and the privilege of life lies in bearing the sorrows of others on our hearts.

If . . .

MORNING

What would happen, if Jesus came again? Suppose Jesus were to be born into our town and our community today, what would happen to him?

There is no doubt that, by some, he would be crucified again

There is a famous story of an almost savage saying of Thomas Carlyle. One evening he was at a small literary gathering. There was present a gushing, sentimental lady who was inveighing against the Jews for what they had done to Jesus. She insisted on how terrible and how wicked these people had been. She was so sorry, she said, that Jesus had not appeared in her time, for she at least would have delighted to honor him and to welcome him. "How delighted," she said, "we would have been to throw open our doors to him, and to listen to his divine precepts. Don't you think so, Mr. Carlyle?"

Carlyle answered, "No, Madam, I don't. I think that, had he come fashionably dressed with plenty of money and preaching doctrines palatable to the higher orders, I might have had the honor of receiving from you a card of invitation on the back of which would be written 'To meet our Savior'. But, if he had come uttering his sublime precepts, and denouncing the Pharisees, and associating with publicans and the lower orders, as he did, you would have treated him much as the Jews did, and have cried out, 'Take him to Newgate and hang him.'"

The terrible truth is that anyone who does not wish to be disturbed necessarily wishes to eliminate Jesus.

EVENING

When Jesus did enter this world, there was no room for him to be born in the inn

Of all the attitudes to Jesus Christ, that is the commonest. There are so many who do not hate him, and who do not even dislike him, but in whose life there is simply no room for him. To them he is simply an irrelevance who does not matter.

There would be some few who would still welcome and adore

There would be some few who were still waiting for the consolation of Israel; and they would receive him—but they would be few. "He came unto his own and his own received him not" (John 1:11).

We think what would happen if Christ came again. Some would crucify him; some would disregard him; some few would welcome him.

When we examine ourselves, what would we do?

Prayer

MORNING

I remember a ten-days' motoring holiday we once had. In that ten days we covered no less than 1,467 miles. We went first to Fort William, then to Mallaig, to Inverness, and then from there we went right up to the far north, to Wick and to Thurso.

You can see from that list of places that we traveled through some of the loneliest places in Scotland. And over some of the most difficult roads.

As we were traveling, one thing struck me particularly. Wherever we went, even in the loneliest parts of the country, we would pass a telephone box. In the middle of a moor, or on a lonely stretch of road, all of a sudden one of these little red boxes would come in sight.

That is very valuable because it means that no matter where you are, if you do get into trouble, somewhere not far away there is one of these little red telephone boxes, from which you can call for help.

It means that even in the remote country places, if there is no telephone in the house, and if there is sudden illness or trouble, people can go to one of these little red boxes and send a message for help.

And you can do it twenty-four hours a day, at any time of the day, or at any time of the night, because there is always someone in the telephone exchange waiting to answer a call for help.

Life is like that. No matter where we are, we can send out a call to God for help. All the great men have known that.

EVENING

One of the very great generals of the 1914-18 war was the French general Marshal Foch. He was in command of all the Allied armies in Europe and of course that was a terrible responsibility.

On one occasion a staff meeting had been called, and all the officers and commanders turned up. Foch himself was not there.

One of his officers said, "I think I know where we can find him." He went round to a little ruined church that was near army headquarters and there was Foch kneeling in prayer before the altar.

These men knew that whenever they were in trouble and up against it, they could send a message to God, and God would hear it.

We don't have to do things all by ourselves.

God is always there to help.

Memory

MORNING

I was born in Wick. I had not seen it since 1912, but the extraordinary thing is that when we went back to Wick recently, I immediately and without hesitation recognized the street where we used to stay and could go straight to the house where I was born. That set me thinking about memory.

We should be careful what we look at

Sir Joshua Reynolds, the great artist, used to refuse even to look at an inferior painting, because, he said, even to look at an inferior picture had an effect on his own art.

Somewhere, everything that we have seen is buried in the unconscious depths of our memories. Whether we know it or not, memories are affecting us.

If we allow ourselves to look at soiled and smutted things, there is defilement within our memories, even if we are unaware that it is there.

EVENING

If memory retains everything, we should be very careful what we listen to.

Old Thomas Fuller once said: "Almost fifty years ago I heard a profane jest and still remember it. How many pious passages of a far later date have I forgotten!"

He listened to the soiled thing, and it stuck on the surface of his memory. We should be careful what we listen to, for every soiled and questionable thing is there somewhere in our memories.

We should be careful what we read

The classical psychological example of the way in which a thing is never forgotten is the story of a certain servant girl. She fell ill, and in her illness she suffered from delirium. In her delirium she poured out a flood of language which no one could understand. Then someone who knew Hebrew happened one day to be visiting her during one of her fits of delirium, and discovered that this servant girl was actually reciting whole chapters of the Old Testament.

She, of course, had never studied Hebrew. What had happened was this. At one time she had been a serving maid in a manse. The minister who lived there had been in the habit, each morning, of reading aloud to himself a chapter of the Hebrew Bible as he walked up and down his study. While he read, this servant girl had been brushing and dusting and polishing the landing outside the study door.

She had heard this Hebrew, and, all unknown to her, it had lodged in her memory. In her fits of delirium, it came up from her "unconscious", and she recited it.

In that, lies a warning!

Spiritual growth

MORNING

Because something is buried in the depths of our unconscious, it does not mean that it is not having its effect upon us.

We should never willingly let our eyes rest on soiled and questionable things. Certainly we should never let our eyes rest on them in order to get a mistaken pleasure out of them.

There is many a man still suffering from the hidden taint of the evil thing which he allowed himself to look at, to listen to or to read.

"Whatsoever things are true, whatsoever things are honest, whatsoever things are just, whatsoever things are pure, whatsoever things are lovely, whatsoever things are of good report; if there be any virtue, and if there be any praise, think on these things" (Philippians 4:8).

EVENING

It is curious how sanctification has become a kind of lost doctrine of the Christian faith.

The Greek word for sanctification is *hagiasmos*.

All Greek nouns which end in -*asmos* describe a continuing process, and hagiasmos could well be translated "the road to holiness".

Are we every day a little farther along the road to holiness, the road to loveliness, the road to beauty? Or are we pretty well stuck in the one place, no better than we were a day, a week, a month, a year ago?

If we are going to make any progress along the way to holiness and beauty, there are certain things we need.

We need first a bit of self-examination
W. H. Davies said that there was something wrong with life, if we had no time to stand and stare. But we should not only take time to stand and stare at the world. Every now and again we should take a good look at ourselves.

Dr. Johnson used to say that this was one of the greatest uses of the Sunday. Sunday ought to be used for self-examination. We should always examine ourselves to see if we are a little farther on than we were the week previously.

No one wants a morbid self-examination, but there is undoubtedly a place in life for a periodical stocktaking of ourselves.

Pressing on and more prayer

MORNING

On the road to holiness *we need something to aim at.*

When we are going on a long journey in a motor car, we take out the map and look at the route, and we say: "We'll get to such and such a place by tonight, and we'll spend the night there." We are so determined to get there and so confident that we will get there that we book rooms in an hotel there before we even start!

When a lad is studying, he knows that he has got to get to a certain stage for the examination. He has got to get to that chapter, that theorem, that section in the book, that line in the text.

Even in games a man sets himself a certain standard. He sets himself a figure and makes up his mind to get his golf handicap down to that.

In every sphere of life we set ourselves an aim and a goal. Strangely enough we seldom do that in the business of life itself.

We would get on a great deal better and go a great deal farther, if we set ourselves deliberately to gain this new virtue and to lose that old fault.

But we need someone to help

Harry Emerson Fosdick has a sermon somewhere—I have forgotten the sermon, but I can't forget the title! — entitled: "No man need stay the way he is."

If Christianity means anything, that is exactly what it does mean. It is Jesus' power that he can enable us to get farther and farther along the road to holiness, if we will ask for and take the help which he continually offers to us.

"I press towards the mark," said Paul (Philippians 3:14). It is not enough for a Christian to accept a life which is stuck in the one place.

Life for him should be this road to holiness, the upward and the onward way.

EVENING

There was a noted bishop called Bertram Pollock. A bishop is a very busy man, with all kinds of meetings and calls on his time. But Bertram Pollock had three times every day when he spoke to God. Once, just as one of these times was about to begin, a visitor came to the door. His servant came to Bertram Pollock to tell him that a visitor had arrived. Bertram Pollock said, "Put him in an ante-room and tell him to wait for a minute or two. I've got an appointment with God."

Every day we should have our appointments with God, when we pray to him and speak to him and tell him of our needs.

Prayer is our way of asking God for help, and of talking to him. The Psalmist said: "This poor man cried, and the Lord heard him, and saved him out of all his troubles" (Psalm 34:6).

Trust

MORNING

I got out of my car and I was sitting on a rock.

Two small girls appeared. They would not be any more than six or seven, and they were both pushing prams in which there were children younger than themselves.

One was another little girl of about three or four, and the other was a baby of about six or seven months old.

The three-year-old was duly disentangled from her pram, but the baby was left in his.

They played around for a bit, and then one of them said to me: "We're going along the shore and up another way, and back round by the sea-front. Will you look after the baby till we come back, mister?"

Off they went. And they were away so long that I began to think that they had either abandoned the baby or forgotten about him or got lost. Then I began to get anxious about the time. If I wanted to get home at the right time, it was time that I moved. But I couldn't leave the baby.

At last the little girls turned up again.

"Look," I said. "I thought you were lost. Aren't you frightened to go away and leave the baby like that?"

Back came the answer from one of them: "Oh no, mister, I knew you would take care of him." "Aye," said the other, "I knew he would be all right with you."

EVENING

There is no obligation in this world like the obligation of being trusted.

It is impossible to fail or to let down someone who trusts you.

God has trusted us

Surely that is what the fact of free will means. God could have made us automata who were compelled to be good whether we liked it or not, creatures who had no choice. But God gave us free will to obey or to disobey himself, to accept or to reject himself, to bring joy or sorrow to himself.

Jesus trusts us

That is really what Paul meant when he spoke about the church being the body of Christ (1 Corinthians 12:27; Ephesians 1:23). Jesus is no longer in this world in the flesh, and therefore the plain truth is that if Jesus wants a task done, he has to get a man to do it for him.

In the most literal sense we have to be hands to do his work, feet to run upon his errands, a voice to speak for him.

Jesus has entrusted *his* work to *our* hands.

The love of learning

MORNING

There is nothing in this world worth learning that can be learned without a struggle.

That is, in fact, the thrill of learning. If a thing was easy to learn, there would be no kick in mastering it. The thrill is to struggle away with some subject for a long time, and then quite suddenly to have the excitement of discovering that one understands what before was unintelligible.

Paderewski, perhaps the greatest of the pianists, thought nothing of going over a bar of music as many as forty times until he was sure he was playing it exactly as it ought to be played. Before a concert he always played through his entire program though no doubt he had already played the pieces of which it was composed times without number.

One day he played before Queen Victoria, and the Queen was deeply moved by his performance. "Mr. Paderewski," she said, "you are a genius." That may be," answered Paderewski, "but before I was a genius, I was a drudge."

No one will ever acquire any kind of knowledge or any kind of greatness without a struggle. But in the struggle lies the thrill.

EVENING

The most tragic example of indiscipline in English letters is the career of Coleridge. Never was a man blessed with so great a mind, and never did a man do so little with it.

He left Cambridge to join the army. He left the army because, with all his erudition, he could not rub down a horse. He came to Oxford and left without a degree.

He began a paper called the *Watchman* which ran for ten numbers and then died.

As has been said of him: "He had every gift save one — the gift of sustained and concentrated effort."

He himself said that he had all kinds of books ready for printing "except for transcription". He would never face the discipline of writing them down.

There are many ministers and laymen in pulpits today whose ministrations fail to be as effective as they might be, for the simple reason that they will not accept the discipline of writing out every word of their sermons, and of carefully preparing their prayers.

It is the tragedy of the church that there are too many preachers who are seeking to render unto God that which costs them nothing, or at most, that which costs them very little.

New views

MORNING

It is real life that Jesus offers. "I am come," he said, "that they might have life, and that they might have it more abundantly" (John 10:10). What is it that Jesus does to life?

He gives us a new view of the world

If all that Jesus said is true, this world is the training ground of eternity. The value of any action is dependent on the end for which it is done.

Bernard Newman tells somewhere of being in a peasant house in the remote places of the Balkans.

The daughter of the house spent all her time sewing. Bernard Newman thought that she must be laboring away to earn a little more money at this sewing which never seemed to stop. "Don't you ever get tired, stitch, stitch, stitching away?" he said, "Oh no, sir," she said. "You see this is my wedding dress."

The object for which the dress was being made, made all the difference in the world to that which she had to do. It made the difference between drudgery and glory.

EVENING

Jesus gives us a new view of life

If Jesus is right, life becomes a pilgrimage to eternity, and every act of service to our fellow-men is a milestone on it.

No teacher ever linked eternity to time as Jesus did. To other teachers the philosopher sitting in his study thinking his long, involved, abstruse thoughts was the man who was dealing with eternity.

To Jesus the man who was giving a cup of cold water to the thirsty, the man who was visiting the sick and those in prison, the man who was feeding the hungry and clothing the naked, and welcoming the stranger was the man who was dealing with eternity.

Jesus gives us life because he teaches us to see life *sub specie aeternitatis*, in the light of eternity. We see this world in the light of eternity and it becomes no longer a world of drudgery and unimportant tasks, but a world which is the training-school for the life which is beyond.

When we see our fellow-men in the light of eternity, they are no longer people whom we can despise and dislike, but they are sons of God, whether they know it or not.

When we see life in the light of eternity, it becomes no longer one thing after another in a petty succession, but it becomes the pilgrimage of the soul to God.

Sunday and the sabbath

MORNING

As I was on my way to church, my eye caught a placard advertising a Sunday newspaper. The claim of this newspaper on this placard was that it was *An Essential Part of Sunday*.

I do not suppose that anyone would agree that any newspaper is an essential part of Sunday, if the word "essential" is being used in anything like its true meaning. But, suppose we were asked to draw up a list of the essential things about Sunday, what would that list include?

The commandment says: Remember the Sabbath day, to keep it holy. In the Bible this word "holy" has a very special meaning. "Holy" means different, separate from and other than ordinary things.

A temple is "holy" because it is different from other buildings; a victim for sacrifice is "holy" because he is different from other animals; a priest is "holy" because he is different from other men. God is supremely "holy" because God belongs to a quite different sphere of being from that to which men belong.

So we could say that the commandment means: Remember the Sabbath day, to keep it differently from other days.

EVENING

Wherein then should this difference between Sabbath and Sunday lie?

It is still true that the Lord's Day should be a day of rest
That is not only a spiritual necessity, it is a physical necessity.

Modern life moves at an ever faster and faster pace. The result is that people grow ever more and more tired.

A famous man was asked what he thought was the most characteristic feature of modern people, and he answered: "Tired eyes."

In the days of the French Revolution the Sunday was abolished by law, but it had to be brought back, because the health of the nation would not stand a week without a day of rest.

Everything needs its day of rest.

The old golf green-keeper was right. When he was asked his opinion of Sunday golf, his answer was: "If you don't need a rest, the greens do."

The Lord's Day is a day of rest, and, as such, it is a great social and humanitarian institution.

The Lord's Day

MORNING

The Lord's Day should be a day of family fellowship

It is the one day when the family have the opportunity to be together.

It is the one day when the father has the chance to be with his wife and with his children.

The family and the Sunday are very closely intertwined.

Edwin Muir in his autobiography tells of Sunday nights in his old home in the Orkney Islands: "Every Sunday night my father gathered us together to read a chapter of the Bible and kneel down in prayer. These Sunday nights are among my happiest memories; there was a feeling of complete security and union among us as we sat reading about David or Elijah."

The Sunday ought to be the day on which the unity of the family is rediscovered and confirmed.

EVENING

The Lord's Day ought to be a day of self-examination

In this rushed and busy world we are apt to be so busy living that we have no time to think how we are living. Sunday is the day when we ought to take time to take stock.

We ought to examine ourselves to see if we have advanced or slipped back along the road to holiness. On every Sunday we should hear God's voice saying to us: "Let a man examine himself."

The Lord's Day should be a day of worship

Jesus went into the Synagogue in Nazareth on the Sabbath as his custom was (Luke 4:16).

The worship of God in the company of men was for Jesus an habitual and essential part of God's day.

In the rush and press of things it is easy to forget God.

It is easy to be too busy to pray.

It is easy to be so busy with the things of time that the things of eternity are forgotten.

On the Lord's Day a man should re-establish the bond that binds himself to his fellow men and to his God.

True perspective

MORNING

One of the most staggering things about the human mind is how it can lose all sense of proportion.

It can magnify trifles until they fill the whole horizon.

It can set side by side things that are of no importance and things which are of eternal importance and feel no shattering incongruity in the juxtaposition.

Edmund Gosse tells how his father chronicled his birth in his diary.

His father was a naturalist. It was a household in which the birth of a child was not really welcomed.

When Edmund was born his father entered in his diary: "E. delivered of a son. Received green swallow from Jamaica."

With an astonishing lack of perspective the birth of a man child into the world and the arrival of a green swallow from Jamaica are set down side by side.

EVENING

Mrs. Belloc Lowndes in her book of memories, *A Passing World*, sets down a letter which she wrote to her mother in the autumn of 1914, in the early days of the First World War:

> "London has become very melancholy. The mourning worn by relatives of the soldiers who have been killed is beginning to show in the streets, and strikes a tragic note.
>
> Everything is going to be terribly dear. I got in a case of China tea this morning at the old price, and in the afternoon it went up two pence a pound, so now I wish I had got in two cases."

Here is a woman complaining that the price of China tea is going up two pence a pound when she was moving in a world of broken hearts.

The sheer insensitive blindness of a juxtaposition like that is appalling.

Trifles

MORNING

Somewhere there is an incident told by Dr. Johnson — I quote from memory.

A man who worked in a paper factory came to see him. This man had taken from the factory two or three sheets of paper and some pieces of string to tie up certain parcels of his own. He had convinced himself that by so doing he had committed a deadly sin and he would not stop talking and lamenting about this trivial business.

At last Johnson burst out to him: "Stop bothering about paper and pack-thread when we are all living together in a world that is bursting with sin and sorrow."

We live in a world where people are for ever getting things out of true perspective, a world where one of the rarest of all things is a sense of proportion, a world where people so often seem quite incapable of distinguishing between the things which matter and the things which do not matter.

How often friendships are shattered by some trifle!

How often the peace of a congregation is wrecked on some completely unimportant detail!

There is only one way to get our perspectives right — and that is to see things in the light of eternity, and in the light of the Cross.

EVENING

There is a true story of a young minister in a little country village church. He had invited the congregation to wait after the service for a celebration of the sacrament. Only two people waited. He thought of canceling the whole service; but he went on.

As he went through the ancient ritual he came to the passage: "Therefore with angels and archangels and all the company of heaven . . . "

He stopped. The wonder of it gripped him: "Angels and archangels and all the company of heaven . . ." "God forgive me," he said, "I did not know I was in that company."

If we could see this world against the background of eternity; if we could see it in the light of the Cross; if we could see it in the presence of God, or, if that is asking too much, if we could see it simply against the background of human tragedy and human sorrow and human broken hearts, we would get back the true perspective.

We would recover a sense of proportion.

Trifles would be seen as trifles.

God would come first.

Other things would take their proper place.

Acceptance

MORNING

I was in a house that was a house of grief. In the room there was a humble soul who had come to express his sympathy in that hour of sorrow. Other people were shown in; and this man, although he had been there a very short time, rose to go.

The host of the house asked him to stay. "But," said the humble man, "I don't want to intrude." Back came the answer: "No one can intrude in this house."

It was a noble saying. Here was a man with a sore heart, but an open heart. Here was a house of mourning, but a house with an open door.

Long ago the writer of the Revelation set it down as the invitation of God: "Behold I have set before thee an open door, and no man can shut it" (Revelation 3:8).

We can be sure that there is no such thing as social snobbery with God
Ginger Bailey, a fighter pilot in the R.A.F., had won the D.F.M. and the D.F.C. He went to Buckingham Palace to be decorated by the king. Recounting this experience, he said: "Do you know—after I had done my bow to the king as we were briefed, he bowed back at me."

The fighter pilot was astonished at the courtesy of the king.

Of one thing we can be sure — the humblest man is welcome to the presence of God.

EVENING

God will never despise the poor efforts that we can bring to him
Alasdair Alpin Macgregor was a soldier in the 1914-18 war. It was the battle of the Menin Gate. His father was a disciplinarian and a stickler that things should be done m the right way.

With hell behind and hell in front, Alasdair Alpin Macgregor sat for a moment and scribbled a note to say that he was still alive and put it into one of the green envelopes which soldiers were given to hold their letters.

Two weeks later the letter came back to him, and written across it in his father's handwriting was the sentence: "This sort of letter not wanted here." Alasdair Alpin Macgregor never again wrote to his father.

True, as he lay in hospital later, his father apologized to him for that heartless action, but the wound was there. That is the kind of thing God would never do.

The prayer we may pray, the message we may send to God may be but a poor and a stammering and a halting thing, but God will never despise the prayer of the needy heart.

We are always accepted.

Invitation and glory

MORNING

We can be quite sure that we have an open invitation to the presence of God.

There is a beautiful story of Alexander Whyte of Free St. George's, Edinburgh (as his church used to be known).

At one time A. B. Macaulay was his assistant, and there was a deep bond of affection between the old preacher and the young scholar.

The day came when Macaulay was leaving Free St. George's for a church of his own. He was paying his farewell visit to Whyte's study. Whyte said something like this:

"I wanted to give you a present before you left us. I might have given you a book or a picture, but you have plenty of books and pictures."

Then he put his hand in his pocket and took something out. He held it out to Macaulay. "So," he said, "I decided to give you this. It's the key of my house. Whenever you're in Edinburgh, use it."

He was setting before Macaulay an ever-open door.

That is what God does to us.

He is a foolish man who refuses to accept the ever-open hospitality of the love of God.

EVENING

One of the heroic exploits of the Second World War happened at the siege of Tobruk. The Coldstream Guards cut their way out of Tobruk. When they emerged they were mere shadows of men, and of two battalions only two hundred men were left.

The survivors were cared for by the R.A.F. A Coldstream Guards major was talking to the R.A.F. unit's medical officer. The R.A.F. man said: "After all, as Foot Guards, you had no option but to have a go."

At this another R.A.F. man said: "It must be pretty tough to be in the Brigade of Guards, because the tradition compels you to carry on irrespective of circumstances."

It was simply a sense of duty which turned men into heroes.

It has again and again happened that this sense of duty led a man to greatness.

When Napoleon read Wellington's dispatches, he made the criticism that, in Wellington's accounts of his campaigns, the word "duty" occurred often and the word "glory" never.

Wellington's answer was this: "Does not the foolish fellow see, that even if my aim was glory, duty is the way of it?"

The way of duty may start with a certain stern grimness, but it has a way of ending in a splendor of glory.

Why look at Jesus?

MORNING

Let no man think that this sense of duty is a low and an inadequate and an unworthy motive.

It is a most interesting, and a most moving, thing to go through the gospels and again and again to hear Jesus saying: "I must."

"I must be about my Father's business" (Luke 2:49).

"I must preach the gospel" (Luke 4:43).

He tells his disciples that he "must go to Jerusalem" (Matthew 16:21).

"The Son of Man must suffer" (Mark 8:31).

"The Son of Man must be delivered up" (Luke 24:7).

"I must work the works of Him that sent me" (John 9:4).

"The Son of Man must be lifted up" (John 12:34).

There was never anyone in whom the sense of duty was stronger than it was in Jesus Christ.

He too went to his work saying: "I must."

That sense of duty can be the way to the dawn beyond the dark, for, although Jesus said that he must suffer, he also said that he must rise again.

EVENING

We must keep our eye fixed on Jesus
The writer of the Hebrews tells us to walk looking unto Jesus (Hebrews 12:2).

The word he uses is the Greek word *aphoran*. *Apo* means "away" and *horan* means "to look", so the meaning of the word is to withdraw the eyes from all other things to concentrate upon one.

The concentrated gaze of life must be on Jesus Christ.

In the letter to the Philippians, Paul uses a tremendous phrase. He says, "I press toward the mark" (Philippians 3:14).

The word he uses for "pressing toward" is the very vivid *epekteinesthai*.

It is the word which is used of a runner making his most strenuous effort, his whole body stretched out at an angle as he runs, his head up and his eyes fixed on the tape, his whole being concentrated on that white finishing line in the distance.

It is going to make all the difference in the world to life if we keep our eyes fixed on the ideal and fixed on Christ.

True vision

MORNING

Alasdair Alpin Macgregor, in his volume of autobiography entitled *Vanished Waters*, quotes an old Irish belief and a very charming little poem from Kerry.

The belief is that you can hold a leprechaun so long as you keep your eye on him, but, if you glance aside for even the fraction of a second, the leprechaun is gone. The poem runs like this:

Oh! as I went out one winter's
    night,
A leprechaun I spied,
With scarlet cap and coat of green,
A cruiskeen at his side.
He hammered and sang with tiny
    voice,
And drank his mountain dew;
Oh! I laughed to think he was
    caught at last,
But the Faery was laughing too,
With eager grasp I caught the elf —
"Your faery purse!" I cried.
"I've given it away," he said,
"To the lady at your side."
I turned to look — the elf was
    gone;
And what was I to do?
Oh! I laughed to think of the fool
    I'd been:
And the Faery was laughing too.

So long as you keep your eye on the leprechaun you had him! Take your eye off him for a split second and he was gone!

EVENING

There are other things than a leprechaun that we must keep our eyes fixed upon.

I remember a friend telling me how he and his wife had gone for an evening walk across a Highland moor. It was a lovely evening when they left, but as dusk descended, it brought also mist. They began to find themselves confused in the hazy darkness. They felt a sense of panic beginning to grow. Then for a moment, the mist cleared a little.

Through the haze, they could just see a tiny light. It was the oil lamp burning in the shepherd's cottage. "Keep your eye on that light," said my friend to his wife. "So long as we keep our eyes fixed on that, we can't go wrong". So keeping their eye on that lamp in the window, they came safely through the darkness.

Keep your eye on the light!

The Book of books

MORNING

We do not realize how fortunate we are. Of course, in the early days, books were copied by hand. There was, in the fourth century AD., when the great manuscripts were being copied, a standard rate of pay for scribes. Books for copying were divided into what were called *stichoi*. A *stichos* (the singular form of the word), is not a line. It was originally the length on an average of a hexameter length of poetry — the line in which Homer wrote — and it was counted as sixteen syllables. So the books were classed as having so many *stichoi*, and, of course, however you recopied them and arranged them on the page, the number of *stichoi* remained constant.

Now there is a sixth-century New Testament manuscript called the "Codex Claromontanus" which gives the number of *stichoi* in each New Testament book. Further, there is an edict of Diocletian published early in the fourth century which fixes the prices for all sorts of things; and amongst other things it fixes the rates for the pay of scribes; and the pay is twenty to twenty-five denarii per hundred stichoi. A denarius was about four pence; so we may say that the rate was approximately one hundred pence per hundred *stichoi*.

Now in Matthew there are 2,600 *stichoi*, in Mark 1,600, in Luke 2,900 and in John 2,000. That is to say, in the four Gospels there are 9,100 *stichoi*, which is to say that at that time a copy of the four Gospels would cost ninety-one pounds. If you work it out on the same basis, a copy of the letters of Paul would cost more than fifty pounds!

And now you can buy the whole Bible for less than fifty pence.

EVENING

When Wycliffe published the Bible in English for the first time at the end of the fourteenth century, it was, of course, before printing was invented. The Bible still had to be copied by hand. Later, George Foxe was to say, "Some gave five marks, some more, some less for a book. Some gave a load of hay for a few chapters of St. James or St. Paul in English." Again, remember the price at which we can buy the word of God.

When the Great Bible was published in 1540, Bishop Bonner placed the six copies in convenient places in St. Paul's Cathedral; and such was the eagerness to read them, and to hear them read aloud, that services were rendered impossible and the traffic disrupted and the crowds so great that Bonner had to threaten to take the Bibles away if the eager disorder did not cease.

When George Foxe had spoken of the eagerness of the people to read the Wickliffe Bible and of their sacrifices to pay for one, he went on, "To see their travails, their earnest seeking, their burning zeal, their readings, their watching, their sweet assemblies . . . may make us now in these days of Free profession to blush for shame." It was 1563 when Foxe wrote that, and if it was true for him, it is still truer today.

Debt to life

MORNING

By the time he was thirty, three worlds lay open to Albert Schweitzer for the conquering; and it was then that he embarked upon a course of six years of medical training which was to be the prelude to his life-work in his hospital in Lambarene.

By that time he was a Doctor of Philosophy, and a brilliant academic career was his for the taking. By that time he had studied the organ under Charles Marie Widor in Paris, and, young as he was, he was the foremost authority on the music of Bach.

By that time he was a Doctor of Theology and he was already Principal of the Theological College at Strasbourg, with an attractive residence, a good stipend, and the prospect of an honorable and brilliant career as a theological teacher and thinker.

It was then that he took the road that ended in Lambarene.

It was not a sudden decision: it was a decision that went back to a summer morning, full of happiness and beauty, at Gunsbach nine years before. On that morning, as Schweitzer tells, "There came to me as I awoke the thought that I must not accept this happiness as a matter of course, but must give something in return for it."

EVENING

Certain things stand out in the life of Schweitzer. One is this.

Schweitzer knew his debt to life, and he equipped himself to pay it

No man becomes a Doctor of Philosophy, a Doctor of Theology, a Doctor of Medicine and the foremost authority on the music of Bach without the disciplines of work and of study: to achieve all that he must have toiled terribly. But, being equipped like that, just think of the contribution that he was able to bring to life.

We have become today very largely a people who are looking for an easy way. There are students who want the easiest possible course, with the easiest possible entrance, and the easiest possible examinations and the least possible demands. There are any number of people who want the largest possible rewards for the least possible expenditure of physical and mental energy and toil.

To equip oneself as well as one possibly can is not simply a matter of academic duty or academic ambition or even of academic discipline. It is the duty we owe to God, to man and to the church.

Schweitzer knew the meaning of adventure

"In the many verbal duels I had to fight," he said, "as a weary opponent with people who passed for Christians, it moved me strangely to see them so far from perceiving that the love preached by Jesus may sweep a man into a new course of life." It may indeed!

Drifting

MORNING

One of Tolstoy's fables goes like this:

It was as if I had suddenly found myself sitting in a boat which had been pushed off from an unknown shore, as if I had been shown the direction of the opposite shore, and given a pair of oars and left alone. I ply the oars, I row ahead; but the further I go, the stronger the current becomes carrying me out of my course.

I meet other people afloat, also carried away by the current; some have thrown their oars away, a few are struggling against the stream, but most of them glide with it.

The further I go, the more I watch the long line of boats floating down the current, and I forget the course pointed out to me as my own. From every side cheery voices shout to me that there can be no other direction. I believe them; as men drift down the stream or glide with the current, I let myself drift along with them, until at last I hear the roar of the rapids. Already I can see their boats broken up, and I know I myself must perish.

Then I come to myself.

Before me I can see nothing but destruction; I am hurrying fast towards it. What must I do?

Looking back, I notice a number of boats now struggling to make headway against the current; and then I remember all about the opposite shore, the course, and the oars. I begin at once to row hard upstream to reach the opposite side.

The shore is God; the current is tradition; the oars are free will, given that I may gain union with God.

Here is a fable which tells how a man awoke to the duty and the danger of life.

EVENING

Tolstoy's fable also tells of the glory and the necessity of free will. The Stoics almost mercilessly insisted that virtue can be won by the effort of the mind. A man, they said, learns to walk by walking, to run by running, to read by reading, to write by writing. Just so we learn virtue by being virtuous.

When a boy is learning to wrestle and when he is thrown, the gymnastic master simply says to him, "Get up and wrestle again until you are strong."

You have but to will a thing and it has happened, the reform has been made; as, on the other hand, you have but to drop into a doze and all is lost. For it is within you that both destruction and deliverance lie.

It is just there that Christ comes in; and the dynamic of Jesus Christ gives a man power to be what by himself he could never be, and to do what by himself he could never do. As we are, the whole problem of life is that our wills are not free, they are in chains; and it is the power of Christ which alone can make them free.

It's not worth . . .

MORNING

I sometimes feel that the most dangerous phrases in our vocabulary are the phrases which begin: "It's not worth . . ." I can think of several of them which can do infinite harm.

The other day I found myself well behind with my work. I had to go out to an engagement. I had half an hour before I needed to leave my desk, and I had a definite job that ought to have been done. But I found myself saying to myself, "I've only got half an hour: *it's not worth starting.*"

Often we find ourselves with a small amount of time; and often we know that there is something that ought to be done; and often we say, "It's not worth beginning with so little time available."

It is a dangerous phrase, because it means that the half hour is wasted — and wasted half hours soon mount up to a considerable amount of time. If we work a five-day week and waste half an hour each day that is two and a half hours. Over a year that is one hundred and thirty hours; and one hundred and thirty hours is not much short of a week — a whole week's time and work wasted and gone.

J. E. McFadyen, my old teacher, used often to tell with great delight how he learned Italian during the tram run from Pollokshields in Glasgow, where he lived, to the college where he taught. I suppose the tram run took about half an hour in the mornings, and in that time he learned a new language, by using the half hours each day.

EVENING

Sometimes we say, *"It's not worth bothering about."*

In some ways this is the most dangerous saying of all. We may know that there is some quite little thing wrong; we may know that some quite little mistake has been made. In either case at the moment it is quite easy to put it right. But we let it go. "It's not worth bothering about."

That is the way in which real trouble can grow and in which a really unmendable situation can arise. That is why a man can lose his health for ever, and perhaps his life. The continual lament of doctors is that people will not come to them in time, when they feel the first little symptom of something wrong. They say, "It's not worth bothering about," and by the time they decide to do something about it, so often there is nothing that can be done.

Life would be very much better if people would stop consenting to push things through somehow, and would take that extra trouble and go that extra mile to make them just exactly right. It is always worth the trouble to get something as perfectly done as we can do it.

When we catch ourselves saying, "It's not worth . . ." let us beware. That way trouble and danger lie.

New translations

MORNING

Why then are the new translations necessary?

The Authorized Version emerged in 1611. The basis of the Greek text from which its translation was made was from the text of Erasmus, whose first edition was published in 1516.

Now obviously, the older a Greek manuscript of the New Testament is, the more likely it is to be correct. Every time a manuscript was copied, new errors crept in; the nearer a manuscript is to the original writing, the less chance there is for error, and the more likely it is to be accurate.

The earlier manuscript Erasmus used for the Gospels belonged to the fifteenth century; the earliest he had for Acts and for the Pauline letters was from the twelfth to the fourteenth century; the earliest manuscript he had for the Revelation belonged to the twelfth century, and it actually broke off at Revelation 22:15. The last verses of Revelation Erasmus supplied himself in Greek by translating the Latin of the Vulgate back into Greek.

This is the Greek text from which the Authorized Version was made. No manuscript was used earlier than the twelfth century.

As the years went on, far older manuscripts were discovered. In the nineteenth century, Tischendorf discovered "Codex Sinaiticus", and "Codex Vaticanus" became available, and both of these manuscripts date back to the fourth century. In the present century, in 1931 the Chester Beatty manuscripts were discovered and they date back in some cases to the early part of the third century. As recently as 1958, the Bodmer manuscripts were discovered and they date as far back as AD 200 or thereby.

This means that we now possess manuscripts of the New Testament which are one thousand years older than anything from which the Authorized Version was made, one thousand years nearer the originals, and which are therefore very much more accurate.

EVENING

The language of the Authorized Version is inevitably the language of 1611, and is therefore archaic. So we need new translations.

When the New Testament was first written in the original Greek, it spoke to men in the ordinary everyday language that they used to each other daily. The English of 1611 cannot be like that to us. The Bible ought to speak to men in their own contemporary language; that is the way it originally spoke; and only a modern translation can make it so speak again.

Today we have aids to the translation of the New Testament which did not exist in 1611; and to refuse to use them is to despoil ourselves of a new knowledge which can make the Bible more meaningful than ever.

Neglect of knowledge is always a sin.

Authority

MORNING

Where, for the Christian, does authority lie?

Does the authority for the Christian lie in conscience?

There are those who have held that conscience is instinctive, inherent and innate.

Epictetus used to say that no one is born with a knowledge of music or geometry, but everyone is born knowing the difference between right and wrong.

But there is no solution here. Conscience is a variable thing. The conscience of a child is not the conscience of a mature man. The conscience of a civilized man is not the conscience of a primitive man.

A man may so silence, stifle and blunt his conscience that it ceases to operate as sensitively as it should operate. Anything so variable and so much the product of circumstances as conscience cannot be the final authority.

Does the authority of the Christian lie in the church?

It does for the Roman Catholic. But the church has been guilty of the cruelty of a Spanish Inquisition, of the unspiritual commercialism of a traffic in indulgences, of Pharisaic discipline, of rank obscurantism, and often of the total inability to make any precise pronouncement on the very things on which the ordinary man desires guidance, as, for instance, on the issues of peace and war. The church on earth is far too human an institution to have any kind of infallibility attached to it.

EVENING

Does the authority of the Christian lie in the Bible?

The trouble about the Bible is that no sooner have we quoted one text on one side than it is so often possible to quote another text on the other side. We could find authority in the Bible for destroying our enemies and for forgiving our enemies, depending on which part of it we use. We could find authority for arguing that there is no life after death and for arguing that life after death is the very center of Christian belief, depending on whether we choose to quote the Old or the New Testament.

No man alive accepts every word of the Bible as authoritative. He is bound to select, and he uses some other principle to guide his selection.

There is no such thing as a final authority which can be externally imposed on any man. It is God's method that man is compelled to use his own mind, his own heart and his own judgment. And for the Christian there is only one authority, and that authority is Jesus Christ interpreted by the Holy Spirit.

To know Christ is to have the authority to which all things can be submitted for judgment and decision.

Whence? Where? How?

MORNING

Where do I come from?

There is more than one answer to that question. A man comes from an act of intercourse between a man and a woman, who are his father and mother, and therefore, humanly speaking, a man may be the product of a great and pure love, or of a moment's uncontrolled passion.

It can be argued that a man comes from purely material things. Fosdick quoted the chemical analysis of an ordinary man. In such a man there is enough fat to make seven bars of soap, enough iron to make a medium-sized nail; enough lime to whitewash a henhouse; enough sugar to fill a sugar sifter; enough magnesium for a dose of magnesia; enough potassium to explode a toy cannon; enough phosphorus to tip 2,200 matches; and a very little sulphur. That then is, in one sense, the origin of man.

But if you ask Christian theology and the Christian thinkers where man comes from, the answer is very different. The Christian answer would be that every man comes from the mind of God; every man is a thought of God; every man is a child of God for whom God has a special task and a special destiny in the world.

Life, as the Christian sees it, is no chance production; life is not a kind of amalgam of chemical elements; life essentially comes from God.

EVENING

Where am I going?

There is more than one answer to that question. There are some at least who would say that we are going nowhere. They would say that we are destined for death and that there is nothing beyond. There are those who would say that the end is nothingness, obliteration, disintegration, extinction.

The Christian answer is very different. The Christian answer is that, just as a man comes from God, so a man goes to God. It is precisely for that reason that this present life matters so much to the Christian.

How do I get there?

In the Bible the Christian has the map and the route-book of the good life to show him the way to his goal. But a map may be difficult to read and to understand and to follow, and there is an even better way to make sure that on a journey we do not lose the way, and that is to get for ourselves a guide who knows the way and who can guide us on the way.

That is what the Christian has in Jesus Christ. If we are Christians, we believe that we came from God and we go to God and that Jesus Christ is the guide upon the way.

Jesus had to . . .

MORNING

No matter what we are called on to suffer and to bear and to endure and to accept, Jesus had it worse.

Jesus had to accept insult, and he had to accept slander

They called him a gluttonous man and a drunkard; they said that he was the friend of tax collectors and sinners and they implied that he was like the company that he kept.

Sometimes we feel insulted and slandered. Whatever is said about us, let us remember that they said still worse things about Jesus — and he was the sinless One.

Jesus had to accept the failure of friendship

If ever a man \vas let down by his friends, Jesus was. In the hour of his deepest and bitterest need, in the hour when loyalty would have been infinitely valuable, they all forsook him and fled.

Sometimes our friends fail us; sometimes they are disloyal to us; sometimes they break their promise and their pledge. Often it is hurting, but it is not really the end of all things.

When that happens to us, let us remember that it happened to Jesus and that one of his friends was the traitor who delivered him to death. No matter what has happened to us, worse happened to Jesus — and Jesus was the one, who, having loved his own, loved them to the end.

EVENING

Jesus had to accept ingratitude and thanklessness

When Jesus was on trial for his life, when Jesus was led out to die, when Jesus was crucified, where were all the hundreds and the thousands whom he had fed and healed and whom he had saved from death? There was apparently no voice raised on his behalf and no one prepared to stand by him in that hour.

There was no one who gave as much to men as Jesus did, yet, in his hour of need, there was not a single person to speak for him or to stand by him.

Jesus had undeserved suffering to bear

No man ever deserved suffering less, and no man ever experienced suffering more terrible. He had done nothing but love people; he had lived a life of moral and spiritual perfection; and yet he came to the end in the agony of the Cross.

There is nothing that we have to experience which Jesus has not already experienced. And it is because he went through it himself that he is able to help others who are going through it.

Dilettantes and the Church

MORNING

We have those who are not very good church members, but who are honestly doing their best. Sometimes we think it would be nice to have a kind of standard of church membership and to insist that all should conform to it. But clearly we can't do that. To them we owe sympathy and help and encouragement, not criticism and irritation.

But we have the other kind of church member. We have the kind who are very slow and very safe, quite unadventurous, who won't be hurried, whose battle-cry is, "We never did that here." They hold things up because they refuse to move any faster. And they can come near to breaking a minister's heart.

Worst of all. we have the members like the drifting drivers out for pleasure. We might call them dilettante Christians. They drift comfortably along, continuously holding up those who want to get the church somewhere. For them religion is a saunter and not a pilgrimage, a drift and not a drive.

It is the stragglers who hold up the traffic on the roads, and who, with their dilettante Christianity, hold up the church.

EVENING

The first duty of the church is to build people, not buildings

The word church never means a building anywhere in the Bible. If you said to an early Christian, "What a lovely church," and you were referring to a building, he would not know what you were talking about. To him "the church" was a body of men and women and children who had given their hearts to Jesus Christ.

This means that when we build churches today, they should be the best that today can build in its own idiom and its own style

The church has an odd habit of stopping at certain periods. Its liturgical language stopped five hundred years ago in Elizabethan English. Its architecture stopped even before that. Even the robes that preachers wear are an anachronism and belong really to the traveling monks and friars of past centuries.

This means that church building must be functional; it must be such that the work of the church can be adequately done in it

There are two things we must aim at — reality and "contemporariness". So long as the church continues to live in the past in liturgy and architecture, so long people will regard it as an archaic survival and not a living power.

Life and death

MORNING

There is a certain impermanence in life.

"The world is a bridge," says the unwritten saying of Jesus. "The wise man will pass over it, but will not build his house upon it." Man is all his life a resident alien and a pilgrim in the world.

Away back in A.D. 627, the wise men of the ancient kingdom of Northumbria were meeting to discuss whether or not they would accept the new faith of Christianity which Edwin their king had already accepted. And an aged counselor drew the famous picture of life: "So seems the life of man, O king, as a sparrow's flight through the hall when you are sitting at meat in wintertide, with the warm fire lighted on the hearth, but the icy rainstorm outside. The sparrow flies in at the one door, and tarries for a moment in the light and the heat of the hearth-fire, and then, flying from the other, vanishes into the wintry darkness whence it came. So tarries for a moment the life of man in our sight; but what is before it, what after it, we know not."

There is a pessimism there that is far from Christian belief, for we know that we come from God and we go to God. But there is the essential truth that life is only a moment in God's eternities. Life is not a settled possession; no man has a prescriptive right to life; life is basically and essentially an impermanent moment of time in the midst of eternity.

EVENING

If there is this rhythm of life and death, and of sorrow and of joy, it must be true that whatever is happening, life must go on

We cannot stop the world and get off; we cannot opt out of life. There is therefore in life the need for acceptance of life as it is, and the necessity to go on.

Resentment, bitterness, the refusal to accept things as they are can cause nothing but a frustrated beating of the head against the bars of life.

A man must therefore always be ready to lay life down

In life there is not only impermanence, but there is also uncertainty. No man knows the day or the hour when the last call will sound for him, coming at morning, at midday or at evening. And therefore, if he is wise, he will have life so ordered, and peace with God so made, that he can at any time answer serenely to his name.

A wedding and a funeral, and between them an ordinary week — that is life. That is life's rhythm. Just because of that a man does well to remember that he is not a resident on earth but a pilgrim of eternity.

History

MORNING

One of the most famous remarks ever made was Henry Ford's dictum that "History is bunk". But Henry Ford went on to add something to that dictum. He went on to say that the history which really matters is not the history that is past and done with, but the history which in our day and generation we are consciously engaged in making.

We may place beside Henry Ford's dictum the saying of Oliver Cromwell. When he was arranging for the education of his son Richard, he said, "I would have him learn a little history."

Here are two points of view about history. Which is the right one? As so often happens in cases like this, they are both right, for history has its uses *and* abuses.

History can lead to pessimism or it can lead to optimism

It can be quoted as a proof of all the things that cannot be done, and it can be quoted as a proof of all the things that can be done.

Take, for instance, the dictum that we cannot change human nature. We can point at war, at graft, at racketeering, at victimization, at prostitution, and we can say, "You will never get rid of these things, because you can't change human nature."

On the other hand, history justifies a glorious optimism in the power of the Christ who can do things like that.

History can teach hope and history can teach despair; it all depends how you look at it.

EVENING

History can lead to cynicism or to faith

Take for instance, two contrasting verdicts on history. One student of history has said that history is the record of the sins, the follies and the mistakes of men. On the other hand, J. A. Froude, the historian, said that history is a voice sounding across the centuries that in the end it is well for the righteous and ill for the wicked.

The one man sees in history nothing but the human race staggering from error to error; the other sees in history the action of the justice and the providence of God. This much is true, that there is a moral order in the world, and the man or the nation which breaks that moral order comes in the end to disaster. *Magna est veritas et praevalebit*, runs the Latin tag; great is the truth and in the end it will prevail; and, even though sometimes the triumph took the long way round, that triumph has always in the end appeared.

Pessimism or optimism, cynicism or faith, soporific or stimulus — history can bring them all. It is for us to make the choice.

Unity

MORNING

I once spent a thrilling and a fascinating week at a Summer School for Christian Education. Here was unity founded on three things.

It was founded in a common love for scholarship

The basis of the school was Bible Study. Here is the very basis of unity. No matter who we are and what we are, we can sit down before the Bible together, and we can ask what this book says to us, when it is interpreted with all that modern scholarship can bring to it.

It was founded on a common love of worship

It was founded on devotion as well as on scholarship. It was not that the demand to worship was obtrusive or regimented; it was simply that its atmosphere dominated all the fellowship of more than a hundred people. Night and morning we prayed together, and the whole tone of the school was set by that prayer.

Again, in this sphere today we have a most hopeful situation. In the last twenty years or so there has been a notable blurring of the lines between what we might call the liturgist and the advocate of what is usually called free prayer. The people who need pugnaciously to insist on free prayer are coming to see the beauty and the use of liturgy and order, and the liturgist is coming to see the value of an element of spontaneity added to the fixed forms. In the sphere of worship people of opposite traditions are stretching out hands to each other in a very wonderful way, in the new discovery that each has something to offer the other.

EVENING

It was founded on personal relations

For me the most interesting part was when we talked late and argued late, when mind sharpened mind as iron sharpens iron. Here again there is a notable blurring of differences. There is a new willingness for Roman Catholic to talk with Protestant and for Jew to talk with Gentile. There is a new willingness at least to try to understand each other a little better.

Scholarship, prayer, human relationships brought us together; but we knew, however, there was a limit. The Sacrament was never celebrated.

What then kept us apart? I think we could call the separating force ecclesiasticism. And in ecclesiasticism I see four things:

Ecclesiasticism is worshipping systems more than worshipping Jesus Christ.

Ecclesiasticism is limiting the operation of the grace of God.

Ecclesiasticism is making the tradition of the past more determinative than the need of the present.

Ecclesiasticism is holding an exclusive rather than, an inclusive view of the church.

Procrastination and knowing yourself

MORNING

Often when we say, "I'll think about it," all that we really mean is that we don't want to decide

There is a famous story of how in a moment of crisis in the history of Greece, Agesilaus, the Spartan king, assembled his men and prepared to go into action. He sent word to another of the Greek rulers asking him to come to help in the hour of their country's peril. The other king replied that he would consider it. Agesilaus sent back the answer: "Tell him that while he is considering it we will march."

We ought to be very careful that, when we say, "I'll think about it," we do not mean precisely the opposite, and that we are not simply evading a decision that we ought to make.

Another way of putting this is that when we say, "I'll think about it," we are often simply postponing something that we ought to do

Sometimes, perhaps unconsciously, we labor under the delusion that, if we talk about a thing for long enough, in some mysterious way we will find that it has happened. No one is going to deny the usefulness of thinking about things and of discussing them, but perhaps we should remember oftener than we do that thought and talk are in the last analysis no substitutes for action. There comes a time when talking and thinking must become doing, and when the phrase, "I'll think about it", ought to be left behind.

EVENING

It is by no means easy to meet oneself and to know oneself.

There is a very real sense in which no one knows himself

It is, for instance, true that most people receive a shock when they hear their own voice, when they hear themselves speaking on the tape of a recording machine, or when they hear themselves in a recorded broadcast.

It is very hard to know any man as he really is; and perhaps it is hardest of all for a man to know himself as he really is.

It is very easy to have a quite mistaken notion of ourselves

A man may be just plain conceited, and he may think of himself as being much more charming and witty and clever than he really is. He may think himself charming when he is really smarming; he may think himself witty when he is merely irritating; he may think himself clever when he is really only smart and slick and worldly wise.

We can look at ourselves through a golden haze of self-idolization; we can look at ourselves through a black cloud of self-criticism.

We ought to be profoundly grateful to those who help us to know ourselves and to see ourselves as we are.

Religion

MORNING

A correspondent from Canada, who is one of the few surviving people who actually heard Henry Drummond preach and teach, sent me, in a letter, a story about Moody and Drummond.

Moody and Drummond were very different and yet for many years they worked hand in hand. Moody was very conservative and was what would now be called fundamentalist in his standpoint. Drummond willingly accepted a modem scientific view of the universe, welcomed developments in biblical scholarship and was much more liberal in his outlook.

Certain of Moody's followers and associates were highly suspicious of Drummond, and were very critical of Moody for accepting Drummond as a helper. They questioned Drummond's orthodoxy and would, if they could, have insisted that Moody should break with him. To those who attacked Drummond's orthodoxy and who questioned his suitability as a partner in evangelical work. Moody answered, "Henry Drummond is a scholar. I am not; I wish I were. But this I know, that I can only hope to spend eternity with Henry Drummond."

As Moody quite clearly saw, the main thing which clearly matters is not theology but personality. Let Henry Drummond's theology be what it might be, D. L. Moody was quite prepared to take his chance in eternity with Henry Drummond as a person.

EVENING

This saying of Moody's turned my thoughts to an article on Stephen Colwell. Colwell was troubled about the aridity of so much religion of his day, for Colwell was one of the first prophets of the social gospel. In 1851 he published a book entitled *New Themes for the Protestant Clergy: Creed Without Charity, Theology Without Humanity, Protestantism Without Christianity*. That seemed to him an apt description of the official religion of his day.

Colwell spoke of creeds without charity
There is a certain type of Christianity so-called which joins together an unimpeachable orthodoxy and an almost complete lovelessness. It is much more concerned with smelling out heresy than it is with helping human need. It carries with it an atmosphere of permanent disapproval. It is incapable of believing that there is any other way to God than its own way. It may possibly blast men with truth; it will certainly never warm them with love.

Colwell's complaint is still valid. Orthodoxy, intellectualism, Protestantism in the narrower sense, cannot win men. What does win men is a Henry Drummond in whom others catch a glimpse of the love of Jesus Christ.

No "Act of God"

MORNING

I had to go to visit a mother who had lost a daughter in the most tragic circumstances.

The death of the daughter had taken place as a result of an accident that was in any ordinary way impossible. To this day no one knows just how this accident happened, yet happen it did.

Now, when the accident was being investigated, a certain phrase was used by one of the chief investigators, a man with a long experience in such investigations. He said that the accident was so impossible that all that could be said was that it was "an act of God".

It is difficult to imagine a more terrible and a more blasphemous phrase. What kind of God can people believe in when they attribute the accidental death of a girl of twenty-four years of age to an act of God? How can anyone who is left possibly pray to a God who would do a thing like that?

During my own parish ministry I was never able to go into a house where there had been an untimely and a tragic death or sorrow and say, "It is the will of God." When a child or a young person dies too soon, when there is a fatal accident, maybe due to someone's mistake or misjudgment, that is not "an act of God", neither is it the will of God. It is, in fact, the precise opposite of the will of God. It is against the will of God, and God is just as grieved about it as we are.

I do not think that anyone can calculate the vast amount of damage that has been done by suggesting that terrible and tragic events in life are the will of God.

EVENING

When Jesus was on earth in the body, he healed the sick; he raised to life the little daughter of Jairus and the son of the widow at Nain. Quite clearly, Jesus did not think sickness and illness and untimely death the will of God. Quite clearly, he thought them the reverse to the will of God. They were the very things that he had come to help and to overcome.

What, then, can we say at a time like that?

We can say that Christianity has never pretended to explain sorrow and suffering

It may often be that in any tragedy there is traceable an element of human fault, human mistake, human sin; in any disaster the reason may well lie in human error. Yet even when all such cases are taken into account there remains much that is simply inexplicable.

Christianity offers no cheap and facile explanation. In face of such things we have often to say, "I do not know why this happened." But what Christianity does triumphantly offer is the power to face these things, to bear them, to come through them on your own two feet, and even to transform them so that the tragedy becomes a crown.

Second

MORNING

In the New Testament we have a supremely wonderful example of someone who was content to remain in the background and that at no small cost to herself. Of all Paul's helpers there was none so near and so close to him as Timothy. "I have no one like him," said Paul (Philippians 2:20). More than once Paul calls Timothy his beloved and faithful child (1 Corinthians 4:17; 1 Timothy 1:2; 2 Timothy 1:2). To Paul, Timothy was like a son.

It was at the beginning of the second missionary journey that Paul as it were took Timothy on to his staff. Timothy's mother's name was Eunice (2 Timothy 1:5). It is in Acts 16:1-4 that we read the first connecting of Timothy with Paul. Now from that passage there is every reason to believe that Eunice was a widow. There are Latin manuscripts which in the first verse call the mother of Timothy *vidua*, and there are certain Greek manuscripts which call her *chera*, and both words mean widow. And it may be in verse 3 that we could translate, "For they all knew that his father *had been* a Greek."

Now, if Eunice was a widow, and if Timothy was her only son, and beyond doubt a good son too, it must have been not only a wrench but a very considerable sacrifice to see her son go off adventuring with Paul for Jesus Christ. Surely the home of Eunice must have been an emptier and financially a much poorer place without the young Timothy there. It may well be that in the background of Timothy there stands a mother, Eunice, of whom the church at large never heard, but to whom the church owed Timothy.

EVENING

There are in life very many to this day who are still described in terms of someone else. They are known as someone's husband, someone's wife, someone's brother, someone's sister, someone's son. For the most part they never complain and they never grudge the limelight and the leading place to their more famous friend, relation, or partner. They are content and well content to take the second place.

The world needs such people, the church cannot do without such people
True, we can never do without our leaders, but there is many a Timothy who could never have become a leader in the church unless at home there was a mother or a father or a family who made it possible for them to go out.

When we give thanks for those who were first, let us never forget to be equally thankful for the great and noble army of those who are content to take the second place.

Caring for the fellowship

MORNING

One Sunday I was preaching in a church which has a very large congregation. The Sacrament was due to be observed two weeks later.

The minister made the intimations. Several were about the communion services. He said that there would be communion services at eleven a.m., at two p.m. and at three-thirty p.m.

He then said something about the service at three-thirty p.m. That service would be a service specially for the aged and the weak and the infirm. He said that it would not last more than half an hour.

He went on to say that if there were any who were unable to walk to the church the elders who had cars would call at their houses and bring them.

They would be brought to a door of the church that would save them a long walk up the aisle to the pews. They would be helped, and indeed, if need be, carried every step of the way; and at the end of the service, they would be carefully and lovingly taken home again.

I thought that was lovely. There would be many on that coming Sunday who loved God's house and "the place where his honor dwells", and who would be enabled to share in the fellowship of the church in a way that would not be possible had transport not been provided and all things arranged for them, who would be glad when someone came to say, "Let us go to the house of the Lord."

EVENING

My minister friend had another intimation to make. He announced that on the Friday before the Communion Sunday the "Preparatory Service" would be held in the evening. At that service the new members from other congregations, and the new members who had professed their faith would be welcomed and received into the fellowship of the church.

So far the intimation was normal. But then came the extra bit!

After the service there would be a cup of tea in the hall and all the office-bearers and all the congregation present were invited to come and to meet the new members to give them a greeting and to make them welcome.

It is always a bit difficult to make an entry into a new church. People coming from other churches always feel strange. But here indeed was the open hand, the open door and the open heart. I wonder how many strangers have been made to feel welcome by that simple custom in that church.

Perhaps we could do a little more to make the stranger feel at home. Even just through cups of tea.

Your view of life

MORNING

I met a distinguished minister in a group of people. I asked him how things were going with him.

Most ministers with large congregations are feeling a little weary in the early spring before the busy time comes to an end. He said that it was tough going, but he said it very cheerfully.

I said: "Well, you're in good heart about it anyway."

"Yes," he said, "when I feel a bit under the weather, and when things are worse than usual, I always remember a Scot I served with in the First World War. Things were at their worst — mud and blood and wounds and general agony.

"This chap described it all with a wealth of unrepeatable and unprintable adjectives; and then at the end of it he used to say: 'Och well! We're having a rare time!'"

There was a wealth of philosophy and of Christianity in that Scottish phrase.

Even when things are at their hardest and their sorest, you've just got to "kid yourself on" you're "having a rare time".

It is amazing how the gloom will lift, if you can see things in that way! Try it!

EVENING

It is amazing how two people can go through exactly the same experience and get almost precisely opposite things out of it

The old rhyme has it:

Two men looked out through the prison bars;
The one saw mud; the other stars.

There is an old story about two girls who went for a walk in the country together.

When they got back home, they were asked how they had got on.

One talked about nothing but the dusty roads and the flies and the heat and the general discomfort.

The other talked about a drift of bluebells in a wood and a glimpse of the sea at a turn in the road that she would never forget.

Keep your eyes open.
There is much to see.
And keep open your hearts.

Through the rain and laughter

MORNING

It really is astonishing how much of this world's work has been done by sick men. I've mentioned some of these facts elsewhere, but it is worth recalling them again.

Julius Caesar was an epileptic.

Augustus had a stomach ulcer.

Nelson was wretchedly sea-sick every time he put to sea.

Paul had a "thorn in his flesh" which twisted like a torturing stake in his body.

Just when things were at their toughest and when he thought that he could not go on any longer, Paul heard God saying to him: "My grace is sufficient for you, for my strength is made perfect in weakness" (2 Corinthians 12:9).

At the end of the day, after more than three years in prison, after shipwrecks and beatings and batterings and stonings and all kinds of things, this same Paul is singing out: "Rejoice in the Lord always; and again I say, Rejoice." He is telling the world: "I can do all things through Christ who strengthens me" (Philippians 4:4,13).

The sun can start to shine again — even if it is shining through the rain.

EVENING

It is good to laugh.

It was that supremely lovable soul, Haydn, who said: "God will forgive me, if I serve him cheerfully."

The doctors tell us that it is a medical fact that he who laughs most lives longest, for laughter expands the lungs and makes a man breathe deeply. I've said this before, but I like to emphasize it!

It is strange how often the church has been suspicious of laughter. There was a time — not completely at an end yet — when it was a heresy to make a congregation smile.

One schoolboy's school report once stated: "On the whole he is doing fairly well, but he is handicapped by a sense of humor."

Jesus could teach with a smile.

What a picture he drew when he talked about the man with a plank in his own eye gravely trying to remove the speck of dust from someone else's eye! (Matthew 7:3-5).

How the disciples must have appreciated it when the nickname "Sons of Thunder" got itself attached to that tempestuous pair James and John!

It is indeed good to laugh!

Consistency

MORNING

A friend of mine met a woman in a hospital. She was waiting for treatment to help a condition which was a result of an accident that she had had at her work. It was the second time she had had an accident, and the second time that she had received a long course of treatment. In both cases the accident was due to the conditions under which she had to work.

She worked in a factory where the conditions were bad, where the wages were shockingly small, and where the workers had no Trade Union to take up and to plead their case.

In neither accident had the woman received any compensation, and she was not likely to receive any unless she went to law, and then every effort would be made to fight the case against her. She went on to tell how the owner of that factory had the reputation of being a very religious man. Indeed he had the reputation of being an exceptionally able and brilliant preacher of the gospel.

The woman said: "Me and my husband went to hear him preach one night. He's terrific; he's a spellbinder. But I don't believe he means a word of it, for I know how he treats his workers."

Here is one man whose daily life is canceling out his preaching.

EVENING

If I wanted to know if a man was really saved, I would ask his wife.

If I wanted to know if a woman was really saved, I would ask her husband.

If I wanted to know if a lad or a girl was saved, I would ask his or her father or mother.

If I wanted to know if an employer was saved, I would ask his workmen.

If I wanted to know if a man was saved, I would ask his boss.

No one knows better than I do how far I fall short of that standard myself. But we see young people caught up in some evangelistic movement and enthusiastic for Bible study circles and prayer groups and such things, yet never doing anything to make things easier for an overworked mother in the house.

When Jesus prayed, he prayed in order that he might come back from the solitary place better equipped with the peace and the power of God for the battle of daily life and living.

Christianity should make a difference in the conscientiousness of our work, and in the courtesy with which we serve the public and in the consideration with which we live within our own homes.

Christian witness is not one moment's profession of our faith, however brave that moment may be. Christian witness is a whole-time job every day.

All in a day's work

MORNING

You never know what will happen when you set out on a journey.

In the Bible there is a vivid story that proves that. It is told in 1 Samuel 9. A young man, Saul, set out with a servant to look for his father's asses. The asses had strayed away, and he had set out to find them; and at the end of the journey he found, not the asses, but a kingdom; for before he came home, Samuel had anointed him as the king of Israel.

He set out to look for his father's asses, and he found a crown.

It is wonderful what the routine of a day's work will produce, if we go about it faithfully and diligently.

Take the case of Johann Sebastian Bach, the great composer. For years he was teacher and organist in St. Thomas's School in Leipzig. For one hundred and twenty-five pounds a year he had to train the boys" choir, play at services, weddings and funerals and — most amazing of all — to produce new compositions every week to be sung and played each Sunday.

In Leipzig, Bach produced 265 church cantatas, 263 chorales, fourteen larger works, twenty-four secular cantatas, six concertos, four overtures, eighteen piano and violin concertos; 356 organ works: and 162 pieces for the piano.

Bach's masterpieces were produced all in the day's work.

EVENING

Jesus told a story about a man who found a tremendous treasure in a field (Matthew 13:44). That man must have been ploughing or digging or weeding that field, and it was in the day's work that he found the treasure.

Every day in life brings its opportunities — the opportunity to practise the greatest of all heroisms, the heroism of carrying on when we are up against it; the greatest of all conquests, the conquest over our own selves; the greatest of all honors, the honor of serving and helping someone in need.

Emily Dickinson has a lovely and simple little poem:

> If I can stop one heart from
> breaking,
> I shall not live in vain;
> If I can ease one life the aching,
> Or cool one pain,
> Or help one fainting robin
> Unto his nest again
> I shall not live in vain.

For the man who walks with Christ, there is glory along every way and at every journey's end.

Coping with a task

MORNING

I heard one of our greatest theologians begin a paper on a very difficult subject in a very simple way. He depicted an imaginary conversation between a student and an examiner.

"I can do nothing with this paper," said the student. "It is quite hopeless."

"Why?" said the examiner.

"Because," said the student, "it is far too difficult for me."

"Then," said the examiner, "put down what you know."

Life can at times be very difficult, but even at its most difficult times a man can put down what he knows. It is surprising sometimes how much you know!

When we cannot see all the way, we can at least take the next step

When we set out in a motor car for a place that is fairly far away, at first its name does not appear on the signposts at all.

We have to go on the journey stage by stage without even seeing the name of our destination. But if we have taken the first steps right, then sooner or later for certain the desired name will appear and we will know that we are on the way to our goal.

EVENING

When we cannot see how we are to complete a task, we can at least begin it

Suppose a minister goes to a new church "extension" parish in a new area where the church is beginning for the first time. He may have three or four thousand houses to visit. It may seem a hopeless task with no end to it, but he won't get it done by sitting down and thinking how hopeless it is. He can at least start on the nearest street of houses.

Any writer of books or articles would tell you that the universal experience of the writer is that the hardest sentence to write in any book or in any article is the first. I know that! But nothing will be done if we sit forever looking at a blank sheet of paper.

The end of the task may not even be in sight, but the first step in the task is waiting to be done. We can always take that step.

Do it *now*!

No interruption

MORNING

I remember some years ago being on my way by plane to Germany. BEA (now BA) supply their passengers with an excellent little handbook of information and of maps. One sentence in that book seemed to me a great ideal. "We have a motto, 'Our passengers are the purpose of our business — not an interruption in our work', and we shall try in every way to live up to it."

Not long before, the booklet had already said: "The bell at the side of your seat will bring your steward or stewardess to you. You have only to ask. Their job is to make your flight comfortable and pleasant."

A request for help is not an interruption or a nuisance; it is something that their staff exist to serve and satisfy.

Big business is built on nothing else than the Christian ideal of service! The more it fulfils that ideal, the more successful it is.

It is so easy to regard people as a nuisance. It is so easy, when people come with some wearisome request, or some interminable problem to discuss, to regard them as an unwarrantable interruption.

But people matter.
As we all do.
To God.

EVENING

Kermit Eby, that great American teacher, tells how it is his deliberate principle always to be available and always accessible to his pupils and students. The door to his house and to his help is always open.

"I know," he says, "that research is important; yet I also know that a man is more important than a footnote."

Nobody was an interruption or a nuisance to him.

The Salvation Army people tell of a certain Mrs. Berwick who retired from active work with the Army in Liverpool, and who came to spend her old age in London. She had been engaged for years on social work. The war came with its terrible air raids. People somehow or other got the idea that her house was safe.

She was old but the experience of her Liverpool days had never left her, and her first instinct was to bind up wounds and do what she could for the sufferer. So she assembled a simple first-aid box, and she put a notice in her window: "If you need help, knock here."

Knock! Help will come!

Two kinds of nuisance

MORNING

William Corbet Roberts was the somewhat unconventional but greatly beloved Rector of St. George's, Bloomsbury.

A stranger was one day looking for information and left a message with one of the church cleaners.

The stranger said: "I hardly like to trouble him." Back came the cleaner's answer: "Nothing's a trouble to our Rector."

That was indeed a compliment.

When we are in the middle of writing a sermon or an article or a lecture, when we are comfortably settled down in front of the wireless or the television set, when we have some plan of our own, it is so easy to think of the chance visitor, the one who comes appealing for our help, as an interruption and a nuisance.

Jesus was not like that.

Luke tells how Jesus tried to get away, how he took his disciples into a desert place privately to be alone, and how the crowds with their unceasing demands chased after him. He might so easily have told them that he must have his quiet time, his rest, his prayer, his preparation; but he didn't. He received them.

"He received them and spake unto them of the Kingdom of Heaven, and healed them that had need of healing" (Luke 9:10, 11).

No man can be like Jesus Christ and find another man in need an interruption or a nuisance.

EVENING

The men who have done most for the world have been nuisances.

Antisthenes, the great Cynic philosopher, used to say that truth is like the light to sore eyes, and that he who never hurts anyone, never helps anyone either.

Jesus likened the Kingdom to leaven, and when leaven is put into the dough, it makes the dough bubble and seethe and erupt (Matthew 13:33).

The Thessalonians characterized the Christians as those who were turning the world upside down (Acts 17:6).

There is a sense in which the man who would help men must be a nuisance.

The way to amendment is never to regard rebuke and criticism as a nuisance but as a blessing

"Thank you," said our chairman, "for being a nuisance." He who will not listen to criticism can never hope to see, or to overcome his faults, and he who does not wish to be disturbed can never bear the presence of Jesus.

The man who would help the world must run the risk of being a nuisance; and the man who would be helped must have the grace and the humility to accept criticism. By seeing his faults in the light of Christ, and by conquering them in the grace of Christ, he will rise to higher things.

Independence and guidance

MORNING

One of the great errors in life is the error of trying to maintain an unreasonable and an impossible independence.

To do so is the surest way to end in disaster.

There are some people who are too independent to take advice

It was in the snows and ice and the blizzards of Russia that Napoleon's Grand Army perished, and that the beginning of his ultimate destruction emerged.

He was warned not to invade Russia. He was told by the experts that in that particular year the birds had migrated far earlier than usual, and that that was a certain sign of a specially severe winter to come.

Napoleon laughed at advice.

Advice might be useful for lesser men, but not for him.

He refused advice.

His army perished.

It is one of the tragedies of life that so many errors and so much heartbreak could be saved, if people were only humble enough to accept advice.

EVENING

There are some people who are too independent to ask for help

There is a famous legend of the death of Roland, the greatest of Charlemagne's paladins. Along with his friend, Oliver, he was the rearguard of Charlemagne's army. All unexpectedly he and his little force were suddenly surrounded by the Moors.

Now Roland wore at his side the great horn whose blast could be heard miles and miles away. "Blow the horn," said Oliver, "and Charlemagne will come back and help." But Roland refused; he was too proud to ask for help.

The battle raged, and always Roland refused to sound the call for help. One by one his men were slain, till only he and Oliver were left. Oliver was slain and Roland was wounded unto death.

Then and then only did he send the call for help across the hills and valleys. Charlemagne came hastening back; but Oliver was dead and Roland was dead, and not a man was left alive.

Roland had sent the call for help too late.

Blow the horn when you need to do it!

JULY 26

Pride and punishment

MORNING

Sometimes, in our pride, we think that we can cope with life ourselves. We think that we can bear the burdens and conquer the temptations and face the sorrows alone.

There is a pride in life that will not ask for help. That pride is folly. If we would be safe, we must be humble enough to ask for advice and guidance and help before it is too late.

There are two texts that should be written on our hearts. The first is: "Without me ye can do nothing" (John 15:5); the other is: "With God nothing shall be impossible" (Luke 1:37). I can't quote either often enough.

A false independence is the way to disaster.

The humility to ask for help is the way to safety.

There is no man who can deal with life alone.

There is no man who needs to deal with life alone.

EVENING

It is true that the approach to religion must be positive, but it is equally true that it is not possible to eliminate from religion all the "thou shalt nots".

There was a time when religion was far too much built on "thou shalt not"; but in our permissive society the pendulum has swung so far the other way that there tends to be no "thou shalt nots" at all.

It is time that the church said uncompromisingly that there are certain things which are wrong, and wrong under any circumstances.

It is true that the Christian object towards the wrongdoer must be the wrong-doer's reformation, but it is equally true that the element of punishment cannot be entirely eliminated.

It is, nowadays, almost to be labeled "unchristian" to speak of punishment at all. But it is not punishment in itself which is wrong. What matters is the spirit and the aim of punishment.

Punishment administered in vengeance and in retribution is wrong.

Punishment administered in pride or in the delight to hurt is wrong.

But punishment administered in the spirit of discipline that is part of true love may often be right.

It will always be true that some people have to be taught that wrong-doing has its inevitable consequence, and that some people have to be shocked out of evil into good.

Learning from the unlikely

MORNING

I remember talking to a minister friend whom I know very well indeed. He told me something that I had never suspected — that he had a very fiery and violent temper. He also told me of a lesson that he had learnt a long time ago, one which had enabled him to control and to master that temper.

My friend had been other things before he was a minister. At one time he had worked out in the East.

One morning when he was shaving, his native servant came in and said or did something which annoyed him, and which made his temper blaze out.

My friend took the soapy shaving brush that he had in his hand and hurled it at the native boy. The brush missed its target and fell on the floor.

Without a word, the native boy stooped and picked up the brush, and with a courteous bow handed it back to him.

My friend told me that that incident taught him a lesson which he never forgot. Here was a so-called Christian, a member of a so-called more civilized race, losing his temper like that. Here was the boy, who was a heathen and not a Christian at all, showing a perfect example of courtesy and forbearance.

So my friend learned the lesson of courtesy and self-control from an Eastern native boy who was not a Christian.

EVENING

The Christian can often learn a lesson from the Communist

There is never any doubt that a Communist knows what he believes. He knows exactly the creed of Communism and all that it means and all that it stands for.

How many Christians know and understand their creed and their faith as a Communist knows and understands his?

The Christian can often learn a lesson from the atheist

It is very often a feature of discussion that the atheist knows the Bible far better than the Christian does. When it comes to an argument about what the Bible says, the atheist time and time again will know the Bible in far greater detail than most church members do.

The people in the church can often learn a lesson from people like Jehovah's Witnesses

The members of that sect will go from door to door selling their literature and pleading their case, and arguing their case with the greatest enthusiasm and the greatest intelligence.

How many of our church members could we persuade to go round the doors spreading propaganda for their church?

Know-how

MORNING

There was a certain firm that had installed in their works a very complicated machine. One day the machine went wrong. The firm's own mechanics were unable to deal with the fault, so they sent out an S.O.S. for help to the makers of the machine.

In due course a man arrived. He looked at the machine, and all he seemed to do was to give a certain part of it a slight tap with a hammer and the machine was going as well as ever again.

At the end of the month the account came in the account read: "To repairing the machine — £5.12s.6d."

This seemed a very large sum to charge for effecting a repair with a single tap with a hammer.

So the firm wrote to the makers of the machine asking them to detail the account and to explain how this sum of £5.12.6d. was arrived at. Soon an answer to this demand arrived and now the detailed account read: "To mechanic's time in repairing machine — 12s.6d.; to knowing how to do it— £5."

The crucial part is to know how to do it.

EVENING

There is nothing more pathetic in this world than the sight of a man who drifts from job to job because he has no real trade and no real skill, because he has never accepted the discipline, the training, the work involved in knowing how to do anything in this world.

"It is good for a man," said the old prophet, "that he bear the yoke in his youth" (Lamentations 3:27).

There may be times when the yoke of discipline and the task of learning seems hard, and when it seems much more attractive to take an easier and a more immediately profitable way, but the rewards of life are for the man who has borne the yoke in his youth and who has learned how to do it.

The greatest of all knowledge is the knowledge of God. As the old preacher said: "Remember now thy Creator in the days of thy youth" (Ecclesiastes 12:1).

Get that knowledge early!
And hold on to it!

Nameless

MORNING

For the simplest and the most essential things we are dependent on a nameless army of helpers.

I wonder how many hundreds of people from how many different countries it takes to produce one breakfast table. The farmer and his workers who grow the grain from which the bread is made, the people in India or China or Ceylon who grew the tea from which the tea is made, the sugar, the milk, the bacon, the eggs, the oranges for the marmalade, the people who grew them, the sailors who carried them across the sea, the transport workers who brought them along the roads and the railways, the people in the factories who manufactured them, the shopkeepers who sold them — the list of people who give us our breakfast each morning is endless.

Our dependence on the nameless host of people is an amazing thing. "I am a debtor," said Paul (Romans 1:14). "We are members one of another," he said (Romans 12:5). Just as the body cannot do without its many parts, so we cannot do without each other. There is that strange, vivid phrase in the Old Testament which speaks of being "bound up in the bundle of life" (1 Samuel 25:29).

We are all dependent on the nameless hosts who help.

EVENING

We are all dependent on nameless workers

We know the names of the great statesmen and the great artists and the great musicians and the great writers and the great philosophers, but no man knows the name of the man who invented the wheel or the water tap, on which so much depends.

We should stop and remember those on the work of whose hands we are dependent. Sometimes there is a tendency to despise those who work with their hands. But they are the people without whom we could not do.

We are dependent on nameless witnesses

We know the names of the great saints and martyrs, but there are thousands upon thousands of simple men and women, whose names are forgotten, but who chose to die rather than to deny their Lord.

There is a story that Martin Luther was marching through the streets of Worms to that mighty conflict in which the fate of the Reformation was finally decided. The streets were crowded. The multitudes were silent. The leader of the new faith pressed steadily, almost stonily, on. Suddenly a voice, clear as a bell, rang through the air. "Play the man, play the man. Fear not death. It can but slay the body. There is a life beyond."

Might it be possible that we owe the Reformation, our church, to the cry of encouragement of a nameless witness, when Luther's heart was near to shrinking from its task?

The church is built on the witness of the nameless host of faithful ones.

Christ's army and the Church's new young members

MORNING

We enter into other men's labors; so they must enter into ours. We are dependent on the work of the host of nameless ones, so we must work with diligence that others may reap the benefit of the work we do.

We are dependent on the witness of the nameless host, so we too must bear our witness so that we may make it easier for others to follow Christ.

In the army of Christ we may not be the leaders and the generals whose names are on every lip; but we can at least be the private soldiers, whose names are unknown, but on whose valor the outcome of the battle must depend.

EVENING

I see three characteristics of our present-day church young people.

They think

They are not content to be told. They want to discuss and to argue and to think things out for themselves.

They do not believe that reverence consists in a hushed acceptance of ancient creeds and dogmas. They believe with Plato that "the unexamined life is the life not worth living".

I believe that we are building up today a generation who have thought out the faith which they hold. They may abandon many things in the process, but what is left is really and truly theirs, at first hand.

They speak

These young people can put their thoughts and beliefs into words in a way that would do credit to anyone. I believe that we are building up today a generation which is articulate and one which can tell the world what it believes.

They criticize

But their criticism is the criticism of love.

They criticize the church, not because they wish to destroy the church, but because the church as it stands does not come up to their ideal of what it should be. They have not yet reached the stage of accepting second bests and of writing off ideals as impossible — and thank God for that!

The future of any church lies in its young people. As a teacher in a university and as one who sees much of the youth fellowship movement, it is my conviction that the future of the church was never brighter than it is today — if judged by our young people.

Working and waiting

MORNING

The more one reads of the life and of the work of great men, the more one sees that they had a twin capacity — the capacity to work and the capacity to wait.

The capacity of the great writers to work is an extraordinary thing. It was said of Southey that "he was never happy unless he was reading or writing a book".

Perhaps the supreme example of a writer's industry was that of Anthony Trollope.

Trollope was an inspector with the Post Office, first in Ireland and then in England. His work made it necessary for him to be traveling constantly every day. He devised a certain kind of writing pad which he could hold upon his knee, and by far the greater part of his early novels was written during journeys in railway trains.

On one occasion he had to go on postal business to Egypt. He describes the voyage, and how not even its difficulties were allowed to interfere with his prescribed output. "As I journeyed across France to Marseilles, and made thence a terribly rough voyage to Alexandria, I wrote my allotted number of pages every day. On this occasion more than once I left my paper on the cabin table, rushing away to be sick in the privacy of my state room. It was February, and the weather was miserable; but still I did my work."

The man who has learned the secret of work knows that in everyday things perspiration has done more than inspiration has ever done.

It would not be a bad thing if preachers were chained to their desks at least four mornings a week and forbidden to rise until they had produced something to show for their labors!

EVENING

Equally the great men had the ability to wait. There is a time for a wise inactivity, an inactivity which in a sense is creatively active.

Strangely enough, Anthony Trollope himself tells us of Thomas Carlyle's reaction to his writing in trains. "Carlyle," says Trollope, "has since told me that a man when traveling should not read, but "sit still and label his thoughts"."

Dr. Johnson used to say that one of the great uses of the Sunday was that on it the ordinary affairs of life were laid aside, and it gave a man the chance and the obligation to sit quietly and to take stock of himself and of his life.

"I must work the works of Him that sent me, while it is day," Jesus said. "For the night cometh when no man can work" (John 9:4). Yet this same Jesus said: "Come ye apart yourselves into a desert place, and rest awhile" (Mark 6:31).

In the fully organized life there will be rhythm in a life in which a man works for men and waits with God.

Help for the unhappy

MORNING

The mottoes of the Scottish clans are very intriguing. Let us look at some of these during August.

The Macmillans come from more than one particular part of the country. They come from Knapdale in Argyllshire and from Galloway as well.

Perhaps they began by being a family of holy men connected with the church, for it may be that the name of Macmillan is connected with the Gaelic word *moal*, which means bald or tonsured, as a monk is tonsured.

The Macmillans have a very fine Latin motto — *Miseris succurrere disco*, which means, I learn to succor the wretched, or, as we might put it, "I learn to help the unhappy".

There could be few finer mottoes than that.

If we are to learn to help the unhappy, certain things have to be remembered.

It is perfectly possible to walk through the world and not even notice the pain and the sorrow that are there.

EVENING

We must learn to see the unhappiness of others

In the old days in America Dwight L. Morrow was a very influential man who had a great deal to do with decisions as to whom his party would run as President. He had a daughter called Anne Morrow, who, when she was a child, used to be present almost unnoticed at some very important gatherings.

At one meeting the question was whether or not Calvin Coolidge was a suitable candidate for the Presidency. Coolidge had been invited to be there. He had been interviewed, and sized up. He had left the meeting, and now they were discussing whether or not he would do. Suddenly Anne's voice interrupted the discussions of the statesmen. "Of course he'll do," she said. Her father asked her why she was so sure. She lifted up a rather grubby thumb decorated by an even grubbier bandage. "He is the only one of you," she said, "who noticed that I had a sore thumb, and who asked me how it was getting on."

It was a child's test, but a good test.

It is so easy to be so aloof, to be so wrapped up in one's own self, to be so blind and deaf and insensitive that we never even notice the unhappiness of others.

Action and prayer

MORNING

"I learn to help the unhappy."

We must learn to feel the unhappiness of others.

It is not enough simply to see. When we see, we must also feel.

It is quite possible to see the unhappiness of others and to think — perhaps even unconsciously — that it has nothing to do with us. It is quite possible to see the unhappiness of others and to accept it as part of the landscape, as just one of these things which are in the nature of things.

William Morris used to say that every time he passed a drunken man on the street he felt personally responsible for that man.

The sight of human need, human unhappiness, human misery should always make an answering sword of grief and pity pierce our hearts.

We must learn to act for the help of others

To see is not enough; even to feel is not enough; the seeing and the feeling must be turned into action. And that is so for a very special reason.

Help given to a brother man in trouble is help given to Jesus Christ

Therein is the reason for every Christian to take as his motto: "I learn to help the unhappy, I learn to succor the wretched."

"Inasmuch as ye have done it unto one of the least of these my brethren," said Jesus, "ye have done it unto me" (Matthew 25:40).

EVENING

Ramsay is the family name of the Earl of Dalhousie, who is the head of one of the most ancient and famous Scottish families. The motto of the Ramsays is the Latin phrase *Ora et Labora*, which means, "Pray and Work".

There are no two activities more closely connected than prayer and work.

The one is always incomplete and often futile without the other.

To prayer must always be added work and labor and toil

No man need think that all he has to do is to pray for something and that then that something will fall into his hands. It is always wrong to look on God as the easy way out, to look on God as the person who will do for us what we are too lazy to do for ourselves.

Nowhere are we better taught this than in the Lord's Prayer Jesus taught us to pray: "Give us this day our daily bread." But we cannot thus pray and then sit back and wait for our daily bread to fall into our hands.

Prayer and action

MORNING

There was a man who had an allotment. Once it had been rough, unsightly, weed-infested ground, but he had labored and toiled until it bore the loveliest flowers and the largest vegetables.

A pious friend was being shown over the allotment. He naturally commented on the beauty of the flowers and the excellence of the vegetables.

Then he said: "Yes, it's wonderful what God can do with a piece of ground isn't it?"

"Yes," said the man who had toiled in the sweat of his brow over the allotment, "but you should have seen this piece of ground when God had it to himself!"

All great things come from the combination of God's help and man's toil.

A Christian man must pray, and must then do everything possible to make his prayer come true.

EVENING

One of the noblest of the unwritten sayings of Jesus, the sayings which are not in our gospels is: "Raise the stone and thou shalt find me; cleave the wood and I am there." Jesus Christ is there to help the mason as he dresses the stone and the carpenter as he handles the wood.

It is one of the basic rules of life that no man is ever left to do any task by himself. Whenever he sets his hand to any good and useful undertaking Jesus is with him to strengthen and to help.

That is why time and time again men have been enabled to do things which humanly speaking were impossible; and that is why men have been prepared to put their hands to tasks which are obviously beyond their powers.

Jesus said to his disciples: "Go ye and teach all nations" (Matthew 28:19). That was a command addressed to no more than one hundred and twenty men, and they were men without influence, without money, without learning, without prestige (Acts 1:15). Yet these men laid their hands to that impossible task because Jesus had made another promise to them: "Lo, I am with you always even unto the end of the world" (Matthew 28:20).

With the task there always comes the power to do it

Prayer and work must always go together. God's grace and Christ's presence added to our toil make all things possible.

Glory and virtue

MORNING

The Robertsons came originally from the Atholl country. Their motto is a Latin phrase: *Virtutis gloria merces*, which means: "Glory is the reward of virtue." Here is a great truth. The only way to glory is the way of honor, of honesty and of virtue.

Glory is a deceptive word. It is a word that sounds as if it was clothed in glamour and in romance. But glory is always the product of unremitting toil

Anyone who achieves glory in any sphere of life has to work for it.

The great musician or the great singer comes only to his glory by way of ceaseless practice for many hours a day every day.

The great athlete comes only to his through unremitting discipline and training.

There is no easy way to glory. *Per ardua ad astra*; the way to the stars is always steep.

"The gods," said Hesiod, "have ordained sweat as the price of all things precious."

Not the dilettante, but the toiler reaches the glory.

EVENING

There is a group of words all closely related, but all with very different meanings. There is "fame", there is "notoriety", there is "glory"

They all imply that there is something outstanding about the person to whom they are ascribed.

To be "notorious" is to be known for things which are discreditable.

To be "famous" is to be known for great things, good and bad alike.

To have "glory" is always to be known for good.

Sometimes the Bible has a way of summing up a man in one sentence. It dismisses Nadab, king of Israel, in little more than one sentence: "He did evil in the sight of the Lord" (1 Kings 15:26).

Life has a way of summing up in one sentence. When a man is gone from this earth, he always leaves a memory that is so often summarized in one sentence. Many will say of him that he was sarcastic, that he was unreliable, that he was kind. But always for good or for bad there is the one sentence verdict.

What will that sentence be about us?

Notoriety, fame, or the glory which comes from goodness?

Which shall we leave behind?

For the King

MORNING

The Macfies or MacPhees originally came from Colonsay, and their motto is *Pro Rege*, which means "For the King".

Here is the motto of loyalty, the motto of men who will never betray their king.

One of the great stories of loyalty is the story of the eight men of Glenmoriston.

It was in 1746 after the Duke of Cumberland had annihilated the armies of Prince Charlie at the Battle of Culloden. The Prince had escaped; and he was wandering literally in rags with one companion. The government had put a price on his head, offering the sum of £30,000 for him dead or alive.

He came to Glenmoriston and was all but starving. He saw smoke coming from a hut and he determined to go there, although there might be enemies there, for anything was better than slow death by starvation.

In the hut there were eight men, two Macdonalds, three Chisholms, one Macgregor, one Grant and one Macmillan. They were all thieves and criminals and had taken to the hills to escape justice.

When the Prince entered the door one of them recognized him, but hid his recognition. But the others had to be told, and, when they were told, for weeks these eight Highland outlaws guarded and protected and cared for the Prince. There was £30,000 on his head, but not one of these men was prepared to play the Judas.

They even made a journey to Fort Augustus at the peril of their liberty and lives to buy the Prince a pennyworth of gingerbread.

EVENING

For weeks the Prince sheltered with the men in Glenmoriston. When in the end he left them, he shook hands with each of them.

The years passed by and the time came when men in Scotland forgot danger and looked back on the Jacobite rebellion as a romantic episode.

By that time one of the eight men was in Edinburgh; his name was Hugh Chisholm. People would ask him to tell the tale of the days when he and his friends had sheltered the Prince in Glenmoriston and he would willingly tell it.

But one thing Hugh Chisholm always did; he would always shake hands with his left hand, for he said that he would never give to any other man the hand that once he had given to his Prince.

There is loyalty.

Would that our loyalty to God our King was of that standard!

Never behind

MORNING

The Douglases take their name from the moorland country in Lanarkshire and their motto is *Jamais Arrière*, which means, "Never Behind".

There are indeed certain things in which the Christian should never be behind.

The Christian should never be behind in generosity

His heart should be the first heart to be pierced with the sword of grief and pity for the pain, the sorrow and the want of others; and his hand should be the first hand stretched out to help.

The Christian church has always been in the very forefront of all work to alleviate pain and suffering.

The first blind asylum was founded by a Christian monk, Thalasius, and the first free dispensary by Apollonius, a Christian merchant.

The first hospital of which there is any record was founded by a Christian lady, Fabiola.

During the great Decian persecution the church in Rome had under its care a great crowd of widows, orphans, blind, lame and sick folk.

The heathen prefect broke into the church and demanded that the congregation should hand over its treasures to the state.

Laurentius the deacon pointed at the crowd of poor and sick and maimed and lonely and said: "These are the treasures of the church."

EVENING

What is true of the church should be true of the individual Christian

There is a story which tells how a crowd was watching a disaster which had befallen a carter and which had wrecked his cart. Amongst them there was an old Quaker. Many were the expressions of sympathy for the carter in his loss.

Amidst all the words the old Quaker stepped forward:

"I am sorry five pounds," he said, handing a note to the carter. Then he turned to the crowd: "Friend," he said to each, "how much art thou sorry?"

The Christian should never be behind in backing the sympathy of words with the sympathy of deeds.

The Christian should never be behind in forgiveness

The Christian should always be ready to be the one who makes the first approach. Many and many a quarrel and a bitterness would long since have been healed, if someone had had the grace and the humility to take the first step towards healing it.

Through

MORNING

The Hamiltons are one of the greatest Scottish families. The Duke of Hamilton is the premier peer of Scotland, the hereditary keeper of Holyroodhouse, the royal palace of Scotland, the peer who had the first vote in the Scottish Parliament, and who had the privilege of leading the vanguard of the Scots in battle.

The Hamiltons, like the Cummings, have a motto of one word, "Through".

It is a magnificent motto.

It is a Christian duty to think things through

"Prove all things," said Paul, "and hold fast that which is good"
(1 Thessalonians 5:21).

If a faith is only held with the surface of man's mind, if to him it is only a conventional thing, which he has learned secondhand, if he has never made any attempt to think it out and to think it through, then, when it is put to the test, it will certainly collapse and fail.

Dr. J. S. Whale has said that "it is a moral duty to be intelligent".

It is not of doubts that a man should be ashamed. What he should hate is the failure to face his doubts.

We can only acquire a faith that will stand the test when we think things through.

EVENING

It is a Christian duty to see things through

There are many more glamorous virtues in this world, but there is no virtue which is more valuable than the virtue of perseverance, the power to see things through.

During the war in Bristol there was a boy cyclist messenger called Derek Belfall. He was sent on his bicycle with a message when a raid was threatening. He was almost at the post to which he was to deliver his message when a bomb fell. He was blown from his bicycle and mortally wounded.

When they came to pick him up, he was barely conscious. With a last effort he held out the message he had been given to deliver. "Messenger Belfall reporting," he whispered, "I have delivered my message."

"I have finished the work which thou gavest me to do," said Jesus (John 17:4).

The deepest satisfaction in life is to see something through, and the tragedy is that the world is full of people whose lives are filled with uncompleted tasks and with things half done.

Courage

MORNING

The Cumming family trace their ancestry all the way back to Robert de Comyn who came to this country with William the Conqueror in 1066. Their motto consists of only one word: "Courage."

Courage is the one virtue which all men recognize and which all men admire.

Quintin Reynolds, a famous American journalist broadcaster, told, in a war book, of something that he saw in London during the days of the war.

He was walking down a London street. On the other side of the street a commissionaire was standing in a doorway. He was not very young; and in those wartime days of shabbiness, his uniform was not very resplendent.

As Quintin Reynolds watched, an army officer came down the road, and as he passed the old commissionaire, his arm swung to the salute and he passed on.

Why, thought Mr. Reynolds, should this officer salute this old commissionaire? A moment afterwards a high-ranking R.A.F. officer passed, and, as he passed, he too swung to the salute as he passed the old commissionaire. By this time Mr. Reynolds was watching in astonishment. Then down the street there came nothing less than a major-general; and, as he passed the old commissionaire, he too gave him a sweeping salute. Mr. Reynolds was astonished at all this. He crossed the road to have a closer look at the commissionaire. As he came closer to him he suddenly caught sight of something. On the left breast of the old man's tunic there was a ribbon, a dark red ribbon, the ribbon of the Victoria Cross, the highest of all awards for gallantry.

Courage demands the admiration of all.

EVENING

Every Christian needs courage, and, in these days in which we live, when the church and the faith are under fire, the courage which we need most of all is the courage to witness to Jesus Christ, the courage never to be ashamed to show whose we are and whom we serve.

Tertullian was one of the greatest of the early Christian fathers. They say that, at one time, he may well have been the attorney general of the Roman Empire. He was certainly a lawyer, and he was so impressed with the dauntless courage of the Christians whom he prosecuted that he enquired what made men like that, and he became a Christian.

Courage!

It is a great motto.

It ought to be the Christian motto too.

"I am not ashamed of the gospel of Christ," said Paul (Romans 1:16).

Try

MORNING

The Dundases originally came from the country south of the Forth around Dunbar. Their motto is one French word: *Essaye* which means: "Try!"

This is surely one of the greatest of all mottoes. It is surely a word which Jesus Christ is speaking to everyone who desires to be his follower.

Men are divided into two classes, when they are confronted with any demand, or task, or challenge. There are those who say, "It's hopeless"; and there are those who say, "I'll try"

When we read the stories of the healing miracles which Jesus worked, again and again we see that it was the man who was prepared to try who received the miracle.

Jesus said to the paralyzed man whose friends carried him into his presence: "Take up your bed and walk" (Mark 2:11). The man might well have answered: "That is precisely what it is hopeless for me to try to do."

But he tried and the miracle happened.

Jesus said to the man with the withered hand: "Stretch out your hand" (Mark 3:5). It would have been easy for the man to say: "Can't you see that it is hopeless for me to try to do that?"

But he tried and the miracle happened.

There are many things which, tackled by ourselves, are hopeless. There is nothing that is hopeless with Jesus Christ.

EVENING

Men are divided into those who say, "It's impossible", and those who say, "If you tell me to, I'll try"

One of the most astonishing things that the risen Christ ever said to his men was: "Ye shall be witnesses unto me both in Jerusalem, and in all Judea, and in Samaria, and unto the uttermost parts of the earth" (Acts 1:8). "Go ye and teach all nations" (Matthew 28:19). There were about one hundred and twenty of them (Acts 1:15).

They went

If ever men would have been justified in saying, "It's impossible", it would have been these men. A command to one hundred and twenty uneducated Jews to evangelize the world looks like insanity. But they tried.

They did.

Dread God

MORNING

The Carnegies are one of the great Scottish families connected with Southesk and with Kinnaird. They take their origin from a man called Jocelyn de Ballinhard who lived as long ago as 1203. Their family motto is "Dread God". A great motto it is.

This motto speaks to us of the need of reverence

The fear of God, said the Hebrew sage, is the beginning of wisdom (Proverbs 1:7). By "beginning" he may well mean not the thing with which wisdom begins, but the chief thing in wisdom.

It is true that, through Jesus Christ, there has come to us the friendship of God, and that we can come to him with childlike confidence and boldness without dread. But there is a familiarity that can breed contempt in a man with an insensitive heart.

When we are in God's house, we should behave with reverence, remembering that the place whereon we stand is holy ground.

When we are in God's world we should behave with reverence, remembering that the whole world is the temple of the Spirit of God, and that in him we live and move and have our being.

God is Father; but God is also God. The way to approach God is on our knees.

EVENING

This motto speaks to us of the secret of courage

If we really fear God, we will never fear any man. When they laid John Knox to rest in his grave, the Earl of Morton looked down, "Here lies one," he said, "who feared God so much that he never feared the face of any man."

To fear God is to find forever the secret of courage in the face of man.

There is a craven and a cowardly fear. There is an abject and a humiliating fear. There is fear of the consequences, fear of the things that men can do, fear of the things that life can do.

That kind of fear has no place in the Christian life.

There is a cleansing and an antiseptic fear, a fear that is awe, reverence, dread of God. It is not fashionable now to think much of "the fear of God". It is much more fashionable to think sentimentally that God is a good fellow and all will be well!

The fear of God is the beginning of wisdom.

The fear of God is the foundation of reverence, the mainspring of obedience and the secret of that courage which will be true to the end.

AUGUST 11

Never unprepared

MORNING

The Frasers come from the Buchan country in the northeast of Scotland and the Johnstones come from the Borders.

Their mottoes are almost the same, one in French and the other in Latin. The motto of the Frasers is *Je suis prêt*, which is old French for, "I am ready".

The motto of the Johnstons is *Numquam non paratus* which is Latin for, "Never unprepared".

No man will ever seize his opportunity unless he is prepared

Sometimes, a reserve is pitchforked all unexpectedly into a team and seizes his opportunity and plays a wonderful game.

Sometimes an actor or actress who is an understudy has at a moment's notice to play the star's part, and scores a personal triumph. But the success would be quite impossible unless the reserve had trained himself to physical fitness and unless the understudy had memorized and studied the part, to be ready to seize the opportunity when it came.

That is why study, discipline and preparation are of such tremendous importance when we are young. It is only the man who has made himself ready for it who can be offered the bigger job when it comes along.

We must remember the example of Jesus. It was not until he was thirty years old that Jesus left Nazareth to begin upon his task (Luke 3:23).

All these years he had spent preparing himself for the great task that God was one day to give him to do.

EVENING

To preparation must be added watchfulness. A man must seize his opportunity when it comes

The Romans always painted the picture of Opportunity as a figure with plenty of hair in front but quite bald behind. If you meet opportunity face to face and recognise her, you can grasp her by the forelock and hold on to her, but, if you let her past, she is gone for ever, because there is no way of catching and holding her.

To watchfulness must be added obedience

Opportunity is always a challenge and a summons. Opportunity does not give a man some great thing ready- made, dropping it, as it were, into his lap. Opportunity gives him the chance to get it for himself.

A man must obey the call of opportunity when it comes; if he does not, he has no grounds of complaint, if forever after, his life is lost in shoals and shallows and amongst the little things that could have been so much greater.

Don't forget

MORNING

The Campbells and the Grahams have the same motto, the former in Latin and the other in French. The motto of the Campbells is *Ne obliviscaris*, and the motto of the Grahams is, *N'oubliez*, both of which mean, "Don't forget".

That is indeed a fine motto, a motto that expresses a duty that falls on every man.

Sometimes a man claims to be a "self-made" man. There is no such thing in this world as a self-made man. As Ulysses said, a man is a part of everything that he has met.

We should never forget our debt to the past

No generation starts from scratch; every generation enters into the heritage which the past has left it.

No scientist and no doctor and no scholar has to begin at the beginning; he begins where his predecessors left off.

Every man enters into a heritage of civilization, of liberty, of freedom, a heritage which was bought at the cost of the agony and the toil and the death of those who went before him.

It is our duty to remember those who made life what it is for us.

It is our duty to hand on our heritage, not weakened and soiled and tarnished but enhanced.

EVENING

Harry Emerson Fosdick, the great American preacher, tells somewhere of a lad who was living recklessly. He was studying biology.

One day he was shown under the microscope the life of little creatures which are born and breed and die all within a matter of minutes.

He literally saw the generations of these microscopic creatures rise and pass away before his eyes. It made him think of life, and he suddenly said: "I resolve, God helping me, never to be a weak link in the chain."

We must remember *our debt to the past and our duty to the future*. This will involve remembering our teachers, our parents, our church, and all the great and the good and the sacrificial men and women who made us what we are.

We should never forget Jesus Christ and all that he has done for us

Jesus knew how easily men forget, and he gave them his sacrament in which he said: This do in remembrance of me" (Luke 22:19). Every man can know what the sacrament means as an act of remembering Jesus Christ.

"I help the brave"

MORNING

The territory of the Buchanans is mainly in Stirlingshire, in Central Scotland. The motto of the family is *Audaces iuvo*, "I help the brave".

I suppose that we might put this in the form of the popular proverb: "Fortune favors the brave."

The church needs those who are brave in action

The most difficult thing in life is to be different. The easy thing is to be a "yes-man", to go with the crowd.

Robert Louis Stevenson's advice to a young man was: "Stop saying 'Amen' to what the world says, and keep your soul alive."

The church and the world needs those who are brave enough, when it is necessary, to defy public opinion, to swim against the stream, to be different from the crowd, to have the courage to follow the voice of conscience, the demand of principle and the summons of God, to be in fact nonconformist.

The church needs those who are brave in thought, and who are brave enough to express their thoughts

It needs courage to follow where the truth leads. It is very much easier to go on repeating outworn slogans, to go on reciting outworn creeds, to go on using conventional and pious language, to confound fossilized orthodoxy with living faith.

EVENING

The church needs those who are brave enough in purpose

The Christian should never forget that he is a man who is bound to attempt great things for God and to expect great things from God. The basic fault of so many congregations today is that they are well content to keep things as they are. For so many the task of the church has become a holding engagement rather than a campaign of advance.

Neither a person nor an institution can stand still. It must either advance or retreat. It must either progress or decay.

We need those who are brave enough to think and plan and purpose and act adventurously.

The church needs those who are brave in their Christian witness

A certain great preacher used to speak of the scandal of the ordinariness of the lives of so many who are claiming to be Christian. There is no sphere of life today which is not crying out for witnessing Christians, Christians who are prepared to take their Christianity into the arena of life along with them.

Fortune favors the brave. God needs and helps the brave.

Unity

MORNING

The Brodies are originally a northeast country family, who came from around Nairn; and their motto consists of just one word: "Unite!"

It is a magnificent motto for unity is always strength.

There must be unity in the family

William Soutar, the Scottish poet I referred to earlier, had a gift for epigrams. He once said in one flashing sentence:"A ruined world is rebuilt with hearth-stones."

He meant that the only thing which can give a shaken civilization stability is the home.

We are all appalled by the problem of juvenile delinquency. The cure for that problem is not in the law, and not in the educational system. It is in the home.

Where the home stands supreme, there will be no juvenile delinquency.

There must be unity in the church

At a time when church union is so much in the air, one sometimes has to ask with shame: How can we expect union between different branches of the church, when so many congregations in every church are torn and rent in two, and when every one of the churches is itself divided into differing sects and parties?

Where there is bitterness, strife, hatred, envy, discord, the work of Christ can never be done. God's greatest gift to the church on earth is those who sow peace. The devil's greatest allies are those who sow strife.

EVENING

There must be unity in the nation

Bit by bit the old class distinctions that divided men are being broken down. There are few places today where the old feudal distinctions between master and servant still obtain.

I have been at more than one function at which the Provost of the Burgh (or, as they say in England, the Mayor) who occupied the place of honor was an ordinary workman in a public works, and at which one or more of the guests was the managing director of the same works!

That is as it should be. But one of the great national problems today is the fact that time and again one section in the community, one trade in the community, one set of craftsmen in the community, demand for themselves rights and privileges at the expense of the whole community.

Unity in the nation can only come when men set Christian duty and Christian responsibility far above party interest.

Displacement

MORNING

A certain man was sitting in his garden suffering agonies with toothache, trying to make up his mind to visit the dentist.

He thought that he would have a cup of tea and a piece of bread and jam. He got the tea and the bread and jam; he took a bite of the bread and jam without noticing that a wasp had settled on it. When he took the bite, the wasp stung him extremely painfully in the gum. He dashed indoors and saw in the mirror that the gum was swollen and inflamed; he treated it and bathed it and gradually the pain subsided; and when the pain of the wasp sting had subsided, he suddenly realized that the pain of the toothache was gone too.

A medical man, commenting on that story, said that it is medically quite common for two pains to cancel each other out. In other words, paradoxically the best way to get rid of one pain is to get another, and then they will eliminate each other.

In life the way to get rid of a bad thing is to displace it with a good thing. This is a lesson of the parable of the empty house (Luke 11:24-26). The demon was ejected from the house; the house was swept clean; but it was left empty; and the consequence was that the demon came back with seven demons worse than himself and reoccupied the empty house. To keep the demon out, he should have been displaced by good occupants.

Not emptiness, but displacement must be the principle of life.

EVENING

It is this way with thoughts

No man ever got rid of evil and unclean thoughts by simply saying, "I will not think of this or that." The more he does that, the more in fact he concentrates his thoughts on the thing of which he does not wish to think. He can only get rid of the evil thought by thinking of something else. He must get a new interest, a new thought. You cannot empty your mind; you must displace one thought with another.

It is this way with disappointment

A person may be disappointed in some hope. It is not enough simply to accept it; one hope must be displaced by another hope. This is in fact very largely what the psychologists mean by sublimation. When something vital is taken out of a man's life, the way to handle the situation is to displace the lost thing by something else, to give all the thought and energy which would have been given to the lost or unattainable thing to something else, not simply to leave an empty hole in life, but to displace the lost thing with some new interest and activity.

God

MORNING

How do we feel about God? What is our attitude to what God sends?

You can have three attitudes to what happens in life.

You can accept it just because God is bigger than you

In the last analysis you can't do anything about it anyway, so it is better to accept it and to be done with it.

That was the Stoic point of view. The Stoics believed that everything that happened was according to the will of God. They therefore said that the one thing to learn was to accept everything without complaint. Not to do so was simply to batter your head against the walls of the universe, a painful process that got you precisely nowhere. So the Stoics said epigrammatically, "If you can't get what you want, teach yourself to want what you can get."

EVENING

You can accept things because God is wiser than we are

This is better, but it is still not the best. We have all known the kind of people who have a passion for arranging the lives of others. They know best and they genuinely think that you ought to accept their guidance. Now these people are not usually popular, because no one likes being pushed around.

If we could say no more than that God is wiser than we are, there might well be a kind of cold impersonality about the way God deals with us. We might think of God sitting in a vast superiority arranging people's lives with a kind of intellectual benevolence, meticulously dealing out what is best for us, but regarding us rather as the pieces in a pattern than as persons with hearts that can be touched and feelings that can be hurt.

You can accept things because God is a God of love

God has the wisdom to know, and the power to do; he is bigger and wiser than we are. But God also has the love to understand; and so he does not move us around like pieces on a board who cannot say "No" anyway. He does not arrange things with a distant superiority. He appeals to us; he trusts us; he leaves us free to say "No"

and to go our own way if we want it that way.

But when we realize that at the heart of things there is love, then we can say, not in resignation, but in joy, "Thy will be done."

Clothes

MORNING

I wonder how many congregations still make it a rule that their elders should, at the sacrament of Communion, wear a morning coat, striped trousers and perhaps a white tie?

What is to be said for it, and what is to be said against it?

To dress all alike certainly obliterates differences

The likeness does away with the differences, and therefore does away with any kind of competition — although without being cynical one may well say that any such competition is much more likely to arise among the female membership of the church than among the male membership. Still, there is something to be said for uniformity.

To have a dress which is a uniform is no bad thing

It does appear to show a man is on duty, and that he is not ashamed to show that he is on duty. It identifies a man as doing a particular kind of job, and as being the kind of man who is perfectly willing to show that it is so.

It is the sign of respect

We normally dress carefully if we are going to any social or important function. It could be argued that the same principle should apply to those who go to serve in the house of God.

I do not think that there is really anything else to be said for this custom. To many, these three reasons will seem good enough reasons for conserving it.

EVENING

Now we turn to reasons that oppose formal dress on Communion occasions.

Certainly such dress is archaic and anachronistic

It is seldom or never worn anywhere now except at weddings.

This was not so forty years ago or so. My own father usually wore such clothes every day in life for his work as a bank manager; but now such dress has almost entirely passed from the scene. This may be yet another of the many things which, to the ordinary person, are an image of the church as an institution which lives in the past.

It could be argued that there is a certain social snobbery in this

It could be argued that this is a symptom of the fact that perhaps there was a day when the church did in fact draw its office-bearers from that class of the community that wore such clothes.

It is men we need — what they wear within the limits of decent respectability is totally irrelevant.

Conflict

MORNING

I write this on the Saturday evening following the tragic death of President Kennedy, and like most other people I have a personal sense of loss at the death of this man, whom I never saw in the flesh.

But it is not about that that I write. I write about one of the most significant things that I have seen for a very long time in regard to the place of the church in modern life and society.

There is an evening newspaper, which on a Saturday has a certain amount of space given to the news of the churches and to articles on religion. *This Saturday evening that page is missing.* The news of the Kennedy assassination has driven it from the paper.

The situation was desolatingly plain — when something had to go; that something was the news of the churches and the religious articles.

I have seldom seen anything which, without a word of comment, showed more devastatingly the twilight of the church.

EVENING

But why should anyone really be surprised at the newspaper's action, because this is what is happening in the personal life of so many people? If there is a clash of times and engagements, it is so often the church and the religious meeting which have to go. People will go to church, but if there are visitors on a Sunday, if someone suggests an excursion on the Sunday, it is the church that goes.

There are very few like a great scholar whom I know. He belonged to a group engaged on fairly important work; it was difficult to get the group, widely scattered, together through the week, and it was suggested that the group should meet and work at weekends. This man said gently but firmly, "No! I worship on Sunday." And the astonishing thing was that the whole group accepted this as a final verdict and, in fact, did not meet to work on Sunday.

The tragedy is not so much that the action of the newspaper shows how expendable the voice of the church is; the tragedy really is that the church is so full of people for whom their religion is only on the periphery of their lives that we, in fact, have no right to expect anything else.

If we are living in the twilight of the church, there is no one but ourselves who can usher in a change.

One step

MORNING

A well-known bacteriologist tells me about a little assistant that he had. About 300 samples of milk had come into his laboratory for testing; and it was the assistant who had to do the testing. He was sorry for her, faced with such a task; so he said to her, "Isn't that far too much for you to do?" "O no," she said, "I'll just do them one at a time!"

Can you think of a better way?

And then my bacteriologist friend went on to quote a Chinese saying to me: "A journey of a thousand miles begins with one single step."

There is sound advice here to anyone who has a great deal of work to do, and who does not know where to start.

When we have a great deal of work to do, the first thing to do is to make a start

That sounds as if it was hardly worth saying, but it is. When we have a great deal of work to do, one of the greatest of all temptations is to sit and look at it. At a time like that, a kind of lethargy seems to descend on us, and we tend to sit and look at, and think about, all that has to be done. In such a situation, whether it be concerned with writing letters, washing dishes, composing sermons, paying visits, working for examinations, the first rule is to make a start somewhere.

To start is half the battle.

EVENING

Remember that it is steady and consistent even if slow work that gets things done rather than brilliant spasms of work

It is worth setting down Aesop's old fable of the hare and the tortoise.

A hare one day ridiculed the short feet and slow pace of the tortoise. The latter, laughing, said, "Though you be swift as the wind I will beat you in a race." The hare, deeming his assertion to be simply impossible, assented to the proposal; and they agreed that the fox should choose the course, and fix the goal.

On the day appointed for the race they started together. The tortoise never for a moment stopped, but went on with a slow but steady pace straight to the end of the course. The hare, trusting to his native swiftness, cared little about the race, and lying down by the wayside, fell fast asleep. At last waking up, and moving as fast as he could, he saw that the tortoise had reached the goal, and was comfortably dozing after her fatigue.

As the Preacher had it many centuries ago: "The race is not to the swift, nor the battle to the strong." (Ecclesiastes 9:11). Steady perseverance will, in the end, achieve far more than spasmodic brilliance.

Under-rating people

MORNING

There are at least some of us who under-rate people very badly indeed.

We often under-rate children

We quite certainly under-rated our granddaughter Karen's intelligence on one occasion and we under-rated her ability to take what we thought would be news that she wouldn't like.

Perhaps we sometimes keep from children what they could perfectly well be told. Sometimes we don't even try to explain to children that which they could perfectly well understand. We often brush off a child's question to which we might well give a straight and honest answer. One of the worst faults in our bringing up children and our teaching of children is that we under-rate their intelligence and their power to take things.

EVENING

There are very many preachers and teachers who completely under-rate their congregation and their audience

There are very few preachers who make any attempt to pass on to their congregations any of the results of modern scholarship or modern thought; and the main reason for this failure is, bluntly, that they are afraid to do so. So long as they do the thing positively, and so long as they do not deal in destructive negatives, their fears will nearly always be quite unjustified.

Well over a quarter of a million people bought John Robinson's *Honest to God*, and practically no one would buy the normal book of sermons if any publisher would publish one.

People want honesty. They want to be treated as theologically and intellectually adult. They want to know how the case stands and what a man thinks.

I do not wish to tread on dangerous ground, nor do I wish to confound legitimate criticism with conceit, but I am bound to say that this seems to me specially true of broadcast and televised preaching. There is here given to the church an incalculable weapon of systematic Christian education, and yet so often a preacher spends the precious moments trying to be entertaining rather than informative.

As the writer to the Hebrews saw long ago, there is nothing worse than feeding people with milk when they need strong meat and of making babies out of adult men and women (Hebrews 5:12-14).

Comfort and care

MORNING

It is extraordinary how mindful the Bible is of the brokenhearted. I turn to only one prophet, to Isaiah. "Comfort, comfort my people, says your God" (Isaiah 40:1). "I am he that comforts you." (Isaiah 51:12). "The Lord has comforted his people." (Isaiah 52:9).

You remember how the prophet interprets his commission from God — and here none of the newer translations can ever really take the place of the Authorized Version. It is to bind up the broken-hearted; to give beauty for ashes, the oil of joy for mourning, the garment of praise for the spirit of heaviness (Isaiah 61:1-3). "As one whom his mother comforts, so will I comfort you," (Isaiah 66:13).

Sunt lacrimae rerum, said Virgil in that phrase at once unforgettable and untranslatable. There are tears of things. And the Bible never forgets the tears of things. And yet it can so often happen that a person can go to a service of the church and find that the note of comfort is forgotten.

It must never be forgotten that the Latin root of the word comfort is *fortis,* which means brave. The true Christian comfort is no easy and sentimental thing, but something that puts courage into a man when life is threatening to take his courage away.

In any service, there should be that word of comfort that will keep men and women on their feet.

EVENING

There were two brothers in a family who were very close to one another. In their school days the younger one was crippled and could not walk. Every day the older brother carried his little crippled brother on his back to school.

One day a stranger met the two of them, the older brother tramping along a little bent with the effort and the little lame lad on his back.

The stranger stopped.

"That's a heavy burden you've got on your back," he said. And like a shot, back came the answer: "That's no burden; that's my brother."

Sometimes — God forgive us — we think the sick and the aged and the infirm a burden. They are not a burden. They are our brothers and sisters.

We *are* our brothers' keepers.

I am my brother's keeper.

Self-discipline

MORNING

I suppose that W. B. Yeats was one of the most musical and the most mystical of modern poets. Anything less "made to order" than Yeats' poetry would be hard to imagine. But he himself, in a scrap of autobiography, gives us a curious glimpse of his work.

He had been ill, and the illness had left him indolent and lethargic and unwilling to work. He had gone to stay with Lady Gregory, and afterwards he said that he owed everything to her.

"I asked her," he said, "to send me to my work every day at 11 a.m., and at some other hour to my letters, rating me with idleness, if need be, and I doubt if I should have done much with my life but for her firmness and her care."

It sounds an extremely odd thing that anyone should say to a poet at 11 a.m., "Go to your desk and write poetry," and yet that is precisely what Yeats did, and there is no poet in whom the stream of true poetic inspiration is clearer.

EVENING

One of the difficulties of the work of the ministry is that a man has no necessary office hours. There is no one but himself to see that he does his work. But there are certain things that he might well keep before his mind and his conscience.

What is the scholar or the preacher really thinking about when he is waiting for the mood or waiting for an idea?

Certainly, if we have no method in our preaching, we may well be searching for an idea even late on a Saturday night

But the essence of a teaching ministry is that a man does not preach as the whim or the preference takes him. He preaches his way systematically through the Christian faith and through the Bible.

It is far easier to preach systematically — and it is far better. If a man does not do that, the unfortunate congregation will get all the things the man likes and all the things the man prefers and all the things in which he is interested — and not a total and rounded exposition of the Christian faith.

Does this mean that I must preach on things in which I am not interested, on things which do not attract me, on things which at the moment I know nothing about?

That is precisely what it means. And, if one man's experience is worth anything at all, I think that it is quite certain that the things we thought uninteresting become filled with interest when we work at them, and the books of the Bible we never opened become very arsenals of sermons when we study them, and the things we knew nothing about are very likely the very things we need to know about.

It takes self-discipline to do this, but as Winston Churchill said: "It's the only way."

Wrong emphasis

MORNING

There is in Khartoum a very famous statue of that great Christian soldier. General Gordon. It shows Gordon mounted on his horse. One day a small boy was taken to see the statue and was told that it was a statue of Gordon. At the end of the day, his father said to him, "Well, you saw Gordon's statue today and that was something worth seeing and remembering." "Yes," said the small boy, "I liked seeing it very much. It's a lovely statue. But tell me. Dad, who is the man on Gordon's back?"

To the small boy the most important thing about the statue was the horse. To him it was not the statue of a man on a horse; it was a statue of a horse with a man on it.

This is an example of getting the emphasis all wrong, and of letting the quite unimportant thing overshadow the important thing.

A famous, or notorious, example of that comes from Edmund Gosse's *Father and Son*, his study of his youth and of his relationship with his parents. His father was a zoologist and a writer of books on natural history and he was immersed in his zoology. He was fairly old when he was married, and so was the lady whom he married. Maybe against all their expectations, Edmund the son was born to them. And Edmund tells how the event was described in his father's diary: "E. delivered of a son. Received green swallow from Jamaica."

The arrival of the son and the arrival of the green swallow are set down as if they were equally important. The emphasis had got itself wrong. Edmund Gosse's father was a zoologist as much as he was a father.

EVENING

In a home, the emphasis on the material rather than the spiritual can spoil everything

When a home begins to assess everything by the amount of money which comes into it, by the number of things which it can buy, by the number of enjoyments which more money can purchase, then it is on the way to trouble. Long ago the wise old Hebrew sage said, "Better is a dinner of herbs where love is than a fatted ox and hatred with it" (Proverbs 15:17). When those in a home forget that it is love that makes a home — not things — then the home is in danger.

In a church, the emphasis on self rather than on service can spoil everything

It so often happens in a church that someone resigns office or refuses to go on with work because he or she did not get his or her place, or things were not done as they should have been done. Anyone who does that has been working for no one else than himself. Anyone who does that hurts the church, hurts the kingdom of God, hurts Jesus Christ — and in the last analysis hurts himself or herself most of all.

In the long run, the real loser is the person who permits himself to act like that.

On the road

MORNING

Anyone who is interested in railways is bound to know the books of O. S. Nock. In his book *British Steam Railways*, he has a chapter about the early days of railways, when the railways were growing up, and when travel was still an adventure.

In it he tells how, more than a hundred years ago now, there was published a little book of official advice to travelers entitled *Official Guide to the North Western Railway*, solemnly dedicated to The Most Noble The Marquis of Chandos. One section of this little Guide was entitled "Hints Before Starting".

The first three hints were as follows:

"Before commencing a journey the traveler should decide:

1. Whither he is going.
2. By what railway train and when.
3. Whether he will have to change carriages at any point, and where."

Then later on there is this: "The traveler is advised to take as little luggage as possible; and ladies are earnestly entreated not to indulge in more than seven boxes and five small parcels for the longest journey."

There is a good deal of sense in this for travelers in more than railways; there is a good deal of sense for those making the journey of life. You could hardly give a young person beginning on the journey of life better advice than is contained in these rules.

EVENING

Anyone setting out on the journey of life ought to make up his mind clearly, firmly and early where he is going

He may not get there, but he will at least be trying to get somewhere. The person who does not know where he is going, will literally get nowhere fast.

Broadly speaking, the young person who starts out on the journey of life will have one of two aims — he will start out either to give or to get; either to do all that he can for the world and his fellow men, or to try to make the world and his fellow men do all that he can make them do for him.

He will think either of the satisfaction of a job or of the pay for a job. To put it crudely, he will either want a job where he can be of service to his fellow-men, even if the pay is not lavish, or he will want the kind of job which he visualizes as finishing up with a Rolls-Royce and an unlimited expenses account.

In making his choice he will do well to remember something Dean Inge once said: "The bored people are those who are consuming much but producing little."

Conversion

MORNING

George Ingle in his book, *The Lord's Creed*, wrote, "Someone once said that there are three conversions in a man's life — first to Christ, then to the church, and then back to the world."

This is a very wise and a very true and a very penetrating saying. The first step in conversion is for a man to be convinced of the wonder of Jesus Christ, and to know that Jesus Christ can do for him what he can never hope to do for himself.

The second step in conversion is the conviction that this experience brings both the privilege and the responsibility of becoming a member of the fellowship of people who have had the same experience and who share the same belief.

The third step in conversion is the awareness that we are not converted only for our own sake that we are not converted to gain the entry only into a society of believers, but that there is laid on the Christian man the obligation to take upon his shoulders and into his heart the sin and the suffering and the sorrow of the world.

From this we can see ways in which an alleged conversion may be incomplete and imperfect.

A conversion is incomplete if it does not leave Jesus Christ in the central place in a man's life

Any alleged conversion which does not leave a man totally committed to Jesus Christ is incomplete and imperfect.

EVENING

A conversion is incomplete if it does not leave a man integrated into the church

By this we do not mean any particular part of the church; what we do mean is that conversion must leave a man linked in loving fellowship with his fellow believers.

Conversion is not something between man and Jesus Christ, with no other person involved. True, it may start that way, but it cannot end that way. Conversion is not individualistic. It is in fact the opposite of individualistic. It joins man to his fellow-men and certainly does not separate him from them.

A conversion is incomplete if it does not leave a man with an intense social consciousness, if it does not fill him with a sense of overwhelming responsibility for the world

The church must never be in any sense a little huddle of pious people shutting the doors against the world.

Committal to Jesus Christ, integration into the fellowship of the church, active, caring love for our fellowmen — these are the marks of the threefold conversion that is real conversion.

Frontiers

MORNING

There had never been a war between the Argentine and Chile, but in 1899 there was a frontier dispute that had highly explosive possibilities. By Easter 1900 the two armies were poised to strike and war seemed inevitable.

During Holy Week, Monsignor Benavente preached in Buenos Aires on Easter Day a sermon that was a passionate appeal for peace. News of the sermon carried to Chile and a bishop in Chile took up the message. Both these bishops set out on a preaching campaign for peace. At first little seemed to be happening and then bit by bit the whole country in both nations was caught up in a great movement for peace. In the end, the two governments were forced by the will of the people to submit the frontier dispute to the arbitration of King Edward VII of Britain.

A treaty was entered into which promised in the future to submit all matters of dispute to arbitration, and then the wonderful thing happened. The guns of the frontier fortresses were now useless and irrelevant. They were taken to the arsenal in Buenos Aires and melted down and out of them there was cast a great bronze figure of Jesus. The right hand is stretched out in blessing; the left holds a cross. It was decided to carry this great statue 13,000 feet up the mountains to the frontier. It was taken by train as far as the railway went; it was then taken on gun carriages drawn by mules; and for the final steep rise to the top of the mountain it was dragged up with ropes by soldiers and sailors.

On March 13, 1904, it was erected and unveiled, and there it stands.

Beneath it there is written the words: "These mountains themselves shall fall and crumble to dust before the people of Chile and the Argentine Republic forget their solemn covenant sworn at the feet of Christ." On the other side there is inscribed the text: "He is our peace who hath made both one." The text is Ephesians 2:14.

EVENING

There is no doubt that, in the early days of the faith, the most miraculous thing about Christianity was its astonishingly unifying influence. The ancient world was full of lines of division: the line between Jew and Gentile with its embittered hatred on both sides; the line between Greek and barbarian with the Greek contempt; the line between the slave and the free man with the slave regarded as a thing, no better than a living tool, and the line between male and female with the woman also regarded as a thing with no legal rights whatsoever.

Yet Paul can say: "There is neither Jew nor Greek, there is neither slave nor free, there is neither male nor female; for you are all one in Christ Jesus." (Galatians 3:28).

Now, as ever, Jesus Christ is the hope of the world, and in the Christ of the Andes we can see the foreshadowing of the day when men will be one in Jesus Christ.

Felllowship and friendship

MORNING

Fellowship is by no means blind. When people are in fellowship together they are certainly not unaware of each other's faults. They can see them quite clearly.

You remember the schoolboy's definition of a friend: "A friend is someone who knows all about you and still likes you."

True friendship and true fellowship can never exist so long as we insist on wearing rose-colored spectacles. Any kind of friendship or fellowship or love which is based on illusion or on a refusal to see each other's faults is doomed to grave disappointment.

It is always important to remember that, in true fellowship, we take each other exactly as we are.

How then does fellowship overcome consciousness of each other's faults? It does so in two ways. It does so, first, by doing things together. There is no better way to friendship and to fellowship than joint action and activity.

Here is a lesson for the churches. The church has no greater handicap than its divisions. It may be that these differences cannot as yet be solved round a conference table, or from a theological or an ecclesiastical point of view, but they can be solved in action together. This in fact is the natural way to solve them.

If ever there was a time, the time is now, when we should say with Wesley: "Is your heart as my heart? Then give me your hand."

EVENING

The Greeks had a phrase which speaks of "time which wipes all things out", as if the mind of man were a slate and time a sponge which passes across the slate and wipes it clean. There are friendships that vanish with the years; there are people from whom we were once inseparable, with whom nowadays we would even find it difficult to make conversation.

There are people and friendships from which we quite inevitably grow away. But the real friendships are victorious over the years. You may not see a real friend for months and even years at a time, but you can take up the friendship just where you left it off.

Time is the great destroyer but time cannot destroy the link which true friendship has forged.

In all the ups and downs of life, in the chances and the changes, when the light shines and the shadows fall, true friendship remains the same.

The writer of the Proverbs said a wonderful thing: "There are friends who pretend to be friends, But there is a friend who sticks closer than a brother." (Proverbs 18:24, RSV) How true!

Loyalty and extravagant love

MORNING

This generation is very unwilling to make decisions.

There are certain things that ought to be a matter of decision

Our job in life should be a matter of decision. One of the tragedies and disasters of life is that for the majority of people this is not true. Their job is not what they chose, but what they more or less drifted into because there was nothing else available.

This, of course, is not so true of the professions, but it does tend to be true of the man who cannot enter one of the professions. And this is in large measure the cause of discontent and unrest and even of inefficiency and bad workmanship, for there are few people either settled or efficient in a job in which they are not really interested.

Our acceptance of membership of the church should be the result of a perfectly definite act of decision

Too often it is no more than a kind of hallmark of respectability. Too often it is entered upon because a young person has reached a certain age, or because a friend is doing it.

If church membership is to mean what it ought to mean, it ought to be a deliberate and conscious pledge of loyalty to Jesus Christ, made in such a way that it will be impossible to forget it.

EVENING

Surely John told us the loveliest story in the Gospels when he told us about the woman who anointed Jesus' feet with the perfume (John 12:1-8). The perfume could have been sold for three hundred silver pieces — about fifteen pounds in modern money — a colossal sum. A *denarius*, one of these silver pieces — about four pence — was a working man's wage for a day. That phial of perfume cost almost a year's wages.

There were extremely sensible people there who were horrified at the extravagance and who thought that the perfume should have been sold and the proceeds given to the poor.

No one loved the poor more than Jesus did—but he didn't stop to think. It was the very extravagance of the gift, the very fact that it was fantastically generous and reckless, that went straight to his heart. And he promised that all the world would know about the lovely thing that this woman had done.

What's in a name? (1)

MORNING

I once heard of a new baby who was to be named Tiffany — if that is the right way to spell it! Here is one of the changes in family customs that have come in my lifetime.

There was a time when the selection of a name was no trouble. You simply called a son after his father, who had been called after his father, and a daughter after her mother, who had been called after her mother.

Names, like the family estate, descended from generation to generation. But nowadays this custom is often abandoned, or, if it is still maintained, the family name is the second or the third name, and the name for general use is something quite different.

There are many ways of choosing a name
Tiffany, I gather, is one of James Bond's heroines! Chrysostom, in the fifth century, tells of one odd way of choosing a name in his day. The parents would get a number of candles. They would give each candle a name. They would then light all the candles, and the child was given the name that had been attached to the candle that burned longest!

EVENING

Very often in the Bible a name is the expression of a parent's faith
Elijah means "Jahweh is my God," and this name was given to the young Elijah when Baal worship was very prevalent, and in giving it to their child the parents asserted their faith. The Puritans did this in a way that reduced the whole thing to the ridiculous. So Macaulay tells of the man called Tribulation Wholesome and another called Zeal-of-the-Lord Busy.

The most notorious example of this is the name that the Fleet Street leather-worker, himself called Praise-God Barebones, gave to his son. He called him If-Christ-had-not-died-for-thee-thou-wouldst-have-been-damned Barebones, a name which was, unfortunately, regularly shortened to Damned Barebones.

Perhaps the most unfortunate way of naming a child is to give the child, usually a girl, a name that is at the moment very popular. We have girls named in this way called Marina and Marlene and Marilyn. The unfortunate thing about that is that with a little mental arithmetic it is no trouble to guess the age of the person involved!

What's in a name? (2)

MORNING

Nowadays one of the commonest ways of naming a child is just to give the child a name you happen to like. My two granddaughters are called Jill and Karen, for no particular reason other than that their parents liked the names, although these two have other names which retain the family tradition.

I have often thought that it would be a good idea to delay naming a child finally until you could see how the child turned out! There is not much point in giving a name like Lynette to a chunky little tomboy! It is unfortunate to saddle a small, self-effacing, diffident little boy with the name Hector, greatest of the Trojans, or to call a young tough Lancelot or Gareth! There would be something to be said for waiting: for a name to fit.

Chrysostom, who did not like the candle method one little bit, was all for giving a child one of the great saints' names and then telling the child the story of the name so that he would become like the saint after whom he was called. I once knew a girl called Elizabeth Margaret, who was thrilled when she discovered that she bore the names of the most famous queens of Scotland and England. It is quite something to be able to tell a child to be true to his or her name.

EVENING

There have been some names too sacred to use, and some too terrible. In New Testament times Jesus was a very common name. It is the Greek form of the name Joshua, but it is easy to understand how both Jews and Christians ceased to use it. Just so, Judas was a common name, but in Christian circles it became very rare.

It is good to know the meaning of your name
Here are some examples:

> Margaret, the pear;
> Katherine, the pure one;
> Jane, the grace of God;
> Peter, the rock;
> Andrew, the courageous one;
> Alexander, the defender;
> Irene, peace.

It is good to have a name to live up to.

And we have a name which we all share — the name Christian. Christ's man, Christ's woman, Christ's boy, Christ's girl, the name of the person who has been with Jesus and who is on Jesus' side.

Delegate

MORNING

I am sure that no one is indispensable, and that no one should try to be

David Sheppard tells in his charming book. *Parson's Pitch*, about a rector who paid a return to his old congregation. A lady met him and said, "Oh, rector, the church has gone splendidly since you left!" And, you know, that was just about the greatest compliment she could have paid to a man's ministry.

Often a man has what is regarded as a highly successful and even a great ministry. And when he retires, or when he leaves to go to another charge, the whole life of the congregation almost collapses.

Attendances dwindle; the life of the congregation sags; life has gone out of the place. Now, in the real sense that was a bad ministry.

It was a ministry that made the life of the church dependent on one man.

Any person should pray to God that his congregation will go on even better and better when he leaves it. And it won't if he tries to make himself indispensable.

No congregation should ever be dependent on one man. And a ministry after which there is a sag and a collapse is essentially a failure.

EVENING

This leads to a second conviction.

I am sure that no man should ever try to do everything himself

I am bound to admit that this has been my own failure. I have always been bad at delegating work. And my good doctor has now taught me that work must be delegated.

Not to delegate work is to pass a vote of no confidence in one's staff and one's helpers. It may well be to cheat and rob someone else of the opportunity to do work that he ought to be made to do, and perhaps very much wishes to do. When anything becomes a one-man show, it is on the way to failure. Any wise leader and any faithful parson must learn to delegate work. He must see that his duty is not to do all the work himself, but to train others to do it with him.

Here we are very near to the heart of the failure of the church. The failure of a church may well be due to the fact that it has come to be centered far too much round one man, the minister or the parson, and that we have all delegated far too little work to the laymen and the laywomen whom we should have been training to do it.

Mistranslations

MORNING

The more you hear about the Bible, the more you are certain that it is a very wonderful book.

One of the extraordinary things about the Bible is that a man can take the wrong meaning out of it and still get himself something of infinite value for life.

Some time ago I received a letter from a person who has lived a hard life and who still has a great faith. It finished with thanksgiving and with a quotation from the Authorized Version of Psalm 139:13: "Thou hast possessed my reins."

Now I think that the writer of that letter took "reins" in the sense of the reins which guide a horse, and that he took it to mean that God had guided him all through life. And he was profoundly and devoutly thankful for the loving guidance of God which he found within this text.

But in point of fact that is not the meaning of this text at all. True, any ordinary twentieth-century person would almost certainly take the word reins in that sense, for it is the only sense of the word that he knows, but the word here literally means the kidneys; and the meaning of the text is that God knows a man because God has formed even his inmost and his most secret parts. The R.S.V. has: "Thou didst form my inward parts." Moffatt has: "Thou didst form my being." Goodspeed has: "Thou didst create my vitals".

EVENING

There is one Authorized Version mistranslation which Westcott once called "The most disastrous in idea and influence."

This is the notorious mistranslation in John 10:16. The Authorized Version runs: "Other sheep I have, which are not of this fold: them also I must bring, and they shall hear my voice; and there shall be one fold, and one shepherd."

In the English of the Authorized Version, the world "fold" occurs twice in that translation, but the words are quite different words in the Greek. In the first case the Greek word is *aule*, which is correctly translated "fold"; in the second case the Greek word is *poimne*, which means "flock", not "fold".

Any modern translation — Moffat; R.S.V.; Goodspeed — will show that the last part of the verse should read: "There will be one flock, one shepherd."

The seriousness of the mistranslation of *poimne* by the word "fold" is that this is the text which the Roman Catholics use to prove that there is only one church, and that outside that church there is no salvation. But Jesus said nothing like that. He said that there was one flock, which is a very different thing, for a flock could be distributed throughout many folds and still remain the same flock and the flock of the one owner.

There is nothing in this text which proves that there can be only one church.

Discipleship and in the background

MORNING

A thing to be worth giving must cost something

That which is done slickly and easily will have very little effect. It will sound slick and it will sound easy; it may gain admiration, but it will not move and penetrate the heart.

I do not envy the man who is not nervous before he preaches or conducts the public worship of God. I am quite sure that no musician, no actor, no preacher will ever give anything worthwhile unless he is tensed and strung up before he begins.

This is not a case of lack of faith; this is not a case of not committing oneself and one's message to God. It is simply that no man can ever rise to any heights without a humble sense of the greatness of the occasion, and what greater occasion can there be than to enter into the holy place in the company of the people of God?

When Jesus helped the woman with the issue of blood, he knew that power had gone out of him (Mark 5:30). He felt the strength drain out of him.

In order to help, there must be total involvement with and identification with the sufferer. Even so, Matthew quotes the prophetic words about Jesus: "He took our infirmities and bore our diseases." (Matthew 8:17; Isaiah 53:4).

To help others was for Jesus a costly thing. It cannot be otherwise for us.

EVENING

The more I think of life, the more I am impressed with our complete dependence on other people who do their job without ever being heard of.

I am quite sure that, far oftener than we do, we should stop to think how we are all bound up together in the bundle of life; that we should stop every now and again to remember our utter dependence on other people; that sometimes we should stop to look at our own work to see in it, whatever it is, not something by which we earn a wage, but something which is contributing to keeping the world going, and something in which we must therefore take a pride.

We ought at least sometimes not only to thank God for our work, and not only to thank him for health and strength and knowledge and skill to do it. We ought also to thank him for the great number of ordinary people doing ordinary jobs for they are the most important people of all. Without then no one would ever be able to get any work done at all.

Thank God for the men and women in the background.

Golden moments

MORNING

We had just come out of morning prayers in the wonderful chapel with the pulpit from which John Knox once preached. It was a beautiful July morning, with a sky of cloudless blue and a sun of summer heat shining on the green of the lawns and the colors of the flowerbeds. As I walked along the cloisters to the lecture room for the morning lecture, a lady turned to me and said, "if we could only stop the clock now!" It was a golden summer morning and she would have liked to stop just there. And I suppose that all of us have had times and moments when we would have liked time to stand still and things to remain forever just as they were.

But even the golden moment would lose its charm, if it were indefinitely extended, because the interest of life lies not in sameness but in contrast

It is hunger that gives food its taste. It is thirst that makes cool clear water taste like nectar.

It is tiredness that makes sleep a boon.

It is toil that makes rest the thing that the body and the mind long for.

It is loneliness that gives friendship its value.

It is the rain that gives the sunshine its joy.

It is the dark of the night that gives the dawn its glory.

It is parting that makes reuniting a happy thing.

EVENING

It is its very kaleidoscopic quality that makes life what it is

As Shelley had it in the famous simile:

Life, like a dome of many colored glass,
Stains the white radiance of Eternity.

If life consisted of only one kind of experience, then it would lose the very quality which makes it life. It is just because life is interwoven of sorrow and of joy, of gladness and of grief, of laughter and of tears, of silence and of song, that it is as it is. It is the many-colored texture of life that creates the fullness of life.

A life that had no experience of tears would lose something of infinite value, for, as has been well said, "all sunshine makes a desert". A life that never had a problem, a faith that never had a doubt, would be sadly lacking in something of infinite value.

However golden the moment, it is only golden when it is part of the ever-changing kaleidoscope of life, and when it is a moment and not a permanent condition.

The Lord's Day

MORNING

The use of the Lord's Day is still a living issue. I would like to do no more than state one or two facts from which discussion must start, and ask one or two questions which must be answered.

The Sabbath and the Lord's Day are different days

The Sabbath is Saturday and the Lord's Day is Sunday; the Sabbath is the last day of the week and the Lord's Day is the first day of the week. It is therefore clear that the Christian does not observe the Sabbath, and that terms such as "Sabbath school" are both wrong and misleading.

The Sabbath and the Lord's Day commemorate different events

The Sabbath commemorates the rest of God after the six days of creation; the Lord's Day commemorates the rising of Jesus from the dead.

The two days therefore have different objects

The object of the Sabbath is to perpetuate that rest, that cessation from work, which ended the work of creation. It will therefore be very properly a day when human work also stops.

The object of the Lord's Day is to perpetuate the experience of the resurrection.

The first reference to the Lord's Day is in Revelation 1:10

By the early second century, at least in Asia Minor, the observance of the Lord's Day was universal in the Christian church, and Ignatius could speak of Christians as no longer "sabbatising" but keeping the Lord's Day.

EVENING

Now for some positive feelings about the Day — not without their questions.

Since the Lord's Day demands that I remember God and Jesus and his resurrection, it will naturally and inevitably be the day of worship

But must I "go to church" to worship? Is the only way to worship to attend a church service?

The Lord's Day should surely be a family day; it may be the one day of the week when the whole family can meet and eat together

When I moved from the work of a parish to the work of a university, Sunday became to me the day when I was able to lunch with my family, the only day. The Sunday midday meal is not a joke. It comes near to being a sacrament.

Salvation

MORNING

The Christian assertion is that God cares; and the Christian proof of that is that God sent his Son Jesus Christ into the world to live and to die for men. The Christian believes that God is and that God cares.

We might say that the Christian believes that God is both mind and love. But the Christian assertion goes one step further. The Christian believes that God is not only love, but that he is also holiness.

If then God is holy, he cannot look with indifference at sin and disobedience to his law. Therefore, there enters into life the necessity for repentance.

Repentance is very liable to be misunderstood. Repentance involves three things. It involves the realization that we have done and been wrong. It involves sorrow that we have done and been wrong. Now it is here that, for some people at least, repentance stops; and, if it stops here, it is not repentance at all in the Christian sense of the term. For repentance involves not only realization and sorrow; it also involves reformation; it involves the amendment of life to match the realization and the sorrow. It involves fruits meet for repentance, as the Bible puts it. Repentance means sorrow for sin and new goodness.

For the Christian the whole matter centers in Jesus Christ

It is in Jesus Christ that we see what God is like; it is through him that we see what sin is like and that we are moved to repentance; it is through him that we know that sin is forgiven; and it is in him that we find the picture of the new life that we must live and the strength to live it.

The process of salvation begins, continues and ends in Jesus Christ.

EVENING

Billy Graham tells how in an American university he and his team had been answering questions for two hours. At the end of the session one of the students said to him, "All right, tell me what you want me to do. What must I do to find God?"

In answer Billy Graham laid down what you might call four steps on the way to salvation.

"First," he said, "you must be willing to admit that God is, that he exists.

"Second, you must accept the fact that he loves you in spite of your sins, failures, and rebellion. This is why he gave his Son to die on the Cross for you.

"Third, you must be willing to repent of your sin. Repentance means that you confess your transgression of moral law and that you are willing to give up your sin.

"Fourth, you must receive Jesus Christ as your own Lord and Savior."

It would be difficult to find a better summary of the way of salvation.

Training

MORNING

I have come across a very remarkable and interesting document. It is the outline for the training of Salvation Army officers, put together by Mrs. General Booth in 1884,and contained in the fourth, volume of the *History of the Salvation Army*.

The training of the Salvation Army officer had six aims in it.

First, we begin with the heart

If the heart is not right, the service cannot be right, therefore, the heart comes first. The first essential for the ministry is a heart that has responded in love to the love of God in Jesus Christ.

Second, we try to train the head

The Salvation Army planners saw quite clearly that the officer must in his knowledge be in advance of those whom he seeks to teach. An academic training is an essential, for youth especially will only listen to those whom it can respect.

Third, we teach them how to appeal to the consciences of the people

The Salvation Army officer is taught to present a God who is love, but also a God of justice and of judgment. The preacher has to learn to tell men, not what they want to hear but what they need to hear; not to lull them comfortably to sleep with an easy gospel, but to stab them broad awake with a Gospel which condemns that sin for which it brings the remedy.

EVENING

Fourth, we teach them how to inspire hope in the most hopeless

The Salvation Army has always gloriously walked in the footsteps of that Jesus who was the friend of outcasts and of sinners.

Fifth, we try to show them how to exhibit the Savior as a full and sufficient sacrifice for sin.

This salvation is seen, not only in terms of forgiveness for past sin, but also in terms of strength in the future to conquer sin and to overcome temptation.

Sixth, we teach them how to utilize the trophies they may be permitted to win

By this Mrs. Booth meant that it was the task of the Salvation Army officer to turn every converted man into a converter of others.

To this day it, it would be difficult to better this scheme. It has in it the essence of a training that is religious, intellectual, theological and practical, and those who legislate for the training of the ministry today might still do worse than study it.

Too busy

MORNING

Often we are too busy talking to listen
Really good talkers may be scarce, but really good listeners are much more scarce. We are usually much more eager to tell people what we think and what we have done than we are to listen to what they think and what they have done. Most people don't really want a dialogue. What they want is a monologue, with a few polite murmurs of respectful agreement just to keep things going.

Often we are too busy earning a living to live
We live in a society in which there are so many things to buy, and things to buy cost money. And so you get a man working so much overtime, or doing so many money-earning small jobs that he has hardly time to know his family. Or you get the woman going out to work and — not always, but certainly sometimes — neglecting the children God gave her and the home of which she ought to be the center. They are so busy earning a living that they forget how to live.

Be careful you are not too busy to have time for the things that matter.

EVENING

Life is full of occasions when we are too busy to remember the most important things of all.

Often we are too busy arguing together to pray together
The odium theologicum, the hatred of theologians for each other, is notorious. There are few spheres of life in which there is such violent argument as there is in theology. There are even certain theologians who will attack a man's character because they do not agree with his opinions.

Often we are too busy planning to think
It is very easy to get into a state of mind when we think that action as such is the most important thing in life.

There are some people whose principle of life is, "Do something". It doesn't really matter what it is, so long as we do something. Such an attitude is rather like hailing a taxi and saying to the driver, "Drive like fury," and when he says, "Where?" saying "It doesn't matter where, so long as you drive like fury."

Of course it is true that too much deliberation paralyses action: but it would save a lot of trouble and it would make action much more effective if we really thought before we acted.

Time spent in thinking is never time wasted.

The unseen cloud

MORNING

I have always remembered the thrill I had in preaching in the University Chapel in St. Andrews and in being told that the very pulpit in which I was to stand had been the pulpit of John Knox. As every day in my own classroom I step on to the rostrum. I remember the men who went before me in that New Testament classroom—A. B. Bruce, James Denney, W. M. Macgregor, O. H. C. Macgregor — what a company!

Now when this kind of thing happens it has two effects.

It makes one very humble

It gives one a feeling of complete astonishment that one should be walking in such a company. There is nothing like the memory of the unseen cloud to keep us humble.

Do we never sometimes stop to think of the great souls who were within this church of ours, the saints, the martyrs and the prophets who were part of it, who maybe worshipped in our very town and buildings? Do we never think of the succession in which the humblest Christian walks? And do we never think of how unworthy we are of all that has gone before? To remember the unseen cloud is to be humbled to the dust.

EVENING

But to remember the unseen cloud is to be more than humbled

It is equally to he challenged. We have entered into the labors of other men; we must so labor that other men may enter into ours. The generations are each like links in a chain, and we must surely see to it that ours is not the weak link.

Memory is always a challenge. Am I lessening or am I enhancing the tradition which has come down to me? Do I bring joy or sorrow to the unseen cloud as they look down? When I meet them on the other side of death, will I have to meet their eyes with pride or with shame?

No man lives to himself, and no man dies to himself, and no man can honorably forget those who have given him what he has and in whose footsteps he walks.

If I am humbled and if I am challenged by the memory of the unseen cloud, then still another thing emerges

I can only be true to them, I can only not fail them, I can only walk in their company if I in my life have the same daily and hourly dependence on Jesus Christ that they had.

The generations rise and pass away in the unending panorama of the years, but Jesus Christ is the same yesterday today and for ever (Hebrews 13:8). His arm is not shortened, and his power is not grown less. His presence is still with us as it was with them, mighty to help and mighty to save.

Christian qualities

MORNING

In regard to people, the Christian life should be characterized by what the Bible, in the Authorized Version, calls "charity".

Maybe the best modern equivalent of "charity" is kindness. The Christian should be kind in his judgments: kind in his speech; and kind in his actions. It is characteristic of the world to think the worst, and put the worst construction and interpretation on any action.

It is characteristic of the world to say the cruel and the cutting thing; it is characteristic of the world to be so taken up with self that it has little time for kindness to others. But the judgments, the words, and the deeds of the Christian are kind.

In regard to self, the Christian life should be characterized by humility

There are few things so common in this life as conceit, and there are few of us who are not fairly well pleased with ourselves. Humility really means the extinction of self. It is only when self is extinguished that a man can learn, for the first condition of learning is the admission of our own ignorance. Above all, it is only when self is extinguished that a man can really see the beauty and the necessity of service, and that he can discover that the essence of life is not in being served by others but in serving others. The world wants to make use of others for its own purposes; the Christian wants to be used for the purposes of God.

EVENING

John W. Doberstein in *The Minister's Prayer Book*, makes three quotations, one after another, all on the same subject,

Of the first two the author is nameless! "The life of the clergyman is the book of the layman." "The life of the clergyman is the gospel of the people."

The third is from Kierkegaard: "Order the parsons to be silent on Sundays. What is there left? The essential things remain: their lives, the daily life which the parsons preach. Would you then get the impression by watching them that it was Christianity they were preaching?"

These three quotations are all saying something that has been said over and over again. They are saying that the most effective sermon is a life; they are saying that Christianity must be demonstrated in action rather than commended in

words.

These three quotations all speak specifically of the parson. But this is to limit the matter far too much.

In regard to life, the Christian life should be characterized by serenity. There should be in the life of the Christian a certain calm. A worried Christian is a contradiction in terms.

Needs to meet

MORNING

What would you say is the great characteristic of the work of a minister of the church?

Raymond Calkins tells how, in the old provincial town of Saumur in France, there stood the great and ancient Roman church of St. Peter. At its entrance, in the pre-war days, there stood a placard the object of which was to challenge young men to enter the ministry. The placard said: "There are just four days in anyone's life: birth, confirmation, marriage, death. Would you not like to be the one who would be needed on all four of those days?"

The one who would be needed. Here should be the first great characteristic of the ministry. The minister is a man dedicated to the needs of men. He is involved with his people in the great moments of joy and of sorrow: like Ezekiel, he sits where they sit. His people need him in their joys and in their sorrows alike. The true minister is one who is needed by his people.

On the arch of the gate of the seminary at Wittenburg there is an inscription directed towards students for the ministry. The inscription is a saying of Luther's: "Let no one give up the faith that God wants to do a deed through him." So then in the second place a minister is a *man whom God wants to use and who wants to be used.*

EVENING

There is a third thing about the minister.

One of the great Scottish preachers in the days of James VI was Robert Bruce. "No man, since the apostles," they said of him, "spake with such power."

Once Bruce was preaching in Larbert, as Adam Bumet tells. He was in the vestry before the service and someone was sent to fetch him when the time was near. The person who was sent returned saying that he did not know when Mr. Bruce would be free to come . . .

There was somebody with him, for he heard him many times say with the greatest seriousness that he would not, he could not, go unless he came with him, and that he would not go alone; but the Other did not seem to answer. And when at last he came out of the vestry to preach, and after he had taken that service that day, it was said of him that "he was singularly assisted".

Here then is the third and the dominating fact about the minister. He is a man who, if he will have it so, is always singularly assisted. God does not call any man to a task, and then leave him alone to do it. With the vision comes the power; with the call comes the strength.

Hard work

MORNING

Tolstoy somewhere has a story of a nobleman who always kept open house. At evening anyone could come and have a meal at his open and hospitable table. And when anyone came, he was never turned away, but there was one test. The nobleman always said, "Show me your hands," and, if the hands were rough and scarred with toil, then the man was given a seat of honor at the top of the table, but if the hands were soft and flabby, then his place was low at the foot of the table.

It always takes self-discipline to be a workman who has no need to be ashamed, and I am certain that there is no job where that self-discipline is more essential and yet harder than in the work of the ministry.

Let us remember that the man who is prepared to do an honest day's work is indeed the conqueror. There are some victories that we cannot all win; but the victory of honest work is a victory that is open to all to win.

EVENING

Apolo Kivebulaya was one of the great saints of the African church and in the book *African Saint,* Anne Luck has told his story.

One of the most characteristic stories of him tells how he arrived at Mboga in the Congo. He was not the first Christian missionary to arrive there. Two African missionaries had been there before him, but they had had to leave, because people would not give them any food. These two former missionaries had been members of the proud Baganda tribe in which menial work is for women and slaves. So, when the people of Mboga refused them food: they had been far too proud to cultivate the land themselves and so they had to starve or go.

Apolo knew this, and he was well prepared to grow his own food. As he passed through the patches of forest on his way to Mboga. he stopped to cut some hoe handles to be ready to get to work on some patch of ground whenever he arrived. When Tabaro, the ruler of Mboga, saw Apolo coming into the village carrying his hoe handles at the ready he said, "Here is a man who is going to conquer."

A hoe handle may be an odd sign for a conqueror, and an odd crest for a victor, but the very sight of it marked out Apolo as the man who would conquer. And why? For the simple yet sufficient reason that here was a man who was clearly prepared to do a day's honest work.

It is hardly an exaggeration to say that what the world needs more than anything else is men who are ready and prepared and willing to do an honest day's work.

SEPTEMBER 12

(R)evolution

MORNING

Christopher Maude Chavasse, who was Bishop of Rochester, once spoke about what was going to happen after the Second World War. He was thinking about the brave new world that everyone hoped would be born. He was remembering too the failure to build any kind of new world after the First World War, which he so well remembered. So he said that when it came to facing a new situation, people had three different attitudes — there was the reactionary attitude; there was the revolutionary attitude; and there was the evolutionary attitude.

There is the reactionary attitude
The reactionary attitude resents all change. It wishes to keep things as they are. It characteristically looks backward; and it has a built-in tendency to say "No" when any new course of action is suggested.

Very often, perhaps even as a general rule, the reactionary attitude springs from the determination to hold on to some state of privilege. The reactionary attitude was 'specially evident when, thirty or forty years ago, the social differences began to be ironed out.

That reactionary attitude is rampant in the church. The reactionary attitude lives in the past; it tries to stop the tide of progress. Change accepted is good; change refused can turn to explosive destructiveness.

EVENING

There is the revolutionary attitude
A revolution may be a good thing; it may in fact be an essential thing. All great nations have, somewhere in their history, a revolution.

But there is one thing to remember about a revolution — it is necessarily destructive — and it is necessarily temporary. It is not possible to live in a permanent revolution. A revolution can never become routine. A revolution could be compared to a demolition squad. Here is some slum-infested area; a new transformation is dreamed of and worked out; the demolition squad is called in. That is the revolution. But you do not leave the area looking as if it had been hit by high explosive. You begin to raise the new buildings out of the rubble.

We come to the evolutionary attitude, which is the attitude that is prepared to grow
It is the attitude that is constantly willing to adjust itself to the challenge of changing circumstance.

Change and growth are the characteristics of life. The church should be a growing and a changing church. Since the grace of God is sufficient for all things, the church can find the grace to deal with any situation — if it is living enough and flexible enough to take it.

Blame

MORNING

Usually we have no difficulty in finding someone or something to whom or which the blame may be attached.

We blame other people for our sins and our mistakes

We blame someone else's influence for the mistake we have made, or for the trouble in which we have found ourselves. When Burns as a young man went to Irvine to learn flax dressing, he fell in with an older man who led him astray. He said afterwards, "His friendship did me a mischief."

It is no doubt true, but it is also true that no one needs to say "Yes" to someone else's suggestions and no one needs to yield to someone else's seductions.

No one would wish to deny or to belittle the evil influence that a bad association can cause, but even in such a circumstance a man has still to say "Yes" to the tempting voice, and he might say "No".

EVENING

We blame life for our sins and our mistakes

Sometimes we think that if life had been different there would have been things we would not have done and mistakes we would not have made. But the truth is that, if we are that kind of person, if life had been different we would simply have made other mistakes to match other circumstances.

Sometimes we say, "It's my nature. I can't change myself." But if there is any truth in the Christian claim at all, then any man who will submit to Jesus Christ can be changed and made new. We cannot change ourselves, but we can submit to being changed. We can receive grace to live triumphantly in any circumstances and we can receive grace to make any life new.

We almost blame our sins and our mistakes on God

Bums wrote:

Thou knowest thou hast formed me
With passions wild and strong,
And listening to their witching voice
Has often led me wrong,

as if to say that, if God had made him differently, he would not have made the mistakes he did make. But a man is not so much what God made him as he is what he has made himself.

There can be neither forgiveness nor amendment until we admit our own fault and say that we are sorry. The way to forgiveness and to betterment begins when we learn to say, "God, be merciful to me a sinner!" (Luke 18:13).

Women and men

MORNING

One day, Themistocles, the great Greek statesman and soldier, the leader of Athens, was looking at his baby son. "Do you know," he said to the person who was with him, "that little baby is the ruler of Greece!"

The friend asked him to explain this astonishing statement. "Well," said Themistocles, "this baby rules his mother; his mother rules me; I rule the Athenians; and the Athenians rule Greece; therefore this baby is the ruler of the whole of Greece!"

So Themistocles was another man fortunate enough to be ruled by his wife.

There are good reasons why the mother is bound to be the ruler of every home. She is concerned with the most essential things. The essential things are the simple things. The food, and health, the warmth, the comfort of the family are in the mother's hands. It is the hardest job of all; it never stops; there will be sheer disaster if ever women want an eight-hour day and a five-day week, and if they demand overtime for any hours worked in the home beyond these!

EVENING

What are the qualities that you would expect a real man to possess?

I would want him to possess vitality

Julian was the Roman Emperor who wanted to put the clock back. By this time Christianity had been accepted, but he wanted to go back to the old ways and the old pagan gods. And his complaint, as Ibsen put it into his mouth, was like this: "Have you looked at those Christians closely? Hollow-eyed, pale-cheeked, flat-breasted all; they brood their lives away, unspurred by ambition; the sun shines for them but they do not see it; the earth offers them its fullness but they desire it not: all their desire is to renounce and suffer and die." Swinburne turned the words of the same Julian into verse:

> Thou hast conquered, O pale Galilean;
> The world has grown grey from Thy breath.

Julian — and Ibsen and Swinburne agreed with him — saw in Christianity a colorless and anemic thing. And the trouble is that it is often too true. The Christian church is so often represented by people who are lack-luster and depressed and depressing, preaching the Good News, as someone has said, like a wireless announcer announcing a deep depression off Ireland.

Encouragement and criticism

MORNING

Canon A. C. Deane, in his autobiography *Times Remembered*, tells of his old English teacher, a Mr. Barkworth. When he corrected "he did not only score and underline; he rewrote and transformed. He always wrote encouraging comments. One of these I have never forgotten, a scribble at the foot of the page which read: 'Capital! Read all the good English you can, take pains, and presently you will do something worth doing'."

You can imagine what the encouragement meant to a boy of twelve or thirteen who was anxious to become a writer. Anyone who has reached my age will, during his life, have received a prodigious quantity of advice, for which, as he looks back, he is still grateful. Yet his warmest gratitude will be felt for those who gave him little advice but real encouragement.

It was said of Florence Allshorn, the great teacher, that when she had to criticize, she did it with her arm round you, so that the very criticism was an encouragement.

It is a terrible thing to quench the light in someone's eyes.

Encourage!

EVENING

To accept such criticism we need three things.

We need humility
The man who cannot conceive that he is ever wrong is a sorry case.

We need to love truth more than we love self
When we resent criticism, we are in effect more concerned with the preservation of our self-esteem than we are with the truth — and that is the way to lose truth.

We need to love progress more than a static immobility
To refuse to listen to criticism is never to move, never to advance, never to improve—and that is death in life.

The greatest men and the greatest scholars welcomed criticism.

That is why they were great.

The happy critics

MORNING

On any grounds, William Tyndale is a prince of translators. In the Preface to the reader in his 1534 translation he writes:

"As concerning all that I have translated or otherwise written, I beseech all men to read it for that purpose I wrote it: even to bring them to the knowledge of the scripture . . . And where they find faults let them shew it to me, if they be nigh, or write to me if they be far off: or write openly against it and improve it, and I promise them, if I perceive that their reasons conclude (i.e. are conclusive) I will confess mine ignorance openly."

Here is the great scholar and translator asking for criticism and promising to welcome it when it comes.

In almost the next year another man who has written his name on the English Bible published his translation, and in his address to the Christian reader Miles Coverdale wrote:

"Lowly and faithfully I have followed my interpreters, and that under correction. And if I have failed anywhere (as there is no man but misseth in something) love shall construe all to the best without any perverse judgment . . . If thou (the reader) hast knowledge therefore to judge where my fault is made, I doubt not but thou wilt help to amend it, if love be joined with knowledge. However whereinsoever I can perceive by myself, or by the information of some one else, that I have failed (as it is no wonder), I shall now by the help of God overlook it better (revise it), and amend it."

Here is a second great translator asking for criticism and welcoming it.

EVENING

As a contrast to Tyndale and Coverdale — and remembering that he is writing in jest — Ronald Knox, one of the greatest of modern translators, writes in the preface to his book *On Englishing the Bible*:

"I have long since given up protesting when controversialists misquote me, or newspaper columnists credit me with authorship of limericks that are none of mine. But if you question a rendering of mine in the New Testament, you come up against a parental instinct hardly less ferocious than that of a mother bear. I shall smile it off, no doubt, in conversation, but you have lost marks."

No one likes the criticism of ignorance, or the criticism that is designed to hurt; but wise and kindly criticism is something of infinite value.

Determination

MORNING

A certain newspaper had an interesting article on those unfortunate people who suffer from kleptomania, that twist in a mind which drives a person to put out his hands and take what he should not take.

It appears that women suffer from this strange urge far more than men. A psychologist set down some useful advice to people so tempted and so afflicted.

Clasp your hands together as tightly as you can, interlocking the fingers. It symbolizes determination not to stretch out your hands to crime. As such it can be a powerful psychological aid.

Then go to a quiet corner and think hard of your husband and children, of how they would feel if, in the week before Christmas, you appeared in a dock and shamed them before the world.

Best of all, get out of the store immediately and away from these tempting counters. A great man once said that he could resist anything—but temptation. That is true for many of us.

EVENING

Here is a prescription for the defeat of temptation. In it it has three most valuable ingredients, but the greatest and most powerful ingredient of all is missing.

There are three ways to beat temptation: by determination, by remembering those we love and by never flirting with it.

Determination

Determination is a strong weapon wherewith to defeat temptation.

There is a world of difference between having a vague desire to do something fine, or a lurking sense that we should not do something, and an utter and deliberate determination to do it or not to do it.

The cases in which we really and fully and finally make up our minds about anything are far too few.

Practice the art of making up your mind!

Temptations

MORNING

Here are the two other ingredients present in our prescription for temptation.

The memory of those we love is a powerful aid wherewith to resist temptation

There is nothing that so delights those who love us as when we do well. There is nothing that so hurts them as when we do badly.

Even if a man has a certain right to do what he likes with his own life, he never has any right to break someone else's heart

Never flirt with temptation

It is an error of judgment to allow ourselves to think about the forbidden thing, to look at it, to cast longing eyes upon it. To avoid it, to stay as far from it as possible is neither weakness nor cowardice. It is common sense.

There are times when the business of life means that we cannot escape tempting things but to linger needlessly in their presence is to court disaster.

EVENING

The greatest of all the ingredients in this prescription is however missing. For prayer is the greatest of all defenses against temptation.

Edgar N. Jackson, in an excellent book on preaching entitled *Preaching to People's Needs*, writes this: "One psychiatrist has reported that though he himself does not pretend to be a religious man, he cannot help being impressed by the fact that, in twenty-five years of active practice in New York City, he has never had a patient who really knew how to pray."

It was his experience that it was the people who did not know how to pray who got life all tangled and messed up.

When we are in difficulty there is no help like the help of God, and no safeguard like the memory of the living and ever- present Christ. The human will can prove weak. Even the thought of those who love us can fail to restrain our passions. There are times when escape seems impossible.

Then is the time to remember that we do not fight this battle in our own strength, and that we do not struggle alone.

He who knew temptation in the wilderness and in the garden is with us.

In that presence alone is the grace which can make us clean and keep us clean.

The dignity of work

MORNING

Jesus was a man who worked with his hands. He was thirty-three when he died upon his Cross and for thirty of his thirty-three years he was connected with the carpenter's shop in Nazareth.

There is an old legend that tells how Jesus was the best maker of ox-yokes in the whole of Galilee, and how people from far and wide came to Nazareth to buy the ox-yokes that Jesus of Nazareth made, for they were the best of all.

One of the most famous and beautiful things that Jesus ever said goes back to the days when he was a carpenter. "My yoke is easy," said Jesus, "and my burden is light" (Matt 11:30).

The Greek word for "easy" is *chrestos*, and *chrestos* really means "well-fitting".

In Palestine ox-yokes were made of wood. The ox would be brought to the carpenter's shop and its measurements taken. The yoke would be blocked out, and then the ox would be brought back for a fit-on. This curve would be deepened, that rough place would be smoothed until the yoke fitted so exactly that it would never gall the backs of the patient beasts.

That is the kind of work Jesus did.

In those days, shops had their signs over them just as they have now; and it has been suggested that the sign above the shop of Jesus was a wooden ox-yoke, with the words painted upon it: "My yokes fit well."

Jesus was not ashamed to work with his hands.

EVENING

Thomas Carlyle was one of the most voluminous of authors. His father, a good and godly man and an elder of the Kirk, was a stonemason in Scotland.

There are places in Dumfriesshire where the bridges which Carlyle's father built still stand.

Carlyle said that he would rather have built one of his father's bridges than have written all his own books.

Thomas Carlyle did not despise a man who worked with his hands.

God save us all from that false sense of values which issues in that senseless snobbery which looks down on the man who works with his hands.

It was the hands of a working man that were nailed to the Cross on Calvary's hill.

Lessons on prayer

MORNING

There is much to be learned from the physical attitude of men when they pray.

Jesus told of a tax-gatherer who came to the Temple to pray

He would not even dare to lift up his eyes to heaven, but beat upon his breast, saying: "God be merciful to me a sinner" (Luke 18:13).

That is the prayer of the *downcast head*; that is t*he prayer of the heart that is ashamed.* That is the prayer of the man who has sinned, and who is seeking only the mercy of God.

No man can even think of approaching God without thinking of how unworthy he is to enter into the presence of the God who is of purer eyes than to behold iniquity.

Once Abraham Lincoln said: "I have often been driven to my knees in prayer because I had nowhere else to go."

That is the prayer of the downcast head; that is the prayer of the bended knee and the outstretched hand, the prayer of the man for whom there is nothing left to say but: "God help me! God help me!"

EVENING

Once Jesus prayed to God in the garden of Gethsemane and when he prayed his sweat was as drops of blood

At that moment the Cross was facing Jesus. He was only thirty-three. No man wishes to die at thirty-three, and least of all does he wish to die upon a cross.

That *is the prayer of the man who wrestles in prayer.*

Sometimes we know what is right, but it is desperately hard to do it.

Sometimes we have to face things that are apparently impossible to face.

Sometimes a man has to wrestle in an agony of prayer until in the end he can say: "Thy will be done."

Sometimes a prayer can be an agony of a struggle to gain that self-conquest which will make us accept the will of God. But when we do reach acceptance, then comes peace.

"More things are wrought by prayer than this world dreams of," said Tennyson.

There is a prayer for every moment and for every need in life.

No matter what a man's need may be, that need will find its answer in God.

SEPTEMBER 21

Defender of the faith

MORNING

In ancient Greece the Spartans were always proverbial for their courage. They might lack the finer virtues of the more cultured Athenians, but no one ever questioned their courage and their loyalty.

In his life of Lycurgus, the Spartan king, Plutarch tells a great story.

There was a certain Spartan wrestler competing at the Olympic Games. An attempt was made to buy him off by the offer of a large sum of money. He completely refused it. After a long struggle he outwrestled his opponent and won his victory.

He was asked: "What advantage, O Spartan, have you gained from your victory?" He answered with a smile: "I shall stand in front of my king when I fight our enemies."

The greatest privilege of which the Spartan could conceive was to defend his king, if need be with his life, in the day of battle.

It must be so with the Christian.

The greatest privilege the Christian has is the privilege of being the defender of the faith, the champion of Jesus Christ.

EVENING

Are you a defender of the faith?

We are always faced with the temptation to play down our Christianity

We are faced with the temptation, if not to attempt to conceal, at least not to stress the fact that we are Christian, and that we belong to Jesus Christ.

We may fear the laughter of the world. We may fear to be different from others. But the real Christian is the man who in any company says along with Paul: "I am not ashamed of the gospel of Christ" (Romans 1:16).

The Christian must defend the faith in his words and with his arguments

The opponents of Christianity know what they believe. They have been drilled and schooled into learning the tenets of the particular political or philosophical faith which they happen to profess.

Too often the Christian is a man who, to put it bluntly, does not really know what he believes.

Too often he is a man who has never even tried to think things out for himself.

Too often the church has forgotten her teaching ministry, and has sent out her members ill-equipped to meet the arguments and the criticisms of the opponents of the church and the critics of Christianity.

If the Christian is to be a true defender of the faith, he must be ready to give to all who ask him a reason for the hope that is in him (1 Peter 3:15).

Rules for work

MORNING

I have had a letter from "Raymond". He asks me how I get my work done! There are three rules that I want to mention.

(1) My first rule is BEGIN EARLY

I have just been looking at a concordance, and I find that the phrase "early in the morning" occurs about forty times!

Raymond is a Methodist, so it is easy to remind him that John Wesley preached forty-two thousand sermons in fifty-three years, that he averaged four thousand five hundred miles per year in travel, and that he wrote or edited four hundred and fifty books.

John always got up at 4.30 a.m.! I can't claim to emulate that! But, though my classes don't normally begin till 11.30 a.m., I always leave home at 8 a.m., getting to my desk at the University by 8.30 a.m. Without these three morning hours, I can honestly say that I would not get any work done at all!

(2) My second rule is KEEP GOING!

One of the greatest time-wasters, I find, is the habit we have of saying: "I've only got twenty-five minutes. It's not worth starting." But I find it is always worth starting!

To return to John Wesley, he did most of his reading on horseback!

It is amazing how much you can get done in the odd quarter-hour or half-hour. There is no unit of time that cannot be used.

EVENING

(3) My third rule is KEEP TO SCHEDULE!

I have no use for the idea of waiting for inspiration! When I was a minister in a parish, I don't think I ever wrote a sermon after Thursday morning.

Beverley Nichols tells of a conversation he had with Sir Winston Churchill. Churchill asked him how long it took to write "Prelude". Nichols said that it was written in spasms over five months.

Churchill asked if he did not write regularly. Nichols said he had to wait for the right mood.

"Nonsense," said Churchill. "You should go to your room at 9 a.m. each day and say 'I'm going to write for four hours'."

"Suppose you can't," said Nichols.

Churchill replied: "You've got to get over that. If you sit waiting for inspiration, you'll wait till you are an old man."

He went on: "Writing is like any other job . . . like marching an army . . . If you sit down and wait till the weather is suitable, you won't get very far with your troops. Kick yourself, irritate yourself, but write. It's the only way."

Words! Words! Words!

MORNING

I am recovering from an attack of speechlessness. A week ago I lost my voice completely and could only communicate with the outside world in a hoarse and almost inaudible whisper. This failure of voice came upon me quite suddenly in the middle of a day's work.

On the way home I thought it would be a good idea if I called in at a chemist's shop and obtained something to gargle with; and so I did. I explained to the girl behind the counter what I wanted. I didn't need to tell her that I had lost my voice! She recommended what she thought would be most helpful.

As she wrapped up the bottle and handed it across the counter to me and took my money, she smiled brightly, and said: "You must have been talking too much!"

Her diagnosis was correct—far more correct than she knew, and correct in a far deeper way than she meant, because the basic trouble with every one of us is that we talk too much.

Torrents of talk inundate this world. Floods of the highest sentiments flow over the world. Oceans of good advice are poured out. Cataracts of sermons are unleashed.

There is enough Christian talk in this world to reform half a dozen worlds! The trouble is that for all the talk there is so little action!

EVENING

I know that I am going to be accused of being a moralist, and of preaching that Christianity consists of doing good. I am quite content to be so accused, for that is what Jesus said.

Jesus insisted: "By their fruits ye shall know them. Not everyone that saith unto me. Lord, Lord, shall enter into the kingdom of heaven; but he that doeth the will of my Father which is in heaven" (Matthew 7:20,21).

When Jesus painted a picture of the judgment of God, the basic question was simply had or had not a man been kind (Matthew 25:31-46).

James, whose epistle had the ill-fortune to be called "a right strawy epistle" by Martin Luther, laid it down: "Pure religion and undefiled before God and the Father is this, to visit the fatherless and the widows in their affliction, and to keep himself unspotted from the world" (James 1:27).

This is a call, not for words, but for action.

What did it do?

MORNING

Thomas Chalmers was one of Scotland's great orators. After a masterly speech in the General Assembly he was congratulated by all his friends. "Yes," he answered, "but what did it do?"

Had the words simply gone whistling down the wind?

There never was a time when religion was so much discussed as it is today. But someone has said that half the trouble is that people tend to think that they are being religious when they are discussing religious questions.

The church is littered with discussion groups — and discussion groups can be intensely valuable, but they are not valuable if people are sitting talking when they ought to be acting, and if they do not result in any action to follow the discussion.

EVENING

Florence Allshorn was one of the great missionary teachers. She was principal of a great women's missionary college. She was always infuriated by the type of person who suddenly discovered that her quiet time for prayer was due just when the greasy dishes were waiting to be washed in the kitchen.

There is not much virtue in discussing or even in praying when we ought to be giving a hand to make someone's work easier about the house.

Robert Louis Stevenson turned on someone who expressed the highest sentiments with no accompanying action with the words: "I cannot hear what you say for listening to what you are."

Am I being a little unfair? Perhaps. But this I do know —that people will remember a minister's kindness in a time of trouble when they have forgotten every sermon that he ever preached.

I also know that many of the finest advertisements for Christianity I have ever known would have been like fish out of water at a discussion circle which was sunning itself in its own intellectual brilliance.

I wouldn't say I was the only one who produced too many words and too few deeds to fit them.

Grin and bear it

MORNING

A minister I knew joined the Royal Navy in the First World War. He is a big man, easily the biggest in his squad. So he soon found himself with the nickname "Lofty".

In charge of the squad there was a cockney petty officer. This petty officer was also a champion navy boxer. He was a small man, and he wanted some special practice before a certain tournament.

It struck the petty officer that Lofty was the very man to give him some practice. The fact that Lofty was big and he was small would make the practice all the more useful.

He asked my friend if he would put on the gloves with him. The latter said he had never boxed in his life, but he would try it if he liked. So he put on the gloves, and the petty officer told him to bore in and try to hit him. Lofty bore in all right, but left himself wide open. The petty officer stopped him, and told him to cover up his chin, or he might get hurt.

They started again. This time Lofty's wide open chin was too much of a temptation for the cockney champion and he hit Lofty, and hit him so hard that Lofty hit the ground. Lofty jumped up ruefully rubbing his chin.

The little petty officer stopped him: "Lofty," he said, "if ever you're boxing, remember one thing — and don't forget it. Don't ever let your opponent see that you're hurt."

It is good advice for a boxer —and for any man.

EVENING

Don't ever let them see that you're hurt. The world seems to be so full of the people who are always getting hurt and telling all the world about it.

A man doesn't get his own way in a committee meeting — and he just won't play any more.

A church member doesn't get things done the way he thinks they should be done — and he constitutes himself a kind of permanent opposition in the church.

A choir member doesn't get the solo he or she thinks was due—and the voice that once made music becomes huffily silent.

Someone is not thanked for some bit of service, someone is accidentally omitted in a vote of thanks — and that person's feelings are not only hurt, they are lacerated, and the whole community hears about it. Someone is not invited to the platform party — and the injured one has a grievance which all the world can see. Churches are all too full of people who get hurt and let everyone see it and know it.

There is a phrase which tells us "to grin and bear it". It is good advice.

Be an example

MORNING

I stepped off a bus, my journey ended. Without thinking what I was doing, I threw my ticket away.

I was hurrying away when my eye was caught by an oldish man who had stepped off the same bus. He also had a bus ticket in his hand. But he didn't throw his away. He walked over to the little wire basket for litter which was attached to the nearest lighting standard and neatly dropped it in.

I found myself then running after my thrown-away ticket, retrieving it from the pavement and also neatly placing it in the litter basket.

What a power of good an example can be!

Human nature is essentially suggestible. King Edward accidentally left the bottom button of his waistcoat unfastened, and before very long, every well-dressed man was doing the same.

A certain statesman wears a certain kind of hat, and soon the hat becomes the uniform of the well-dressed businessman.

A certain film star adopts a certain hairstyle, and soon all women are doing their hair in the same way.

A certain comedian develops a certain catchword, and soon everybody is repeating it.

A certain "royal" uses a certain gesture, and soon everyone is copying it.

Example is one of the most powerful forces in this world.

EVENING

H. L. Gee tells of a moving event which happened in the days of Dunkirk.

On the quay of an English port a number of French troops had been disembarked. The spirit had gone out of them, and they were lying there in a dull lethargy of despair, for they knew that they had lost, not a campaign, but their country.

Another ship came in, and from it there embarked a detachment of the Brigade of Guards. The Guards" discipline had never relaxed. In so far as it was possible their uniforms were still perfect and their equipment precisely as it ought to be. On the quay they formed up, and marched away as if they had been changing the guard.

Some of the Frenchmen looked up listlessly. Slowly in their eyes a light began to be reborn. Stiffly they rose, squared their shoulders, and marched off after the Guards and before that movement had finished every one of the Frenchmen bad fallen in and was on the march.

The power of an example had changed dispirited, defeated men into men who had got back their hope and their self-respect.

Responsibility and generosity

MORNING

I do not think that we realize that someone is always watching us.

The little boy watches the big boy, and models himself upon turn.

The child watches his father or mother, and unconsciously copies his or her mannerisms and actions.

The Sunday school scholar watches his or her teacher.

We all remember how the Pied Piper of Hamelin piped the children away, and as someone has put it, "Everyone pipes for the feet of someone to follow".

When Paul was writing to Titus, he told him what to say to other people about their Christian duty, and then he says: "In all things show yourself a pattern, a type, an example of good works" (Titus 2:7).

When he writes to Timothy, he says: "Be thou an example to the believers, in word, in conduct, in love, in spirit, in faith, in purity" (1 Timothy 4:12).

Here is our responsibility.

EVENING

My wife attended a city clinic in Glasgow at one time for treatment for fibrositis. She had many talks with an old lady who came to the clinic from the other side of the city. As they were talking one day, the old lady asked my wife if she could lend her a penny.

In the afternoon old age pensioners get a concession fare on the tramcars, and the old lady had nothing but one single pound note, and she wanted the penny to pay her penny fare home on the tramcar, because she did not wish to bother the tram conductress by presenting her with a pound note for a penny fare.

My wife opened her purse and gave the old lady the penny she wanted; and then laughingly my wife pointed at all the money she happened to have in her purse at the moment — a ten-shilling note and two florins (a total of seventy new pence)— and said by way of a joke: "Look! That's all I've got until Tuesday (this happened on a Friday) when I get my housekeeping money."

The old lady's reaction was immediate. She held out the pound note: "Take this, my dear," she said. "It'll help you over the weekend anyway, and you can give me it back when you get your money."

Here was an old lady, an old age pensioner, offering her only pound note to someone she scarcely knew, because she thought that the stranger was worse off than herself.

If there is one thing that moves the human heart, it is generosity — especially spontaneous generosity.

True giving

MORNING

There is not only a generosity in money. There is also a generosity in talent, a giving of whatever gifts we have, to other people.

Bruno Walter tells how Kathleen Ferrier, that wonderful singer who died too soon, was in America. Because he himself had engagements in New York, he could not play the host to her when she was in Los Angeles as he would like to have done. So he did the only thing he could — he gave her the use of his house in Los Angeles that she might stay in comfort and in peace there.

He goes on: "When we came home after she had left, our faithful domestic helpers, a married Austrian couple, told us that Kathleen on her free evenings used to call them to the music room, where she sat down at the piano, shed her shoes, and sang to them to their heart's desire, and, of course, to their utter delight."

A true giving!

EVENING

You would not think that meanness could ever be a vice of a Christian.

It is James who speaks of God who gives generously to all men, and never grudges the gift (James 1:5).

It is Paul who speaks of the Lord Jesus Christ who, though he was rich, "yet for your sakes he became poor, that ye through his poverty might be rich" (2 Corinthians 8:9).

It is not a case of giving big gifts.

At the Feast of Purim the Jews have a lovely custom. It is laid down that at the Feast which is the time of the giving of gifts, even the poorest person must search for someone poorer than himself and give him a gift.

Sometimes we feel we live in a drab enough world, but the world's grayness is lit by every act of generosity.

For in every such act, there is the reflection of God.

Character and potential

MORNING

T. H. Huxley, in one of his published essays, puts forward a very interesting point of view. He writes:

> "That which is to be lamented, I fancy, is not that society should do its utmost to help capacity to ascend from the lower strata to the higher, but that it has no machinery by which to facilitate the descent of incapacity from the higher strata to the lower . . . We have all known noble lords who would have been coachmen, or gamekeepers, or billiard-markers, if they had not been kept afloat by our social corks; we have all known men among the lowest ranks of whom everyone has said: 'What might not that man have become, if he had only had a little education?'."

So Huxley makes the point that we rightly do everything to enable a clever man to rise in the world, but we have no corresponding machinery to bring the foolish and the useless man down in the world.

Character is always more important than birth.

EVENING

The value of a man lies not in his social status, but in his efficiency. The true value of a man lies in the contribution he can make to the community. The true aristocracy lies not in lineage but in service.

All social claims are valueless and baseless unless they are backed by usefulness in the community of men.

The important thing about any man is not his ancestry but his potential, not his past but his future.

Sir Linton Andrews, the famous journalist, tells of the editor who greeted all candidates for jobs, when they produced their references and their testimonials, by saying: "Never mind what you did last year, or even yesterday. What can you do today, and tomorrow and next year? It is your future work I have to assess."

The really important thing about a man is that he should be able to produce, not a pedigree, but a potential. This is not to say that blood and ancestry and heredity do not matter, but it is to say that the judgment of any man is based on what he is, not on what his fathers were.

The possibilities only God can help a man to realize.

God sees what a man is; God knows what a man can be.

Only God can turn the one into the other.

Learning from journalists

MORNING

In *Faith in Fleet Street*, Robert Moore tells of one of his early experiences as a journalist. He was sent out on a special story and assignment, and he could get absolutely nowhere with it.

He was worried about this and he was also not a little alarmed. The investigation had been asked for by Lord Beaverbrook personally on the information given to him by one of his senior editors.

In spite of the source of the story, Robert Moore knew that the story was inaccurate. In great trepidation he had to go back to his editor and say so.

The editor told him to drop the investigation at once, and then he went on to say something which, as a journalist, Robert Moore never forgot.

The editor said: "Anyone who spends his time and energies and his experience fully proving that there is not a story to write has done just as good a day's work as someone who proves that there is a story."

What the paper was interested in was not in getting a story but in getting the truth. So Robert Moore writes of "the temptations and opportunities for a journalist that are lined up on every bar counter: stacked high in every whisper and gossip and which sometimes shriek at him on that blank sheet of paper in his typewriter at which he has been staring seemingly for hours".

He says: "I can never, must never, say that my journalism is the truth, the whole truth, and nothing but the truth. But this I do say, that my journalism is the result of looking for the truth."

EVENING

The ethics of the Christian should be equal to the ethics of the journalist. And yet it is so often true that the so-called Christian will repeat the story, the rumor, the piece of gossip, which he knows perhaps only by hearsay, and of the truth of which he is by no means certain.

The journalist has to resist the temptation to write the spicy and malicious story. Too often the Christian falls to that temptation, for there are no hotbeds of gossip like churches and congregations.

We should never repeat the story about the truth of which we are uncertain

During wartime there was actual legislation to punish, and to punish severely, the person who disseminated alarmist and defeatist rumors.

The proverb has it that three things can never come back — the spent arrow, the spoken word, and the lost opportunity. There is nothing so attractive as gossip, and there is nothing so dangerous as gossip.

We might well remind ourselves more often than we do that we shall one day give account for every idle word that we have spoken (Matthew 12:36).

Be welcoming

MORNING

A brother minister rang me up on the telephone. He is one of the princes of the church, a far bigger person than ever I will be, and he is a man with the grace of God on him. He wanted some information that he believed that I could give him.

After he had talked and apologized that he had troubled me — not that to speak to him could ever be any trouble, I made the conventional reply, but I did not mean it merely conventionally. I said: "It's a pleasure." And he answered: "It's a pleasure to me to have the right to bother you whenever I like."

It was only a great man's humility that made him speak to me like that, but it set me thinking, and I came to see that the really valuable people are the people whom you *can* bother — at any time!

It is so easy to get so immersed in work — work which may be very important — that we cannot be bothered with people, and that we find them a trouble.

EVENING

Luke has a wonderful incident in his gospel. He tells how Jesus went round the north end of the Sea of Galilee to Bethsaida Julias. "He went aside privately into a desert place." He wanted some peace and quiet for himself and for his men.

But the people marked where he had gone and followed him in their hordes, and his peace was wrecked and stolen away.

Luke says: "And he welcomed them, and talked to them about the Kingdom of God, and healed them that had need of healing" (Luke 9:11).

It would have been so easy to regard the people who had invaded his privacy as nuisances. They had interrupted his rest and spoiled his chance of praying and teaching his disciples. But no — *he welcomed them.*

If we are to have this priceless quality in our lives, this precious ability to be bothered, we must have certain qualities.

We must always be ready to welcome people at any time.

We must be really and truly interested in people.

We must come to see that individual people are the most important beings in the world. Every individual man is dear to God.

Our most precious right is that we have the right to bother God with our troubles at any time. The right God gave to us, we must learn to give to other people.

Brightness and vision

MORNING

I have been looking at the advertisements again! As Shakespeare had it, there are

"... Tongues in trees, books in the running brooks,
Sermons in stones, and good in everything."

There are certainly sermons on the advertisement posters for him who has an eye to see!

There is a certain well-known washing agent that commends itself to the public in two words. Its claim is that it "adds brightness".

I don't know if there could be a better definition of the effect of the Christian life. If a person is a true Christian he or she will add brightness everywhere.

It was said of Alice Freeman Palmer, the great American teacher, by one of her pupils, "She made me feel as if I were bathed in sunshine."

Is it not of Phillips Brookes, the great American preacher, that a lovely story is told?

He was going down the street one winter day of snow and ice. He stopped to buy a newspaper from the scantily clad and shivering lad at the street corner. As he turned away he smiled at the boy and said: "It's cold today, isn't it?" Whereat the boy flashed back: "It was, sir, till you passed."

There is an unwritten saying of Jesus that states: "He who is near Jesus is to be in the presence of a warm comforting glow. And those who are followers of Jesus should also bring to others this glow of warmth and they also should add this brightness to life."

EVENING

Roger Fry, writing on what he calls the "Artist's Vision", once said that anyone who is to be a great artist must have four different kinds of vision.

Not only the artist, but the Christian also needs these four visions.

The first necessity is practical vision

"Practical vision" sees what demands to be done in any given situation.

So many people can look at a situation, can look at someone's sorrow and need and distress, and the sight conveys no challenge to their hearts and no summons to their hands.

In the parable of Dives and Lazarus (Luke 16:19-31), Dives, the rich man, finishes up in hell, not because he was in any way deliberately cruel to Lazarus, the poor man, but because he simply accepted him as an inevitable part of the landscape and did nothing about it.

The Christian has the practical vision to see what needs to be done, and the loving heart to do it.

Curiosity and creative vision

MORNING

The second necessity, Roger Fry says, is curiosity vision

"Curiosity vision" is the vision which moves a man to ask, "Why?"

"Curiosity," Plato said long ago, "is the mother of knowledge."

Many people have seen apples fall from trees, but only Newton asked, "Why?" In doing so, he discovered the law of gravity.

A man loses half his life when he loses that faculty of wonder that makes him seek and search for reasons.

The soul is half dead when we take things all for granted and stop asking, "Why?"

The third necessity is aesthetic vision

"Aesthetic vision" is the vision that sees loveliness everywhere. There is loveliness everywhere for him who has the eyes to see it.

Henry Ernest Hardy, who wrote the loveliest poems under the name of Father Andrew, has some wonderful verses entitled "Mystic Beauty", in which he writes of the beauty that can be seen in any London street.

> I've seen a back street bathed in
>   blue,
> Such as the soul of Whistler knew;
> A smudge of amber light,
> Where some fried fish shop plied
>   its trade,
> A perfect note of color made —
> Oh, it was exquisite!

Here is the man whose eyes can see beauty and find value even in the glow of the window of the fish and chip shop.

EVENING

The fourth necessity, says Roger Fry, is creative vision

"Creative vision" is the vision that sees the possibilities in any situation.

Here are two men looking over a remote area in the Western Highlands. They look at the bracken and the bogs. They look at the glint of the little lochs and the spume of the waterfalls on the hillside.

One man says "What a wilderness! There is nothing on earth to be done with a waste land like this!" The other man is a hydroelectric engineer. He says: "Let me build a dam here; let me harness these waters there; and I'll give you power to drive the machines and light the lamps of half a dozen cities."

Jesus saw the possibilities in every situation and in every man.

Retiring

MORNING

I well remember that time when there came to me the summons to leave the one pastoral charge that I ever had. I had been with my people for more than thirteen years, and I was happy. I was torn in mind as to whether to stay in my parish, or to go to teach.

I was talking to an old man who was a member of my congregation. He was a most distinguished engineer, with a name known far beyond Scotland, but he had never lost the broad Scottish speech of his boyhood. I told him of my problems and of my indecision.

He was silent for a moment, and then he said quietly: "It's a wise man that kens when tae lay doon the barra'." (Being translated into English, it means: "It's a wise man who knows when to lay down the barrow.")

There was a lifetime of wisdom there. He is a wise man who knows when the time has come to go. The man who hangs on too long is a sad spectacle.

EVENING

It is one of the lovely facts of life that the great men have always had the gift of retiring gracefully.

Once William Gerhardi was at a dinner party with H. G. Wells, when Wells was an old man. As they rose to leave the table to join the ladies, Gerhardi courteously stood back at the door to allow Wells to pass before him. "You first," said Wells. "You are tomorrow and I am yesterday."

When Sir James Barrie made one of his amazing speeches to the Rhodes Scholars, he said: "If to despise us helps you in your enthusiasm, then, gentlemen, continue. Far worse than your scorning us beyond reason would be your not having a cheery belief that you can do better. If in firing at some of our performances you feel that the straightest line is through our bodies, still fire."

And there is one tremendous instance of this in the New Testament itself. When Jesus emerged, John the Baptist said: "He must increase, but I must decrease" (John 3:30).

John had held the center of the stage, but now he knew that it was time to go.

Wrong way, wrong destination

MORNING

I had occasion to make the journey from Glasgow to London. I was traveling by the "Royal Scot" which did not stop at any station between Glasgow and London. More than once a railway inspector passed up and down the train calling out: "First stop London!" It was as if he said: "Remember where you are going to finish up if you start out on this train!"

Now that is a thing that life is always saying to us. Life is always saying to us: "If you start this way, remember where you're going to finish up!"

There are some who discover too late that they have taken the wrong destination

Cardinal Wolsey was Henry's great Prime Minister. For a time he flourished; and then the policy of the king demanded that Wolsey be jettisoned. For a time Wolsey managed to buy security, but in the end his execution came.

As he lay in the Tower awaiting the end, he was talking to the Lieutenant of the Tower.

"Master Knygton," he said, "had I but served God as diligently as I have served the king, he would not have given me over in my gray hairs. But this is my due reward for my pains and study, not regarding my service to God, but only my duty to my prince."

Wolsey had made a mistake. Wolsey had not realized where he was going. The end was tragedy.

EVENING

There are some who have known the way they were going, and who, because they knew the destination, did not care how hard it was.

Barrie tells of the students who took the way to knowledge:

I knew three undergraduates who lodged together in a dreary house at the top of a dreary street. Two of them used to study until two in the morning while the third slept. When they shut their books they awoke number three who rose and dressed and studied till breakfast time; among the many advantages of this system was that, as they were dreadfully poor, one bed did for the three of them. Two of them occupied it at one time and the third at another.

The students knew where they were going, and the hardness of the way was as nothing.

In every decision in life, before we allow ourselves any pleasure or indulgence, before we take the first step towards developing any habit, we ought to ask: "Where is this way going? What is its destination?" It is better never to start than to arrive at the wrong destination.

The law

MORNING

There is in our days an extraordinary contempt for the law. It may well be that we are living in one of the most lawless ages in history, and we are living in a time when there is less confidence between the public and the guardians of the law than there used to be.

A good deal of this is to be explained by three facts about the law.

An unenforceable law is a bad law

A law which cannot be enforced should not really be enacted. If the national or civic authorities are not prepared to enforce laws, then they should not lay them down.

Every time a threat is made and not carried out, respect for the law grows less and less

No man bothers about a law which he is fairly certain that he can flout with impunity.

Erratically applied law is the biggest cause of resentment and trouble between the authorities and the ordinary man

There can never be any satisfactory relationship with law and authority when the same action may be on one occasion punished and on another unpunished, or when the law punishes one man and lets another go free for precisely the same fault.

EVENING

Let us bring this nearer home.

What we have been saying of the law is equally true of the family. The parent who lays down family laws which he cannot enforce, the parent who makes a threat and does not carry it out — and some parents are for ever doing just that — the parent whose justice is erratic and unpredictable, can look for nothing but family trouble.

A child is not a fool. He very soon sees when threats are not going to be carried out. A child has a vivid sense of justice and will soon resent erratic justice.

In the family and in the community, law must have respect. People must observe laws, or law and order will necessarily come into disrepute. Perhaps this is exactly what has happened.

Last words and an epitaph

MORNING

There are those who discover too late that the easy way is not the happy way

Once Cranmer stood for the real faith, but in face of Mary's persecution he signed his six recantations, by which he hoped to purchase his life.

But no sooner had he signed them than he was wretched. In the end he recanted his recantations and went to be burned.

As he spoke to the people before he was burned he said:

Now I come to the great thing that troubleth my conscience more than any other thing that ever I said or did in my life, and that is the setting abroad of writings contrary to the truth: which here I now renounce and refuse as things written by my hand contrary to the truth which I thought in my heart, and written for fear of death, to save my life, if it might be. And forasmuch as my hand offended in writing contrary to my heart, my hand therefore shall be the first punished; for if I come to the fire, it shall be the first burnt.

He came to the stake: "This was the hand that wrote it," he said, "therefore it shall first suffer punishment." And holding it steadily in the flame "he never stirred nor cried" till life was gone.

Cranmer thought that the destination of the easy way was peace. It wasn't.

EVENING

Epitaphs are often dull and even distressing things, but sometimes one comes across one which has a touch of genius.

In Liverpool Cathedral there is a tablet on the wall, part of which reads like this: "Here lies in honor all that could die of a pioneer in orthopedics. Sir Robert Jones."

"Here lies all that could die."

Centuries before Horace, the Roman poet, had said: *"Non omnis moriar,"* "I shall not all die."

There is a part of man which is laid in the tomb, and there is a part of a man which lives on.

Sometimes a man's words live on

Horace wrote in his Odes: "I have completed my work, and I have raised a monument more lasting than bronze."

It is not only the words of the great that live on. It can happen that the wise word of a parent can live in the heart of a child until that child becomes an old man. Over a lifetime that life has been kept nearer to God by such a good word.

Lasting influences

Sometimes a man's teaching lives on

A great teacher marks his scholars. He lives in them. Some of these scholars may themselves become teachers, and they pass on the mark of their old teacher, and so an influence begins which passes from generation to generation.

A. J. Gossip reminds us that Principal John Cairns once wrote to his teacher. Sir William Hamilton: "I do not know what life, or lives, may lie before me. But I know this, that, to the end of the last of them, I shall bear your mark upon me."

Sometimes a man's memory and influence live on

There are some people who are talked about whenever those who knew them meet together.

There are some people about whom we find ourselves thinking whenever we are up against it. In the hard times and the sore times, their memory comes back.

There are certain influences that do not die. A man tells how once, when he was staying in a village in Cornwall, a fishing village, he was impressed by the atmosphere of sheer goodness in the place.

In talk with an old fisherman, he asked what the explanation was of the atmosphere of simple goodness that pervaded this village. The old man bared his head: "There came a man amongst us," he said. "His name was John Wesley."

Whatever else is true, a man's soul lives on. All that can die of him is placed in the tomb, but there is a part of him that cannot die.

That is what makes life so important.

Life is the training school of eternity.

Life is the apprenticeship for glory.

All the time we live in this world, we either fit ourselves or unfit ourselves for the greater life of the world to come.

In this life all our days we are either winning or losing a crown.

Life is always infinitely worth living, because on how we live life depends eternity.

For all

MORNING

In Cheltenham there was an inn called The Five Alls. And its sign was most interesting.

On the sign there was a king, with the motto: "I rule for all."

There was a bishop, with the motto: "I pray for all."

There was a lawyer, with the motto: "I plead for all."

There was a soldier, with the motto: "I fight for all."

And there was an artisan in working clothes, with the motto: "I work for all." There indeed is a program for all.

I rule for all

If it should happen that we are in control of many people, the motive that should animate us is not our private profit, but the good of all.

If we are simple ordinary people, servants and not masters, there is one person whom we can rule, and that is our self, for only he who is master of himself is fit to be the servant of others.

EVENING

I pray for all

Jowett, the great preacher, used to tell of a girl who came to join his church. She was a servant girl, not well off, and not well educated. He wished to make sure that she knew what she was doing and that she was in earnest about her profession, and he asked her how she proposed to live the Christian life.

"I haven't much time off, sir," she said, "and I can't attend many meetings or even many services."

"Well," said Jowett, "what do you do?"

"Well, sir," she said, "I always take the daily paper to bed with me at night"

Jowett was puzzled, as well he might be. "What's the good of that?" he said.

"Well, sir," she said, "I look at the first page and I read the birth notices and I pray for the babies that have been born; and I read the marriages and I pray that they may be happy and true; and I read the deaths and I pray that God's comfort may come to these sorrowing homes." Is it not a staggering vision — the waves of prayer that went out from that attic beneath the tiles?

I pray for all. The servant girl did. So can we.

Three alls

MORNING

I plead for all
The writer to the Hebrews has the most tremendous vision in the New Testament. He speaks of Jesus in the heavenly places and he says of him: "He ever liveth to make intercession for us" (Hebrews 7:25). Even in heaven Jesus is pleading for men.

I fight for all
That is what the great lovers of humanity have all done. They saw some wrong, some iniquity, some oppression, some distress, some need and they fought that it might be removed.

Often they themselves were well-to-do and comfortable and lived in ease. The conquest in the struggle of social reformation was not going to profit them. But they spent themselves for the sake of others.

Where there was poverty, oppression, sorrow, distress, they must fight the battle for others.

It is too often the case that so long as things are well with us, we do not mind very much what is happening to others.

The great men were the men who bore the sorrows of the world upon their hearts, and who were God's crusaders in the battle for the downtrodden and the under-privileged and the oppressed.

EVENING

I work for all
Do we?

The tragedy of things today is that hardly anyone does! Some of us work for ourselves, a bigger bank balance, a television set, a refrigerator, a motor car—these are the things for which we work.

Some of us go a little further and work for our families, a better chance for our sons and daughters, a better start in life for them, a better job than we have — these are the things for which we work.

Some of us work for the class to which we belong, more privileges, higher pay, shorter hours, longer holidays, better conditions for ourselves and our mates — these are the things for which we work.

But there are so few, so very few, who work for all, who have the spirit of service which sees beyond the boundaries of self and selfish interest.

The social and the economic millennium will come when master and man work, not for self, but for God and for all.

God so loved the world . . . His love is over all.

And we, who are his servants, must ever seek to be like him.

Light and glory

MORNING

During a visit to Banbury Cross I went to its very handsome church where I saw a very wonderful thing.

As I came in through the front door the church looked very dark, for there was no lighting. Then my eye traveled to the faraway end of the building. On the altar there was a polished brass cross and that cross was shining like a star through the dark. There was no artificial lighting on it.

With its own light, that cross was shining so that it stood out in the dark even from far away.

A war journalist, in one of his war books, tells of a conversation he had with a fellow journalist on the morning after London's most devastating air raid.

The journalist said to him: "Did you see the cross on St. Paul's, old boy? Nobody has ever seen it shine and glow as it did that night. Clouds of smoke rolled by it, an unearthly beauty was over it."

In the destruction and the devastation, the cross shone out.

EVENING

Our future depends on how we use this life

No scholar or student is allowed to pass to a higher class and a higher study until he has mastered the junior class and the more elementary study. Life is like that.

There is one sense in which each day is sufficient to itself.

The New Testament forbids the anxious looking forward of the worried mind and the distrustful heart.

But there is a sense in which a Christian man is always looking forward; for he must see life in the light of eternity.

If we will remember that, the tasks of this life are the tests by which we prepare ourselves for a higher service, if we learn to look on this life as the training ground for eternity, then even the smallest and the most routine tasks will be clothed with glory.

For then it will be literally true that, whatsoever we do in deed or word, we will be doing it in the name of the Lord Jesus (Colossians 3:17).

The light of the cross

MORNING

The light which shines from the Cross has always brought wonders in the dark.

It shone in the dark for the sick and the suffering and the weak

Dr. A. Rendle Short wrote in *The Bible and Modern Medicine*:

> "We know from Jerome's writings that the first hospital of which we have any record . . . was founded by a Christian lady, Fabiola."

He goes on to tell how the plague smote Carthage in AD 252. The heathen flung out their dead and fled.

But Cyprian, the Christian bishop, assembled the Christian congregation to care for the sick and to bury the dead, and so saved the city from desolation.

The love, the care, the tenderness that the sick and the ailing and the weakly and the deformed received was quite absent from heathen civilization; it shines from the Cross.

EVENING

It shone in the dark for the morally helpless

The tragedy of the ancient world was not lack of knowledge of the good. It was powerlessness to do it. Seneca said that men loved their vices and hated them at the same time. He bewailed what he called "our inefficiency in necessary things".

Men knew that they were sinners, and yet were helpless to do anything about it.

But Paul can write to the Corinthians, making a list of the foulest sins and sinners — fornicators, adulterers, homosexuals, drunkards — and then at the end add triumphantly — "And such were some of you" (1 Corinthians 6:9-11). The Cross has always shone with power to overcome and to defeat the moral helplessness which has man in its grip.

The light of the Cross shines for the sick and the sinner.

Not all the darkness in the world can quench that light.

The sanctuary

MORNING

In London there is a little row of houses between Westminster Abbey and Dean's Court.

One day I was going along it and looked up to see its name.

Its name is a lovely name.

Its name is "The Sanctuary".

As I walked along it I glanced at certain of the buildings of which it is composed, and quite suddenly I noticed that two of them stood out as insurance offices!

Here is a parable of modem life. Men seek their safety in earthly insurance. They seek a sanctuary in insuring themselves in material things.

Now, in one sense, there is nothing to be said against that, and everything to be said in its favor, for once a man has acquired a wife and a family he has, in the old phrase, "given hostages to fortune". And he is a reckless man who, in the face of the chances and changes of life, will leave them entirely unprovided for.

But there is a sense in which this modern identification of insurance and sanctuary is a wrong thing.

EVENING

In these days men are searching for security.

The real Christian has never sought security.

Think of the old days in the Roman Empire.

A man might say to a Christian preacher: "If I become a Christian, what may I expect?" The honest answer would be: "You can expect imprisonment, crucifixion, the fight with beasts in the arena, the stake and the flames. You will become an outlaw and your life will never be safe again."

Unamuno, the Spanish mystic, used to pray for those he loved: "May God deny you peace and give you glory."

There is a great prayer of the Christian church which runs like this:

O Jesus Christ, the Lord of all good life who hast called us to build up the city of God, do Thou enrich and purify our lives, and deepen in us our discipleship.

Help us daily to know more of Thee, and, through us, by the power of Thy Spirit, show forth Thyself to other men. Make us humble, brave and loving; make us ready for adventure in Thy cause.

We ask that Thou shouldst keep us loyal, who for us didst face death unafraid and dost live and reign for ever and ever.

Ready for adventure?

Security

MORNING

A man came to Tertullian with a problem. His problem was the difficulty of earning a living in a heathen world.

> What if the mason was asked to build a heathen temple?
> What if the tailor was asked to make clothes for a heathen priest?
> What if the soldier must daily bum his pinch of incense on the altar of the camp?
> The man finished up by saying: "I must live."
> And Tertullian answered him in one immortal question: "Must you?"

If it came to a choice between our Christian principles and our job, honestly, what would we do? Have most of us ever really taken a risk for our Christian faith in all our lives?

When we do seek for security, we seek for it in the wrong place.

We seek for it by taking earthly and material precautions.

We seek to ensure earthly security by earthly insurance.

But there is safety far beyond that, and it is this other safety that matters.

EVENING

In the 1914-18 war Rupert Brooke wrote his poem "Safety".

> Safe shall be my going,
> Secretly armed against all death's endeavor;
> Safe though all safety's lost; safe where men fall;
> And if these poor limbs die, safest of all.

The Roman Catholic cardinal threatened Martin Luther with all kinds of vengeance. He told him that his present supporters would soon leave him in the lurch.

"Where will you be then?" he demanded menacingly. "Then as now," said Luther, "then as now — in the hands of God."

There is not much use in a man insuring his life unless his life is safe with God.

The way to be safe with God is always to take the risk of staking everything on Jesus Christ.

A welcoming church?

MORNING

I know a lady whose household moved to a new house in a part of a town not very far away from where her home used to be. She is not young and she is not old. She is by no means shy. She is a good talker and meets all kinds of people with the greatest of ease. She was brought up in the church and has always had the closest connection with the church.

Now, I have always believed as a matter of principle that a family ought to go to the church of their parish or their community area, and that to travel long distances to maintain an old connection is neither wise nor right.

I said to this lady: "I suppose you will be leaving your church and you will be joining a congregation nearer at hand."

"No," she said, "I am going to stay in the church of which I am a member just now."

"Why's that?" I asked, surprised.

She looked at me and said: "I just couldn't bear to make the effort to break into another congregation."

The effort to break into a congregation!

EVENING

Does the church welcome sinners as it ought to welcome them?

Suppose someone has made a mess of things, suppose someone has fallen into some of the sins into which a passionate nature may bring a man or a woman, is that person likely to receive a warm welcome, if he or she tries to break into a church?

Hugh Redwood somewhere tells a terrible story.

There was a woman in the dock district of London. She associated with a Chinese and bore him a half-caste child.

She found her way to a women's meeting in a certain church, taking her child with her. She liked it and she came back. She came back a third time. The minister of the church came up to her. Awkward and embarrassed, he said to her:

"I'm very sorry but I must ask you not to come to this meeting again."

"Why can't I come?" she said.

He answered: "The other women know about you, and they say that, if you keep on coming, they will stop."

The woman looked at the minister with poignant sorrow on her face. "Sir," she said, "I know I'm a sinner but isn't there anywhere a sinner can go?"

Fortunately the Salvation Army got hold of her. But "the church" had slammed the door in her face.

It is not a question of taking sin lightly, but it is a question of remembering that Jesus said: "Him that cometh unto me I will no wise cast out."

The shy stranger

MORNING

Does the church welcome strangers as it ought to welcome them?

Does a stranger feel a stranger when he enters a church, or does he feel he has come among friends?

One of the great tributes that Homer paid to one of his characters was: "He dwelt in a house at the side of the road, and he was the friend of wayfaring men."

Can we really say that about the church?

Was it not Sir Walter Scott about whom they used to say that when he shook hands with you, he was never the first to withdraw his hand?

Does the church give you a welcome like that?

One of the strange, disturbing features of many churches is the "possession" of pews by their members.

There is something radically wrong, something totally unchristian in the sight of any man having an exclusive right to eighteen inches or two feet of seating accommodation in any church.

True, in most cases the stranger will be shown to a pew — as if he was there by grace and favor. In most cases he will receive some kind of welcome. But there is a kind of malign fate that will sometimes lead him to the one pew where he will be met with blank hostility.

It is not a case of a backslapping, vociferous, overwhelming welcome. It is just a question of Christian kindliness to the stranger in a strange place.

EVENING

Does the church welcome shy people as it ought to welcome them? There are far more shy people in this world than we realize.

Sometimes I wonder if young people who leave home, and then stop going to church, do stop going just because they are too shy to go.

Surely we ought to try to meet people halfway.

Surely we ought to try to get alongside them better than we do.

Surely we ought to make the family of God the one place where shyness is at home.

Will you think of all this?

Is your church a place where it needs an effort to break in?

Son of Abraham

MORNING

A true son of Abraham must have the humble mind

The greatest necessity for the humble mind lies in the fact that there can be no learning without humility, for the very simple reason that there can be no learning without prior realization that we do not know. The man who knows all the answers already obviously cannot learn.

In learning there is one kind of humility which is both specially valuable and specially difficult. It is the humility to sit down in front of the facts and look at them just as they are.

He must have the humble spirit

No one can ever solve the problem of personal relationships without the humble spirit. For without the humble spirit two things are impossible. No one can see any beauty in service without the humble spirit. Service and pride are mutually contradictory; service and humility are almost synonymous.

It is only the man with the lowly spirit who really believes that he who serves is the greatest of all, and he does not think in terms of greatness at all.

So, the good eye, the generous eye, will give us the secret of right seeing; the humble mind will give us the secret of right learning; the lowly spirit will give us the secret of right relationships. These things are worth praying for.

EVENING

Abraham was the friend of God. To a Jew the highest compliment that can be paid a man is to say that he is a true son of Abraham. There is a Jewish saying which tells of the three things that a true son of Abraham must have. He must have "the good eye, the humble mind and the lowly spirit".

He must have the good eye

Here the word good is not used in the physical sense of having good sight; it really means the generous eye. So a good man will look generously at people.

He will be generous with praise

We have quite enough critics in this world; it is encouragers who are in short supply.

He will be generous to give

One of the most valuable things in the world is the sensitivity which can see the need of people before they are compelled to ask for help. To see need sensitively and to help need quickly are great qualities.

Our ally

MORNING

If we have God for our ally, then we have an ally for victory. But we must be quite clear what this means.

This does not mean that we are not going to have any trouble; it does not mean that we are going to have a peaceful and a protected life

This very Paul who was so sure that, if God was for him, it did not matter who was against him, was the same Paul who wrote that he had been scourged five times, that he had been beaten with rods three times, that he had been stoned once, that he had been three times shipwrecked, that he had been in prison, that he had looked death in the face often, that there was no kind of peril and no kind of weariness and no kind of exhaustion that he had not gone through (2 Corinthians 11:23-28).

No, the fact that God is on our side does not mean that we will enjoy a comfortable trouble-free existence. What it does mean is that, no matter what comes to us, we can face it erect and foursquare and we can emerge triumphant from it.

If God is for us, then life will be no escape, but conquest.

EVENING

If God is for us, it does not even mean that life itself is safe

It will not necessarily save us or those we love from the last enemy. But it does mean that we will be very sure that not even that can separate us from the ally of victory.

This is precisely what Paul went on to say. He went on to affirm that in his belief nothing in life or death, in time or in eternity could separate him from the love of God in Christ Jesus our Lord.

To be able to say that God is on our side is not to say that we think that life is going to be easy and protected, and trouble free: it is not to say that we will win the victories which the world counts victories: it is not even to say that we will go on living this earthly life. But it is to say that no matter what happens to us, we can bear it and face it and conquer it and transform it; and it is to say that even the last enemy has lost his terrors, for ours is the ally who has already conquered him.

Cruelty

MORNING

When I am writing, Rusty, the Staffordshire bull terrier who stays with us, is usually lying at my feet or across my feet. No one in this family ever comes in without a tumultuous welcome from Rusty. And usually at meal times he is sitting hopefully near the table just in case someone forgets the way a dog ought to be treated and throws him a scrap.

But Rusty is not here at the moment. He has had an experience that has wounded his heart!

Board and Lodging

Within the next day or so we have to pay a visit to the south of England and we cannot take Rusty with us. So Rusty had to have his board and lodging fixed up in kennels where they will be very kind and good to him.

One day last week Rusty was taken to the kennels, but Rusty refused to enter them. He shook and shivered and wept and slipped his collar and ran away, and in the end had to be bodily lifted and carried in and left.

Rusty was of course broken-hearted and terrified at leaving the people he knows and loves. But it is all right. We phoned to see how he was getting on (you would think he was an invalid in a nursing home) and he has settled down and is quite happy.

EVENING

Roam the Streets

I have just been reading an article in a newspaper that horrifies me. This article says that every day strays and homeless cats and doers are picked up. But in the summer months, in June, July and August, every week they are picked up literally by the hundred and many roam the streets homeless until they starve to death. This is because there are people who, when they go on holiday, simply turn their animal out and make no provision for them.

This article goes on to say that quite often children get a present of a kitten or a puppy for Christmas or for a birthday. For a week or two, or a month or two, some of them are thrilled with their new friend. Then they get tired of it, and the animal is put out and left to wander and get lost and get run over perhaps or starve.

I hope no reader of this book will ever do this cruel thing to an animal. An animal cannot complain and cannot appeal for itself, and that makes the cruelty all the worse.

Cruelty is always an ugly thing; and cruelty to animals in their dumb helplessness is specially an ugly thing.

The love of God is the love that stretches out over man and beast.

The more we are together

MORNING

One of my difficulties in worship has always been that I have never been happy about the reputation of the Creed. The Creed is, of course, part of the service of the Church of England; it is not nearly so universally part of the service of the Church of Scotland, which is my own church.

My trouble has always been that there were certain statements in the Creed that I am not prepared to accept, and I have always felt that to repeat them as an act of worship was dishonest. But here is what Dr. Barry says: "In saying the creeds we identify ourselves with the total faith and experience of the church, trusting that, as our Christian life develops, we may grow into fuller understanding of it. No one Christian can apprehend it all; and indeed the original form of the credal statement is 'We believe' rather than 'I believe'".

Here is something that is infinitely worth repeating and remembering. And here for many years has been my mistake. Although it may be that I cannot say "I believe", it is blessedly true that I can say "We believe".

I can lose my uncertainty in the certainty of the whole church, of the whole company of God's worshipping people. It will be a really notable day when we introduce our credal confessions not by "I believe", but by "We believe".

EVENING

When we worship, even with the two or three, we too are compassed about with a mighty cloud of witnesses (Hebrews 12:1).

If we think at all, we are bound to think of things as they are and then to think of things as they should be. The difference is daunting, and sometimes we feel our own weakness and helplessness so much that we come to the conclusion that it is hopeless to do anything about it.

Once again, that is the result of thinking as an individual. At such a time we must remember that we are one of a great body and community of people, a church scattered throughout every nation upon earth, and that there are so many besides ourselves who share our concern and who share our effort. And we remember that at the head of them, there is Jesus Christ.

Nothing is hopeless with a fellowship and with a leader like that.

Life alters when we lay down our foolish individualism and remember that we are one of the community of Christ.

Contentment and creativity

MORNING

Last week I accidentally came across a copy of the *Strand Magazine* for Christmas 1894. In its day the *Strand* was perhaps the most famous of all magazines; it was in it, for instance, that the famous Sherlock Holmes stories first appeared. But what interested me were the advertisement pages.

It was interesting to note that, in the many pages of advertisements, there was not a single advertisement for cigarettes or for coffee, and very few for liquor. It seems that seventy-five years ago people were not the slaves to tobacco and to drink that they now so largely are!

The advertisements fell into certain classes, however.

There were many advertisements for *food* and for *clothes*. Here are the basic needs. Men need to know what they are going to eat and what they are going to put on.

There were many advertisements for *medicines*, for *toothpastes*, for *medicines for babies*, for *reducing treatments* and *slimming diets*, for *electrical machines, which* were guaranteed to cure all ills. Men, then as now, were interested in their health.

From these advertisements it is possible to draw certain conclusions.

The basic needs of men do not change.
Throughout the centuries there are needs which remain the same and which will always remain the same.

But there were far fewer advertisements for luxuries
The sophisticated and the affluent society have developed far more needs. As time goes on, men's needs become more and more complicated and elaborate. The more sophisticated men become, the more they think they need to make them happy.

EVENING

There are certain things in life that almost everyone can make, or at least can share in making.

We can make a home
Home making is a co-operative effort in which young and old can and must join.

We can make a friend
"A man that hath friends must show himself friendly," as the old saying has it. No one can expect to have friends who will not go to the trouble to be a friend.

We can make a character
We should always ask, not, "Why has God sent me this?" but, "What does God mean me to do with this?"

Be your age!

MORNING

In *An Introduction to Pastoral Counseling*, Dr. Kathleen Heasman talks of the ages of man. There are three main ages each with its own characteristics.

"The first reaches its peak in youth when the achievement are reached in spheres involving physical attributes such as strength and speed. The second is in middle age when a state of maturity and self-confidence has been reached and when the successful have attained the height of their profession or career. The third is in old age when mental attributes such as experience and systematic thinking are the crucial factors and when wisdom has been learnt."

One of the supreme mistakes in life is to try to remain at a stage from which we should have moved on.

It is a mistake to try to remain young

There is wisdom in knowing when the time for competitive games has come to an end. There is still more wisdom in learning to leave young people to themselves.

Peter Pans who refuse to grow up, are tragic rather than attractive figures. Youth is a magnificent time — but it does not last. We must accept that.

EVENING

Dr. Heasman says that *middle age* is the time when a man reaches the height of his profession or career. Here the temptation is to stay on too long.

There can be such a thing as the delusion of indispensability. There are few people who are immune from the conscious or unconscious desire for power. Power is difficult to lay down. To be able to leave the top is in its own way as great an achievement as to be able to reach the top.

Age too has its problems. Age has to have a care that it does not become self centered and crotchety. It is no good "being yourself, if "being yourself simply brings you into collision with other people.

One of the biggest problems in life is to remember that one's children and the people whom one taught are now grown up. The transition from authority to equality is something which is not always easy to make. But if personal relationships, and the closest personal relationships, are to be right, it must be made.

There is the popular saying, "Be your age!"

It is good advice.

Discouraging enthusiasm

MORNING

When any new ideas are around, there are those who wave the red flag and there are those who wave the wet blanket.

There can be no possible doubt that is the right thing to do.

It is always a sin to discourage enthusiasm

One of the surest signs of age in any man is when youthful energy and enthusiasm on someone else's part leave him feeling tired and disapproving.

A man was once walking along the promenade in Brighton with his little grandson. They met an older minister. The old man was sadly disgruntled. Nothing in this world was right; everything and everybody was all wrong, and to make matters worse he was suffering from a slight touch of sunstroke.

The little grandson had been silently listening. When they had left the gloom-stricken old man and had walked on for a short distance, the little grandson said, "Grand-dad, I hope that you never suffer from a sunset."

Maybe the little fellow hadn't got the word quite right, but he had got the idea all right. There are some people who suffer from a sunset. They live in a dark and discouraging world.

The Christian should be a man, not of the sunset but of the sunrise, a man of encouragement and not discouragement.

EVENING

There are some people who have a very highly developed faculty of criticism. They see faults much more easily than they see virtues, and they find it much easier to criticize than to praise. There is one principle of criticism that we should always observe.

No man has any right to criticize any other man, unless he is prepared to do the thing better himself, or unless he is prepared to help the other man to do it better.

The world and the church and life would all be infinitely poorer without the critics.

Only the man who is prepared to have a go himself, or at least to lend a hand, has the right to criticize.

Of all flags to wave, the wet blanket is the worst of all, and yet there are a large number of people in the church and in the world, for whom the wet blanket is the national flag. We will not go far wrong, if we make it our aim to go through life always encouraging and never discouraging those who are willing to adventure and those who are doing their best.

People and construction kits

MORNING

People are the most important realities in the world. We must remember this.

And so must some others.

The scholar must remember it

Kermit Eby, the great American teacher, in his book *The God in You* tells how he feels about teaching. "I know," he says "that research is important, yet I know also that a man is more important than a footnote."

He is.

The social reformer must remember it

"Do not try to convert them," was the advice given to worker priests in Paris. "Love — for you are placed beside one another for this."

The social reformer can be tempted to forget people and concentrate on conditions. But it is people who matter. Change them, and conditions will change!

The ecclesiastic must remember it

The ecclesiastic's danger is that he may begin to believe that the most important things in life are ecclesiastical systems, forms of church government, rituals, liturgies, vestments. etc! In fact it is living souls that matter.

EVENING

Construction kits, for me, are parables of life. God does not give us a completed life; he gives us the raw materials out of which to make a life.

God gives us ourselves, with all our gifts and our abilities; he gives us the world, with all its beauty and its bounty, and its resources; he gives us the people we live with; and he says to us, "Out of all these things, make a life that is worthwhile."

It is never God's way to give us the finished article; he gives us the raw materials. It is never God's way to do things for us; it is always his way to enable us to do things for ourselves. God's whole method is to encourage and enable us to do things for ourselves.

But you would never get your construction kits to come out right unless you followed the instructions. So it is with life. God gives us the raw materials of life, and God gives us the instructions how to turn them into a real and worthwhile life. He gives us his law and his commandments in his book; he gives us conscience within to tell us what to do and what not to do; he gives us the guidance of his Holy Spirit; he gives us Jesus to be both our example and our power.

God has given us all we need to make a life; God has given us the rules and instructions to follow: and God has given us his Son to help us to do the things we could never do ourselves, and to make the life we could never construct ourselves.

God, sin, and the Church

MORNING

We all have this habit of calling something that we do not wish to face by a different name.

Men do this with God

Men are often quite willing to speak of a First Cause, a Creative Energy, a Prime Mover, when they will not speak of God.

Many people continue to use all kinds of circumlocutions to avoid speaking and thinking of a personal God — but you cannot banish God by simply changing the name of God.

This is even truer of sin

It is nothing less than characteristic of modern thought and speech to talk of everything except sin.

We cannot escape from God by changing the name of God; we cannot escape from our own responsibilities by talking of sin under names that are evasions. "A rose by any other name would smell as sweet." God by any other name is no less God; and sin by any other name is still nothing less than sin.

EVENING

Generalizations are hardly ever true universally. To argue from one particular instance to a verdict on a whole institution is grossly unfair. It is no more fair to say that churches are packed because one is full than to say that churches are deserted because one is two-thirds empty.

There are very few statements made about "the church" today that would stand up to a cross-examination in a court of law.

It is time that we all — ministers, laymen, journalists, authors, supporters and critics of the church — stopped making large and general statements about the church, often out of ignorance rather than out of knowledge.

What we can do is to take the New Testament picture of the church and compare our own congregation to it — and then we shall be compelled, not to criticism, but to search our consciences.

Kindness

MORNING

Long ago, Seneca said that what men need above all else is a hand let down to lift them up.

To be kind is always better than to be clever — not that the two things are mutually exclusive, but they so often tend to be.

One of the greatest scholars under whom it was my privilege ever to sit was John E. McFadyen, who taught so many of my generation Hebrew, and who opened our eyes to the wonder of the Old Testament. But it is not "Johnnie's" scholarship that we who knew him remember; it was his almost Christlike kindness.

I remember a college football match at which Johnnie was present — he always came to them. One of our Glasgow boys was hurt — he was assistant in a certain church with responsibility for services in a mission. That evening there was a knock at his door. He opened it to find Johnnie on the doorstep. "You were knocked out at the match today," said Johnnie (it was Saturday), "and I've come to see if I could take your services for you tomorrow."

It is kindness that matters.

No one can think along these lines at all without the thought of the mind going back to the saying of Jesus: "Inasmuch as you have done it unto one of the least of these my brethren you have done it unto me" (Matthew 25:40).

EVENING

There are some people whose lot in this world owes almost everything to Christianity.

There is the workman
Aristotle was quite definite: "Master and slave have nothing in common; a slave is a living tool, just as a tool is an inanimate slave."

Varro is equally definite. Writing a treatise for the Romans on agriculture, he divides the instruments of agriculture into three classes — the articulate, the inarticulate, and the mute. "The articulate comprising the slaves, the inarticulate comprising the cattle and the mute comprising the vehicles". The only difference between a slave and a beast or a cart was that a slave could talk.

When Lord Shaftesbury was asked why he toiled so hard for chimney sweeps and factory workers and coal miners, he answered, "I have undertaken this task, because I regard the objects of it as being, like ourselves, created by the same God, redeemed by the same Savior, and destined for the same immortality."

A new image

MORNING

L ooking in a mirror can produce many reactions!

You can look at yourself with a certain admiration

Narcissus, the handsome young Greek, was not much concerned for anyone else, but he did like himself. Looking into a pool of clear water one day, he saw his own reflection and he fell in love with himself. He just wanted to keep looking and looking at his own lovely appearance. But he was so entranced with himself that, wholly occupied in gazing at his own reflection, he pined away and died. At death, he was changed into the Narcissus flower. And the truth in that story must never be missed. Self-admiration is the death of the soul. To admire ourselves as we are is to have no wish to change. And with those who don't want to change, the soul is dead.

You can look at yourself with a certain bewilderment

A famous cartoonist drew a little man on a vast pile of books, looking into a mirror. The books were labeled history, philosophy, biology, theology, etc.

The little man was clearly an academic who knew the contents of all the books and probably understood them. As he looked in the mirror, there was sheer bewilderment, and above his head there was a question mark. He understood everything — except himself!

It is wise to "look in the mirror" and take stock every now and then. But we must not just look. We must act. And in Jesus we can. He can give a new image to us all.

EVENING

The Incarnation takes away our ignorance of God

Long ago, Plato said that it was impossible to find out anything about God, and, if by any chance you did find out anything, it was impossible to tell it to anyone else.

The essence of Jesus Christ is that in him we see what God is like.

The Atonement takes away the barrier of sin

The church very wisely has never had one official and orthodox theory of the Atonement. But every theory of the Atonement says one thing, although the different theories may say it in different ways. Through the life and death of Jesus Christ, the relationship between man and God was completely and totally changed.

The one idea that is common to all theories of the Atonement is the idea of reconciliation. Because of what Jesus Christ is and what he did and does. the fear and the estrangement and the distance and the terror are gone.

We know that even to us the friendship of God is open.

Destiny and a bleak future

MORNING

We are living in an age of power, an age when men control forces the like of which even their fathers never even dreamed of. The mind of man has penetrated the secrets of Nature. "The nature of the Universe," said Hegel, "hidden and barred from man at first, has no power to withstand the assaults of science; it must reveal and lay bare the depths of its riches before man, ready for his enjoyment."

Bertrand Russell once said, "Science as technique has conferred a sense of power; man is much less at the mercy of his environment than he was in former times."

Man has power today such as no other generation ever possessed. Distance has been annihilated, and space is on the way to being spanned. The means of mass communication make it almost as easy to speak to a continent as to a single individual. Speeds that would once have been thought incredible are commonplace. Measured in terms of sheer destruction, the power which man controls is like a devilish and satanic miracle.

It is this power which has presented man with a life and death problem.

The problem is not now the acquisition of power. The problem is the use of power. All power is in itself quite neutral. It is neither good nor bad. It is potential for goodness and for evil, for blessing and for destruction.

The important thing in relation to all power is the character and the quality of those who possess it. In the hands of good and loving men, power is a blessing; in the hands of selfish, self-seeking, reckless men, power is an evil.

EVENING

I have come across one thing that tells of very real threats to the life of man in the time to come.

In the *Lancet* Dr. Reginald Passmore, Reader in Physiology in Edinburgh University, says that a new species of man is emerging in the West — a species which takes in too much food (often of the wrong sort), in relation to his energy output, and becomes diseased as a result. He calls this species *Homo sedentarius*, which literally means "sitting down man".

Here is the description of the kind of life that many people, perhaps most of us, lead. We drive sitting down to our work in a motor car; we do our work sitting down at a desk; we eat meals which are too large and too rich; we drive home again at night; and we spend the evening half-sitting, half-lying, in a chair, half-awake, and half-asleep.

OCTOBER 29

A house of your own

MORNING

Virginia Woolf said that all she asked from life was a room of her own.

The great souls knew the value of a house of their own — Francis of Assisi "loved mountains". Paul went to Arabia to be alone. Jesus was often alone.

We need to be alone to meet ourselves

We are so often so busy making a living that we do not stop to think whether we are making a life.

We need to be alone to meet God

We do not really know a person if we have only met him in crowds.

We need to withdraw to meet others better

It is not so that we may live alone that we need a little house. It is to help us to serve others better.

EVENING

A family cannot really be a family until it has a house and a key of its own.

In this life we need at least sometimes to be alone

It is one of the problems of modern life that people have lost the art of being alone.

Friendship is good, and doing things together is fun. Man is instinctively a gregarious animal. But there can get into life a restlessness, an inability to bear one's own company, which ends in making life a neurotic and a discontented business.

We have the example of Jesus

After a busy day at Capernaum in which he gave himself unreservedly to people, he rose early in the morning and went away to be alone (Mark 1:35). After the days of teaching and the feeding of five thousand he sent the crowds, and even the disciples, away on ahead across the lake that he might be alone (Mark 6:46).

It is necessary sometimes to be alone with ourselves and alone with God. It is not that this loneliness is an end in itself. Jesus did not want to be alone for the sake of being alone. He wanted to be alone so that he could meet God, and then come back stronger and calmer to meet people. His loneliness was only a withdrawal to fight the better. And so it must be with us.

The people God needs

MORNING

At a recent conference I heard the story of an older minister who, when he was informed that a certain younger man was the possessor of a B.A. degree, said, "The only B.A.s we want here are those who are Born Again."

And I heard that the story sometimes circulated in the form that the only M.A.s who were wanted were those who were Marvelously Altered!

A man must have certain things before he can effectively serve the church.

He must have a real religious experience

No man can teach what he does not know; and no man can bring other men to Jesus Christ unless he himself has met Christ and knows Christ. It is not possible to introduce others to someone whom we do not know ourselves.

He must have a real training in thought

No man will ever be an effective force as an evangelist if he can do no more than repeat like a parrot that which he has been told. Any real course of education must teach a man not only what to think, but far more, how to think.

Any man who is to become preacher, teacher, witness for Jesus Christ must know what the great minds and hearts of men have thought and said of Christ, and must also have thought the matter out for himself until he comes to a faith which is his faith.

EVENING

The student for the ministry must have a real training in the technique of communication

One of the most damaging of all mistakes is the idea that in the work of the minister and the evangelist and the witness for Jesus Christ, technique does not matter. Many a man's work has been spoiled and rendered ineffective for the simple reason that he never took the trouble to study the technique of how to get this material across.

He must have a real ability to understand his fellow men and to get on with them and to get alongside them

There was a great deal to be said for the Jewish regulation I have mentioned earlier, that a Rabbi must have a trade. There would be much to be said for making it the practice that all who seek to enter the ministry should have had some time at some ordinary work amidst men. Still further, the Jews had a saying: "An irritable man cannot teach." It is quite certain that the man who has never solved the problem of living at peace with his fellow men will never be an effective servant of the church.

To all this, there must be added staying power. That staying power can only be acquired by the ability daily to live close to God.

The individual and Philemon

MORNING

The pastoral gift is a supreme interest in people and in *individual* people. This makes a man a great minister of a church.

This ability to remember things about individual people is not only the mark of a great minister; it is also the mark of a great doctor, and it comes first and foremost, from sheer interest in people.

Paul Tournier in his book *A Doctor's CaseBook* says that sometimes a patient says to him, "I admire the patience with which you listen to everything I tell you." Then he says, "It is not patience at all, it is interest."

God is like that

In another part of his book, Paul Tournier speaks of what he calls the personalism of the Bible. Most people find the long lists of names in the Old Testament and in the New Testament sometimes quite irrelevant. But Paul Tournier is fascinated that God should know so many people by name. "I know thee," God said to Moses, "by name" (Exodus 33:17). "I am the Lord," God said to Isaiah, "which call thee by thy name" (Isaiah 45:3).

God, with a world to sustain, knows each one of us by name.

EVENING

In many ways the letter to Philemon is the strangest book in the New Testament. What is a little personal letter about a runaway slave named Onesimus doing in the New Testament?

How did that letter get into the New Testament? We cannot tell for sure, but we can guess. Scholars believe that it was in Ephesus about AD 90 that Paul's letters were first collected and edited and issued to the public as a book. Now some years after that Ignatius, the Bishop of Antioch, was writing letters to the churches of Asia, as he was being taken to Rome to be flung to the beasts in the arena.

Amongst the letters there is one to Ephesus which pays rare tribute to the Bishop of Ephesus and to his beautiful nature and to the usefulness of his life — just like his name.

And what is the name of this Bishop of Ephesus? It is Onesimus.

There are scholars who believe that the runaway slave, Onesimus, and the bishop, Onesimus, are one and the same person, and that when Paul's letters were collected at Ephesus, Onesimus insisted that this little letter to Philemon must go in, that all men might know what once he had been and what Jesus Christ had done for him.

Mothers

MORNING

Mothers never get tired!

If a so-called "working" man had to work a mother's day he would both strike and collapse. (Twenty-first-century readers will recognize that a mother very often has a job outside the home, in addition to the following):

Mother's day begins at 6.30 am to get the family on the way by 8 o'clock and at midnight Mum will still be working.

An eight-hour day? Payment for overtime? These are things that mothers know nothing about. Mother works as long as her family need her.

Mother knows nothing about demarcation disputes

We get a good deal of industrial trouble about who does what. Duties are strictly delimited and defined. But Mother is the cook who cooks the meals; the chambermaid who makes the beds; the cleaner who cleans the house; the laundrymaid who washes the clothes; the waitress who serves the meals; the dishwasher who washes up; the nurse who looks after us when we are ill; the child psychologist who knows what to do with the child; the teacher who helps the child with his first steps in learning; the priest who hears the confessional; the disciplinarian who keeps order; and at all times the lover and the friend.

Mothers don't stop to argue what is their duty and what is not. Where they are needed they act.

EVENING

The Bible is rich in mothers

There is Rebekah the mother of Jacob (Genesis 27).
There is Hannah the mother of Samuel (1 Samuel 1).
There is the anonymous mother of Peter's wife who served Jesus with a meal (Mark 1:29-31).
There is Eunice, Timothy's mother (2 Timothy 1:5).
And there is Mary, the mother of Jesus.

Protestants are often angry about what they call Roman Catholic "Mariolatry". But I sometimes wonder if behind so-called Mariolatry, there is the recognition of what all mothers are and do; that, even if it has become debased and exaggerated, there is something of human value there.

Don't let us ever forget the tireless ones: Mothers!

Modern pilgrims

MORNING

I admire the adventurousness of young people today. They are ready to go off alone into the blue, without a tremor!

My granddaughter Karen, when she was seven, went off to Ireland where she was to spend her holidays, by boat from Stranraer all by herself. True, she would be looked after on the boat and she would be met at Lame, but I'm pretty sure that at seven I wouldn't have made that journey!

My daughter Jane went off to France on her own when a teenager. True, we knew the people she was going to, and she was met at Paris, but I very much doubt if, at her age, I would have gone off with so much confidence.

I knew a young man who, when still at the university, made the most incredible journeys. On one occasion his brother drove him to the nearest motorway and left him to hitch a lift just anywhere. The boy finished up in Salonika! And the only money he spent on travel was for the boat from Dover to the Continent.

These modern pilgrims show faith in action

There are three kinds of faith here. They have obviously *faith in themselves*. And there is *parental faith* too. There is *faith in the essential decency of other people*. For every one case where there is trouble and even tragedy, there are thousands in which everything goes well.

This is faith.

EVENING

Again, all this adventure of pilgrimage does two things to young people.

It removes their insularity. And it ensures that there is growing up a race of young men and women whose outlook is international. It is part of an exciting new world.

I am convinced that it would be — thank God — very much harder to persuade people to go to war today than ever before, because no one wants to fight the people with whom he has eaten and drunk and hiked and swam and climbed and sung and talked.

The modern pilgrims are pioneers of a movement by which the world can become one. Let us encourage them!

Do it badly!

MORNING

There is nothing quite like the D'Oyly Carte performance of the Gilbert and Sullivan operas. A performance by that company is as near perfection as any human production can possibly be.

There is nothing quite like the D'Oyly Carte performances! There would be a girl singing Frederick's part in *The Pirates* because the school hadn't any boy tenors. The curtain would stick when it was supposed to open on the scene. And so on. But in the hearts of many of us in Dalziel High School it put a love for these operas that time has done nothing to lessen.

No school could possibly perform these operas like the D'Oyly Carte Company; *but if a thing is worth doing, it is worth doing badly.* We did them badly, but we got one of the treasures of life out of them.

We do not stop playing golf because we cannot score like Tony Jacklin. We do not stop playing the piano because we will never be concert pianists.

We do not stop preaching because we will never be Spurgeons. It is worth aiming high even if it seems beyond us.

EVENING

The choir *ought* to have a go at the really great music.

The preacher *ought* to attempt the great and difficult subject.

The congregation *ought* to launch out on this or that impossible scheme.

If it is worth doing, it is worth doing badly.

But — and it is a big but — it is also true that *the thing must be done, as well as ice can possibly do it.*

The choir need not start on the big work if the members have come to a stage when they think they do not need to attend practices.

The preacher need not start on the big subject unless he is prepared to read and think. The congregation can hardly launch the big effort if 50 per cent of the members propose to do nothing.

If a thing is worth doing, it is worth putting our best into it.

Let us "have a go" at the big thing. If it is worth doing, it is worth doing badly, so long as it is done as well as we can possibly do it.

Bible study

MORNING

How ought we to study the Bible so that we may overpass the barriers and come together?

We have to ask of the Bible first of all: What does it mean?

This is one of the great reasons — perhaps it is the only reason — why we must never fail to teach our students and our preachers the original tongues, the Hebrew and the Greek, in which the Bible was written.

This is why the study of words is all-important.

This is why the study of the background of the Bible is of intense importance, because we can never really find the meaning of a saying until we also find the circumstances and the situation in which it was written.

EVENING

We must always study the Bible as a whole

The battle of proof texts is a battle with no victory. Isaiah says, "They shall beat their swords into ploughshares, and their spears into pruning hooks; nation shall not lift up sword against nation, neither shall they learn war any more" (Isaiah 2:4). Joel says, "Beat your ploughshares into swords, and your pruning hooks into spears; let the weak say, I am a warrior" (Joel 3:10). In the Bible we are constantly being confronted with this kind of contradiction. Clearly, what we must do is to find the total message of the Bible and to think about it.

There must be an end of the belligerent hurling of texts at each other, and a real attempt to bring the whole gospel to the questions we discuss.

We must try to find out, not just what the Bible means in general, but what it means for us

If we are to do this, there is one thing that, perhaps above all we must try to avoid.

We must try to avoid going to the Bible in order to find in it material to support ideas and theories which are in fact our own.

When we study the Bible we must sit down in humility before it and listen, not to our own voices extracting our own meanings from the Bible, but to the voice of God as it speaks to us in his book.

It will be an exercise in humility, but it will also be a path to truth.

We are one!

MORNING

I belonged to a small group of people who met together several times a year to work on a task which had been assigned to them. People who meet together might learn from this little group.

All the meetings of the group are begun with prayer

It would be wrong to say that we ask for the presence of God, because we very well know that, even if we wished to do so, we could not get out of the presence of God; but what we do ask for is that we should be made aware that we are working in the presence of God.

How different many a meeting, even many a church meeting, would be, if we remembered that God heard and saw everything that was said and done!

No one in the group ever hesitates to express his opinion

It may well happen that his opinion is very much his own, and that it is startling and unusual and even unlikely to meet with agreement. But everyone in the group feels quite free to say what he thinks.

If a person has something to say, he should say it at the right time and in the right place, and it is the reverse of helpful to be quite silent at the time when things ought to be said, and to be extremely talkative when the right time for saying them should be over and past.

There is always some hope of meeting a man's objections, if you know what they are.

EVENING

The group is prepared to give anyone of its members a hearing

There is never any impatience; no one is ever snapped at; no one is ever made to feel that he is a time-waster. The members of the group are prepared to listen to anyone who thinks that he has something to say.

All the members are prepared to admit that they were wrong

On occasion it is the work of one of the group itself which is under the microscope and under examination; but no one ever resents criticism, however drastic. It often happens that a member of the group will express an opinion with conviction, but it may be that after he has heard the others speak, he will admit that he was in error.

Attendance at the group of which I have been writing is one of the joys of life. I wish that all church groups were like this one!

Discouragement and encouragement

MORNING

Discouragement has three terrible consequences.

Discouragement kills a man's enthusiasm
So long as a man is enthusiastic about something, life is bearable, but take that essential enthusiasm away and there is very little left.

Discouragement ends by making the person discouraged come to the conclusion that it is simply not worth trying any more
A psychologist tells of being in a home where there was a small child. In a visit of an hour he heard that small child either told to do or told not to do eighteen different things, and told to do them or not to do them in a tone of the utmost severity. There can be only one result of that. The child is bound to come to think of himself, consciously or unconsciously, as a useless bungler who can do nothing to please his parents.

Constant discouragement can make a person lose all self-confidence
There is a vast difference between the arrogant self-confidence that is based on an inflated idea of one's own ability and importance and the quiet confidence which knows that it can cope with life and with the situation. But constant discouragement can cause so much self-doubt that it can leave a person quite unable to face life at all.

EVENING

There is nothing in this world which will pull the best out of a man as encouragement will. To feel that someone is with you, to feel that someone is willing you on to achievement is one of the great things in life.

Parents should encourage their children
Let parents encourage their children. "Fathers," said Paul, "do not provoke your children, lest they become discouraged" (Colossians 3:21).

Employers should encourage their employees
If you want to get the best out of a man, the best way to do it is to rive him some praise.

Congregations ought to encourage their ministers
A word of encouragement to a preacher can be a thing of infinite value.

There is criticism enough in the world. Let's try some encouragement instead.

Home sweet home (1)

MORNING

Queen Victoria was almost entirely dependent on the Prince Consort, Prince Albert. When Albert died all too young, Queen Victoria was grief-stricken with a grief which lasted for many years; and all her sorrow was summed up in a thing she once said: "I have no one to call me Victoria now."

She had plenty of people to call her "Your Majesty", but no one left to do the little personal things which mean so much.

Here, there is something to be said about the modern setup of life. This is one of the great problems — and even disasters — in the house and home in which the mother goes out to work. There is something fundamentally wrong with a home in which there is no one there to welcome a child when he or she comes home.

When money is earned at the cost of a child coming home to an empty house, that money is money dearly earned. Being a wife and mother is not only far and away the greatest job in the world; it is also a fulltime job that takes everything any woman has got to give to it.

At the end of all the roads there is no empty house, but a home where we shall, face to face, receive the welcome of him with whom we have walked so long.

EVENING

The more "human" you are the more you love your home. It is a very strange person who does not love home. Dogs are next door to being human and they love their homes. I love cats, but I am bound to say that they are remote and inhuman animals, and home does not mean nearly so much to them, unless they are like Sammy the Siamese whom we still mourn and who was more like a dog than a cat.

The poets have all loved home. You remember Byron's lines:

'Tis sweet to hear the watchdog's
    honest bark
Bay deep-mouth'd welcome as we
    draw near home;
'Tis sweet to know there is an eye
    will mark
Our coming, and look brighter
    when we come.

Or do you remember the story in the Bible about Hadad the Edomite who, when he was a little child, was taken in exile to Egypt? He was well treated there, but the day came when it was safe for him to go home. "Let me depart that I may go to my own country," he said to Pharaoh. And Pharaoh, who had loved him and treated him well said, "What hast thou lacked with me that thou seekest to go to thine own country?" And Hadad answered, "Nothing, howbeit, let me go" (1 Kings 11:21, 22).

Let him who has a home thank God for it, and let him remember with sympathy and kindness those who have not.

Home sweet home (2)

MORNING

There are at least three reasons why in this age in which we live the home is supremely important.

We live in a worried age

It is of supreme importance that we should have some place in which we can relax, in which we can find people to whom we can really talk and really open our hearts, knowing that they will neither laugh at our dreams, mock at our failures, nor laugh our troubles out of court.

My old teacher, W. M. Macgregor, used sometimes to talk of the work of the ministry and the importance of getting married in order to do it well! Thinking of the worries and the frustrations and the problems and the annoyances and the irritations that the running of a congregation is always bound to bring, he used to say, "Happy is the man who has someone at home to whom he can explosively unburden himself!"

There are many of us who simply do not know what we would do, if we had no one to talk to at home.

EVENING

We live in a tired age

One of the features of this age is the number of people whom one sees asleep! In buses, in trains, on any journey, in restaurants and in clubs you see people who obviously have been unable to keep their eyes open.

It is one of life's supreme gifts to have some place in which we can fully and completely relax.

Sometimes we may think that it would be pleasant to live forever in some luxury hotel with all kinds of service at our beck and call. But experience teaches us that there is literally no place like home — and the supreme thing about a good

home is that it is the one place where we can find the peace our soul's desire.

We live in an age of insignificance

Today, we all tend to be names on a card, numbers on a card index, specimens of some kind of class or group. The individual has come to matter less and less as an individual.

Jesus spent thirty years in fulfilling home duties and only three in the world of men.

Let us thank God for the home and for the family which, in his goodness, he has given to us.

Creation and instinct

MORNING

The joy of making things is one of the elemental joys of the human situation. The more ambitious the project, the better.

I have a friend who decided to try woodwork. Most people, when they embark on woodwork, start with something like a pipe rack; my friend's first production was a most elaborate, built-in, fitted wardrobe for his and his wife's bedroom! There is nothing like starting in a big way!

To know the joy of creation is to share the joy of God, for it was at creation that, in Job's magnificent phrase (Job 38:7)

> The morning stars sang together,
> And all the sons of God shouted
>   for joy.

The man who refuses to use his gifts misses the greatest thrill in life, the joy of making something, the pride in the finished product, and the thrill of seeing others use what his hands or his mind have made.

EVENING

Instinct is the raw material of life; and as with all raw material, everything depends on how you use it.

There is an instinct of acquisitiveness
We can use it to develop a wise and prudent independence, to support ourselves and our loved ones by our own efforts and to build up a home.

There is an instinct of self-defence and self-production
We can use it to seek a wise safety and to avoid a foolish recklessness; or we can use it to produce, within ourselves, a weak cowardice which will face nothing, and whose one policy in life is to run away from things.

There is an instinct of sex
We can use it to ennoble life, to be in the closest and most perfect relationship with someone else; or we can use it to become kin to the beasts, and even to ruin life for ourselves and for other people. It can lead life to the greatest of joys and to the deepest of tragedies.

There is the instinct of motherhood
We can use it to be the foundation of a home, to lead to one of the most perfect relationships in the world.

God gave us the raw material of life. The question is, What are we going to make of it?

Responsibility and irresponsibility

MORNING

There is no more delightful passage in Boswell's *Life of Johnson* than the passage which tells how a certain Mr. Edwards stopped Johnson one Sunday on the way home from church.

Fifty years before, he and Johnson had been fellow students at Pembroke College and their ways had never crossed since.

In the conversation between Edwards and Johnson, there is a passage which must make every minister of the church and of the gospel pause for thought.

Edwards is talking about what he wished he had done. "I wish I had continued at College," he said. "Why do you wish that, sir?" asked Johnson. "Because," answered Edwards. "I think I should have had a much easier life than mine has been. I should have been a parson and had a good living like Bloxham and several others, and lived comfortably." "Sir," said Johnson, "the life of a parson, of a conscientious clergyman, is not easy. I have always considered a clergyman as the father of a larger family than he is able to maintain. I would rather have Chancery suits upon my hands than the cure of souls. No. sir, I do not envy a clergyman's life is as an easy life, nor do I envy the clergyman who makes it an easy life:"

Surely this must make every minister of the gospel think.

EVENING

There are some people who claim that they live entirely by faith. They go off to the mission field, for instance, entirely on faith. It is their conviction that God will provide; they pray, and money for some needed purpose has an extraordinary habit of turning up.

I am becoming less sure that there is any virtue in that.

Recently I received a letter from abroad. The writer said that he had given up a good position in life to become a missionary. He had no financial resources, but that did not worry him. Somehow or other he got all he wanted; God never let him down. Then the letter went on to say that this man had heard of certain books. He would like to have them. Would I send them to him — "complimentarily" — or, to put it crudely, for nothing? Of course, the man got his books: I was very glad to send them to him.

But the incident set me thinking. People who rely on faith for everything, who never think of money, who trust God for everything, are in a very curious position. They are, in fact, completely dependent people who *do* think twice about money and how to earn it.

Dietetic discipline

MORNING

I am still thinking about the problems of dieting and slimming. I have learned a great deal of great value in doing so.

I have learned that to lose weight, the only way is to stop eating!

At least, I must stop eating the forbidden things. There is no short cut. Nor is there a short cut to anything worthwhile in this life.

I have learned that the supreme danger is little relaxations

Someone hands you a plate of biscuits and says with a smile, "One won't hurt you!"

Someone offers you the chocolates and says appealingly, "Just one!"

Someone says, "Go on! Take a spoonful of sugar in your tea, just for energy!"

If you give in to this you're sunk!

There is no halfway house. You either take the things, or you don't take them. The little relaxations are fatal.

When you take a decision, you have to take it. No halfway house, and no let-up, just as in a diet.

EVENING

I have learned that your worst enemies are the people who want to be kind to you

They are the people who encourage you to take just one — "it can't do any harm".

How unwise love and kindness can be! I think that it was Seneca who said: *Ama fortiter!* "Love courageously." If you love a person, the love must be strong, not sentimental. The best sympathy is a bracing, not an enervating thing.

You must never invite temptation. Someone says: "Just one!" And I used to say, "I would love to, but I mustn't." And that in effect was to say. "I know I shouldn't do it. but I might be persuaded if you coax me!" The way to say "No" is to say "No", and not to give any chance for a persuasive comeback.

We would fall far less often to temptation, if we did not put ourselves into situations in which we are tempted.

Without discipline, there is no such thing as real life.

Sinful pride

MORNING

I met a man today who said rather a wise thing to me. He said to me, "I've been reading about your slimming successes!" "Yes," I said, "I've removed two and a half stones in three months." He smiled at me: "I think you ought to write a piece about pride!" he said.

He was quite right, because I was really much too well pleased with myself! And we are all very apt to be pleased with ourselves for the wrong things.

There is no point in being pleased with ourselves for doing the things which it is our duty to do

In my own case it would have been better to be ashamed of letting myself get overweight rather than be proud of myself for having taken weight off!

Jesus had something to say about this. He said, "When you have done all that is commanded you, say: 'We are unworthy servants; we have only done what was our duty!'" (Luke 17: 10).

Too many people seek praise and thanks for doing what it was only their duty to do. No man has any right to be well pleased with himself when in fact all that he has done is what he ought to have done.

Jesus wanted to know what case for pride a man had if he loved the people who loved him, and if he greeted his brothers enthusiastically. That is the kind of thing anyone does. So Jesus asked, "What more are you doing than others?" (Matthew 5:47).

EVENING

There is no point in Christianity unless it has the something extra special.

This is the really Christian question. There are a great many people who will claim: "Well, I'm as good as the next man anyhow." But the whole point of the Christian life is that the Christian should not he as good as the next man; *he should be a great deal better than him!*

Not only has the Christian the obligation to be something special. He has also the power to be something special. For he has God.

This is his real reason for pride. "Let him who boasts, boast of the Lord," said Paul (1 Corinthians 1:31). The only thing about which the Christian can have a just and legitimate pride is the fact that God so loved him that he gave his Son to die for *him.*

That is the pride which brings with it the obligation to be a little more worthy of that love.

Laughter

MORNING

Beyond doubt there is a ministry of laughter

I know well there is laughter and laughter. There is a wrong kind of laughter, the bitter laughter of the cynic laughing someone's faith away, the snigger of the dirty mind laughing at some smutty joke, the cruel laughter which can find delight in someone else's pain. But beyond doubt, laughter is one of God's great gifts to men.

"Laughter," as Thomas Hobbes the philosopher said, "is nothing else than a sudden glory."

There is no doubt that the great laughter-makers are exercising one of God's ministries.

I am profoundly grateful to the great laughter-makers; they too are serving men and serving God, for he who brings sunshine into the lives of men and women, if only for an hour, is doing something well worth while.

EVENING

Laughter is one of the greatest of God's gifts. And here are three questions.

Can you make others laugh?

There are some people, and if they are in a group or company, you can be sure that very soon everyone will be laughing: you feel happier just for meeting them. There are other people v,-ho are like a douche of cold water, or a black cloud, or a deep depression over Iceland; you feel chilled just for meeting them.

Alice Freeman Palmer was a great American teacher, and one of her students said of her, "She made me feel as if I were bathed in sunshine."

The laughter-bringers are doing God's work.

Can you bear being laughed at?

There are some people who are deeply offended if they are laughed at. There are some people who promptly lose their temper if they are laughed at. One of the most difficult things in the Christian life is to be regarded as a fool for the sake of loyalty to Jesus.

Can you laugh at yourself?

In many ways the greatest gift in life is ability to laugh at oneself. If we can really see how silly we are sometimes, if we can really see how ridiculous we often are and if we can laugh at ourselves with all our queer ways, life will be very much easier.

Laughter is always a cleansing thing, but it is never so cleansing as when it is directed by ourselves at ourselves.

Giving and receiving

MORNING

A small church I know has raised ten thousand pounds to renovate their church building. This I find incredible. How have they done it?

They had an aim and an object

That object was the reconstruction and the rebuilding of the sanctity of the church.

It is easier to raise money for a concrete cause than for a general appeal.

The whole parish was brought into this, not just the congregation

In other words, the project became a community undertaking and ambition.

There was the full support of the minister

It is true to say that the leadership lay largely in the hands of lay people. When there is lay leadership at the top, everything becomes much more attainable.

The congregation called in the experts

If a job is to be done it is wise to get the expert to do it. The expert will only achieve his best results when the spiritual tone and atmosphere of the congregation is also high.

A church is not a business, but that is no reason why it should not be run in a businesslike way.

EVENING

There is a royalty in receiving. When a gift is offered, there are, I think three necessities.

A gift must be accepted

There are few things more wounding than to have a gift refused.

A gift must be appreciated

This is where the courtesy of a thank you comes in. Sometimes we send a gift to a person and there is not a word, spoken or written, of thanks; and it is only long after that you can even be sure that the person got the thing at all.

A gift must be used

Half the joy of giving a gift is to see the gift used by the person to whom it is given. This is where Jesus was so wonderful. He took the smallest and apparently most inadequate gifts and used them gloriously. The giver whom Jesus praised most of all was a woman who put a couple of coins worth together less than a farthing into the Temple treasury (Mark 12:41-44).

Differences

MORNING

I have just been reading two interesting books. The first is the life of Sir Halley Stewart, churchman and industrialist, founder of the Sir Halley Stewart Trust, who was born in 1838 and died in his hundredth year in 1937.

The other is the *History of the Highland Railway* by O. S. Nock.

These two books have shown the wide difference between the Victorian and Elizabethan ages.

There is the difference in the family

Halley Stewart's father, Alexander Stewart, was one of twelve children; he married a girl who was one of a family of seven daughters; he himself had fourteen children, of whom Halley was the tenth. To use an Irishism — if Halley Stewart had been alive today, the chances are he would never have been born at all! Here we have three marriages, with a product of thirty-three children — common enough a hundred years ago, almost impossible today.

There is the difference in the Sunday

Alexander Stewart ran a school, and we are told of the time-table of the ordinary Sunday: 7 a.m. prayer meeting for the scholars and the family. 8.00. breakfast; 9.00, School Scripture class: 9.30, Sunday School:11.00, church service; 1 p.m. dinner; 2.30, Sunday School followed by a walk; 5.00, tea: 6.30. church service; 8.00 singing in the home. That was a Sunday in a pious home a hundred years ago. Today it feels incredible.

EVENING

There is the difference in the employment of so-called servants

Halley Stewart did not run a very big house, but there is a photograph of the house staff taken about 1896 or thereby. There are three gardeners, a coachman, a cowman, cook, scullery maid, parlourmaid, housemaid, washerwoman and two other assistants who were gardeners' wives.

For the fourth difference I turn to O. S. Nock's railway book

In the new Elizabethan age the child-bearing mother becomes the wife who goes out to work; the regimented Sunday becomes the day for golf and a run in the car; the servant in a big house has become the wage-earner in the factory; the discipline of work has been devalued in the permissive society. It may be that in the Victorian age the pendulum swung too far to one side and in the Elizabethan age it has swung too far to the other. Our task is to get discipline and permissiveness into proportion.

Dependent, yet independent

MORNING

One of the hero stories of modern times is the story of the Scottish poet, William Soutar. He died in 1943 at the tragically early age of forty-five.

He died after twenty-five years of illness and ten years of complete helplessness.

There was a time when he could do nothing more than move his head.

That situation Soutar met with gallantry. When at twenty-five he knew that he was doomed, he said. "Now I can be a poet."

When he became increasingly helpless, as helpless as a child, he said: "One's core of manliness must be preserved."

"Life," he said, "demands something more from a man than a handful of lyrics," and life received more from William Soutar.

EVENING

The story of that life was admirably written recently by Alexander Scott in his biography of Soutar entitled *Still Life.*

In that book two sayings of Soutar are quoted.

The first is an incident related by Soutar himself. He was thinking of his earliest memories and he describes the "first important symbolic episode in his life".

He and his mother had set out for a walk one afternoon when he was about three years old. Suddenly the walk was interrupted, when the little lad ran from his mother with the words which he flung over his shoulder: "Get back, get back, I don't require a mother."

There was the child's desire for independence.

But this very same William Soutar was later in his manhood also to say: "If I have been privileged to catch a more comprehensive glimpse of life than many other men, it is because I have stood on the shoulders of my parents."

There is the declaration not of independence, but of dependence.

Little things

MORNING

William Soutar was not only one of the great Scottish poets. He was also a prose writer of more than ordinary distinction, often with a touch of wit and humor. Sometimes he used to write parables. Here is one of them:

"There was once a woodcutter's wife who forgot to salt her husband's porridge, and when the woodman reproved her she retorted that he was a fool to make a fuss about so small a thing.

This angered the woodman and, coming to his task, he began to smite at a tree furiously, so that in a back swing his axe-head flew off to a great distance and injured a favorite horse of his master's which was being led to be reshod.

Now on that day this very horse was to have borne the nobleman to a meeting of noblemen who were gathering to discuss their grievances against the king.

It was therefore in a disgruntled mood that the woodcutter's master joined his peers; and under compulsion of his anger, eloquently counseled his confederates to revolt.

In the subsequent tumult many were slain by the sword, pestilence and famine; and for a generation afterwards the people bowed under the burden of great taxation.

There came a rebellion, and a generation of suffering all because a woodman's wife forgot to salt her husband's porridge!"

This is a parable of the greatness of little things. "Who hath despised the day of small things?" said Zechariah (Zechariah 4:10).

EVENING

There are times when small things can save a man

This was something William Soutar found out himself. In his increasing helplessness, it was inevitable that more and more things should vanish from his life.

He writes: "So much can wither away from the human spirit, and yet the great gift of the ordinary day remains; the stability of the small things" of life, which yet in their constancy are the greatest."

Again and again a man finds salvation in the things of every day. In sorrow, worry, indecision, there is nothing that so saves a man's sanity and life as simply to go on with the ordinary routine things of life.

To sit down amidst regrets, to sit and do nothing but worry is fatal.

Ordinary duties enable us at these times to go on.

The parent's task

MORNING

There are in the two sayings of William Soutar which we have quoted a summary of the task of the parent — and it is a task almost impossibly difficult and hard.

There is a time when the child is utterly dependent. Everything has to be done for him or he would literally die. There is a time when the lad or girl, or the youth or the maiden has to be gently but firmly guided and controlled. But all this dependence and all this guidance have but one end — the production of a person who some day will be able to stand up and meet life on his own two feet.

In life there is nothing more difficult than the duty of the parent to guide and control and yet to render strong and independent his child. And today that duty is infinitely more difficult than it used to be.

So often the tendency is to hold on to people too long, to try to keep them dependent, consciously or unconsciously to resent the day when they must live their own lives and come to their own conclusions.

EVENING

We must let go material things; we must let go preconceived notions and ideas. So far these are conventional preaching points. But then this young man added something startling — *we must let people go*. We must never hang on to people when the time has come for them to be themselves.

We must never smother them when they ought to be breathing a larger air.

We must never try to make them dependent when they ought to be independent.

There is a wonderful text in Deuteronomy 32:11: "As an eagle stirreth up her nest, fluttereth over her young, spreadeth abroad her wings, taketh them, beareth them on her wings, so the Lord alone did lead him."

The eagle has to teach her young to risk the adventure of flight. At first she rouses them, takes them on her broad wings; carries them; but then bit by bit she withdraws her wings and the young eagles find themselves in the sky alone. She carries them — but only to launch them out in flight for themselves.

Those of us who are older, and those of us who are parents, must remember that we have a double duty — the duty of guidance and of control, and yet at the same time the duty of making young people independent, able to live their lives on their own.

To be great . . .

MORNING

There is no finer storehouse of stories than classical literature. Let us think then of some of the great stories of the Romans and the Greeks.

The greatest of all the Greek kings was Alexander the Great, the man who before he was thirty wept because there were no more worlds left to conquer.

The most illuminating story of Alexander comes from his Persian campaigns.

He had put Darius into a position in which ultimate defeat was certain. Darius recognized this and offered Alexander terms which were very favorable. He offered Alexander a great ransom for the captives which had been taken, a mutual alliance, and the hand of one of his daughters in marriage.

All this Darius offered, if Alexander would halt and stay his hand and be content with that which he had won. Alexander told Parmenio, his chief of staff, of the terms which had been offered.

Parmenio said: "If I were you I would accept them." And Alexander replied: "So would I — if I were Parmenio."

Alexander was Alexander, and for him there was nothing less than absolute victory. A lesser man would be content, and well content, with lesser things, but for Alexander it was all or nothing.

Great men have always had a sense of their own greatness.

EVENING

To be great one must have a sense of greatness. But this is a very different thing from conceit. How shall we get that sense of greatness?

We get it from self-respect

When Nehemiah was urged to seek a cowardly safety in the hour of his danger, his answer was: "Should such a man as I flee?"(Nehemiah 6:11).

Many a man has been compelled to greatness, because he respected himself, and would not let himself down.

We get it from the fact that others are thinking of us, hoping for us, believing in us, praying for us.

George Washington once said: "I shall not despair so long as I know that one faithful saint is praying for me."

We have God behind us

Every time we say good-bye, and every time we use the word "good-bye", we are listening to the words, or we are saying the words: "God be with you!" We go in the strength of the Lord. The world needs men and women who can think and act greatly.

The sparrows

MORNING

In Manchester Exchange Station there was a tea bar.

It was typical of that station at that time that there was not even room there in which to drink your cup of tea. There was a makeshift counter and one or two comfortless forms.

But it was a wonderful experience to have a cup of tea there.

Why?

Because the station sparrows try to share it with you! They were so tame that they hopped about on the counter within inches of you to ask for crumbs and to eat them.

I shall never forget the friendly sparrows in Manchester Exchange Station.

EVENING

Jesus would have liked the stories about the sparrows I told in this morning's entry. He too said something about sparrows.

Matthew and Luke tell it differently.

Matthew says: "Are not two sparrows sold for a farthing? And one of them shall not light on the ground without your Father" (Matthew 10:29). (It's not a case of the sparrow falling dead; it's a case of the sparrow hopping on the ground; God sees even that.)

Luke has it: "Are not five sparrows sold for two farthings, and not one of them is forgotten before God?" (Luke 12:6). Something wrong with the arithmetic? Two sparrows for one farthing — five sparrows for two farthings — someone slipped up in counting? No! In Palestine two sparrows cost a farthing, but if you were prepared to spend two farthings, an extra sparrow was flung into the bargain for nothing.

A sparrow that was literally worth nothing—and yet God sees and cares for that sparrow!

Jesus used that saying for a purpose. If, he said, God cares for sparrows like that, if God cares even for the sparrow that is worth nothing at all, the sparrow that is just flung into the bargain and given away as worthless, how much more will he care for you?

God cares for the sparrows.

Are you not of more value than many sparrows?

Jesus speaks to everyone

MORNING

There was once a Welsh girl who went to work in an English town.

In the English city there was a Welsh church, but it was a long journey from where the girl worked and stayed, yet Sunday by Sunday, she made the long journey to worship with her own people in her own tongue.

The people with whom the girl stayed and worked were kindly people, and they invited her to save herself the trouble of her long Sunday journey and to come with them to their own church. The girl courteously refused, saying that she would rather make the journey to share in worship in the tongue which she knew and loved so well.

Not at all critically, and in spite of faultfinding, but very gently the master of the house said to the girl: "You must remember that Jesus wasn't a Welshman."

The girl answered: "I know that, sir, but it is in Welsh that he speaks to me."

Jesus speaks to every man in the tongue and the language that he can understand.

EVENING

Jesus speaks to men of every nation

Christianity is the one thing that can overpass all national barriers and boundaries. The church is not a human institution which belongs to any one land or nation or continent or color.

Within the church all nations are gathered. Christ comes to every man in that man's own tongue.

Jesus speaks to men of every condition

The philosopher with his wisdom, and the simple man who has no book learning, the great man with the cares of great affairs upon him, and the humble man of whom no one has ever heard, the saint who walks in holiness and the sinner who is soiled with sin— Jesus Christ speaks to each in a language that he can understand.

Christ speaks to each in a language that he can understand.

The reason? The language that Jesus Christ speaks is the language of love.

It is the wonder of Jesus Christ that he speaks to every man in his own tongue.

He is the spiritual linguist.

The rough and the smooth

MORNING

In any day and in any week and all through life you get the rough and the smooth, the sunshine and the shadow, the prizes and the spots.

Life is bound to be a mixture.

It is of the greatest importance to remember that life is a mixture and to accept it as it comes.

In life there are things we can do and things we cannot do

There is nobody in the world who can do everything equally well. Each of us has his abilities and each of us has ineptitude in some areas.

One of the great secrets of life is to realize what we can do and to do it, and to see our limitations and to accept them.

There are pleasures we can have and pleasures we cannot have

That is more than a matter of merely being able to afford them. One of the strange features of life is that in every pleasure there is an element of danger.

It is so very easy for a pleasure to become an addiction, and for a habit to become a master, and even a tyrant.

It is a wise man who realizes the pleasures which are not for him.

EVENING

There are things in life that we get and things that we do not get

In this world there are two kinds of people. There are the people who are constantly surprised that life has been so good to them — and they are by no means always the people who have the most. And there are the people who are always bitter and resentful because life has — as they see it — withheld so much from them.

There are a great many things which may not be for us, so it is well to begin to count the blessings which are for us.

The number of them will surprise us!

Life has its prizes and life has its blots. It has the things we can do and the things we cannot do, the pleasures we can have and the pleasures we cannot have, the things we get and the things we do not get.

But for those who love God it can still be harmony, for God always works things together for good to them that love him (Romans 8:28).

Dreams

MORNING

The fable of Perette and her milkpail is one of the oldest fables in the world. Perette was a girl who worked on a farm, and one day the farmer's wife gave her a whole pailful of milk for herself. So Perette put the pail of milk on her head, and she set off to the market to sell it; and as Perette went she was dreaming her dreams. Perette's dreams went something like this.

"I'll sell this pail of milk, and with the money I get for it I'll buy some eggs, and I'll soon have some chicks, and I'll keep them and I'll fatten them, and when they are grown into hens, I'll sell them. And with the money I get for the hens, I'll buy a little pig, and I'll keep him and I'll fatten him and I'll sell him."

And then she began to smile with anticipation. "And with the money I get for the pig. I'll buy a real silk dress; and I'll put on my dress, and I'll go to the dance, and Robin will be there, and when he sees me all dressed in silk, he'll ask me to marry, but I'll show him how particular I am; I'll toss my head and —'

And there and then, in her dream, she tossed her head, as she would do at Robin, and when she tossed her head, off fell the pail, and the milk all spilled, and all Perette's dreams were gone.

EVENING

Like all fables, the story of Perette has its lessons for life.

We cannot do without our dreams

It was the tragedy of the days of Eli that there was no open vision in the land (1 Samuel 3:1). As the writer of the Proverbs had it: "Where there is no vision, the people will perish" (Proverbs 29:18) — which may be a wrong translation, but which none the less, even if it be by accident, contains a great truth.

All the men who have done great things have had their dreams, dreams of the distant places, dreams of a New World, dreams of the defeat of pain, dreams of harnessing new power.

Always behind the action there lie the dreams.

But the dream needs an interpreter

The complaint of Pharaoh's butler and baker, when they were in prison, was: "We have dreamed a dream, and there is no interpreter of it" (Genesis 40:8).

The interpretation of the dream can make all the difference. One of the great things about Jesus Christ is that he is the interpreter of men's dreams. In him men find the satisfaction of their highest longings, the meaning of their dream.

What is the point?

MORNING

What is the point of so much of our business and of our hurry and our worry and our effort and our anxiety?

We strive so hard to get a little more money, to get a little farther up the ladder — but in the end, what's the point of it all? What good is it really going to do us?

We worry about this and that and the next thing — and in the end, what's the point about it all? Even if the things we worry about do happen, the heavens won't collapse. As a friend of mine often says, "it will be all the same a hundred years from now".

I do sometimes wonder what the point is of many of the arguments that go on in committees and all kinds of church bodies. We get so hot and bothered about a comma in a report. A trifle can be magnified into a matter of epoch making principle.

We would save time and trouble and wear and tear, if, before we started an argument, we would say: "What's the point of it anyhow?"

EVENING

I hope that I won't be misunderstood, if I say that there is a great deal of scholarship of which one is sorely tempted to ask: "What's the point of it anyhow?"

There are many books that have undoubtedly taken years of research, and which, regarded as pure scholarship, are monuments of erudition, but what's the point of them?

Epictetus used to say: "Vain is the discourse of philosophy by which no human heart is healed."

It is an interesting test

If it were applied, quite a number of erudite works would emerge as vanity.

But there is a bigger question than any of these — What's the point of life?

The point of life is to know Jesus Christ, and through him to be ready, fearlessly, to meet the call of God when that call comes.

If we see life that way, then all other things would take their proper place.

What's the point of it all?

It might enable us to see a little better what things are important and what things, ultimately, really do not matter.

Silence is golden

MORNING

There is nothing worse than talking at the wrong time. There is nothing so valuable as knowing when to keep quiet.

It was said as a tribute to a great linguist, not that he could speak seven different languages, but that he could be silent in seven different languages.

There are times when we ought to keep silent.

We ought to keep silent when we are angry

If we speak when we are in the grip of anger, we will say things that will hurt others and hurt ourselves, when we remember them.

We ought to keep silent when we want to criticize

Most criticisms are better never uttered. No one has the right to criticize at all, unless he is prepared himself to try to do better what he criticizes.

It is a good rule never to be slow with praise and never to be quick with criticism.

Anaximenes, the old Cynic philosopher, used to say that there are only two people who can tell us the truth— an enemy who hates us bitterly and a friend who loves us dearly.

The truth can hurt.

It is sometimes better to suffer in silence.

EVENING

There is certain company in which we ought to keep silent

Boswell tells how once Dr. Johnson was enjoying himself with freedom of jest and talk in a company of friends. He saw a foolish man approaching.

"Let us be silent," said Johnson. "A fool is coming."

There are some people in whose presence it is dangerous to talk. They will repeat our confidences. They will twist our words. They will broadcast in public that which was said in private. In the presence of such people — and it is not long before we are able to identify them — a wise silence is better than words.

There is need for silence, if ever we are to hear the voice of God

It is quite possible that we hear the voice of God so seldom because we listen for it so seldom!

Sometimes we may feel that God does not speak to us. But "Do you ever give him the chance to speak to you?"

The Psalmist heard God say: "Be still and know that I am God" (Psalm 46:10).

Knowing people

MORNING

It is knowing people that matters. Compared with knowing people, knowing things is not of any very great importance.

It is from knowing people that certainty comes

It would be quite possible to have an argument with an atheist, or an agnostic, or a communist about Christ and about Christianity, and to be quite unable to meet and to counter the arguments he advanced against Christianity. But, if we know someone who is really and truly a Christian, a person in whom Christ lives again, then we can say: "I know that I can't meet your arguments. But I know so-and-so, and so-and-so is the living and indestructible argument that the Christian faith is a fact."

A human being is always the best argument for the Christian religion.

People can do what print can never do.

God sends his comfort through people much more than through any written word.

EVENING

It is from knowing people that courage comes

It is always easier to walk some frightening road, to do some difficult thing, to meet some hard situation, if there is someone there to meet it with us.

Loneliness is the great begetter of fear. At such a time it is often possible to know all the promises of God and of Jesus Christ, and to believe them in a kind of way; but again and again they come alive in a person.

It is through the company and the influence of somebody that we really lay hold upon them.

It is God's way to work through people. Blessed are those who know the people who can bring us certainty and comfort and courage.

It is never enough to know the creeds; it is not even enough to know the print of the Bible. It is only enough to know him whom the creed seeks to define, and him of whom the Bible tells. Jesus himself said it: "This is life eternal, that they might know Thee the only true God, and Jesus Christ whom Thou hast sent" (John 17:3).

Christianity never consists in knowing what; it always consists in knowing whom.

The value of a life

MORNING

There are many things in this world whose life-span is far beyond the life-span of a man. Man is by no means the living creature with the longest life on earth.

So length of life is not the most important thing about life.

Shelley, Keats, Rupert Brooke, Schubert, Mozart all died long, long before they had attained even middle age.

The value of a life lies in the intensity of its living

It is better to live for a shorter time with a kind of passionate intensity, stretching out eager hands to grasp life, enjoying life to the uttermost, living life to the full, than it is to live for a much longer time with care and prudence and careful calculation never to become excited and never to do much.

Sir Walter-Scott used the famous lines as a chapter heading in Old Mortality:

> Sound, sound the clarion, fill the
>   fife;
> Throughout the sensual world
>   proclaim,
> One crowded hour of glorious life
> Is worth an age without a name.

The people we remember with grateful hearts are the people who had the joy of living, even if their time was short.

EVENING

The value of a life lies in the way in which it is spent, not in the way in which it is hoarded

The people whom the world remembers with gratitude are the people who poured out life with a prodigal hand, not the careful souls who jealously hoarded it, lest they should make too much of an effort.

The question about life is not how we have managed to have it, but how we have managed to spend it.

Life is the one possession in which reckless extravagance is better than cautious economy.

In assessing the value of any life, it must always be added to the reckoning that no life stops here

"Whosoever shall seek to have his life shall lose it; and whosoever shall lose his life shall preserve it" (Luke 17:33) — that is the word of him who is the Lord of all good life.

Flesh and bones

MORNING

Edwin Muir, in his autobiography, tells how one of his continental friends, Mitrinovie by name, once said to him of Bertrand Russell: "When he die, the angels they find nothing to eat on his bones."

In some people there is a strange kind of fleshlessness, a kind of inhumanity, a kind of cool detachment from the sorrows and the problems and the passions of mankind.

I have a friend called James Thomas Williams who sent me a poem entitled "The Skeleton", which, with his permission, I pass on:

> With prayer and supplication
> and so much preparation,
> they were so still,
> with so much to be,
> through constant consecration.
> Without adequate preparation,
> one's life is all peroration,
> there's not much bones
> in a life without prayer —
> only continual evaporation!

There are things in life whose very design it is to keep us human, and to preserve us from, or to make us unlearn, this detached inhumanity.

EVENING

Sorrow is designed to make us human
Edwin Muir quotes a wonderful line of poetry:

> A deep despair hath humanized
> my soul.

The Arabs have a proverb: "All sunshine makes a desert."

The land needs the rain and life needs its tears.

Love is designed to make us human
W. B. Yeats says of an Irish writer called Todhunter: "If he had lived anything strongly, he might have been a famous man."

We never really see people as they are, and very certainly we can never help them at all, unless we see them with the eyes of the love of God. One of the great tests of love is that a real and a true love should make us suddenly discover that we love, not only one person, but all men and women everywhere.

No one is expendable

MORNING

The whole experience of life is designed to make us human

That is why the "pure" scholar, the man who lives for ever surrounded by books in a library, can never be really human.

It is only when we have lived amongst men, when we have shared their sorrows, met their temptation, been involved in their sins that we become human.

J. S. Whale talks of a modern habit. He says that we are so apt to scurry round taking photographs of the burning bush from suitable angles instead of taking our shoes from off our feet, because the place whereon we stand is holy ground.

We are apt to sit in an armchair, pipe in mouth, feet on the mantelpiece and talk about theories of the atonement, instead of bowing down before the wounds of Christ.

Long ago Ezekiel saw the valley of dry bones, and heard the voice of God saying to him: "Son of man, can these bones live?" (Ezekiel 37:3). They did live because the breath and the Spirit of God moved upon them.

Love, sorrow, the human sense of human failure and of human sin are meant to humanize us.

We only become really human when the divine heart of Jesus Christ becomes the heart with which we meet all the experiences and all the people of this life.

EVENING

My eye caught the headlines at the top of a column. They read: "Only 80 casualties; only 20 dead." And suddenly I caught my breath — "Only 20 dead."

To the high command twenty dead were as nothing, a very satisfactory figure. But somewhere in Britain there were twenty broken hearts and maybe more.

I remember something I read in that wonderful volume *A Doctor's Casebook in the Light of the Bible*, by Paul Tournier.

Dr. Tournier writes: "There was one patient of mine, the youngest daughter in a large family, which the father found it difficult to support. One day she heard him mutter despairingly, referring to her: "We could well have done without that one!" You can guess the effect of such a remark," says Dr. Tournier, "not wanted by her parents, not wanted in life."

If the New Testament teaches one truth with the greatest definiteness, it is that in God's sight no human being is expendable.

We all matter.

In life, and in death

MORNING

Jesus drove home in his preaching the value of every one.

There was the woman who had the ten silver coins and who lost one. Does one in ten matter so very much? It mattered to her. And she lit a candle and swept and searched until she found it, and, when she found it, she was so happy that she called in her neighbors to share her joy (Luke 15:8-10).

There was the shepherd who had a hundred sheep and one went lost. What was one in a hundred? Did one foolish sheep more or less matter so much? It mattered to him. And the man risked his life on the mountainside and amidst the crags and gullies until he found the sheep that was lost (Luke 15:3-7).

Sometimes we may be apt to look at some peculiarly unpleasant person, or sometimes on the streets we may catch a glimpse of some wretched, dirty, degraded creature; and there goes through us a kind of shudder of disgust; and we wonder how anyone could care for a creature like that.

God does.

The dignity of human life comes from nothing else than the fact that each individual man is dear to God.

No Christian can ever despise a fellow-man, for that man, no matter what he is like, is dear to God.

No Christian can ever ultimately despise himself, for, in his black moments, he must ever remind himself that he is a child whom God cannot do without, and that, even if he matters to no one else, he matters to God.

EVENING

From beginning to the end of Scripture the word is the same.

"You will not fear," says the Psalmist, "the terror of the night, nor the arrow that flies by day" (Psalm 91:5).

Across the waters Jesus comes to his disciples with the words: "It is I; do not be afraid" (John 6:20).

In the heavenly places the words of the Risen Christ to the John of the Revelation are still the same: "Fear not, I am the first and the last, and the living one" (Revelation 1:17-18).

In truth Christianity means the death of fear.

How God is seen

MORNING

God has three problems.

God has to ask, "How can I get men to know me?"

Man, being man, cannot achieve the knowledge of God, being God, Knowledge of God cannot be had by man reaching up, unless God also reaches down. It is through revelation, not speculation, that man must know God.

There are three ways in which God reveals himself to me:
    He reveals himself in the beauty and the bounty of the world.
    He reveals himself in people.
    He reveals himself in Jesus Christ.

EVENING

God has to ask, "How can I get men to heed me?"

The experiences of life are designed to turn the thoughts of a man to God. Sometimes God speaks in suffering or in weakness.

Leighton, you remember, said in a time of illness, "I have learned more of God since I came to this bed than I did in all my life."

Sometimes God speaks out of failure and loss.

Sometimes a man has to lose the non-essential things to be driven back to the things which are essential.

As the poet heard God say, "If goodness lead him not, then weariness may toss him to my breast."

The experiences of life are meant to turn a man's thoughts to God.

God has to ask, "How can I make men love me?"

It would never be enough for God to subject men to himself by force. The only compulsion that God can use is the compulsion of love; and the only submission that God desires is the submission of the loving heart.

So, when we see the love of God in life and in the world, and supremely in Jesus Christ, surely in the end we ought to come to say, "We love him because he first loved us" (1 John 4:19).

Lost property

MORNING

There are certain things we should see to it that we never lose.

We should never lose our temper

The people who fly into a temper are a problem in life. If we know they are like that, we have to handle them as carefully as a stick of gelignite or there will be an explosion. Any man in a temper will say things and do things for which he will afterwards be profoundly sorry.

When a man wished to enter the famous Qumran Community, from which the Dead Sea Scrolls came, the first question that they asked him was about his personal relationships with other people. In other words, the most important question was: How do you get on with other people? I should certainly say to any man contemplating entering the ministry: If you don't get on well with people, stay out! And if you have got a temper, get it cured — or don't begin!

We should never lose our head

When anything dangerous or disastrous happens, the biggest problem is not the people who are injured; the biggest problem is the people who panic.

Kipling said that the sign of true manhood was this: "If you can keep your head when all about you are losing theirs and blaming it on you."

EVENING

We should never lose heart

It is easy to lose heart about ourselves, about our work, about the church, about the world in general.

Most artists have painted Hope as young and eager, with head thrown back and face laughing to the wind. But Watts knew better. He painted Hope as battered and bleeding and tattered, with only one string left on her lyre, but with eyes alight.

This is the hope that matters — the hope that has seen all and still hopes on. For the Christian it is literally true that where there is life there is hope. He has a hope which goes even beyond life and which is immortal and eternal.

Our temper — our head — our heart — these are things we should never lose.

Verdicts

MORNING

In his book *The Day before Yesterday*, James Moffatt set down some verdicts on religion, and on what religion is.

Religion is madness

Robert Owen spoke about "the various phases of insanity called religion".

Religion can be madness in the wrong sense and in a right sense. It can be madness in the wrong sense when it issues in that fanaticism which launches into persecution and savagery.

Madame Roland made the famous statement: "Liberty, what crimes have been committed in your name!" But when we read back into the history of the church, it would often be true to say: "Religion, what crimes have been committed in your name!"

The days when the church burned its so-called heretics, and when it preached the love of God in hate, were, and are, days not of religion, but of madness.

But it can also be madness in the right sense. There was a time when the friends of Jesus said: "He is beside himself." (Mark 3:21). The unswerving loyalty of the Christian, the complete self-forgetfulness, the selfless service, the sacrificial giving, the love which will lay down its life for its friend, can, and do seem like madness to the man who can see no further than the world and the material tests and standards of the world.

Sometimes the man who tries to live like God will seem mad to a godless world.

EVENING

Religion is challenge

Religion has not by any means always been this. George Meredith's objection to religion was that "it belonged to the ambulance corps rather than to the fighting line of life". He felt that religion as he saw it was concerned rather with picking up the pieces of failure than sending men out on a gallant adventure.

Real religion is bound to be a challenge. Real religion is bound to awaken in a man dissatisfaction with himself and dissatisfaction with the world. It is bound to give a man at one and the same time a judgment on things as they are, and a vision of things as they should be, and a summons to turn the one into the other. Real religion presents a man with a challenge to change himself and to change the world.

Thinking of you

MORNING

Charles Wesley was one of the most attractive of men, and the full charm of the man meets us in Frederick G. Gill's biography of him. Unlike John, Charles was ideally happily married, to his wife Sally.

Like John, Charles was much on the road, but even on the road he had a way of meeting his wife across the miles. The idea was that they should agree both to pray exactly at the same time each day and at a certain time on certain other days, and that, though separated, they should at these times meet, as it were, at God's mercy seat.

So during one of his visits to Ireland, Charles writes to Sally, "Remember to meet me always on Monday noon, and every evening at five." At twelve o'clock on Mondays and on each evening at five they kept their pact of prayer, and across the miles they met.

Everyone of us has friends from whom we are separated. Now in real friendship you can take it up again after years of separation as if things had never been any way different. But at the same time, Dr. Johnson's advice is always valid, "A man, sir, should keep his friendships in constant repair." Friendship is like any other plant — it flourishes with nurture and it wilts with neglect. There are certain very simple things that we can say.

EVENING

How often do we write to our friends when we are separated from them?
I fear that most of us are bad correspondents. Happy is the home where there is one person who is the family letter writer.

Nowadays, there is something better than a letter, there is the telephone
When I am away I phone my wife every night without fail. It makes opening the envelope with the telephone account a terrorizing experience — but it's worth every penny of it to meet across the miles. Time and money are never wasted in keeping touch with someone you love.

There is just thinking about each other
There are more things in this world than our philosophy dreams of, and there are things which defy explanation. I am convinced that there is more than something in telepathy, in establishing contact across the miles by the power of thought.

The letter, the telephone, the thought, the prayer—all these can be used to annihilate the miles.

Points of view

MORNING

A Christian and a Communist were in a group run by a pastor in France. It was a group where people of different beliefs and backgrounds could get together and talk — "a house of dialogue". They had been reading the story of the woman of Samaria, and after they had finished the pastor asked each of them what struck him about the story. So he said to the Christian, "What strikes you about this story?" The Christian answered, "What strikes me is that Jesus should ask a favor of that awful woman — an adulteress." So the pastor said to the Communist, "What strikes you about the story?" The Communist answered, "What strikes me is the woman had to come to the well because she had no running water in her house."

Now here are two people speaking from different points of view.

The point of view of the so-called Christian was the point of view of respectability

Respectability was his touchstone — and it certainly is not the Christian touchstone.

You will remember R. B. Duncan's famous saying to the woman at the sacrament. She was plainly hesitating to take the cup. "Take it, woman," said the old saint. "Take it. It's for sinners. It's for you."

The church is the place for sinners, and Jesus Christ is the friend of sinners.

EVENING

The test of the Communist was social service

His aim was to give people better living conditions and better homes to live in. But neither will that do. We have all seen people transferred from a slum to a new house and we have seen them make the new house into a slum in a very short time. That is very far from always happening, but it can and does happen. You do not change a person by changing his or her house.

The real Christian aim is not the collecting of respectable people and not primarily the construction of new conditions. It is the making of new people.

Once you make new people, once you change the heart, then the true goodness and the true holiness follow, and then the new man makes the new conditions.

The Christian aim is not a conventional respectability, not simply the changing of a material situation. It is the recreation of the individual man and woman.

In the last analysis nothing less will do.

Jesus' anger

MORNING

It is much easier to define and describe the abuse of anger than it is to describe and define its use. But there is one sure way to see the proper use of anything, and that is to see how Jesus used it. Let us then see how Jesus used anger. What were the things which incurred the anger of Jesus?

Jesus was angry with anyone who was a hypocrite

In Greek the word for hypocrite is the same as the word for an actor. A hypocrite is a man who plays a part, a man who puts on an act, a man whose whole life is a deception. A hypocrite is a man who says one thing with his lips and quite another in his heart. A hypocrite is a man whose actions give the lie to his profession.

Jesus would prefer honest godlessness to hypocritical piety. The man who is one thing to your face and another behind your back, the man who is ostentatiously pious on Sunday and completely worldly on Monday, the man who professes a religion of love and of service and who lives a life of bitterness and selfishness — that is the man who incurred the anger of Jesus (Matthew 6:2, 5, 16; 7:5; 15:7; 22:18; 23:13-29).

EVENING

Jesus' anger was against those who loved systems more than they loved human beings

There was the day when there was a man in the synagogue, and the orthodox Jews stood and watched to see whether or not Jesus was going to heal him, for it was the Sabbath day. Jesus looked round with anger (Mark 3:1-6).

Jesus was angry with any man who loved a system of theology or a system of church government more than he loved God and his fellow-men. To be more devoted to a system than to God is a common enough fault in the church, and it incurs the anger of Jesus.

Jesus' anger was kindled against all exploitation

This is the background of the cleansing of the Temple (Mark 11:15-19), the story in which John presents us with the terrifying picture of the Jesus with the whip (John 2:13-17). The money changers were charging exorbitant rates for changing the pilgrims' money, and in the Temple booths a pair of doves was costing seventy-five pence while outside they could be bought for four pence. Jesus' anger blazed against the exploitation of poor people in the vested interests of the rich.

Corruption of the best

MORNING

"Lilies that fester smell far worse than weeds." It is one of the tragedies of life that the best things can be perverted into the worst.

Take, for instance, the four virtues which Hitler singled out.

There is love of country

Patriotism can be a noble thing. But love of country can be perverted into the idea of a herrenvolk, a master race, which despises all others. Love of country can turn into apartheid, which looks down on all others. Love of country can turn into the desire for conquest and the lust for power. Love of country can beget the mailed fist and the jackboot and the merciless ambition for mastery.

There is courage in the face of adversity

Courage in the face of adversity has kept men on their feet through thick and thin. But courage in adversity can turn into self-centered stubbornness which is based on selfishness and which will not realistically face the situation.

EVENING

There is loyalty to one's leader

Loyalty to one's leader sounds like a wholly admirable quality. But Paul saw loyalty to one's leader tearing the Corinthian church apart, when men claimed that they were loyal to Cephas and to Apollos and to Paul himself. Loyalty to a leader had become a disruptive and divisive force within the church.

In the church what is required is not loyalty to one's leaders, but loyalty to one's Leader. There is a loyalty to Jesus Christ to which all secondary loyalties must yield.

There is the willingness to accept discipline for the sake of some great cause

It is perfectly true that no great object can be achieved without discipline; but there can come a situation in which discipline becomes discipline for its own sake and not for the sake of some end in view. Asceticism can become asceticism for the sake of asceticism.

No discipline is valuable unless it looks beyond itself to a greater end in view.

It is frightening to see how easily the best can become the worst; and the only way to avoid this is to keep Jesus Christ in the center of the picture, for, when he gets his proper place, all other things will get theirs.

Self-criticism, and taking criticism

MORNING

"Know thyself," said the Greek wise man. Most of us see ourselves through very rose-tinted spectacles, and most of us can be very blind to our own faults. To be able to criticize oneself, and to be able to see one's own faults, is an essential part of the road to self-amendment.

How shall we learn self-criticism? How shall we see our own faults? We can only learn to do this when we have a standard against which to compare ourselves.

There have been men who have had such a purity in them that they made others feel their impurity. Bernard of Clairvaux was like that, and in the days before Bernard had learned gentleness, many of his monks were afraid even to come into his presence, for in his presence they learned how far they fell short.

We have this standard in Jesus.

There is no man alive who cannot benefit from criticism, if he receives it in humility. There is no man alive who would not benefit by learning self-criticism. A man can only see what he is by realizing what Jesus is, who with the humiliation gives grace to us to rise above ourselves.

EVENING

One of the best tests of any man is just how he accepts criticism.

He may receive it with resentment

Anyone who has resented criticism has put himself under three great disadvantages.

First, he can never be a servant of any leader or of any cause, for to himself, he is the most important person in the world.

Second, he can never co-operate in any joint effort, for no one but himself can ever be right.

Third, he will never be able to learn or to improve, for no man can learn, and no man can become better, who refuses to admit that he has any ignorance or any faults.

There are those who receive it in humility

As the ancient wise men used often to say, the really wise man is the man who realizes that he does not know. The man who will make real progress is the man who knows that a job could be done better, and who is anxious only to find out how it can be done better.

The real enemy of all good work is complacency.

343

Being critical

MORNING

There is not only an art in accepting criticism; there is an art in giving criticism.

Criticism can be given almost solely with the desire to hurt

The psychologists will tell us that almost everyone has in some way or other the desire for power; and there are those who criticize acidly or savagely because, whether they admit it to themselves or not, they like to see the other person wince. There is never anything to be said for cruelty and there is nothing to be said for that.

Criticism can be green in conscious superiority

It is possible for us to stand above the other person; and to look down, and to point out his faults, as if we had none of our own. One thing is certain — no man is faultless.

Criticism given in conscious superiority is seldom effective, because it lacks sympathy. When a man has to criticize, he should remember George Whitefield's famous saying as he saw the man going to the scaffold: "There but for the grace of God go I."

EVENING

There are two kinds of right criticism.

There is the criticism which is prepared to try to do better itself

When the young Isaac Watts was returning from church with his father, he complained about the dreariness of the hymns. His father retorted, "Then give us something better, young man." In time for the next Sunday, Isaac Watts started on that career of hymn-writing; which made him one of the two or three greatest writers of hymns in the English language.

There is the criticism of love

Love is not blind; there is nothing so clear-sighted as love; and love cannot rest content watching its loved one living a life which is below the level of what it might have been, wasting the talents which might have been splendidly used, following some course of action which may end in sheer disaster.

But in such criticism there is gentleness, there is sympathy, there is understanding.

The Bible and conversions

MORNING

The book of Esther

In the days of the 1914-18 war, a body of British troops were besieged for a long time. Boredom more than actual danger was the problem. Among them there was a man who was a man of culture, but an atheist.

In the siege he missed above all something to read. In despair he went to the chaplain, thinking that he might have some books. All the chaplain had to offer was the Bible.

At first the man declared that the Bible was useless to him; but out of sheer boredom he took it and began to read it. It opened at the Book of Esther.

Now whatever else Esther is, it is a great story which would make a magnificent film scenario. The man could not lay it down until he had finished it. If the Bible was like this, it was worth reading! So indeed he read on—and he was converted. And it is literally true to say that it was the reading of the Book of Esther which led directly to his conversion.

EVENING

The book of Leviticus

I have been told of an army doctor who was converted by the reading of Leviticus, because its regulations for sanitation and for hygiene were so eminently sensible.

Now, if there are two books which, it has been said, could be removed from the Bible without loss, these books are Esther and Leviticus — and yet in the two cases I have instanced these two books were the means towards conversion.

There is a lesson here. To put it simply — it is safer to leave the Bible alone! Almost the first person to criticize Scripture and to pick and choose the parts he was going to keep and the parts he was going to dispense with was Marcion. who. as Tertullian said, criticized the Scriptures with a pen-knife.

There is a tendency to do just that. No one is going to claim that the Book of Esther has the religious value of, say, the Gospel of John, or that Leviticus has much of the gospel of grace as Luke.

But the lesson of experience is that there is a place in Christian experience for all the books of the Bible, and even the books that seem most unlikely have been for some the way to God and grace.

Leave the Bible alone in its entirety, for no one knows out of which book in it the Spirit of God will speak to the heart of some man.

The Church's image

MORNING

There is a common image of the church.

It is the image of a place whose main clientele is old ladies, whose main aim is the maintenance of respectability in sexual matters, and whose preaching is on the level of a twelve-year-old child. Is the church really like that?

There is enough truth in this to make it sting.

There is no doubt at all that there are far more women than men in the average Sunday congregation, and that the age level is high.

There is no doubt at all that the church's view of sin has identified it with drinking, swearing, gambling, adultery and fornication.

There is no doubt that there are preachers who under-rate their congregations and who deliver pious and harmless essays instead of grappling with the problems which are matters of life and death.

All this may not be typical of the whole church, but the situation does exist.

EVENING

Here is the remedy.

The church must become fearlessly involved in the world

It must show where it stands on great subjects like peace and war, industrial relations, social justice. Then will youth return to it — for to be young is to be ready to crusade.

The church must realize that there are greater sins than the sins of the flesh

There can be a pride, a callousness, a personal and social selfishness, a sheer materialism which are terrible and deadly sins. There can be an external veneer of respectability with a complete godlessness underneath it.

This is just not good enough in Christ's church.

The church must be completely honest in its preaching

There must be no evasions of issues, because to face them might cause trouble.

Preaching must not be following popular opinion, giving people what they want to hear. It must be the statement of inner convictions, even if these convictions are not what some people want to hear.

The church need not have the image it has acquired, if it has the courage to think and to speak.

Crossroads

MORNING

The church is at the crossroads, and the church has to make certain great decisions.

Is the church going to look back or forward?

Is the church going to go on forever speaking in seventeenth-century English, or is it going to use contemporary language to contemporary men and women?

Is the church going to make an honest attempt to think out its message in the categories of the day in which it is speaking?

Are we going to go on saying that something must be good and great because it has been used or done for the last five hundred or a thousand years, or are we going to say that, if a thing has been used for five hundred or a thousand years, then it is near certain that it does not speak relevantly to today?

I am not answering these questions — I am asking them!

EVENING

Is the church going to look out or in?

Is the church going to become more and more a "gathered" community for a comparatively small, and almost certainly dwindling community, or are its eyes to go out to the millions who have lost touch with the church altogether?

Is a congregation to be concerned more with keeping itself together, more with its own congregational activities, than with the hundreds in the parish or area with whom it has completely lost contact?

The greatest problem of the church today is whether to withdraw within itself and become a gathered and separate community, or whether to go out adventurously to those to whom at the present moment the church means nothing.

Is the church going to agree to some extent to conform to the world, or is the church going to insist above all on its difference from the world?

What, for instance, in a new housing area, often a slum clearance area, is the church prepared to allow young people to do on a Sunday night?

Is the church to allow activities and modern ways of enjoyment that may shock many of its members, in order to establish some kind of human contact with the lost generations?

The church stands at the crossroads. The first step to finding the right way is to face the questions with which the present time is confronting us, to stop running away from them and to stop taking refuge in doing precisely nothing but preserve the status quo.

Going to church

MORNING

There are at least five reasons why we ought to go to church. And even if we have been over some of these before, they are worth noting again at the end of the year.

To go to church, and to let others see us going is to demonstrate to the world where our heart lies

Every time we go to church we tell the world where our loyalty is directed.

To go to church is to share in the fellowship of Christian people

To go to church is not only to make a demonstration to the people outside; it is to find the people inside, and with them to be united members of the Body of Christ.

To go to church is to uphold the hands of the preacher

Any minister will tell you that the congregation is far more responsible for the "feel" of the service than he is. It is the people who can create the attitude of eager expectancy in which things really can happen.

EVENING

To go to church is to worship, to wait upon, and to listen to God

Perhaps we connect going to church far too much with hearing a sermon. This is specially so if we belong to the Free churches. This is a mistake that the devout Anglican will not make. But in a service there are prayers; there are scripture readings; there is music, hymns and psalms; there is an offering; there may be a sacrament; there ought to be silence. And it will be our own fault if in some part of the many-sided worship we do not meet God.

To go to church can be, if it is nothing else, an act of discipline

It is fatal to get into a way of life when we only do what we want to do, or when we only do something when we want to do it. There is room for that spiritual discipline which, even when the spirit within us is arid and dry, and even when we feel our hearts cold and unresponsive, sends us out on an act of spiritual discipline. And it has often happened that just on such a day God all unexpectedly has broken into life.

To worship God in God's house is a privilege, but it is also a duty not to neglect, which is to weaken and truncate the spiritual life

It is nearly Christmas. Why not plan to go then?

Age

MORNING

Age is a very indefinable thing. It certainly has very little to do with the date which happens to be entered on your birth certificate.

Where does this essential youth come from? In an aging population, and with social security pensions, there are many more people who now retire from work, because they have to, while they have still a fair time to live. In such retirement, the researches show, there is a good deal of unhappiness, and most of it has its source in boredom.

The thing that keeps a man young and the thing that keeps him really alive is interest. If a man wishes to stay young, the more things he is interested in the better, especially if these things are outside his own job.

The elixir of eternal youth is wonder. So long as a man can find new things at which to wonder, he need never grow old. In this world of God's, and in the world of human relationships, he need never lack for that.

Learn to be interested and stay young!

EVENING

In one of his addresses Pope John XXIII said a very wise thing. He said: "To be guided by Christian principles does not mean to be reconciled with stagnation in obsolete positions; nor does it mean giving up all efforts at progress."

This is well said. There is an approach to Christianity where the instinct is to look back and to keep things as they are.

There can be stagnation in the statement of belief

It is not that the truth changes; it is that the expression of it in every age must change. Truth has to be expressed in the categories of the age to which it is addressed.

Take the idea of "substance"; the old creeds say that Jesus is of the same "substance" as God.

One feature of Greek thought was that it was in the literal sense materialist. It had no real concept of "spirit" other than that "spirit" was infinitely fine matter. And when it said that Jesus was of the same "substance" as God, it literally meant that Jesus was made of the same stuff as God.

We can understand what they were getting at; but we can no longer use this way of speaking!

Every age has to find its own way of expressing the relationship of Jesus to God, and, if that new way of expression is different from the old way, no one should immediately set up a shout of heresy.

Stagnation

MORNING

There can be stagnation in language

For some quite unintelligible reason, religious language petrified in 1611. When the New Testament was first written, it was absolutely colloquial and contemporary. It was written in the everyday language of everyday people. And it must go back into that language. Otherwise, however beautiful it is, it has stagnated into a language which no one now speaks.

There can be stagnation in worship

Worship for so many has got to be in the language of the Authorized Version of the Bible. But surely a twentieth-century man speaks to God in twentieth-century English. The biggest barrier to prayer is the stagnation that insists on a special prayer language which is quite out of date.

But in worship there is also stagnation in the order of service. For the person within the church, and brought up within the church, no doubt the accepted and traditional orders of service are hallowed and dear. But when a man comes in from outside the church, we cannot afford to go through the long preparation of prayer and praise and reading, or we lose him.

EVENING

There can be stagnation in method

Religious institutions change their methods too late. Even today, for instance, we think of evangelism in terms of Moody and Sankey.

One good custom can corrupt the world, as Tennyson said.

The sad thing about the church is that it is forever fighting these rearguard actions. It is seldom out in front. It is always resisting change, seldom initiating it, and rarely welcoming it. It so often confounds stagnation with loyalty to principle.

"Change and decay in all around I see," says the hymn, but there is a real sense in which it is not "Change and decay". It is "Change or decay".

For stagnation leads to death.

Seeing the need

MORNING

I have come across two very interesting and significant incidents in two recent biographies of very great Christians. The first is from Ernest W. Bacon's biography of Spurgeon.

One of Spurgeon's great enterprises was the founding of a college in which students might be trained for the ministry.

One of the earliest students, the Rev. D. J. Hiley, tells of an encounter with Spurgeon when he was a student in that college. He and Spurgeon met one day in the corridor.

"Is that your best coat?" Spurgeon asked.

"Yes, sir," Hiley answered.

Spurgeon was silent for a moment and then he said: "I wonder if you would render me a little service."

Hiley said that he would be delighted to render Spurgeon any service.

The service that Spurgeon required was the delivery of a note at a certain tailor's shop.

Hiley goes on: "I was to wait for an answer. For reply — the tailor measured me for a new suit of clothes and an overcoat, and sent me away with a hatbox!"

Spurgeon had seen that the impecunious student needed a coat and a suit, and did something about it.

EVENING

The other incident is from Richard Collier's biography of William Booth, although the story itself is of Bramwell Booth, when Bramwell had succeeded his father as General of the Army.

Collier writes:

"The Army . . . had become his life . . . His officers' welfare was always paramount; once, lynx-eyed as always, he noticed that several officers taking tea with him bit on only one side of their jaws. Promptly, at his own expense, he sent them to his dentist."

Bramwell Booth saw that his officers needed dental treatment and saw that they got it.

Here we see the same kind of attitude to others in Spurgeon and in Bramwell Booth, who both saw the need.

The universal expert

MORNING

I saw an advertisement recently which first of all amused me and then made me think. The advertisement was that of a firm of painters and decorators, and it said: "Specialists in all kinds of painting and decorating."

At first sight it seems ridiculous to claim to be an expert in everything. To claim to be an expert in everything seems to be a contradiction in terms.

It has been said that a specialist is a man who knows more and more about less and less. If we go to a medical specialist, we go to a man who is an expert on some particular part of the body, like the heart or the lungs, or the ear, the throat at the most.

In sport we do not expect a cricketer to be a specialist in batting, bowling and wicket-keeping; he is a specialist in one branch of the game.

Yes, indeed, the idea of a universal specialist sounds queer indeed. A man can be jack-of-all trades and master of none.

But there is another side to this. We speak of the all-rounder, and a very useful person the all-rounder is. He can bat well enough, and can take his turn with ball, and if need be he can take the pads and gloves and keep wicket.

There is a case for the man who is a kind of specialist in everything.

EVENING

This kind of universal specialism is the sort of thing that people expect from a minister.

He must be a good preacher and an able pastor. He must know something about teaching young people. He must be a good administrator and it will help if he knows something about law and architecture.

But we can go further than that. The Christian has to be a kind of expert in all the conditions of life, a spiritual jack-of-all-trades.

He must be able to meet sorrow without despair. He must be able to meet difficulty without defeat. He must be able to meet success without pride. In the storm or in the calm, in the sunshine or in the shadow, in sorrow or in joy, in success or in failure, in youth, in maturity and in age, he must be the expert who can cope with anything in life.

Jesus can make a man an expert and a specialist in every circumstance in life.

Accidents and spoiling beauty

MORNING

I have been driving a car of some sort since February 1933, and I have been thinking back across the years to see if I could discover out of my own experience, what the main causes of accidents are.

There is irritation with the other driver
Someone wants to pass us and we do not want to be passed, so we take steps to hinder the other man every time he tries. We get behind a slow-moving vehicle and in the end we lose patience and take a risk. We try to pass and there is a smash. This, that and the next thing irritate us, and an irritated driver is a bad driver.

This is true of all life. There is nothing that obscures judgment like anger and irritation. Three times Psalm 37 (verses 1, 7, 8) gives us the advice: "Fret not yourself." "Fret not yourself," it says, "it tends only to evil."

There is a second cause of accidents that every driver must have experienced, and that is a momentary wandering of attention.

What is true of driving is just as true of life. It is so often true that it is the unguarded moment that brings life to shame or even to ruin.

One of the basic demands of the New Testament is: "Watch!"(Matthew 24:42). Life can end in disaster for the man who is even momentarily off his guard.

EVENING

Romans 14:16 has many different translations. *The Authorized Version* has: "Let not your good be evil spoken of."

The Revised Standard Version has: "Do not let what is good to you be spoken of as evil."

Moffat has: "Your rights must not get a bad name."

The New English Bible has: "What for you is a good thing must not become an occasion for scandalous talk."

J. B. Phillips has: "You mustn't let something which is all right for you look like an evil practice to someone else."

I think the best translation of all would be: "You must not do the right thing in such a way that it gets you a bad reputation."

What Paul was saying was this: Don't do a thing which in itself is a good thing in such a way that it becomes ugly and unattractive. Too often Christianity is rendered unattractive by the misuse of good things.

It is a miracle to turn water into wine. It is a tragedy to turn wine into water.

Knowing the great

MORNING

Sometimes a quite simple and ordinary person becomes great, not because he is great himself, but because of some contact with greatness.

Muirhead Bone tells of an old man in the Inns of Court in London. He was long past his work and a little in his dotage. But people still let him come about the place. If anyone spoke to him, before the conversation was five minutes old, he would say to them: I was an office boy to Charles Dickens."

The one thing he remembered of which he was proud was his contact with greatness.

I think it is Leslie church, that very great preacher, who tells that he was preaching somewhere. After the service a very ordinary little man came round to see him, a little insignificant creature. "Sir," said the little man, "you mentioned Nelson in your sermon. My grandfather held him in his arms as he died on board the Victory."

That little man seemed to grow in stature as he remembered his one, remote contact with greatness!

EVENING

That is what the Christian is like.

Peter and Andrew and James and John were fishermen from the Sea of Galilee. Who would ever have beard of them but for their contact with the greatness of Jesus Christ?

Matthew and Zacchaeus were traitors and quislings. Who would have ever known their names but for their contact with the splendor of Jesus Christ?

We have no greatness of our own. We are ordinary, sinful people. Our only greatness is that somehow, in the infinite love of God, we have had our contact with Christ. Let us too remember our contact with greatness. Let us too live as men who have touched the hand of their King.

Remember an astonishing saying of Jesus in the Fourth Gospel. He speaks of the works that he did himself, and then he speaks of the man who in the future will believe in him, and he says: "Greater works than these will he do!" (John 14:12).

It's great to know the great!

The near and the distant

MORNING

It is true that charity should begin at home, but there is something very far wrong when charity ends at home

To be interested in nothing but our own home and our own parish and our own congregation is all wrong.

There are two reasons why it is wrong.

First, broken hearts and smashed lives are broken hearts and smashed lives wherever they happen. No broken heart or smashed life should ever be unimportant to anyone who is trying to be a Christian. Trouble should matter to me, whoever is the victim.

Second, there never was a time when the world was more one than it is today. As things are now, there is no far away. Mankind is bound up in the bundle of life as never before. We are now living in one world, and distress, wherever it is, should matter to me.

The congregation that never looks beyond its own activities and its own needs is not a Christian congregation.

EVENING

It is far more important for a mother to put young children to bed herself than it is for her to serve on any number of committees.

It is far more important for a father to be the friend of his own children than the leader of youth work amongst other people's children.

The Christian has a double duty.

He must be a citizen of the world, for all men everywhere are his brothers in Jesus Christ.

But he must also be supremely interested in that little piece of the world in which life has set him to live and to work.

In other words, we have to hold the balance between the far away and the near at hand.

Jesus did this.

For thirty years he answered the claims of home before he went out to the world; and on his Cross, when he was dying for all mankind, he was not forgetful of his mother (John 19:26, 27).

Liked and loved

MORNING

There is nothing that someone doesn't like. Even if we ourselves think something entirely unpleasant, there will be someone who likes it.

A writer on Sceptic philosophers, Sextus Empiricus, gives us his extraordinary list of people who like unpleasant and even poisonous things.

Rufinus of Chalcis drank hellebore like someone drinking a cup of lemonade.

Andron the Argive was never thirsty, not even when crossing a desert, and never drank water.

Tiberius Caesar could see in the dark.

I have myself known people who love undiluted lemon juice in all its bitterness, and who actually enjoy drinking castor oil!

All this is interesting, but what is more important is that it is the same with people.

There is no one whom someone does not love

EVENING

Love does not see the faults and the failings and the ugliness which spring to the eyes of other people. That is one of the meanings of the Greek saying that "love is blind".

It is one of the loveliest and tenderest things in the human situation that often a parent will love most of all a child who is in some way handicapped.

When Bunyan was under threat of death, the one thing that haunted him most of all was the thought of his little blind daughter.

During the First World War the King and Queen (King George V and Queen Mary) at least on one Christmas sent Christmas cards to all the soldiers in the army.

There was a soldier who had no friends and no relations; he was alone in the world. He had received nothing at Christmas. Then the royal Christmas card came. "Even if no one else remembers me," he said, "my king and queen do."

The Psalmist had it: "For my father and mother have forsaken me, but the Lord will take me up" (Psalm 27:10).

Everyone has someone to love them, even if the closest ties on earth are broken, and that someone is God.

Race

MORNING

In *Race: A Christmas Symposium*, edited by Clifford S. Hill and David Mathews, there is one section that is specially significant for the church. It is a brief section in which an Indian immigrant, a West Indian Social Worker, and an African student in turn take a brief look at Britain.

I want to quote just one sentence from what each of them wrote.

The Indian immigrant writes: "Christianity (in Britain) as a way of life seems practically non-existent, at least not the full-blooded commitment that distinguishes good Christians in India."

The West Indian social worker writes of British church leaders: "Too often the church reflects rather than formulates opinion."

The African student writes: "The biggest shock we receive is in the field of Christianity." He writes of British landladies: "'Knock and the door shall be slammed in your face' is their policy with African students."

This is indeed an indictment.

EVENING

It is always easier to go with the crowd, to swim with the tide, to run before the wind. This must be the conclusion from these quotations from the symposium on race.

It is always dangerous and lonely to stand alone for some great truth or principle which men do not wish to hear.

The first way may be the way to an easy popularity, and the second way may be the way to an agonizing martyrdom; but it will be a bad day for the world when there is no one left to defy the world and to stand alone with God.

The third charge in the quotation is that, in this country too, apartheid may well be practised.

It is by no means impossible to find the apartheid of snobbery and the apartheid of racial prejudice.

It is perfectly true that the colored person will have difficulty in finding lodgings or a house, or just promotion in his job. Have we forgotten that in Christ Jesus we are all sons of God, and that in him there is neither Jew nor Greek, slave nor free, male nor female? (Galatians 3:26-8).

Perhaps we should take a long, hard, honest look at ourselves sometimes.

Ananias

MORNING

It must have been very hard for Ananias to forget the savagery with which Saul had attacked the church in Jerusalem. It must have been very hard for him, knowing as he did why Saul had come to Damascus, to believe that Saul really was a changed man.

It must have been very hard to stifle the suspicion which must have lurked in his mind. And yet the first two words that Ananias spoke to Saul are amongst the most astonishing words in the New Testament. The words were: "Brother Saul" (Acts 9:17; 22:13).

No breath of suspicion, no moment of hesitation, no hint of recrimination, simply the open heart, and the outstretched hand, the man with the welcome.

Ananias is the example of a man who insisted on believing that there are no limits to the grace of God.

He was right.

EVENING

Here are two more points about Ananias. Ananias was a man who was prepared to forget and to forgive the past. He might well have said: "Even if this Saul is converted, we want nothing to do with him in Damascus. He'll have to work his passage before we believe that the man who came to murder us has changed like this."

Whatever Paul's past was like, Ananias was prepared to believe that there was a grace which made all things new.

Because Ananias was as he was, he had the joy of introducing to the church a man who was to prove far greater than himself.

It has often happened that some simple and unlettered person has been the means whereby someone was brought into the church who was due to do great things for the church.

No man can do greater things than to bring someone else to Jesus Christ.

When he does that, he never knows the possibilities he has opened up.

Ananias certainly did more than he understood when he helped to give us Paul.

Christmas Eve and the Christmas message

MORNING

Julian B. Arnold tells of something that happened to himself. He is an Englishman, and on one occasion he found himself all alone in Edinburgh on Christmas Eve.

He walked along Princes Street feeling very much alone, and finally went into a brightly lit restaurant to eat a lonely dinner.

He took a table and sat all by himself.

At the end of the meal he summoned the waiter and asked for his bill.

The waiter said: "Sir, a gentleman sitting at a table nearby instructed me to tell you that he gathered you were a stranger in our city, and therefore he had ventured to give himself the honor of being your unknown host upon this Christmas Eve. He hoped that you would pardon this wish of his to offer you his own good wishes, and the courtesy of his country."

Someone's generosity had lit up a lonely Christmas Eve for a stranger in a strange land.

EVENING

William Booth, at a rally of London Salvationists shouted, "How wide is the girth of the world?" he shouted.

"Twenty-five thousand miles," came the answer,.

"Then," roared Booth, "we must grow till our arms get right round about it."

This is the message of Christmas.

On the second night of the Vatican Council, Pope John XXIII stood in the window of his private study, smiling at thousands and thousands of cheering Romans below in St. Peter's Square. He quieted them. He spoke to them. "Go home," he said, "and make love grow from here to everywhere."

It is the same message.

Nothing less than a world united in the love of Christ will do.

"Love came down at Christmas."

To create love.

Christmas Day

MORNING

The *Sunday Telegraph* once gave the results of a specially commissioned Gallup Poll about Christmas. Thirty-five per cent of the people consulted thought of Christmas as a religious festival. Twenty-six per cent of them thought of it as a holiday. Twenty-three per cent thought of it as an opportunity to meet family and friends. Five per cent thought of it as an opportunity for eating and drinking. Eleven per cent thought of it as none of these things.

Only a third of the people think of Christmas as a religious festival, and 65 per cent of the people consulted think that Christmas is less religious than it used to be. ·

EVENING

An unknown author has written, "One Solitary Life". It ran thus:

"Here is a man who was born of Jewish parents in an obscure village, the child of a peasant woman. He grew up in another obscure village. He worked in a carpenter's shop until he was thirty, and then, for three years, he was an itinerant preacher.

He never wrote a book, he never held an office, he never owned a home. He never had a family. He never went to college. He never put his foot inside a big city. He never traveled two hundred miles from the place where he was born. He never did one of these things that usually accompany greatness. He had no credentials but himself.

He had nothing to do with this world, except the naked power of his manhood. While still a young man the tide of popular opinion turned against him. His friends ran away. One of them denied him. He was turned over to his enemies. He went through the mockery of a trial.

He was nailed to a cross, between two thieves. His executioners gambled for the only piece of property he had on earth, while he was dying — and that was his coat. When he was dead he was taken down and laid in a borrowed grave, through the pity of a friend."

Twenty wide centuries have come and gone, and today he is the example to the human race, and the leader of the column of progress. I am far within the mark when I say that all the armies that ever marched, and all the navies that were ever built, and all the parliaments that ever sat, and all the kings that ever reigned, put together, have not affected the life of man upon earth as powerfully as has that solitary life.

This is a very beautiful description of the life of Jesus, whose birthday is today.

Basic religion

MORNING

The principles of one of the supreme thinkers of Judaism, Maimonides, are found in *The Jewish Religion*, by M. Friedlander.

(1) The Creator exists; there is a God.
(2) The Unity of God : God is One.
(3) The Incorporeality of God; God is spirit.
(4) God is Eternal; God has no beginning and no end.
(5) The Creator alone is to be worshipped; there are no other and no secondary gods.
6) There is such a thing as prophecy. There have been men who had such moral, intellectual and spiritual power that they reached a knowledge not attainable by others.
(7) Moses is the greatest of all the prophets, greater than any before and than any since.
(8) The Law is divine. The Pentateuch, the first five books of the Old Testament, were divinely delivered to Moses, both in their legal and their historical parts.
(9) The Integrity of the Law. Nothing may be added to, or subtracted from this divinely given Law.
(10) God knows the deeds and thoughts of men, and marks them.
(11) God rewards those who keep his commandments andpunishes those who transgress them.
(12) The Messiah will come at a time when we cannot tell. He will be of the house of David and will have extraordinary wisdom and power.
(13) The dead will be raised and the soul is immortal.

EVENING

The thirteen principles can be reduced to three great claims.

There is the fact that God exists
The final argument for God comes not from logic but from experience.

There is the fact that God has revealed himself
The Jews would say that God has revealed himself through the prophets and in the Law; and the Christian would say that God has revealed himself uniquely in Jesus Christ.

There is the fact that this world is not the end
So every action in time is eternally important.
That God is, that God reveals himself to men, that life points beyond itself to eternity — both for Jew and Christian, these are the foundation stones of religion.

The cure

MORNING

I once read an article by Andrew Wilson on lions and lion taming.

One day, a young man called Bobby Ramsay turned up at his zoo asking for a job; he wanted, of all extraordinary things, to be taken on as a lion tamer. When asked why, his reason was still more extraordinary. He was in fact in serious danger of a nervous breakdown, and his doctor had told him that the only thing that would cure him would be to get so nerve-racking a job that he would forget the other fears that haunted him. So he applied for the most dangerous job he could think of, and he became a very well-known lion tamer. His nervous breakdown was cured!

The way to get rid of nerves was to tackle something that demanded nerve.

The way to lighten one's own burden is to help someone else with his

Teilhard de Chardin tells how on his expeditions in the wilder parts of China on horseback, the load would be hung on one side of the horse and on the other there was a stone to balance it.

EVENING

The way to bear one's own sorrow is to share someone else's

We remember the way that Josephine Butler found her life work. One day when she came home, her little daughter ran out of an upstairs room to greet her. The house was built round an open space, and the little girl leant over the railing to see her mother. She overbalanced and crashed to the ground floor and was killed instantly. Josephine Butler was broken-hearted. To her in her sorrow there came an old Quaker lady. The old lady said to her, "I have spent most of my life looking after girls taken from the streets. I am old now and I can no longer handle the work of looking after the home where forty of them live. Come and take my job, and you will forget your own sorrow."

Josephine Butler went. True, she could never wholly forget her own sorrow, but by taking on her shoulders the troubles and the care of others she made her sorrow bearable.

To forget one's own burden in the burdens of others, to lighten one's own sorrow in the sorrows of others, *that* is the cure.

The Lord is risen

MORNING

The central fact of this Christian faith of ours is the resurrection.

We would never have heard of the Cross had it not been for the resurrection

Without the resurrection, the Cross is the tragic death of a good man. A whisper of it might have come down the centuries, certainly no more, probably not even that.

It is because of the resurrection that we know of the Cross at all. It is the resurrection which makes Christ Christ

There is a stage in life when the resurrection will make an impression on a person that the Cross will not.

This is specially so when people are young. It takes the years to awaken that vivid sense of sin which the Cross alone can relieve. But there is no stage in life when the child, the youth and the maiden, the teenager, will not thrill to the message of the possibility of a great companionship with the most heroic soul who ever walked this earth.

There is a time in life when the note of preaching should be the reality of the presence of this princely figure more than anything else. I would be the last to suggest that there is any kind of necessity to choose between the preaching of the Cross and the preaching of the resurrection; but I do say that the common proportion between the preaching of the Cross and the resurrection is wrong.

We cannot preach the Cross too much. This is not untrue. But perhaps some of us preach the resurrection too little.

EVENING

It is clear that very early in the second century, and probably before the end of the first century, the Lord's Day had taken the place of the Sabbath. Ignatius speaks of the Christians as no longer keeping the Sabbath but observing the Lord's Day.

Now the Sabbath, the last day of the week, commemorated God's rest after the six days of creation; the Lord's Day, the first day of the week, commemorates the resurrection.

That is why the day came into being. It is the day on which the Christian church remembers that the Lord is risen.

Here is the proof, if proof were needed, that the resurrection ought not to be the subject of an annual sermon on Easter Day, but the basic memory of every Sunday.

The middleman

MORNING

Tychicus appears four times in the Letter of Paul (Ephesians 6:21; Colossians 4: 7; 2 Timothy 4:12; Titus 3:12), and on every one of these occasions Paul is sending him somewhere with a letter or with a message.

Quite clearly, Tychicus was one of Paul's most trusted go-betweens. We never find Tychicus speaking or writing in his own name; he is always speaking and writing in the name of Paul.

He is Paul's middleman.

The world needs its go-betweens and its middlemen.

The world needs the middleman between person and person

In the New Testament one of the basic meanings of the word "peace" is right relations between person and person. To produce a right relationship between two people, especially if they were estranged, was according to the rabbis one of the greatest things that a man could do.

It was something which brought him joy in this world and honor in the life to come.

Jesus said: Blessed are the peacemakers (Matthew 5: 9). Blessed indeed are the middlemen, who bring people together.

EVENING

The world needs the middleman between the scholar and the ordinary people

This is in fact the function of the preacher.

The world needs a middleman between God and man. We need someone to bridge the gulf of estrangement and fear that stretches between God and man. And we have that person in Jesus.

More than once the New Testament calls Jesus *mesites*. *Mesos* is the Greek for "in the middle"; and a *mesites* was one who stood in the middle, and who brought two estranged people together.

This is exactly what Jesus does with us and God.

He is God's middleman between men and their God.

The all-important moment

MORNING

There is a tide in the affairs of men,
Which, taken at the flood, leads on
   to fortune;
Omitted, all the voyage of their life
Is bound in shallows and in
   miseries.
On such a full sea are we now
   afloat.
And we must take the current
   when it serves,
Or lose our ventures.
So wrote Shakespeare in Julius
   Caesar.

James Russell Lowell, the American poet, in his poem *The Present Crisis* said the same thing:

Once to every man and nation
comes the moment to decide,
In the strife of Truth with
Falsehood, for the good or evil
   side.

As Lowell saw it, God sends to each man some great cause, some new Messiah.

To every man there comes what we call the psychological moment. The all-important moment. It must be recognized. And used.

EVENING

Opportunities do not return
I can't say this too often.

There is a time to speak a word; there is a time to perform a deed; there is a time to learn something; or to acquire some skills; and, if that time is allowed to pass, it very often does not return.

Life is for ever saying to us: "Now is the time."

A man cannot seize an opportunity unless he has fitted himself to receive it before it comes
The understudy in a play cannot step into the part unless he has learned the part.

The reserve for a team cannot step into the team, unless he is physically fit and physically trained for the game.

Two things are necessary for this. One is the patient preparation of body, mind and spirit to fit ourselves for life's opportunities, when they will come, and the other is decision of mind to seize them, when they have come.

On your marks!

Forward

MORNING

Everyone remembers the passage in John Bunyan's Pilgrim's Progress in which Bunyan saw Christian in a time of indecision.

Christian "looked as if he would run, yet he stood still, because, as I perceived, he could not tell which way to go".

Then Bunyan, in his dream, saw Evangelist come up to Christian, and he goes on in the immortal passage.

"Then," said Evangelist, pointing with his finger over a very wide Field, "Do you see yonder Wicket-gate?" The Man said, "No . . ."

"Do you see yonder shining light?" Evangelist said. He said, "I think I do."

"Then," said Evangelist, "keep that light in your eye, and go up directly thereto, so shalt thou see the Gate; at which when thou knockest, it shall be told thee what thou shalt do."

This is the message for a New Year. We may not see the goal, but we need have no doubts as to the direction in which we should be traveling. The gate, Christian could not see; the light, he could see. If he went towards the light, he would surely find the gate. He knew the direction, and for the time being that was enough.

EVENING

We should be traveling forward

When David Livingstone volunteered for missionary service, they asked him where he was willing to go.

"I will go anywhere," he said, "so long as it is forward."

The daunting thing about life is that so often the end of one year finds us no farther on than the end of the year before. We have still the same faults; we are still making the same mistakes; we are still falling to the same temptations.

Let us resolve now to go forward.

Do you see the yonder shining light?

Keep climbing!

NOTES

NOTES

NOTES

NOTES